SYNAESTHESIA AND THE ANCIENT SENSES

THE SENSES IN ANTIQUITY

Series Editors: Mark Bradley, University of Nottingham, and
Shane Butler, University of Bristol

Like us, ancient Greeks and Romans came to know and understand their world through their senses. Yet it has long been recognized that the world the ancients perceived, and the senses through which they channelled this information, could operate differently from the patterns and processes of perception in the modern world. This series explores the relationship between perception, knowledge and understanding in the literature, philosophy, history, language and culture of ancient Greece and Rome.

Published
Synaesthesia and the Ancient Senses
Edited by Shane Butler and Alex Purves

Forthcoming
Sight and the Ancient Senses

Smell and the Ancient Senses

Sound and the Ancient Senses

Taste and the Ancient Senses

Touch and the Ancient Senses

SYNAESTHESIA AND THE ANCIENT SENSES

Edited by
Shane Butler and Alex Purves

ACUMEN

Editorial matter and selection © Shane Butler and Alex Purves, 2013.
Individual essays © the contributors, 2013.

This book is copyright under the Berne Convention.
No reproduction without permission.
All rights reserved.

First published in 2013 by Acumen

Acumen Publishing Limited
4 Saddler Street
Durham
DH1 3NP, UK

ISD, 70 Enterprise Drive
Bristol, CT 06010, USA

www.acumenpublishing.com

ISBN: 978-1-84465-561-8 (hardcover)
ISBN: 978-1-84465-562-5 (paperback)

Marvin Bell, excerpt from "The Book of the Dead Man #10" from *The Book of the Dead Man*, copyright © 1994 by Marvin Bell. Reprinted with the permission of The Permissions Company, Inc. on behalf of Copper Canyon Press, www.coppercanyonpress.org.

British Library Cataloguing-in-Publication Data
A catalogue record for this book is available from the British Library.

Typeset in Minion Pro by JS Typesetting Ltd.
Printed and bound in the UK by CPI Group (UK) Ltd, Croydon, CR0 4YY.

CONTENTS

Contributors   vii

Introduction: synaesthesia and the ancient senses   1
Shane Butler and Alex Purves

1. Why are there nine Muses?   9
   James I. Porter

2. Haptic Herodotus   27
   Alex Purves

3. The understanding ear: synaesthesia, paraesthesia and talking animals   43
   Mark Payne

4. Aristophanes, Cratinus and the smell of comedy   53
   Mario Telò

5. "Looking mustard": Greek popular epistemology and the meaning of δριμύς   71
   Ashley Clements

6. Plato, beauty and "philosophical synaesthesia"   89
   Ralph M. Rosen

7. Manilius' cosmos of the senses   103
   Katharina Volk

8. Reading death and the senses in Lucan and Lucretius   115
   Brian Walters

9.	Colour as synaesthetic experience in antiquity *Mark Bradley*	127
10.	Blinded by the light: oratorical clarity and poetic obscurity in Quintilian *Curtis Dozier*	141
11.	The sense of a poem: *Ovids Banquet of Sence* (1595) *Sean Keilen*	155
12.	Saussure's *anaphonie* : sounds asunder *Joshua T. Katz*	167
13.	Beyond Narcissus *Shane Butler*	185
	Bibliography	201
	Index	221

NOTES ON CONTRIBUTORS

Mark Bradley is Associate Professor of Ancient History at the University of Nottingham. He is author of *Colour and Meaning in Ancient Rome* (2009) and editor of *Papers of the British School at Rome*.

Shane Butler is Professor of Latin at the University of Bristol. He is the author of *The Hand of Cicero* (2002) and *The Matter of the Page: Essays in Search of Ancient and Medieval Authors* (2011).

Ashley Clements is Lecturer in Greek Literature and Philosophy in the Department of Classics, Trinity College Dublin.

Curtis Dozier is Visiting Assistant Professor of Greek and Roman Studies at Vassar College.

Joshua T. Katz is Professor of Classics and Member of the Program in Linguistics at Princeton University.

Sean Keilen is Associate Professor of Literature at the University of California, Santa Cruz. He is the author of *Vulgar Eloquence: On the Renaissance Invention of English Literature* (2006).

Mark Payne is Associate Professor in the Department of Classics, the John U. Nef Committee on Social Thought and the College at the University of Chicago. He is author of *Theocritus and the Invention of Fiction* (2007) and *The Animal Part: Human and Other Animals in the Poetic Imagination* (2010).

James I. Porter is Professor of Classics and Comparative Literature at the University of California, Irvine and author, most recently, of *The Origins of Aesthetic Thought in*

Ancient Greece: Matter, Sensation, and Experience (2010) and *The Sublime in Antiquity* (forthcoming).

Alex Purves is Associate Professor of Classics at the University of California, Los Angeles. She is the author of *Space and Time in Ancient Greek Narrative* (2010).

Ralph M. Rosen is Rose Family Endowed Term Professor of Classical Studies at the University of Pennsylvania. He is author of *Making Mockery: The Poetics of Ancient Satire* (2007), and co-editor (with Ineke Sluiter) of *Aesthetic Value in Classical Antiquity* (2012).

Mario Telò is Associate Professor of Classics at the University of California, Los Angeles. His text of and commentary on the *Demes* of Eupolis appeared in 2007.

Katharina Volk is Professor of Classics at Columbia University. She is the author of *The Poetics of Latin Didactic: Lucretius, Vergil, Ovid, Manilius* (2002); *Manilius and his Intellectual Background* (2009) and *Ovid* (2010).

Brian Walters is Assistant Professor of Classics at the University of Illinois, Urbana-Champaign. His translation of Lucan's *Civil War* is forthcoming.

INTRODUCTION: SYNAESTHESIA AND THE ANCIENT SENSES

Shane Butler and Alex Purves

Synaesthesia is best known as the name of the condition of those individuals who regularly experience one kind of sensory stimulus simultaneously as another – and who almost universally regard their atypical kind of perception as a gift rather than an affliction. The commonest variety of synaesthesia associates particular sounds with particular colours, a phenomenon that is itself best known by the French term *audition colorée*. Roughly contemporary, however, with modern interest in this clinical phenomenon has been the broader application of *synaesthesia* to the sensory blending experienced by all readers, synaesthetes or not. This happens through literature's "use of metaphors in which terms relating to one kind of sense-impression are used to describe sense-impressions of other kinds", as the *Oxford English Dictionary* puts it, providing an example of this usage from W. B. Stanford's *Greek Metaphor* (1936), which introduced the term to many classicists in a discussion "On Synaesthesia or Intersensal Metaphor".[1]

Interest in both kinds of synaesthesia has its roots in the seventeenth and eighteenth centuries, which saw an explosion of philosophical and scientific enquiry into the nature of sensation, cognition and aesthetic pleasure. The very term *aesthetic* in its modern meaning first appeared in this period, applied by the philosopher Alexander Baumgarten to our sensual experience of a work of art, something which, he argued, both preceded and transcended our mental or "noetic" appreciation of the same.[2] Etymologically, *synaesthesia* and *aesthetic(s)* alike can be traced back much farther, to the Greek verb for experience, *aisthanomai*, and its cognates and compounds. These include the verb *sunaisthanomai* and the noun *sunaesthēsis*, though these were used – chiefly by Aristotle – to designate either the shared experience of multiple individuals or the ensemble of perceptions that constitutes an animate being's encounter with the world or with itself. As a theorist of the

---

1. *OED*, s. v. *synaesthesia*; Stanford (1936: 47–62). See also Gage (1988) and, for further discussion, Clements, this volume.
2. Baumgarten (1735: §116) and (1750), where his new term provides his title.

senses, Aristotle's influence stretched well beyond antiquity, and in the main his thought can be characterized as *anti*-synaesthetic (in the modern sense), assigning the work of each single sense to a separate sphere and arranging these into what would become a familiar hierarchy, with sight and hearing (respectively) at the top.[3]

Synaesthesia and the Ancient Senses takes the complex resonances of its title's term to heart, offering a collection that is synaesthetic in a variety of ways. (Indeed, the only sense of *synaesthesia* we shall mostly neglect is the clinical one, regarding which, in the absence of any ancient discussion in which we can identify the same condition, we can only play the tricky game of guessing whether this or that poet was a "geniune" synaesthete.) In the simplest respect, this book is synaesthetic because it embraces between its covers all the senses. More interesting, however, is the synaesthetic reach of our contributors. Many mine the vein of "intersensal metaphor" in classical literature, from "mustard glances" (Clements) to "green taste" (Bradley) to "dark oratory" (Dozier) to "garlicky poetry" (Telò) to the complex metaphors of thought itself, as in "feeling for the truth" (Purves). Three pursue synaesthetic threads of ancient philosophy (and philosophical poetry), synthesizing the senses in order to transcend them (Rosen), surrendering to them in order to find ourselves in the stars (Volk), counting them down as they expire in death (Walters). The complex relationship between sensation and language is a theme that runs through the entire book. One contributor (Payne) examines sound-meaning at and across the divide between human and animal; another (Katz) confronts the inevitably synaesthetic nature of language after the invention of writing, which allows us to see words as well as hear them – and along the way introduces us to a genuine synaesthete, the linguist Ferdinand de Saussure. The remaining essays (Porter, Keilen, Butler) offer explorations of classical literature and its reception in the name of "a kind of syn-aesthetics" (as the first of them calls it); that is, a set of principles about the nature of experience generally and of the pleasure we take in literature and art.

What all of this volume's essays share is their resistance to hierarchies of the senses, Aristotelian and otherwise, especially those which place vision at the top and dissociate it from the other senses. In the original call for papers for the conference from which this volume results, we challenged our contributors to move "beyond the visual paradigm" in order to offer a synaesthetic reading of the ancient world. Two things emerged from our gathering. One was a remarkable body of ancient material that regularly crosses sensory lines and blurs any single, simple "opticentric" focus (even with respect to vision, which our contributors throw into relief as anything but the unfeeling contemplation of flat or text-like surfaces). The other was a shared conviction that the muting of such material in recent humanistic scholarship was the result of methodological limits that needed to be overcome. These limits turned out to have less to do with vision *per se* than they did with the twentieth century's narrowing conception of the work of reading, whether of literal texts or of other things conceived as such. The "visual paradigm" thus revealed itself to

---

3. Aristotle, *On the Soul* 2.6–12 (418a–424b); cf. Sorabji (1971). Not all, however, have accepted this hierarchy, and even Aristotle himself is not consistent in its application: see further Johansen (1997); Jütte (2005: 54–71). On *sunaisthanomai*, see further Porter, this volume, n. 22.

be primarily a hermeneutic one: its vision is that of a reader who reads in order to know. What we seek to recapture here is the reader who reads not just to make sense but also in order to sense.

Long before us, the concept of language as an intersensory experience was the goal of the modern poet most often associated with synaesthesia: Charles Baudelaire. His 1857 poem "Correspondances" poses a "unité" for the space where "les parfums, les couleurs et les sons se répondent", and which leads by the last two stanzas to a place where the poet can smell the colour green:

Il est des parfums frais comme des chairs d'enfants,
Doux comme les hautbois, verts comme les prairies,
– Et d'autres, corrompus, riches et triomphants,

Ayant l'expansion des choses infinies,
Comme l'ambre, le musc, le benjoin et l'encens,
Qui chantent les transports de l'esprit et des sens.

There are odors succulent as young flesh,
sweet as flutes, and green as any grass,
while others – rich, corrupt and masterful –

possess the power of such infinite things
as incense, amber, benjamin and musk,
to praise the senses' raptures and the mind's.[4]

This merging of sound, taste, colour, touch and smell speaks to the Symbolist quest to draw up a list of correspondences between the senses in order to achieve a kind of spiritualist unity.[5] But this synthesis, Baudelaire has already suggested in his opening stanza, is especially difficult for those who rely on "customary ways of looking" ("regards familiers"). His poem, therefore, has been read as a kind of synaesthetic manifesto for breaking into new modes of experiencing and knowing.

It is these "customary ways" that we, too, seek to challenge and reassemble in our call to move beyond the visual paradigm in our engagement with antiquity. A short example (fr. 2) from Sappho provides an illustration of the kind of thickly synaesthetic ancient material available to us:[6]

---

4. Baudelaire (1982: 15, 193, trans. R. Howard). See also Payne, this volume.
5. Cf. Lehmann (1950: 207ff.).
6. Baudelaire initially planned to call *Les fleurs du mal* (the collection in which "Correspondances" first appeared) instead *Les lesbiennes*. Sappho, fr. 2 and "Correspondances" share vocabulary and imagery from similar spheres, despite the fact that Baudelaire would only have known the second and fourth stanza of fr. 2 (believed at the time to be from two separate poems). These two known verses (the remaining verses in the fragment were discovered on a potsherd in 1937) were very popular in Baudelaire's time and often imitated by contemporary poets (Prins 1999: 99–101).

. . ανοθεν κατιου[ς | -
†δευρυμμεκρητεσιπ[.]ρ[ ] | †ναῦον
ἄγνον ὄππ[αι] | χάριεν μὲν ἄλσος
μαλί[αν], | βῶμοι δ' ἔ⟨ν⟩ι θυμιάμε-
  νοι [λι] | βανώτω⟨ι⟩·

ἐν δ' ὔδωρ ψῦχρο[ν] | κελάδει δι' ὔσδων
μαλίνων, | βρόδοισι δὲ παῖς ὁ χῶρος
ἐσκί | αστ', αἰθυσσομένων δὲ φύλλων |
  κῶμα †καταιριον·

ἐν δὲ λείμων | ἰππόβοτος τέθαλε
††τωτ . . ( )ριν | νοις† ἄνθεσιν, αἰ ⟨δ'⟩ ἄηται
μέλλι | χα πν[έο]ισιν [
  [   ]

ἔνθα δὴ σὺ† συ.αν† | ἔλοισα Κύπρι
χρυσίαισιν ἐν κυ | λίκεσσιν ἄβρως
⟨ὀ⟩μ⟨με⟩μεί | χμενον θαλίαισι | νέκταρ
  οἰνοχόεισα

here to me from Krete to this holy temple
where is your graceful grove
of apple trees and altars smoking
  with frankincense.

And in it cold water makes a clear sound through
apple branches and with roses the whole place
is shadowed and down from radiant-shaking leaves
  sleep comes dropping.

And in it a horse meadow has come into bloom
with spring flowers and breezes
like honey are blowing ...

In this place you Kypris taking up
in gold cups delicately
nectar mingled with festivities:
  pour.[7]

---

7. Text following Voigt (1971) and translation Carson (2002: 6–7).

INTRODUCTION

Many of Sappho's verses in this fragment start with one sense and end with another, or transfer an object famous for its impact in one sense over to another act: the water first described as cold, for example, turns out to be making sound, and the roses lend not their perfume but rather their shade to the garden. Sappho allows this imagery to stray into a realm that is oneiric almost to the point of being surreal. Thus it is not the sunlight above that flickers through the tree's branches, but the sound of the water below.[8] Likewise, the rustling of the same branches is first evoked not as a sound, but as the "radiant-shaking" (that is quivering, but also gleaming) of its leaves.[9] Only then, in the next stanza, are the breezes that are the source of this effect named. As the fragment comes to an end, it evokes at least three different senses in quick succession. "Gold cups" sparkle to the eye and are heavy and cold to the touch. "Delicately" implies touch but refers as well to the gentle sound of the liquid as it is poured. "Festivities" translates the sensorily suggestive word *thalia*, "blooming abundance", with a range of possible associations, from the scent of flowers (the cognate verb *thallō*, one stanza before, has described the blossoming of the meadow) to tastes of the banquet, to the singing and dancing of the choral setting Sappho often invokes. Into these pleasures, nectar, the sweet-tasting (but for humans always untasted) food of the gods, is then "mingled" (*ommemeichmenon*), the Greek participle providing an emblem for the mixing of the senses in the poem as a whole.

There are evident points of contact between this fragment and Baudelaire's "Correspondances", and several scholars before us have pointed to the synaesthetic nature of her poem.[10] One could easily claim that Sappho's rich interweaving of the senses here simply draws on poetry's license to push the bounds of the literal and to break categories that are more rigid in ordinary speech. But something is lost when we consider Sappho's move here as simply the dense literary accumulation of imagery and metaphor. Rather, Sappho, like Baudelaire long after her, seems to be asking a question about the complex, synaesthetic nature of experience itself. And as the essays that follow make plain, she is hardly alone among ancient writers and thinkers in doing so.

The material assembled by our contributors comes from a variety of contexts, but it presents a series of closely related questions and problems regarding the translation of experience into language; the role of the senses in criticism and the appreciation of beauty; the relationship of the senses to the mind and memory; and finally, the relationship between the sense organs and what we might call "deep sense" (that is, intuition, "gut reaction", affect, emotion, pleasure, or pain). As a matter of convention and convenience, we have arranged the volume's contributions in a roughly chronological sequence, but other pathways for reading and reflection will be evident.

---

8. Page (1955: 37), suggests that "'sounds through the branches' means 'makes a sound which goes through, can be heard through, the branches'". This may be right, but there is still a transference from the cold water to the effect of its sound as it moves through the air, through the branches, and then to our ears, in the course of its movement through the line.
9. αἰθυσσομένων is very rare (*ibid.*: 37), used first here. *LSJ* s.v. αἰθύσσω, dart, quiver (akin to αἴθω, burn, kindle, glimmer).
10. Carson calls the poem "synaesthetic" in the notes accompanying her translation (2002: 359). See also, among others, Burnett (1983: 259–76), Winkler (1990: 187), Prins (1999: 96–100).

We begin with Homer, whose inconsistency as to the number of the Muses prompts James Porter's investigation into the "plurality" of aesthetic experience. His wide-ranging study culminates in readings of nonsense inscriptions on archaic Greek pottery and "visible sound" in Aeschylus' *Seven Against Thebes*. Focusing, by contrast, on a single sense in a single author, Alex Purves investigates two episodes in Herodotus that call our attention to the function of touch in his work. Like Porter, she focuses on the materiality of language and the senses by seeking to uncover a more haptic, sensorily-integrated way of reading within a discipline – historiography – that has traditionally been understood to privilege only the eye and the ear.

The next three essays in the volume each offer strikingly different takes on the richly synaesthetic world of Greek comedy. Mark Payne offers an examination of the sounds that animals make (and which we may or may not understand) in Aristophanes and pseudo-Oppian, by way of Wagner's theory of the "seeing" and "hearing" eye. His analysis focuses on the imaginative sympathy these sounds forge between animals and humans and its role as a necessary precondition for meaningful sensory experience of all kinds. Mario Telò turns to the fascinating and surprising way in which the olfactory sense operates in the agonistic world of ancient performance, through an exploration of the different smells that the comic genres embodied. Building on smell's ability to reach across time and through memory, his paper facilitates a reading of Aristophanes' aromas as at once nostalgic, political and intertextual. Ashley Clements looks instead at the complex sensory channels through which a single smell is experienced. His careful unpacking of one almost untranslatable word in Aristophanes (*drimus*) demonstrates how ancient comedy lays bare the synaesthetic jumps between the senses already present in everyday speech, revealing a real-life porousness to the senses that philosophers such as Aristotle would later seek to minimize.

The question of the ancient philosophers' approach to the senses, broached already by Porter and Clements, is tackled head on in the next essay, by Ralph Rosen, who addresses a seldom explored tension in Plato's thought between the transcendence of the senses and the possibility of their unity in experience. His essay argues that synaesthesia is represented as the penultimate step in Plato's *Symposium* before the complete, intellectual experience of pure Beauty in its unalloyed totality, through a process where the senses become synaesthetically blended and undifferentiated. Turning to Latin and the *Astronomica* of Manilius, Katharina Volk treats us to a concert of the heavens, in which the "sympathies" of the constellations follow multiple sensory lines simultaneously. Her analysis of how the Stoic principles of *sympatheia* are remapped onto a fully sensory depiction of the cosmos draws a contrast with the earlier work of Aratus: Manilius presents the heavens not merely as a text to be read but as a synaesthetic system that demands the engagement of a plurality of senses, and one where looking, especially, is figured as a sensory experience. Approaching Roman thought from quite a different point of view, Brian Walters examines the horror of death and dismemberment in the poems of Lucretius and Lucan and asks what happens when the senses are extinguished, one at a time, in the process of dying. His essay uses a synaesthetic framework to explore Stoic and Epicurean engagements with the question of where to draw the line between life and death, feeling and not feeling.

The next two essays complicate our understanding of ancient vision. Mark Bradley, in a reading both of literary texts and of ancient material culture, shows how colour, a category that we might presume to be exclusively visual, actually embraced a range of sensory experience for the ancient subject. He argues that a synaesthetic approach (rather than one limited to vision) can help us both to interpret different colour terms and to address the relationship between perception, knowledge and understanding in Roman thought. Further reassessing visual categories, Curtis Dozier turns to the question of darkness in Quintilian, who urges young orators to avoid the obscurity of the poets, since the latter, by the very nature of their art, frustrate our desire to regard reading as a mere process of bringing things into clear view. This does not mean, however, that the orator should illuminate everything; on the contrary, Quintilian instructs, the successful orator will know when and where to cast shadows.

Our final three essays take us beyond antiquity proper and into the classical tradition. Sean Keilen explores the complex and sometimes contradictory sensory invitations of George Chapman's *Ovids Banquet of Sence* (1595), in which the difference between perceiving from afar and sensory immersion from up close offer rival models for ways of knowing. By suggesting that this question of distance mimics our relationship to literature itself, Keilen challenges us to rethink our own habits of reading. Joshua Katz moves us to the twentieth century and some long-hidden texts by Ferdinand de Saussure, whose explorations of, among other things, ancient anagrams reveal a kind of synaesthetic obsession with the tension between sound, sight and sense. Katz takes up what the volume has hitherto explored largely through literature and culture and shows how Saussure sought similar tensions at the level of language itself. Shane Butler transports us to Surrealist Paris, which found a model in the polysensual world of antiquity. He closes the volume with an invitation to break through Narcissus' mirror (and its reconfigurations in psychoanalytic theory) and to embrace the synaesthetic "nonsense" that Ovid, in his telling of the tale, had offered as a far better source of readerly pleasure.

Synaesthesia and the Ancient Senses inaugurates a series of six volumes, each remaining one of which will be concerned with a single sense. By beginning with all the senses, we hope to encourage readers to explore the ensuing volumes in dialogue with this one and with one another. Here in this first volume and in those to come, we trust that the result will be more than the sum of its (bodily) parts.

The volume editors would like to thank the UCLA Center for Medieval and Renaissance Studies and the Ahmanson Foundation for their generous support of the conference that launched this project. We would also like to thank our third collaborator in the organization of that conference, Mario Telò, a contributor to the present volume. In the process of transforming that conference into a book we have benefitted greatly from the suggestions and assistance of the series co-editor, Mark Bradley, our editor at Acumen, Tristan Palmer, and the two anonymous referees who reviewed the volume for the press. Some of our editorial work was conducted in the comfortable surroundings of the Getty Villa through the generosity of the Getty Research Institute. We would finally like to thank all the members of the Department of Classics at UCLA.

1

WHY ARE THERE NINE MUSES?

James I. Porter

If you want to know why there are nine Muses, you just have to ask Homer. Homer knows either one or several nameless Muses of some indefinite number, as at *Iliad* 1.604 ("the antiphonal sweet sound of the Muses singing") or *Iliad* 2.484 ("Tell me now, you Muses, who have your homes on Olympus"), *Iliad* 2.761 ("Tell me, then, Muse, ..."), or *Odyssey* 1.1 ("Sing to me, Muse"). They remain in this indefinite state until the last book of the *Odyssey*, where the Muses are said by Agamemnon's *psychē* in the Underworld to appear finally on Earth – already a peculiar topographical and narrative inversion in itself – in order to lead a *thrēnos* at the funeral of Achilles. Only, they do so *both* as a chorus of nine *and* in the seemingly abstract and faceless singular:

> And *all the nine Muses* in sweet antiphonal singing
> mourned you, nor would you then have seen anyone of the Argives
> not in tears, so much did *the singing Muse* stir them.
> (*Odyssey* 24.60–3; trans. Lattimore 1965)

Hesiod follows suit in the *Theogony*, either conferring or transmitting the nine distinct names of nine Muses, otherwise not functionally distinct, in a gesture that was destined to become canonical.[1]

Elsewhere, their number varies wildly. Ephorus knows three Muses, others give four, five, seven or eight. And the iconography is in agreement. Sappho sometimes makes a tenth, but that is as far as it goes. The disparity in number is telling, but of what? Jean-Luc Nancy, in his brief collection of essays, *The Muses*, is likewise interested in the question,

---

1. *Theogony* 60. See M. L. West (1966) Index I, s.v. "Muses": "—why nine?"; and his note on line 60 (somewhat misleadingly, regarding Homer). Unless, of course, the passage in Homer is a later interpolation, as the scholia insisted, though modern editors do not. Nine muses, it is thought, could easily have been a common inheritance of both Homer and Hesiod, originating, for instance, in one of the Cyclic poems, e.g., in the *Aethiopis*. See Heubeck *et al.* (1988–92) on *Odyssey* 24.60.

which he poses in this way: "Why are there several arts and not just one?"[2] He might have framed the problem in terms of the contrast between one Muse and many Muses and thereby arrived at his signature concept of "the *singular plural* of … art", a concept that for him is informed by a notion of synaesthesia, and behind which lies a view of reality (an ontology, in fact) that is based on the principle of the singular plurality of being or beings.[3] But Nancy doesn't quite make this connection. Instead, he insists, against the facts, that the Muses were plural "from the first": "There are Muses, not the Muse"[4] – probably because he is so keen to conflate each of the Muses with the individual arts individually, whereas in antiquity, at least, the Muses were jointly associated with song, music and dance from early on, tasks they took on in joyous simultaneity, not under separate rubrics. And that is how they continued to be known into later antiquity, despite their changing names and numbers, though gradually and only much later they came to be associated with individual genres of creativity (history, tragedy, music and so on).[5] Whether these associations hampered the joint functioning of the Muses or not remains to be seen. I doubt they did, at least not until post-classical times, and even then not universally or as a rule.

This underlying lack of any functional distinction among the Muses is, I believe, what defines their creative core. It also brings us back to the problem of their number – not their numerical count, but their lack of *fixed* number and their capacity to oscillate between singular and plural without loss of substance or function. This uncanny ability is dramatically on display in the passage from *Odyssey* 24, where Homer shifts from "Muses, nine in all" (Μοῦσαι δ' ἐννέα πᾶσαι) to "the Muse" (Μοῦσα) in the space of three short verses, without so much as batting an eyelash. Are these two expressions equivalent for Homer? Is "the Muse" a shorthand for what the Muses collectively do? Perhaps the Muses were indeed something of a singular plurality, though perhaps not quite the way Nancy had in mind. Nancy's insistence on the plurality of art is aimed against what he considers to be "the modern regime of *art* [which] gets established in the singular", and "tendentiously" so.[6] I find this claim itself tendentious, for more than nine reasons, but I don't want to enter into a detour to prove this point here.[7] Instead, I want to fasten onto the synthetic, or rather synaesthetic, plurality that I believe is entirely symptomatic of Greek views of art and aesthetics, but also of modern art and aesthetics (despite the claims of some to the contrary), though it is the ancient half which will be my main concern in the present context.

One of the advantages of a synaesthetic approach to art is that it allows us to follow the ways in which the materials of art are transformed in their very apprehension, first

---

2. Nancy (1996: 1).
3. See Nancy (2000).
4. Nancy (1996: 1).
5. See generally Murray (2004), esp. 367: "The iconographical evidence confirms [the traditional] conception of the Muses as a chorus who act together as performers and inspirers of the musical arts, without differentiation according to specific functions". Further, *Lexicon Iconographicum Mythologiae Classicae* 7.2, s.v. "Mousa," "Mousai"; Peponi (2009).
6. Nancy (1996: 7). Cf. *ibid.*: 6 "Has art ever had the unity that we project onto the use of a word?"
7. The misguided Kristellerian orthodoxy on the so-called modern system of the (fine) arts, with its debilitating implications for antiquity, is one reason; see Porter (2009).

when they are apprehended *as* (bare) matter or material, and then again when they are apprehended as capable of containing, releasing, or just triggering aesthetic properties, perceptions or experiences. Aesthetic phenomena cannot help but be experienced synaesthetically by their very nature: they are taken in by the eye and the ear simultaneously, but also by other senses, for instance taste, smell or touch, whether it is by feeling objects with our bodies or through the physical impress that non-tactile senses leave on our sensorium. Consider how a piano is both a stringed and a percussive instrument, and hence its sounds create vibrations that touch the ears and other parts of our bodies. The same is true of the Greek lyre, but also of phenomena generally, which rarely appear in one sensory mode alone.[8] This being so, synaesthesia is an ideal way of widening our outlook on the experience of art and the theories of art that attempt to encompass this experience. The Muses work in concert as well as apart.

My comments in what follows will fall into three, related sections:

1. First, I want to indicate how synaesthesia raises a basic issue about aesthetic inquiry, ancient or modern, but with special implications for antiquity. This pertains to the *syn-* half of the term, which points to the complexive nature of aesthetic thought, reflection and practice.
2. Next, I want to suggest that *any* moment of aesthetic sensation is founded on, or contains, a synaesthetic element. This pertains to the *aesthetic* element of the term synaesthesia. Here, aesthetics inevitably becomes a kind of syn-aesthetics. If I do nothing else with this paper, I want to explore a few of the reasons why aesthetics in any era are naturally promiscuous in a synaesthetic way, and why Greek antiquity can help illuminate the problem from a particular angle.[9]
3. Finally, I will turn to two final case studies from Greek antiquity, all I will have space for, in order to illustrate these points in greater detail.

SYN-

Synaesthesia is of critical importance to understanding aesthetics of any era – not in the clinical sense of the term, if by this we understand involuntary sympathetic feeling,

---

8. Cf. the sound sculpture produced and discussed by the Baschet brothers in Baschet & Baschet (1987). For an ancient equivalent, see below and other examples of a verbal equivalent discussed in Porter (2010) (unaware of the Baschets' fascinating work). For a brief historical account of noise relative to tonality in music, see Levarie (1977). That account would need to be greatly modified in the light of ancient Greek experiments along the lines of Sacadas of Argos, Lysander of Sicyon, Lasus of Hermione, Pindar, and the later generation of New Musicians, all of whom tested extended techniques and pressed sound to new limits of "noise" production (and occasionally reduction) in different media (vocal, wind, stringed, choreographic).
9. Although these issues are at the core of Porter (2010) and are touched on in specific instances there (see *ibid.*: Index, s.v. "synaesthesia"), I welcome the opportunity to give synaesthesia more focused attention here.

whereby stimulation of one sense faculty causes a corresponding sensation in another (say, you hear a sound and it conjures up for you the colour blue or a round shape).[10] As fascinating as this phenomenon is, and it is undeniably an element of aesthetics, it is not a core element of aesthetic experience (for starters, it is experienced by a limited population). But something like it is, and I suspect that this is what most of us have in mind when we talk, in aesthetic contexts, about the way language from one sensory sphere is borrowed to describe another. The Greek lyric poets afford plenty of examples of this second phenomenon, as when Pindar uses an architectural metaphor to describe the "golden columns" of the song he has his chorus sing at the start of *Olympian* 6: "Let us set golden columns beneath the well-walled porch of our sanctuary like a much gazed upon palace. For when a work is begun, it is necessary to make its front far-shining" (*Olympian* 6.1–3).[11]

We might be tempted to label descriptions like these grandiose breaches of literal fact. In a strict sense, they are. But in another way they are not. Pindar's odes were sung before sun-drenched columns. They also had an architectural quality of their own in their verbal structure. How could they fail to take on some of the gleam and sturdiness of their surroundings? Similarly, the term *rhuthmos* can be used to capture architectural characteristics, whether designating arrangement, pattern, shape, symmetry, perspectival effects, or simply the movement of a building's appearances in a beholder's eye.[12] *Rhuthmos* is attested in at least one of these senses as early as Pindar's eighth Paean, long before it came to be so used in technical handbooks on architecture: "What *rhuthmos*", he asks, "was shown (τίς ὁ ῥυθμὸς ἐφαίνετο) by the all-capable skills of Hephaestus and Athena" on the third temple of Apollo at Pythia?[13] Finally, Pindar's odes were not simply sung: they were danced to the very same *rhuthmos* to which they were sung.

So, when Pindar's choruses sing about the architectural dimensions of their own song, what they are in fact doing is describing in spatial terms what their audience is taking in not just aurally but also visually, at the very moment the song is being put into rhythmic motion in three or more ways and senses before them: as music, motion, song and language. *A sound is being seen.* Pindar may well be alluding to the architectonics of his own song structure, and not merely to the artisanal, craftsmanlike features of his art (its *facture*), with the dimensional metaphors that characterize so much of his poetry. These building metaphors (which we use today: stanza originally means a room where you stop

---

10. See, e.g., Cytowic & Eagleman (2009).
11. Cf. Pindar, *Nemean Odes* 8.46–8: "But for your homeland and the Chariadai I can erect a loud-sounding stone of the Muses (λαβρόν | ὑπερεῖσαι λίθον | Μοισαῖον) in honor of those twice famous pairs of feet" (trans. Race 1997).
12. Rhythm in the technical sense of musical rhythm is not attested before the late fifth century. For *rhuthmos* as dance movement, see, e.g., Aeschylus, *Libation Bearers* 797. On *rhuthmos* and its connection to *eurhuthmia* in architectural contexts, see Schlikker (1940: 81–95, esp. 83). On its dynamic meaning in Greek generally, see Petersen (1917: 11); Schweitzer (1932: 11); Fritz (1938: 25–6); Benveniste (1971); E. Thomas (2007: 209); Chantraine (2009) s.v. ῥυθμός; Slater (1969) (s.v.) gives "symmetry" (citing this passage, the only occurrence of the word in Pindar). For further discussion see Porter (2010: 436–40).
13. Pindar, *Paeans* 8.65–7. For a more scientific use of *rhuthmos*, see Geminus (?), in Damianus, *Optica* 28.11–19 Schöne (1897): "buildings will … display their underlying rhythms" (τοὺς ὑποκειμένους ῥυθμοὺς ἐπιδείξονται) to beholders.

and stand, and before that, a stay or support, like a *kiōn*, or column of song, in Pindar[14]) are too often construed in recent scholarship as marking a rivalry with the plastic arts, whether sculptural or architectural, and indeed as a vaunting on Pindar's part that declares the superiority of the transportable, mobile word over the materially fixed, immobile works of three-dimensional art, as in the following two representative examples:

> A golden foundation has been wrought for holy songs. Come, let us now build an intricate vocal adornment made of words (εἶα τειχίζωμεν ἤδη ποικίλον | κόσμον αὐδάεντα λόγων) ...
> (Pindar, fr. 194 S.-M.; trans. Race 1997)

> I am no maker of statues who produces figures that stand fixed on their own pedestal; rather, on every vessel and every boat set forth from Aegina, sweet song, proclaiming yourself abroad (στεῖχ' ἀπ' Αἰγίνας διαγγέλλοισ[α]) ...
> (Pindar, *Nemean Odes*, 5.1–3)

While it might be tempting to pin on Pindar a rivalry with the stationary arts of sculpture and architecture, nothing of the sort, I believe, is going on here. Far from rejecting these art forms, Pindar is in fact borrowing the dimensional associations of the neighbouring arts and incorporating these into the experience of his verbal art. He is creating a new, *verbal architecture* and a new kind of *sound sculpture*, with no intention of ousting the plastic arts, but only of basking in their glow. (Nor is he alone. Compare a fragment that is either Pindaric or Simonidean: "I sculpt a measure".[15]) Pindar's poetry wants to be all that the sculptural and architectural arts are and more: palpable, visible, hard, substantial, shiny, reflective and reflexive all at once.

It is worth adding that by taking on these complex plastic features, Pindar is *thickening* the effect of his art, at times elucidating his meaning, at times obscuring it. (In the terms of the Russian Formalist, Viktor Shklovsky, he is making his poetic "forms difficult" and "retarding" their perception by us.[16]) Not all marble or metallic surfaces are transparent, and a reflexive sheen can blind you with its glare even as it lures you into coming closer to examine it. Pindar banks on these congestions of linguistic meaning and material by way of sheer sensory overload, which is one of the most characteristic effects of his poetry:

> Golden lyre, rightful joint possession of Apollo and of the violet-haired Muses, to you the footstep listens as it leads off the celebration, and the singers follow your signals whenever, strings aquiver, you strike up the preludes that lead off the dancing.
> (*Pythian* 1.1–4; trans. Race 1997, adapted)

---

14. *OED*. Cf. Hollander (1996).
15. [μέ]τρον δ(ια)γλύφω, *P. Berol.* 9571ᵛ col. 2.55 (Schubart 1941); Lasserre (1954: 48). Simonides' name was conjectured by Schubart (1941: 28) at l. 53 and in col. 1.17 by Lobel, who hypothesized that the papyrus was a learned commentary on Pindar which also drew on other contemporary lyric poets. Parallels include Aristophanes, *Thesmophoriazusae* 54, 986; *Frogs* 819; [Plut.], *Lives of Homer* (*Vit. Hom.*) 216.
16. Shklovsky ([1917] 1965: 18). On retardation, see Shklovsky ([1921] 1965).

What Kitto says about the tragic chorus applies with equal force here: "metrical structure would have been conceived aurally and spatially, in terms of dance and tune, not simply as poetry".[17] Synaesthetic objects are difficult to process. It is as if the mutual approximation of each of the spheres of sensation comes at an inevitable cost to them all – whenever, that is, we try to analyse them back out again into their separate spheres of activity, and only then.

AESTH-

Pindar is by no means exceptional in antiquity. To begin with, ancient theories of sensation confirm his tendencies. Aristotle once asked a good question: "Why do we have more senses than one?"[18] One of his motives was to understand why the five senses so often overlap even when we have a plurality of them, as in the perception of what is sweet by sight (his example) – as with a sugar cube.[19] At a more general level, as he writes in the *Rhetoric*, "the word *seeing* is not common to sound and colour, but *perceiving* is" (οἷον [ἢ] ψόφῳ καὶ χρώματι τὸ μὲν ἰδὼν οὐ κοινόν, τὸ δ' αἰσθόμενος κοινόν).[20] Here, Aristotle was blocking a move made by some of the sophists, such as Gorgias, who argued – provocatively and aporetically – against the possibility of cross-talk among the spheres of sensation. Aristotle's point is general, and a productive one. Obviously, perception (*aisthēsis*) is wider than, and includes, ocular seeing. The idea that sound and colour are both common to *aisthēsis* points indirectly to Aristotle's theory of common sensibles, or *koina aisthēta*, which he develops in his psychological works. These are the sense objects that can be perceived through the different sense faculties commonly (for instance, movement, rest, number, shape, magnitude, sharpness, bluntness [these last two may be variations of shape], and – controversially – time). More specifically, they are qualities that are invariably co-perceived, for instance, colour and size: if we perceive one, we perceive the other.[21] Thus, movement is common to touch and to vision (as with a pen twirling in your hands), even if feeling (the *sensum* [*aisthēton*] that is felt) is strictly speaking reserved for touch alone.

What Aristotle's theory points to is the intrinsic complexity of all aesthetic perception, since there can be *no* perception that does not take in one or more, if not all of the "common sensibles": all perceived objects are either in motion or at rest, have a number (like the Muses), a shape, a size, and exist in time. You never simply see in some proper sense (colour) but improperly, catachrestically, accidentally: for instance, you see whiteness

---

17. See Kitto (1956: 2).
18. Aristotle, *On the Soul* 3.1.425b4–5.
19. *Ibid.*: 3.1.425a21–7. This is a case of an incidental perception of special objects (two simultaneously *kata sumbebēkos*), not of common objects. See Modrak (1981: 411).
20. Aristotle, *Rhetoric* 3.5.1407b.20–21.
21. Aristotle, *On the Soul* 3.1.425b8–9; Aristotle, *Sense and Sensibilia* 1.437a9. See also Summers (1990: 78–109, 322–35) and E. Thomas (2007: 207–10), two of the rare exceptions who see the relevance of Aristotle's theory for aesthetic theory.

at rest or in motion, in space, of a certain dimension, of this or that texture. (I say "points to", because Aristotle does not make this last argument himself, and it might appear to conflict with his notion of special sensibles.) Finally, *all* sensations are accompanied, for Aristotle, by the awareness or perception that we are perceiving, to which the idea of common sensation may well be linked (Aristotle speaks of "a common power" that is shared by all the sensations but reducible to none of them), and which is prefigured by his own use of the term *sunaisthēsis*: it would later take on this precise meaning (comparable to *conscientia*, or consciousness).[22] Aristotle seems to believe that all sensations are accompanied by this awareness, which adds a further dimension to them. Does this make all of sensation synaesthetic for Aristotle? At the level of *aisthēsis*, it would, but only incidentally (*kata sumbebēkos*); at the level of individual sense faculties, operating in their proper (*idion*) spheres, it would not. What is more, there is a temporality and a built-in aesthetics to second-order perception (that is, the awareness that you are perceiving) that renders such perception a source of potential pleasure and the space of a lingering gaze (not unlike the German *Verweilung*),[23] as a look at *Poetics* ch. 7 can show: "For beauty lies in magnitude as well as in order, which is why a very small creature could not be beautiful, since our view loses all distinctness when it comes near to taking no perceptible time" (trans. Hubbard 1972).

Here, perceptual time *has* a magnitude, and it corresponds to the perception *of* a magnitude. Thus, *pace* Lessing's later desideratum that aesthetic vision should take place in a simultaneous instant (as in the case of an image or statue) and somewhat in line with Shklovsky's notion of impeded perception, Aristotle keenly observes how the eye dwells on its object; it lavishes attention on what it sees: it roves, dallies and lingers. Similarly, in *On the Soul* Aristotle allows that for someone to perceive a stone is for her soul to enclose the form of the stone within itself.[24] What this proves, he says in a striking analogy, is that "the soul is like the hand": it touches, not things, but their forms, which are *quasi-sensuous* things:

> For this reason, no one can learn or understand anything without perception. And when the mind is actively aware of anything it necessarily perceives an image at the same time. For images are like objects of sensation, except that they lack matter.
> (Aristotle, *On the Soul* 3.8.432a7–10; trans. J. A. Smith 2006)

---

22. In brief, it is the idea that answers to the question, "By what faculty do we perceive that we are having sensations?" (Aristotle, *On Sleep* 2.455a15, and more broadly, 2.455a12–26). See Kahn (1966: 73), who notes that *sunaisthēsis* in Aristotle, *Nicomachean Ethics* 9.9.1170b4 means "to perceive at the same time" and may prefigure the notion of "consciousness". For an interesting bridge to shared social perceptions, see *sunaisthēsis* at *Eudemian Ethics* 8.12.1245b24, used of shared social perceptions (among friends and more generally, by extension). More might be done with this extension to the public sphere of experiences (for the concept, see Porter 2010: e.g. 7, 193–6, 454), but this is not the place to do so.
23. *Verweilung* signifies a lingering, dallying, and tarrying of the gaze, from Kant into Hegel: it more or less captures the contemplative stance of subjective aesthetic perception. For more on this term, see Porter (2010: index, s.v.).
24. Aristotle, *On the Soul* 3.8.431b27–432a3.

Touch, after all, is for Aristotle the most primary of sensations. Indeed, it is the thread that connects the soul to life itself.[25] Outside of the Peripatos, other thinkers had other, even more permissive views towards the natural collaboration of the senses. For example, seeing was held to be a form of touching, as were the other senses, according to a number of writers from Homer into later antiquity (though not for Aristotle[26]). Hence, it is safe to generalize that in the ancient world, the senses were in collusion and collaboration at the most basic level of sensation.[27]

That they were can perhaps be illustrated in the area of art, where there have been attempts to exploit the relationship of visuality to tactility, for instance in the school that follows the *fin-de-siècle* Viennese art historian Alois Riegl. Riegl famously introduced (or rather reintroduced) the concepts of the tactual (*haptisch*) and the painterly (*malerisch*) – though for him the two notions tend to be opposed in a historical progression that insists on the liberation of vision from touch rather than on their essential and ongoing co-involvement. On the latter view, which I prefer, what is of interest is how the tactile sense contributes to the visual sense, and vice versa, just as any visual reading of an object involves retracing the material signs of its production (its *facture*). For what a beholder sees are not objects made by and for vision pure and simple but objects that were drawn, brushed, chiseled, scraped and polished: what one takes in through the eye is the work of the hand. To quote Merleau-Ponty, which in ways recalls Aristotle on the common sensibles: "we *see* the depth, the smoothness, the softness, the hardness of the object; Cézanne even claimed that we see their odor".[28] On ancient theories of vision (though not on Riegl's), it would even be acceptable to say that we *touch* these features of objects with our eyes, or even "kiss" them, on the Byzantine extension of this theory.[29] But there were other competing views as well.[30]

Consider a bronze discus, a dedication from Cephallenia (Figure 1.1), dating to around 530–525BCE. It bears an inscription in the form of a spiral that mentions the bronze

---

25. *Ibid.*: 3.13, esp. 435a12–13, 435b15–19: without touch, no other sensation is possible; touch is the mark of the living creature; without touch, the creature cannot be; damage touch (by excess) and the creature dies, etc. Cf. Aristotle, *Metaphysics* 9.14.1051b24; 12.7.1072b21 (on the role of contact in thought). See also S. H. Rosen (1961); Brague (1988: 372–3).
26. See n. 29 below.
27. Hamlyn (1959: 13–15); Gregoric (2007).
28. Merleau-Ponty (1964: 15). See further Merleau-Ponty (1945: 243–4): "Le bleu est ce qui sollicite de moi une certaine manière de regarder, ce qui se laisse palper par un mouvement défini de mon regard. ... Le rouge 'déchire,' le jaune est 'piquant' ..." Similarly, Collingwood (1938: 146). Cf. Scranton (1964: 18), defining sculpture as "an art of the sense of touch".
29. Nelson (2000); further, Pentcheva (2007). For the extension of the haptic (possibly atomistic) model of vision into the Greek novel, see Morales (2004: esp. 130–40). Not even the Peripatetic view is an exception. According to Aristotle, vision receives the form (εἶδος) but not the matter of the object of vision (ἄνευ τῆς ὕλης), the way a seal leaves its imprint on wax, and similarly with all the other faculties of sense (*On the Soul* 2.12.424a17–424b3; 3.2.425b23–4, etc.). Aristotle's strikes a compromise: he is keen, as ever, to stress that it is the *form* that impresses itself on the eye, but it nonetheless does so haptically (though he reserves this last term for the sense of touch). An atomist would naturally disagree with Aristotle on every point: *matter* is transmitted from the object to the eye, through an unabashed touching.
30. See Sorabji (1971: 73–6), on the "non-localization criterion" of sense perception, found prior to Aristotle.

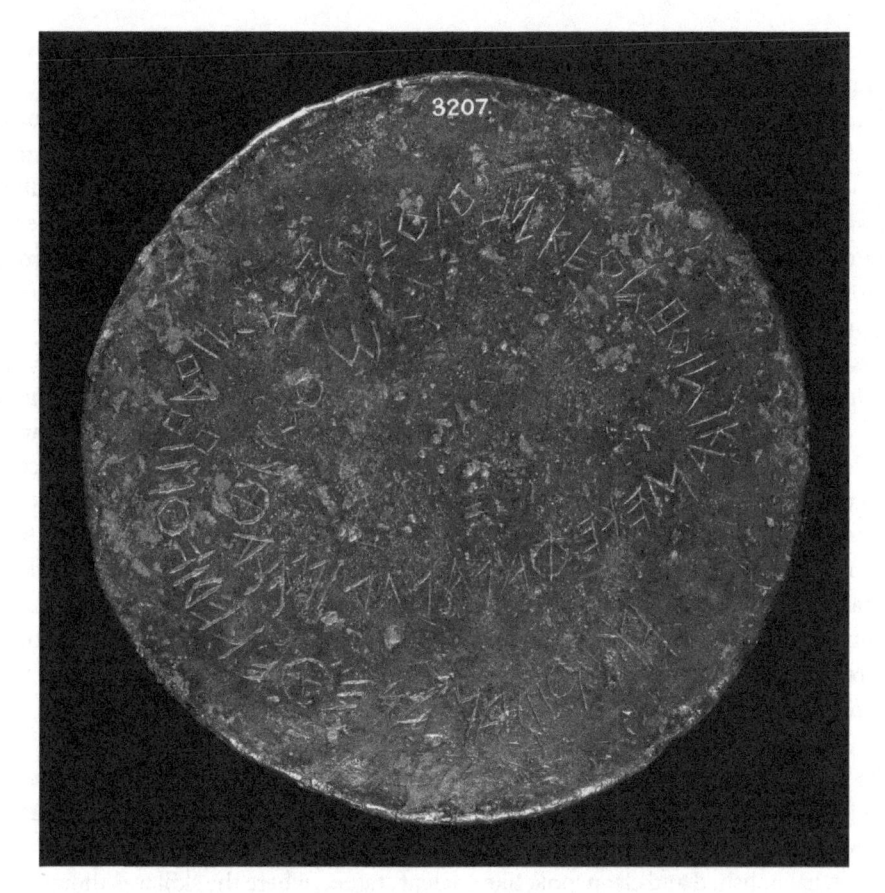

Figure 1.1 Panathenaic bronze discus from Cephallenia, sixth century BCE. 16.5 cm diameter × 0.5 cm thick, 1.245 kg. © Trustees of the British Museum. All rights reserved.

material of which the discus is made (μ' ἀνέθεκε … | χάλκεον) and recalls the circular shape of the object at one and the same time – not an uncommon practice, but neither is it obligatory (the lettering on similar objects can run horizontally, as in regular inscriptions).

Ἐχσοίδα μ' ἀνέθεκε ΔιϜὸς ϙόροιν μεγάλοιο ⋮
χάλκεον hõι νίκασε Κεφαλᾶνας μεγαθύμος.

Exoida(s) dedicated me to the twin sons of great Zeus, [a discus] of bronze, with which he defeated the great-spirited Cephallenians [in competition].
(*CEG* 391 = *IG* IX,1 649)

Here, material, lettering and object-shape all converge in a mutually reinforcing pattern. The discus, a miniature of the original that would have been used in competition, requires a spiral reading that encourages the gaze to do two things at once: to retrace the shape of the object, and to re-enact the spiraling of the discus as it left the hand of Exoida(s) when he vanquished his fellow citizens. The gaze here becomes involved in a motion, while it is simultaneously being asked to register various aspects of the discus as a material object. Stated differently, lineal writing is being put at the service of – is literally recapitulating – motion through space. If the original display of the object permitted its handling, physical tactility and the visual would have been partnered even further. And yet, there is a certain *décalage* palpable here: the writing (which is in retrograde[31]) curves inward, in a motion that runs *counter* to that of the inscribed object, which (in the imagination) is being propelled *forward* in a linear fashion.[32]

Now, when we return to where we began, with Pindar, or the *theatron*, the *skēnē*, and the *orchēstra*, we find that in ancient Greek performance contexts Pindar is the norm. By norm I do not merely mean Pindar's tendency to capitalize on the widest possible canvas available to him as an artist of sights and sounds. I also mean to include his reflexive commentary on his own activity, which surely added a fourth or even fifth dimension to the experience for his audience, one we might call a dimension of proto- or actual aesthetic reflection (analogous to perceiving that one is perceiving), just as his own subtle flecks of metacommentary on his art constituted a proto-aesthetic discourse that would lay the foundations for future generations of critics, artists, sophists, philosophers and other thinkers from the mid-fifth century onwards. So, for example, the author of *On Style* compares writing styles to building and sculptural styles:

> The members of the periodic style are like stones that prop up overarching vaults, while those of the disconnected style resemble stones that lay scattered about without being built into a structure. Consequently, the older style of writing has a somewhat polished and clean look, like ancient statues, where the skill was thought to lie in their spareness and plainness. The style of later writers already resembles the works of Phidias, since it exhibits a certain amount of grandeur and polish combined.
> (Demetrius, *On Style* 13–14)

The capacity of a reader to *see* language in dimensional terms, or rather the incapacity of an ancient reader to do anything *but* view language in such terms – to see sounds, to hear written words and to visualize them as plastic forms – ought to be worthy of being diagnosed as a synaesthetic disturbance of mind today. We might put the phenomenon down to the habits of a culture that never fully emerged from a condition of orality and its accompanying performance contexts, a culture that never ceased to view written texts as embedded and encrypted sound (what was technically called *engrammatos phōnē*),

---

31. The writing thus faces the direction of the inward spiral, which moves from right to left.
32. An intriguing parallel in a different medium is given by Aristotle in ch. 26 of his *Poetics*, where he mentions the case of "objectionable (*phauloi*) aulos-players who spin about if they have to represent a discus" (1461b30–31). Aristotle objects to the cinematic use of synaesthetic *mimēsis* for the same reasons that he rejects *opsis* and *schēmata* (gestures) in his theory of tragedy, though here he has in mind dithyrambic performances, in which musicians are reproducing the whirling motions of a discus in flight either with their instruments in their mouths or with dance steps or both.

and which therefore also encouraged the projection of such aesthetic effects as verbal architecture or sound sculpture that was felt literally to jut off the page:

> The austere style of composition has this sort of character: it wants the words to stand firmly fixed and to occupy strong positions, so that each word can be seen on all sides; and it wants the parts of the sentence to keep at considerable distances from one another, separated by perceptible intervals.
> (Dionysius of Halicarnassus, *On Literary Composition* 22; trans. Usher 1985)

But while conditions of performance were a contributing element, I suspect there were other factors at play as well.

One of these must surely have been the source of the descriptive languages being applied to aesthetic objects. If literary critics resorted to the language of architecture, sculpture, music or art-historical connoisseurship, that is because they were employing inherited criteria of aesthetic judgment that ran across all of these discourses. Thus, literary connoisseurship was grounded in the most immediate and most sensuous properties of texts, the apprehension of which was modelled on the handling of a multi-dimensional art object. Criticism, pedagogy, and reading practices followed the practices of the discriminating connoisseur. Examining a text was a lot like examining a vase, holding it up to the light, feeling its heft, turning it this way and that:

> Unless sculptors and painters had much experience, training the eye over a long period of time by studying the works of the old masters, they would not be able to identify them readily and say confidently that this sculpture is by Polyclitus, this by Phidias, this by Alcamenes, and that this painting is by Polygnotus, this by Timanthes, and this by Parrhasius. So with literature.
> (Dionysius of Halicarnassus, *On the Style of Demosthenes* 50; trans. Usher 1974, adapted)

What lay behind this tactile practice was a general approach to aesthetic experience, available in all levels of society. The intriguing point is not just that these vocabularies were mutually held in common. Underlying these shared languages of art were what may be called a shared public sphere of aesthetic experiences. You can find the same or similar descriptive terms being used and postures being struck among craftsmen and lay persons, in the way rows of shoes or trees are described in the *oikos*, or the way the colours and shapes of everyday objects are being captured on the street or in the public square (to the extent this can be judged today). And all of this in turn points to more fundamental attitudes towards aesthetic experience and objects that need to be uncovered in their own right.

By aesthetic experience we should not understand a privileging of an autonomous realm that results from adopting something like an aesthetic attitude or psychical distance towards things in the world. Aesthetic experience is not reducible to some elite or isolated form of art experience, the way the modern notion of the fine arts has misled generations into believing. It is deeply rooted in the most basic levels of sensation (as the very term *aisthēsis* suggests). To have an experience is to have an empirical contact with the world, and it is to discover this contact in the realm of pain, pleasure, form, shape, surfaces, luminosity, hues and colours, rhythm, sounds, aromas, palpability, the very sense of time, or any aesthetic category you please (the beautiful, shapely, pleasing, ugly or sublime – though we might do better by appealing to a notion of aesthetic "intensities" without appealing to conventional labels) – all of which happen to be both in good supply in the ancient world and found in places where art is not directly discussed (*pace* those who complain that aesthetics is either an impoverished or a non-existent discourse prior to 1750). What *is* being discussed whenever such topics are on the table, on the other hand, is a matter of experience, which is to say, *what passes through the mind and senses in the face of vivid phenomena – the primary features of sentience*. Three things follow from this premise:

1. that aesthetics is fundamentally a question of sensation and perception;
2. that *arts are genres of experience*;
3. that both art and aesthetics are grounded in the ever-changing and ever-adapting *aesthetic public sphere* of antiquity. Such a sphere is constituted by a pool of experiences that cut across boundaries of medium and genre.

When we rethink aesthetics along these lines, we can see how the Greeks and Romans had the capacity to perceive pebbles or gemstones with the same sensibility as they did dance, music, or inscriptional writing, which is to say, in terms of common rhythmical properties, sheen, sound quality – in addition to the general run of aesthetic emotions organized by loftier value schemes (ethical and other). And because they did, we should acknowledge that the ancients were in fact virtuosos of *syn-aesthetics*.

TWO FINAL CASE STUDIES

SEEING SOUND ON STAGE

I want to conclude by glancing at two more instances of the multiply sensuous world of art in Greece prior even to Aristotle, starting with Aeschylus' *Seven Against Thebes*, then a vase.

The *Seven* is a static play, being a preeminent play of language, not actions, and being executed much like a sculpture in the severe style. It is built around a series of ecphrastic scenarios, most famously the seven shield ecphrases, each corresponding to an attack at each of the seven gates of Thebes. To this extent, then, it is a conventional play, even a paradigmatic drama, in that it consists in reported rather than enacted action. In other respects, *Seven* is avant-garde drama, pressing at the physical and aesthetic limits of dramatic and performative representation. But nearly all of Aeschylus' plays were this, so far as we can tell. Think of Aeschylus' Niobe, famously – shockingly – unmoving on the stage, veiled from sight, transformed into a literal stone of unspoken pain for over half to two-thirds of the play.[33] Or consider Prometheus, chained to his rock, immobile, compelling the action to bend towards him in successive waves, making himself the centre of the *praxis* in the present and into the future. Or the blood red carpet scene in *Agamemnon*, which sucks in all the oxygen, and the light, from the stage once it is spilled onto the ground to be admired (a thing of luxury), feared (a harbinger of death), trampled upon, and then played upon as a verbal echo in the remainder of the play and then the trilogy. These are all vivid displays and challenging installation pieces of art that show the enormous potentialities of *opsis*, which is to say the very condition of theatrical performance, in all its mute and resistant material presence, much to the thrill of theatre-goers and later critics, despite the frowning vetoes by Plato and Aristotle.[34] Here, vision becomes tactile, tangible, and palpable, identified with things and therefore itself a thing rather than a medium: it is, in other words, the thing-in-itself of the drama, the very substance of the action, and not the means of conveyance for action. But insofar as it is palpable and sensuous, vision is hardly confined to the visual any more.

Now to *Seven*, a singularly noisy play – even by Aeschylean standards. It presents a city under siege, in a kind of confused mirror-image of the *Iliad* (with Argives made strange and other, yet also Achaean – such is the confusion of internecine fratricide).[35] The war scenes, brought on stage and made vivid for the audience, involve extended accounts of events off-stage, whether retailed by the Messenger or by the Chorus, in which every relevant sense is activated:

> The plains, struck by hoofs, send the noise to my ear.　　　　　　　　　(84)

> Ah, ah, ah, ah, the rattle of chariots round the city, I hear it. O Lady Hera, the naves of the heavily laden axles are shrieking! Beloved Artemis! The air, vibrating with spears, is mad. ... Beloved Apollo! Clashing of bronze-bound shields at our gates!　　　　　　　　　(150–60)

> I was afraid when I heard the rattling din of chariots, the rattling, when the whirling naves of the axles screeched and the fire-wrought bits of the rudder oars of horses roared in their mouths.　　　　　　　　　(203–7)

> But I rushed headlong to the ancient images of the divinities, trusting in the gods, when there was a crash of a deadly blizzard of stones at the gates.　　(211–13)[36]

---

33. *Life of Aeschylus* 331.22-4 Page; Aristophanes, *Frogs* 911–12.
34. *Life of Aeschylus* 333.6-17 Page: "Aeschylus was the first to augment tragedy with effects of the noblest sort and to decorate the stage and to astonish the eyes of his audience (τὴν ὄψιν τῶν θεωμένων) with visual brilliance (τῇ λαμπρότητι), pictures (γραφαῖς) and devices (μηχαναῖς), altars and tombs, trumpets (σάλπιγξιν), ghosts (εἰδώλοις) and Furies. ... One can only be amazed at the poet's intelligence and inventiveness as compared with his predecessors'". Similarly, Quintilian, *The Orator's Education* 11.3.4; Plutarch, *Moralia* 348c.
35. Cf. *Seven Against Thebes* 28–9; 324.
36. Translations are from Sommerstein (2009a), adapted.

As the images accumulate, they grow denser; the language becomes more obscure – and, as a consequence, textual corruptions grow more frequent, reflecting the increased stress under which the language has been put. Meanings are stretched – into a panic of meaning; sensory registers clash; sensations blur; sounds intensify and bleed into the visual, which is where everything in fact started, for as the Chorus say near the outset, compounding what they perceive with what they imagine, "I see the sound!" (κτύπον δέδορκα): "Do you hear or do you not hear the crashing sound of shields? … *I see the sound!* The clatter did not come from one spear alone" (100–103; my trans.). And all the while the chorus are dancing, mainly in excited dochmiacs (though these two lines happen to be in iambs). Presumably, then, the audience can see, in turn, a sound being danced on the orchestra in a corresponding rhythmic pattern as well.

All this initial sensory confusion shatters the perceptual field, or rather fields, and lays the groundwork for the seven shield ecphrases to come. While startling in their imagery, the ecphrases have been fully anticipated aesthetically, and so can do no more than elaborate on the original programmatic statement by the Chorus, "I see the sound". In point of fact, the shield ecphrases are merely the imaginary, or imaged, fulfilment of this remark. The *sēmata* (signs) on the shields effectuate crossovers between images, letters and sounds; they are audible signs ("*With gold letters* [the embossed warrior on the shield] *declares with a loud voice* (χρυσοῖς δὲ **φωνεῖ** γράμμασιν), 'I'll burn the city'", 432–4), some of these painfully loud ("This man too is *crying out loud in his written legend* (**βοᾶι** δὲ χοῦτος γραμμάτων ἐν ξυλλαβαῖς), 'Not even Ares shall throw me off the walls'", 468–9). The overlap and confusion of sensations in the play, this panic of sensations, signals less a collaboration of spheres of sensation than an area of shared limits among them. Sensations are being brought to a point beyond their operational orders. The chorus may see a sound, but the audience sees the chorus, not the sound the chorus sees, which is a sound that goes unheard. And so the rest of the play unfolds in this hiatus between what can be seen and what can be said, which is to say in the gap between these two spheres of sensation, which precisely defines the limits of the tragic in Aeschylus and elsewhere, and as is nicely encapsulated in a single verse towards the end of the play in an exchange between Antigone and Ismene: "Terrible to tell. Terrible to see" (ὀλοὰ λέγειν. ὀλοὰ δ' ὁρᾶν, 993). Tragedy, we might say, is an ecphrasis of an action that cannot be seen, and never truly told. It is the deadly *echo* of a deadly spectacle – less an effect than an *after*-effect.

SEEING SOUND ON VASES

Next, we turn to exhibit B, an archaic Attic vase from the Chazen Museum in Wisconsin (Figure 1.2), which, examined closely, reveals an odd string of written characters (Figure 1.3). The characters appear to be letters of the Greek alphabet, only they form a nonsense inscription, and the most extreme sort at that: not only do they not spell any intelligible words, but in cases they do not even resemble actual letters. An elderly poet, dressed in a *himation* and with a *sakkos* in his hair, is shown seated and playing the *kithara* while singing. The song is represented by nonsense letters flowing from the poet's mouth like

Figure 1.2 Side A of *White-Ground Footed Mastoid Skyphos* c.515BCE. Painter from Pistias Class "M" (Greek). Photo courtesy of the Chazen Museum of Art, University of Wisconsin-Madison, Cyril Winton Nave Endowment Fund purchase, 1979.122.

a fountain (recalling the function of the cup, which is for drinking, but then reversing its directionality; the words flow from the mouth, not into it). The letters are somewhat crudely and illegibly drawn, and some of them only approximate to actual letters, vaguely mimicking rather than consisting of letters. Here is a reasonable guess as to how to decipher them: ηηλολο λοινοχνι.[37] Side B depicts a similar scene with similar writing.

Nonsense inscriptions are a common phenomenon on vases in the archaic period into the early classical period, though their uses vary wildly, and the phenomenon is both greatly understudied and little understood.[38] Here, with the Chazen vase, we have an instance of sound being materialized in a visual form, and so now we can literally

---

37. The first η consists of two vertical strokes, no horizontal bar; the first λ consists of two slanting but non-tangent lines; the next letter (λ) has a slanted right foot (ι?); the first ο is a curved downward stroke that never closes, too round for a *pi*; the dot that follows is the trace of a letter partially preserved on the remains of the slip; the next ι looks more like an inverted *tau*; the following ν is seemingly in retrograde, as is the last ν, if that is what it is. Nick Cahill and Maria Safriotti Dale kindly supplemented my readings of the digital image with their own based on autopsy (flashlight and magnifying glass in hand). The readings presented here are a combination of the two sets of interpretations.
38. See, however, Lissarrague (1987), esp. 124, where the Chazen vase is briefly described ("projetant devant lui des signes incompréhensibles"); Osborne & Pappas (2007).

Figure 1.3 Detail of Figure 1.2. The song of an elderly poet is represented by nonsense letters flowing from the poet's mouth like a fountain.

say that *we see a sound*. The letters conjure up the flowing of song, but that is not all: they conjure up the very *senselessness* of song *qua* music and rhythm, which is to say, *qua* pleasurable reduction of language to sound and sound effects. The very character of language in its signifying capacity is here made insignificant, or nearly so (there is a possible echo with *oinos*, "wine", or *oinochoē*, "wine jug" at the end of the string of letter-sounds) and this reduction is effectuated in the visual destruction of *grammata* or *stoicheia* into meaningless marks that *barely* resemble their lettered counterparts, and in cases may not even try to make a case for actual letters. Tenuously related to language, the letters are allowed to transform into graphic marks, and from there into a further aesthetic element of the vase, visually completing two circles: first that of the lyre to which the song is functionally attached, and then of the seated figure, now made into a literal figure (a shape). Made whole, this circle complements the two palmettes to either side which balance the composition of the whole upper half of the cup's face. Two further tendrils below, looping in opposite directions and recalling the fountain-like spillage of the letter-sounds above, which as it were water the flowers below (and generate a counter-rhythm to the two upward arching handles of the vase), and thus fill out the bottom of the composition.

Here, syn-aesthetics is fully at work. Several Muses are on call at once.

Figure 1.4 Completed pattern of design and decoration including palmettes, tendrils and handles.

TOWARDS A SYNAESTHETIC APPROACH TO ART

Above, we saw how if you want to know why there are nine Muses, you simply have to ask Homer. But by the same token, the Muses in antiquity even from their baptismal moment as nine were a vacillant quantity, never fixed once and for all as nine, and just as often a metonymic one that stood for a complex totality endowed with any number of functions. The simplest explanation to the question, "Why are there nine Muses?" is to say that one was never felt to be enough, while nine was felt to be a good place to stop counting. But the real point is that the exact number is irrelevant. The Muses are a synaesthetic unity, always plural yet always one, a singular plural and a plural singular.

When we finally reach modernity, have things changed? Yes and no. The question is perhaps best got at by way of another: Is aesthetics, the only Muse that modern art knows, itself singular or plural? Consider this: until very recently, the *Oxford English Dictionary* had no separate entry for the word *aesthetics* (all modern evidence to the contrary). If you looked up the word, in a printed copy or online, you would have found it categorized under *aesthetic*, which was classed as an adjective and a noun, even though the very first illustration of "the history of the word" (sc., *aesthetic*) was a quotation, dating from 1832, exemplifying "Æsthetics". Worse (and here nothing has changed), though "commonly" used in the plural, "aesthetics" can also stand for a collective singular. The original entry explains matters thus (under usage "B", where the 1832 example ought strictly to have been located): "*n*. commonly pl. **æsthetics**, as collect. sing.: but also in sing., after Ger. *æsthetik*, Fr. *esthétique*". It is not the editors of the dictionary who were being muddle-headed. The indecision surely stems from the nature of art, which is always perceived *both* as abstractly one *and* as promiscuously plural. The revised entry for "aesthetic" (dated December 2011)[39] makes amends by referring readers to "aesthetics *n*. 1a". The updated entry for "aesthetics", likewise vastly improved – it now reads like a veritable Wikipedia article – recognizes that the word can function either as a singular or a plural noun. Perhaps aesthetics should be abolished and replaced with another, more inclusive term, if not field of inquiry altogether: one that is called "syn-aesthetics".[40]

---

39. "*Æsthetic, a.* and *n.*," www.oed.com/view/Entry/3237?redirectedFrom=aesthetic#eid. I had notified the editors of the dictionary by email about this confusion in February 2006, but doubt I can take credit for motivating the improvements.
40. Thanks to the organizers of this conference for the opportunity to think in a more concentrated way about aesthetic synaesthesia and for editorial comments; to the participants and audience for comments during the event; to Ann Sinfield of the Chazen Museum of Art at the University of Wisconsin-Madison and to the British Museum for permissions; and to Nick Cahill and Maria Safriotti Dale at Madison for indispensable help with deciphering the Chazen vase.

2

HAPTIC HERODOTUS

Alex Purves

> Seeing's Believing, but Feeling's the Truth.
> (Thomas Fuller, *Gnomologia*[1])

INTRODUCTION

Somewhere in the dark a woman's fingers reach across the surface of a man's skin, feeling for something that, as it turns out, is not there. The woman is the wife of a king, and what she reaches for is a pair of ears, hidden beneath the hair of her husband in bed. When she discovers that the ears are not there she learns that her husband is not at all the man she thought he was. In another story, the daughter of a king is set up in a bedroom by her father and instructed to sleep with any man who requests it. If she is able through this method to discern the thief of her father's treasure-house, she is told to grab him and not let him go. The dutiful princess does exactly as she is told, except that, at the very moment when she discovers the thief and reaches out to grasp him in the dark, his arm comes off in her hands. She is then left alone, holding a strange extra part of a body that neither senses nor makes sense.

These two acts of feeling, of grasping for the truth in the dark, are told by Herodotus in the course of narrating the broad sweep of events that lead up to the Persian Wars. Both events are the catalysts for fairly important historical events in Persian and Egyptian history, and both lead to the transfer of power from one king to another. On a quite different level, both of these acts of groping are also creepy, to the extent that we might feel their effect as an involuntary shudder on the surface of our own skin as we confront the unexpected shock of ears that cannot be felt or arms that cannot feel. In this essay, I want to suggest that these two women, who rely on their hands to feel out the truth in passages

---

1. The original proverb, as recorded in Thomas Fuller's *Gnomologia* (no. 4087) from 1732. Since then the second half of the saying has fallen out of use, radically altering its meaning.

where verbs for handling are juxtaposed with verbs of discovery, help us to reflect on the role of the ancient historian – a figure who not only sees but also touches in his effort to discern the past and the material effects of the world around him. Through these two women, Herodotus puts forward the notion that the sense of touch might bring us close to the truth, even when what we find there may be curiously absent or elusive.[2]

These stories, detailing the unmasking of Smerdis, an earless pretender to the Persian throne (3.69), and the attempt of King Rhampsinitus to catch the robber of his treasure house (2.121), provide the backdrop for a sensibility of touching that I want to begin exploring through the hands and fingers of Herodotus himself. In the first part of the essay, therefore – before turning specifically to the hands of the two women we began with – I will consider some of the ways in which Herodotus brings the sense of touch to the fore in his writing of history. In doing so, I will deal with a range of language that is replete with tactile imagery and metaphors that are so familiar that one could argue that we are not conscious of their sensual reference.[3] Without denying their function at the level of plain language, I want to try to look more carefully at this substrate of sensual discourse and to attempt to tease out exactly where and how the sense of touch makes its presence felt in the writing of history.

HISTORY THROUGH THE SENSES

The modern term haptic comes from the Greek verb *haptomai*, meaning to grasp or to put one's hands on something (*LSJ*, s.v.). In Herodotus, we might think in this context of the relation between grasping and power, from the initial act of kidnapping various women to the references throughout the *Histories* to receiving goods, countries or people "into one's hands" (ἐς [τὰς] χεῖρας).[4] But haptic in the modern sense means something quite different from this. It refers, more broadly, to the experience of feeling with or through the body. This kind of feeling might be represented by cutaneous touch, encompassing pressure, temperature, texture or pain, all felt externally on the surface of the skin. Equally, it might be the kind of touch that is located within the body, referring to all sorts of ways in which we feel when we feel *ourselves as bodies*, including the vestibular system (that is, our sense of balance), proprioception (the sense of being able to locate oneself in space), and kinaesthesia (our sense of movement).[5] I will be mostly discussing here the external sense of touch, but occasionally I will refer to the interior of the body as well.

---

2. The verbs of discovery that occur in these passages, underscoring the girls' acts of touching, are: [ἀν]ευρίσκω (Herodotus, *Histories* 2.121α3, ε1); γνωρίζω (2.121β2); πυνθάνω (2.121ε3; 3.68.3, 4); εἰρώτομαι (2.121ε4); γινώσκω (3.68.4 (×3)); μανθάνω (3.69.3, 6); the verbs of handling are: μεταχειρίζω (2.121α3); ἀφάσσω (3.69.3, 4, 6); [συλ/επι]λαμβάνω (2.121.ε2, 5); ἅπτομαι (2.121ε5); προτείνω (2.121ε5); ἀντέχω (2.121.ε5).
3. See Clements, this volume, esp. his nn. 10 and 34, and my n. 13, below.
4. 1.126.6, 1.208, 4.79.1, 6.68.1, 7.8.1, 8.106.3.
5. See further Paterson (2007); Foster (2011: 1–14).

Haptic studies has proven important and adaptable to a number of disciplines, but particularly interesting for my purposes is the movement it has sparked among geographers for a "sensuous geography" – that is, a geography that occurs in the "near-space of haptic exploration" rather than through the distancing space established by the observing eye.[6] If we understand the geographer's body as a body that senses rather than simply observes, these scholars argue, then we are likely to access a new set of ways for thinking about people and place.[7] Yet a truism often expressed in this kind of work is that the "sensuous" or haptic approach to apprehending the world is all the more fluid and evasive for being associated with what is tangible. The touching hand, like the sense of touch itself, is elusive and difficult to grasp. This is partly because, as Aristotle observed, touch is the only one of the five senses that does not have its own specific "organ", such as the nose is to smell or the eyes are to sight. It is also the only sense that does not have a single unifying subject, as light is to vision and sound is to hearing.[8]

There is a blurriness about touch, therefore, which results from the immersion of one's own body within the field of inquiry. Following Merleau-Ponty, scholars often talk about touch collapsing the boundary between subject and object. As Obrador-Pons puts it: "The sense of touch establishes a distinctive relation with the environment, in which there is no clear separation between subject and object as singular coherent entities. Modalites of touch provide a framework of proximity, openness and intersubjectivity, a space 'between-us'".[9] Or, as stated more succinctly by Stewart (1999: 31): "The pressure involved in touch is a pressure on ourselves as well as upon objects".

What, if anything, can be said about Herodotus' sense of touch, and why should touch matter in our reading of the *Histories*? Scholars of Herodotus have been most inclined to turn their attention toward the two organs that are traditionally considered the most distant (or "elevated") from the sensual realm: the ear and the eye.[10] They have wrestled back and forth in adjudicating between what the historian hears and what he sees, from the oral accounts that he reports to the things that he looks at. We have always suggested that it is through the ears and the eyes that the first great historian and geographer of the Greek world gathered his knowledge.[11] But what if this focus on eye and ear is too restrictive and binary, too separatist? What if it dulls our reception to the other senses at work in the text? Herodotus' description of the Pythia at Delphi shows her actively engaging *all* of the senses in her famous proclamation in Book 1 (1.47.3):

---

6. On the importance of the sense of touch in reading history, see Classen (2005a); M. M. Smith (2007: 93–116). On geography: Paterson (2007: 46). Cf. Rodaway (1994); Stoller (1997); Feld (2005).
7. As Hetherington (2003: 1942) has put it: "Places may come to be made at the interface between subject and object, between hand and thing".
8. Aristotle, *On the Soul* 422b19–23. This led Aristotle to suppose that the flesh could only be the *medium* of touch, and that its true *organ* must be located somewhere inside the body, in the heart (*Sense and Sensibilia* 439a1–2). Although note also *Parts of Animals* 2.I 647a14–21, where the flesh does seem to be an organ. See further Johansen (1997: 199).
9. Obrador-Pons (2007: 136), drawing on Paterson (2004) and Hetherington (2003).
10. Cf. Hartog ([1980] 1988: 260–309).
11. For a good framing of these questions, see Marincola (1997: 63–86).

οἶδα δ' ἐγὼ ψάμμου τ' ἀριθμὸν καὶ μέτρα θαλάσσης,
καὶ κωφοῦ συνίημι καὶ οὐ φωνεῦντος ἀκούω.
ὀδμή μ' ἐς φρένας ἦλθε κραταιρίνοιο χελώνης
ἑψομένης ἐν χαλκῷ ἅμ' ἀρνείοισι κρέεσσιν,
ᾗ χαλκὸς μὲν ὑπέστρωται, χαλκὸν δ' ἐπίεσται.

I know (have seen) the number of the sand's grains and the measures of the sea
I understand the dumb man and can hear the mute.
A smell has reached my senses of a hard-shelled tortoise,
Boiling in a bronze pan together with the lamb's meat,
With bronze laid under and bronze on top.

Her vision verges on the synaesthetic, folding sound, sight, texture, taste and smell, as well as the near and the far, into a mixed sensuous perception. The Pythia's act of "seeing" (and scholars are often quick to point out the visual root of the verb *idein*), in other words, takes place through each one of the senses.[12] Even when the Pythia smells the tortoise, its epithet "hard-shelled" brings the quality of touch into her adjudication of what the object is.

We do not have to look far to find other examples of touch in Herodotus. One haptic aspect of his writing that is seldom remarked upon as such is his classification of peoples according to whether they are "hard" or "soft". A culture, according to Herodotus, shares a descriptive or metaphoric language with feelings that are most commonly experienced upon the surface of the skin. I am not suggesting by this that the Greeks thought that they could literally know a culture by somehow touching it, but – as recent research in the cognitive sciences has shown – texture words, even when purely figurative (such as in the English phrase "a rough day") trigger those parts of the brain where the sense of touch resides.[13] The tactile qualities of this hardness or softness are at play in Herodotus' text in sometimes quite specific ways. Wearing soft shoes on one's feet or wearing dresses that allow the legs to move freely will make people's natures (as well as their skin) soft

---

12. The presence of the *vid root (from which *idein,* "to see") within the Greek word for history (ἱστορίη), does not mean that we should necessarily neglect the other senses. A more synaesthetic approach to seeing would suggest quite the opposite, as I discuss in my conclusion. See further Porter (2010), and in this volume, on ancient aesthetics as a mixed and material sensory experience.
13. Lacey *et al.* (2012) show through a series of scanning experiments that the processing of familiar textural metaphors (such as "a hard day" or "a slimy person") activates texture-selective somatosensory areas in the brain. This is consistent with the conceptual metaphor theory of grounded cognition proposed by Lakoff & Johnson (1980). Cf. Paul (2012) and Clements (this volume). Note also Merleau-Ponty's discussion (1962: 273–4) of the body's physical reaction to language: "The word 'hard' [German 'hart'] produces a sort of stiffening of the back and neck, and only in a secondary way does it project itself into the visual or auditory field and assume the appearance of a sign or a word. Before becoming the indication of a concept it is first of all an event which grips my body, and this grip circumscribes the area of significance to which it has reference." What I am suggesting, therefore, is that the haptic quality of these words, even in familiar metaphoric contexts, do matter. As W. E. Connolly (2010: 182–3) has put it, "A philosophy of language that ignores these essential connections may appear precise and rigorous, but it does so by missing circuits of inter-involvement through which perception is organized."

and delicate, as in the famous advice given by Croesus to Cyrus as to how to enervate the Lydians (1.155.4):

> Order them to wear tunics under their clothes and to bind on soft boots, and tell them to play the lyre and the harp and to educate their sons to be shopkeepers. Then quickly, king, you will see them become women instead of men and they will prove no danger of revolt for you.

As a result of wearing these soft clothes and engaging in these pursuits, the Lydians, according to Herodotus, "changed their whole way of life" (1.157.2).[14] As a group, they were stereotyped for their luxurious ways in the archaic period, best summed up by the word *habrosunē*, which involved wearing long hair and soft, flowing garments, scented oils and indulging in an easy, pampered lifestyle. Yet before their defeat by the Persians, Herodotus characterizes them as a strong and warlike people. The advice of Croesus to Cyrus, therefore, pinpoints a "precise historical moment when the Lydians became 'Lydopatheis'"[15] – that is, in Herodotus' version of history writing – soft receptors of external stimuli rather than active doers within the world.[16]

The same can be said of landscapes. Those that are rough (τρηχύς) create men who are tough fighters and who subsist without luxuries (1.71.2):

> King, you are preparing to attack the sort of men who wear leather trousers and who wear other leather clothes as well; they don't eat as much as they want to eat, but whatever they have, since they occupy a rugged land (χώρην ἔχοντες τρηχέαν). On top of that, they drink water, not wine; they have no figs for desert, nor any other delicious things.

While those that are soft (μαλακός), on the other hand, create "soft" men (9.122):

---

14. This can be understood also in terms of the body and its material orientations – actions, objects, orientations and positions all become habitual, "they are repeated, and in being repeated, they shape the body and what it can do" (Ahmed 2010: 252).
15. Kurke (1992: 102). Cf. Xenophon fr. 3 D-K, Aeschylus, *Persians* 41–2, cited in Kurke (1992: 92–3). As Kurke notes (94), Herodotus uses ἁβρός twice of the Lydians (1.55, 1.71). As she also observes, some connect ἁβροσύνη with words denoting swelling or ripeness – qualities that invite equally both the eye and the fingers (inasmuch as we may recognize swelling through sight alone, it always carries with it the idea of how swelling also *feels* to the touch, both internally and externally).
16. This classification of people according to tactile-cultural categories of "soft" and "hard" is a recurring phenomenon. It has played a determinative role in American politics, for example, from Lincoln's tactility (M. M. Smith 2008) to Kennedy's programme for a tougher American body, first published as an article entitled "The Soft American" (J. F. Kennedy 1960; Foster 2011: 118–20) and later the Reagan era's fascination with the "hard body" (Jeffords 1993). By contrast, the famously empathetic Bill Clinton was typically represented by the media during his presidency as soft and even doughy. With softness also comes sensitivity (as in the expression "touchy-feely"), which can muddle the terms of these categories, too. Aristotle believed that the softer one's flesh, the more discriminating one's touch ("men whose flesh is hard are ill-endowed with intellect, men whose flesh is soft, well-endowed", *On the Soul* 421a; cf. *Parts of Animals* 660a11–13; Johansen 1997: 213–14).

"Since Zeus is giving hegemony to the Persians, and of all men to you, Cyrus, now that you have killed Astyages, come – this paltry and rough land (ὀλίγην καὶ ταύτην τρηχέαν) that we possess, let us leave it and possess a better one. There are many neighbouring lands, many far away too, and taking just one of these will make us more wondrous to many people. For it is reasonable that men who rule do such a thing. And when better to do this than now, when we are ruling over many people and the whole of Asia?" Cyrus, hearing this speech, did not admire it; he bid them to do these things, but he cautioned them to prepare to no longer be rulers but to be ruled. For he said that soft people tended to come from soft lands (φιλέιν γὰρ ἐκ τῶν μαλακῶν χώρων μαλακοὺς ἄνδρας γίνεσθαι·).

These passages are often quoted as examples of the concept that a hard or soft landscape will lead, respectively, to hard or soft people.[17] But is this transference, between clothes, landscape and the self, physiological or merely associative? Presumably both. The skin that is caressed by silks and plush garments becomes soft, and that softness – through an osmosis of habit and practice, but also of metaphor – passes through the barrier of the skin and affects the nature of its wearer. The skin that is exposed to harsher elements, on the other hand, such as rough earth, coarse clothes, or wind and sun, is tougher, leading to a corresponding roughness in the texture of its person.

There is a theory in Herodotus, therefore, of what we might call the "haptic effect". Egyptians are black because of the effect of temperature upon their skin (2.22.3), but that need not necessarily stop on the outer surface: illnesses are caused by changes in the seasons (2.77.3) and the Libyans are of the best health because the winds in their land blow hottest and driest upon their bodies (2.24–7). As R. Thomas (2000: 28–74) illustrates, Herodotus' theories are here firmly grounded in the four favourite oppositions of the medical writers: hot versus cold and dry versus wet. His drawing of *ethnos*, *physis* and *nomos* through the grid of the hard and soft may be commonplace, therefore, yet it is striking how haptic the entire theory is. As far as Herodotus is concerned, the way that things feel upon the skin is so important as to even determine historical and ethnographical outcomes, right through to the last paragraph of the *Histories* ("soft people tend to come from soft lands").

Second in the analysis of what might make Herodotus count as a "sensuous geographer" is the way he uses his own hands (and, as I will touch on later, his feet as well). On the site of a sixth-century battle between the Persians and Egyptians, he tells us of a practical experiment he carried out on the skulls of the dead (3.12):

I saw a great marvel here and learned about it from the locals. Of the bones that were lying separated in the battle where they had fallen ... the skulls of the Persians are so soft that, if you tapped them with one pebble, you would break through them; but those of the Egyptians are so firm that you would scarcely break them by

---

17. See especially Redfield (1985).

smashing a stone against them (αἱ μὲν τῶν Περσέων κεφαλαί εἰσι ἀσθενέες οὕτω ὥστε, εἰ θέλοις ψήφῳ μούνῃ βαλεῖν, διατετρανέεις, αἱ δὲ τῶν Αἰγυπτίων οὕτω δή τι ἰσχυραί, μόγις ἂν λίθῳ παίσας διαρρήξειας). They said that the reason for this, and they easily persuaded me, was that the Egyptians from childhood begin shaving their heads and the skull is thickened by the sun (καὶ πρὸς τὸν ἥλιον παχύνεται τὸ ὀστέον). For the same reason they are not bald. For one would see the least bald men among the Egyptians. It is for this reason that they have hard (ἰσχυράς) skulls, and for the same reason the Persians have soft (ἀσθενέας) skulls, for they shade themselves from a young age by wearing felt caps.

Although it appears at first that here, as so often, the historian's principal organs of inquiry are the eye and the ear, Herodotus also stresses his own physical presence at the scene. He tells us that he was close enough not only to see these bones of the Egyptians and Persians, but even to feel them for himself. But in addition, by his use of the second person singular, Herodotus also asks us to imagine performing these actions in an embodied way, just as he asks us to take it on trust that he felt the pressure of each skull with his own hands. As the passage continues, we learn that the reason for the ethnic difference falls, again, on the haptic grid. The Egyptians shave their heads from birth, thereby (in Herodotus' scheme) allowing full exposure to the sun's harsh rays. This, in turn, hardens their skulls. But the Persians from a young age wear caps made of felt. That soft, protective covering, like the cool, soft shade, leads to skulls that are also soft. What Herodotus means by calling these skulls soft is made quite explicit through his experiment of tapping them with a pebble and then watching them crumble.

From the body that is physically present in the environment it studies, that *handles* its data, to the skull that is soft because it has grown accustomed to the delicate feeling of felt, the importance of touch in Herodotus' analysis now seems more palpable than it did before. These examples all suggest that the body and the hands of the historian might be reached for as a constant if unexpressed subtext beneath the surface of so many of his investigations. We might then recognize the haptic folded in with the other sensory modes, when – for example – Herodotus tells us not just what a statue looks like but also how much it weighs, or when he gives us the physical measurements of an object by referring to the span of the hand or forearm, or when he tells us how long a journey might take on foot.[18] In other words, a slightly different conception of historiography can occur, as Paterson has suggested, "by adding once again the concrete experience of hands and feet to the abstract visualism of the eye" (2007: 9). Finally, in this brief overview of some of the

---

18. E.g. Herodotus, *Histories* 1.14; 1.50-51; 5.52-53. Cf. Paterson (2007: 59–77) and Herder on Greek sculpture: "Almost without wishing it our *sense of touch* is *drawn toward* every pliant curve and every delicate form" (Herder 2002: 91, original emphasis). See further Johnson (2002); Hersey (2009: 90–110); Porter (2010: 135–36) and this volume on Riegl. The same can be said of certain forms of painting, as Merleau-Ponty has remarked of Cézanne, in whose work he locates a strong tactile presence within the visual (1969). Weight, too, can only be conceptualized through a summoning of the sense of how something would feel when in the hands. On the haptic qualities of feeling through the feet, see esp. Ingold (2011: 45–46).

ways in which Herodotus might be considered a haptic geographer, it is worth considering how he refers to his historical method at the very opening of the work (1.1):[19]

> This (ἥδε) is the display of the history of Herodotus of Halicarnassus, put forth to prevent what has been made to happen by men from fading with time, and [to prevent] great and marvellous deeds, some accomplished by Greeks, others by barbarians, from losing fame, and in particular through what cause they came to war with each other. (Trans. Bakker 2002, adapted)

The use of the deictic pronoun ἥδε in the opening line suggests that the *Histories* is a tangible object, close enough to touch, and that the first real, demonstrative gesture in the work is the stretching out of Herodotus' hand to point towards it.[20] This does not have to mean that the *Histories* need to be visualized as a material object, but rather that the hand – specifically Herodotus' hand – plays a role in marking the tangibility of the account.

FEELING IN THE DARK

With these general observations about the haptic or sensuous nature of Herodotus' geography in mind, let us turn to the two stories that I mentioned at the outset of this essay, as we move from the practice of history writing to the actions of bodies within it. The hand in Herodotus' *Histories* can grasp, caress, feel for the truth or cling on for dear life, and its presence activates a special kind of proximal, intimate space that it is easier to feel than to see. This is all the more pronounced for a scene that plays out in the dark and that must progress so gently as not to wake the object of its inquiry.

SMERDIS' EARS

In book 3 of the *Histories*, Herodotus tells the story of Smerdis, an imposter king who has no ears. This Smerdis, a Persian magus, has capitalized on the fact that he has the same name as the brother of the dead king Cambyses. By pretending to be the royal (and secretly killed) Smerdis, this second imposter Smerdis has gained the throne. Yet Otanes, a Persian nobleman whose daughter has now become one of Smerdis's wives, suspects that something is amiss. Knowing that the magus Smerdis had his ears cut off by Cambyses for an offence some years before, he instructs his daughter to investigate in bed by feeling

---
19. Cf. Herodotus, *Histories* 2.65.2, where Herodotus uses a haptic metaphor to describe his practice as a historian: τὰ δὲ καὶ εἴρηκα αὐτῶν ἐπιψαύσας, ἀναγκαίῃ καταλαμβανόμενος εἶπον. ("I have only touched the surface of the things I have said, but I spoke compelled by necessity"). The verb ἐπιψαύω is also used at 3.87 of the groom touching the mare's genitals, another passage that might be profitably discussed in connection with the haptic.
20. Bakker (2002); the topic of history as monument also applies here, on which see Immerwahr (1960).

(ἀφάσσω) for his ears once she is sure he is deeply asleep (3.69.3). We are thus prepared for the hand that moves between Smerdis' sheets to go up rather than down, as it feels for the most secret place on her husband's body. The sexual outline of this story is unavoidable – not only is the ear an erogenous appendage, but as Ackerman has memorably put it of a different part of the body: "we most often touch a lover's genitals before we see them" (1990: 109).

The movement of the woman's hand is further pronounced by the darkness and silence of the scene, which narrow our senses to the haptic. The quest for the fleshy, warm ears, those flaps of skin with cartilage bent into their strange and private contours, brings a deeply personal touch to the story. The ears may be visible to the world, but they are not ordinarily open to even the most accidental of tactile encounters. In fact, the only other time in the *Histories* that we find an ear in someone else's hands is at moments of violation, when it is cut from the head in punishment or mutilation.[21]

Herodotus swiftly takes us through the key moments in this small bedroom drama. First, the instructions from the father, then the woman's fear of being caught in the act, and finally the anticlimax of discovering that the task was so easy after all (3.69.6): "Having come to him she slept with him, and when the magus was in a deep sleep she felt for his ears, and then discovered not with difficulty but quite easily that her husband did not have ears ..." (ἐλθοῦσα παρ' αὐτὸν ηὗδε, ὑπνωμένου δὲ καρτερῶς τοῦ μάγου ἤφασσε τὰ ὦτα. μαθοῦσα δὲ οὐ χαλεπῶς ἀλλ' εὐπετέως οὐκ ἔχοντα τὸν ἄνδρα ὦτα ...). Throughout it all, the imposter king sleeps deeply, feeling nothing, as if in uncanny response to the nothing that his wife feels where his ears are supposed to be.

I want to suggest that, although we know that Smerdis is an imposter by the time that the daughter conducts her investigation, the failure of hand and ear to meet at this moment still creates a small shock in the text. Furthermore, there is an interesting turn toward synaesthesia as the organ of hearing and the sense of touch reach for one another in the dark, as if to merge. Smerdis, as we know, is not deaf, and the ears that are being reached for here are important only in their tactile sense. They are instruments of flesh, skin, surface and feeling, not hearing (and the ears are, after all, often very sensitive to touch). Later in the *Histories*, Xerxes specifically locates the seat of one's feelings within the ears – it is there in the *ears*, according to Herodotus' Xerxes, that one's *thumos* is located (7.39.1): "Understand that a man's *thumos* resides in his ears, and when that *thumos* hears good things, the body fills up (ἐμπιπλέει) with delight, but when it hears the opposite it swells (ἀνοιδέει) [with anger]". The overlaying in this passage of the haptic and auditory senses – the twofold use of the participle *akousas* (hearing) and the two verbs denoting the feeling of "swelling" within the body (*empipleō, anoideō*) – expands the sensory potential of the ears. If ears can then be thought of, in this way, as haptically-sensing objects[22] then

---

21. Herodotus, *Histories* 2.162.5; 3.118.2; 3.154.2; [4.71.2]; 9.112.
22. Note also the ancient tradition of locating the seat of memory in the lower part of the ear, as mentioned by Pliny (*Natural History* 11.103) and the cameos such as the one now at the Getty Museum (Roman 400–500 CE) showing a hand pinching an ear between thumb and forefinger and surrounded by the words "Remember me, your dear sweetheart, and fare well, Sophronis".

this perhaps helps us to rethink the words spoken by Candaules to his bodyguard as to the reason why the latter must *see* his wife naked: "men's ears are more untrustworthy than their eyes" (1.8.2). In fact, the ears may both hear and "feel" in a way that is perhaps similar to the way in which the eyes see and "feel" too.[23]

The woman's touch, which is light enough to not be felt but strong enough to grasp the truth, tells a story that contains many familiar themes – touch as a marker of doubt, touch as verifier, touch as carnal union.[24] But still what I am most interested in by this passage is the idea of touch as *sensation,* the strange web of feeling and non-feeling shared between feeler, felt and reader, that holds this short episode in balance. We find similar effects in the touch that is *almost* shared between a woman and a man in the second story I want to examine, concerning Rhampsinitus' daughter and the thief.

TO CATCH A THIEF

In Herodotus' adaptation of a folktale known the world over,[25] a king of unsurpassed wealth asks a builder to construct a storehouse for his treasure. The builder does so, and later, on his deathbed, explains to his two sons that he made one stone on the outer wall of the storehouse removable. The two sons are easily able to remove and replace the stone with their hands, and night after night they subsequently steal the king's treasure. The king, surprised to see his treasure decreasing with no obvious signs of entry into the room, sets a trap within which the first brother is then caught. So as not to reveal the family's identity, the second brother cuts off the head of the body in the trap and takes it home with him. The king, now extremely puzzled, hangs the headless body on the city walls in order to catch the thief, posting guards alongside who are instructed to arrest anyone seen weeping or trying to remove the body. But the thief concocts a clever plan involving wine, bamboozles the guards, and recovers the body of his brother. Next the king's daughter enters the plot, who is required to sleep with man after man in the hopes of catching the thief. Before the sexual act can take place, each man must answer the question of what he has done in his life that is the most clever and the most impious. The thief, who hears about the king's offer of sex with his daughter, cuts off the arm of a freshly-dead corpse, slips it under his coat, and goes to visit the princess. When asked the prescribed question, he tells her nothing but the truth (2.121ε4): "the most impious thing he had done was cut off the head of his brother when he was caught in a trap within the king's treasure house, and the cleverest thing was when he got the guards drunk and retrieved the hanging corpse of his brother".

We might allow ourselves to imagine the excitement of the princess as she reaches out for the thief in the dark at the moment of revelation. Herodotus expresses her action in an economical and balanced phrase in three parts consisting of two words each (2.121ε5):

---
23. As discussed in the conclusion.
24. See further the essays in Classen (2005b).
25. S. West (2007).

Τὴν δέ, ὡς ἤκουσε, ἅπτεσθαι αὐτοῦ ("and she, hearing this, grabbed him"). Although most of Herodotus' sentences are long and paratactic, here it seems as if time is closing together in the simple six words across which the daughter only has to reach in order to hold the thief in her arms. Yet the man makes a counter move of his own, for he – in a parody of the normal gesture for intimacy and embrace – stretches out the dead hand, so that when the daughter touches him she will not feel, as she would expect, the warm spring of flesh responding to her own (2.121ε5):[26]

τὴν δέ, ὡς ἤκουσε, ἅπτεσθαι αὐτοῦ· τὸν δὲ φῶρα ἐν τῷ σκότεϊ προτεῖναι αὐτῇ τοῦ νεκροῦ τὴν χεῖρα· τὴν δὲ ἐπιλαβομένην ἔχειν, νομίζουσαν αὐτοῦ ἐκείνου τῆς χειρὸς ἀντέχεσθαι· τὸν δὲ φῶρα προέμενον αὐτῇ οἴχεσθαι διὰ θυρέων φεύγοντα.

She, hearing this, grabbed him – he in the dark stretched out toward her the hand of the corpse – she grabbed it and held it, holding on tight because she thought it was his hand (but she held the hand of the other one) – and he, giving the arm up to her, left by escaping through the door.

Instead, in an eerie reversal of the Pygmalion story,[27] the thief's flesh here must be disconcertingly cold to the touch. Left behind in the woman's arms, the arm becomes more *her* alien limb than his. Her touch, which was supposed to be felt on the skin of the man she touches, instead doubles back on herself, the touching subject, creating an uncanny echo or short circuit: the weirdness of holding a numb arm, of misjudging the touch. Unlike the hands that elsewhere in Herodotus keep fast their grip to the door handles even after they have been cut off (6.91.2), this hand does not grasp back at all.

In *The Absent Body*, Leder argues that we only really notice the body at moments of dysfunction – by which he means when something goes wrong with it or when it is somehow made to stand apart from itself, to be seen as separate. The body, as the ground of experience from which we sense and perceive, is normally, however, a kind of null point. This is particularly true of the sense organs – we cannot see our own eyes or smell our own noses. In his words, "Insofar as I perceive through an organ, it necessarily recedes from the perceptual field it discloses" (Leder 1990: 14). He notes the oft-cited experiment of the two hands in Merleau-Ponty, which demonstrates that no matter how hard we try, we cannot touch ourselves touching (Merleau-Ponty 1968: 147–8):

---

26. Cf. Paterson (2007: 2–3), on the importance of the difference between whether the object of touch is animate or inanimate: "Reaching out to touch and caress an animate object, such as a familiar cat or a warm-cheeked lover, the immediacy of sensation is affirmatory and comforting, involving a mutual co-implication of one's own body and another's presence". Touch has also long been associated with the bestowal of life (Stewart 2002: 170).
27. Ovid, *Metamorphoses* 10.282-4: "Admovet os iterum, manibus quoque pectora temptat: / temptatum mollescit ebur positoque rigore / subsidit digitis ceditque" ("Again he kissed her and with marveling touch / Caressed her breast; beneath his touch the flesh / Grew soft, its ivory hardness vanishing, / And yielded to his hands ..."; trans. Melville 1986).

> To begin with, we spoke summarily of a reversibility of the … touching and the touched. It is time to emphasize that it is a reversibility always imminent and never realized in fact. My left hand is always on the verge of touching my right hand touching the things, but I never reach coincidence; the coincidence eclipses at the moment of realization, and one of two things always occurs: either my right hand really passes over to the rank of the touched, but then its hold on the world is interrupted; or it retains its hold on the world, but then I do not really touch *it* – my right hand touching, I palpate with my left hand only its covering.

The unsettling presence of the alien hand in the story of King Rhampsinitus and the thief draws attention to the absent body and the overlooked act of touching particularly because of the breakdown that occurs between subject and object, toucher and touched, in the midst of the exchange.[28]

Keats's posthumously published poem, "This Living Hand" offers an illustration of precisely this phenomenon:

> This living hand, now warm and capable
> Of earnest grasping, would, if it were cold
> And in the icy silence of the tomb,
> So haunt thy days and chill thy dreaming nights
> That thou wouldst wish thine own heart dry of blood
> So in my veins red life might stream again,
> And thou be conscience-calmed – see here it is –
> I hold it towards you.

The speaker in the poem stretches out his own living hand to another at the same time as he asks her to imagine it dead. The poem ends by both reassuring us that the hand is alive and confusing us with the detachment of its final words – "see here it is – I hold it towards you", which casts the hand – "it" – as a third party, as if separate from the speaker's body: the arm becomes a thing. From start to finish the hand hovers between the two characters in the poem, interrupting and corrupting the reciprocal act of touch.[29]

---

28. Through a natural empathy, one body is *supposed* to take up the affective responses of another, to engage in a seamless exchange of reversibility and reciprocity between subject and object, toucher and touched. (Leder 1990: 94; Paterson 2007: 160).
29. There has been a considerable amount of speculation concerning this poem: is the hand actually alive or in fact dead? Who is the addressee? See further Hopkins (1989); Bahti (1996: 89–94); Stewart (1999: 35); Culler ([1981] 2001: 153–4); Stewart (2002: 160–78); Dubrow (2006: 267). In his essay on the uncanny, Freud specifically mentions Herodotus' telling of the Rhampsinitus and the Thief story, and this would appear to make sense. There is a girl, there is treasure, there is an arm standing in for the penis, the girl reaches out as if in an act of castration, yet there is some kind of disconnect. But Freud says this passage is not strictly uncanny because we do not experience it from the girl's perspective (Freud 2003: 152, 158; cf. McCaffrey 1994: 96–7). Herodotus tells us that he does not believe the final story involving the princess – claiming that this is where the story loses credibility.

The poem can help us in our reading of the moment of failed touch in the Herodotus story, which – to look at the passage again – is broken up into four cola (2.121.ε5):

τὴν δέ, ὡς ἤκουσε, ἅπτεσθαι αὐτοῦ· τὸν δὲ **φῶρα** ἐν τῷ σκότεϊ προτεῖναι αὐτῇ τοῦ νεκροῦ τὴν χεῖρα· **τὴν δὲ** ἐπιλαβομένην ἔχειν, νομίζουσαν αὐτοῦ ἐκείνου τῆς χειρὸς ἀντέχεσθαι· **τὸν δὲ φῶρα** προέμενον αὐτῇ οἴχεσθαι διὰ θυρέων φεύγοντα.

She, when she heard this, grabbed him; **he (the thief)** in the dark stretched out toward her the hand of the corpse; **she** grabbed it and held it, holding on tight because she thought it was his hand (but she held the hand of the other one); **he (the thief)**, giving the arm up to her, left by escaping through the door.

Here, the reciprocity of feeling that we would expect with the coming together of flesh and flesh instead spills over into a series of sentences where words for "he" and "she" shuttle back and forth, colliding but never settling together. Thus we have four successive phrases beginning *tēn de, ton de, tēn de, ton de … but she, but he, but she, but he*.[30] This reciprocity was supposed to work in at least two different ways. First, as we have discussed, there is the reciprocity of touch – the coming together of the senses of touching and being touched. The fumble in the dark pointedly substitutes for the sexual act that the couple was supposed to engage in, which Herodotus describes earlier in the passage using the verb συγγίγνομαι ("to be together with", 2.121ε2). Second is the reciprocity between the king and the thief, who, as Munson has noted, try to outdo one another with cleverness throughout the story.[31] The triangulation created by the woman just serves to make her more of a third wheel (or fifth arm?) in a courtship conducted between king and thief.

This thief, we already know, has a sure sense of touch. With his brother, he "easily handled" (ῥηιδίως μεταχειρίσασθαι) the loose stone to gain entrance into the treasure house (2.121α3). His deception of the guards relies on some deft fingerwork in the untying of the wine skins, and is also finished off by his shaving the right cheek of each of the guards as they sleep (2.121δ6). The daring and intimate act of drawing a blade across the surface of another man's face shows what the thief has learnt by becoming a thief – to feel his way carefully towards having things, while at the same time leaving skin and the seals on doors undamaged. For when the king first entered his robbed treasure house, he was amazed to see the room untouched, with seals intact and no sign of either entry or exit (2.121γ1: τὸ δὲ οἴκημα ἀσινὲς καὶ οὔτε ἔσοδον οὔτε ἔκδυσιν οὐδεμίαν ἔχον). The missing half of the beard, like the missing treasure, the missing head, and the surplus arm, all speak to the thief's undeniable but elusive presence. Each of these objects carry the

---

30. It is difficult to reproduce the play exactly in English without changing the meaning from "the thief" to "he". In the Greek, the article *ton* is paired with *phōra* (for "the thief"), but because the demonstrative pronoun "he" would also be *ton*, there is an inclination to pair it with its feminine counterpart *tēn* (she) used before and after.
31. Munson (1993).

imperceptible traces of his desire to "get his hands on something" that differ so markedly from the climactic grasp of the princess.

For the princess, on the other hand, the attempt to touch is described with a number of different verbs – συλλαμβάνω, ἅπτομαι, ἔχω, ἐπιλαμβάνομαι – but, still, her grasp is one that cannot hold on to what it wants. We might note that the move from ἔχω to ἀντέχω at 2.121.ε5 (above), from "hold" to "hold fast", contrasts with the simplicity of the phrase wherein the father tells the thieves the secret of the stone (2.121α2) "so that they might have (ἔχω) the king's treasure" (and have it they do).[32] The story ends when the king, impressed by the thief's trick, gives him his daughter to marry anyway (2.121ζ1–2). And so the daughter, also, by failing to catch the thief, gets to have him in the end.[33]

CONCLUSION

The feeling-in-the-dark touch is like that primal feeling-for-the-truth moment in the *Odyssey* when Eurycleia instantly recognizes Odysseus by feeling his scar even after he has first turned toward the shadows, suggesting that a special kind of truth comes from touch alone.[34] The *Histories* is too large and complex a text for me to be able to argue, within the brief compass of this paper, that the over-determined hands of these two relatively minor Herodotean women double for the overlooked hands of the historian. Yet these two small stories that take place in quiet bedrooms in the dark, which are played out on the most intimate and immediately-felt geography of the body, call our attention to the importance of reading Herodotus through the senses.

What these stories can tell us is that, in the *Histories*, the body senses rather than merely observes, and that the act of observing itself is neither simple nor non-sensory. Perhaps the Candaules and Gyges story expresses this best: as if in a critique of Candaules' simplistic statement about eyes versus ears, Herodotus – in the course of playing the story out – not only reveals but even activates the tactile properties of the queen's bare flesh. For when she stands naked with her back to the door, her skin is responsive enough to feel the "palpable" look of Gyges upon it.[35] The naked body is not (just or necessarily) an object to be looked at, but a body that is especially expressive, that feels and senses its physical environment.[36] Haptic theories of sight were commonplace enough in the ancient world

---

32. Similarly, the guards of the headless corpse are instructed to "grab" (συνλαμβάνομαι) whomever they see weeping before the body. The princess is instructed by her father to grab the thief (using the same verb) as soon as she detects him.
33. In a similar way, the touch of the daughter crosses the divide between what is close and what is far away, in a tale that is marked for its extensive use of indirect discourse (S. West 2007). On the coordinates of intimate space in Herodotus, see also Purves (forthcoming).
34. On which, see Montiglio (forthcoming).
35. Cf. Porter (2010: 19, n. 18).
36. Along similar lines, Obrador-Pons (2007: esp. 128–32) argues that – contrary to the popular conception – nude sunbathing is practised because it allows the body to feel its environment (such as sun, water and wind) better, with looking having very little to do with it.

to suggest some kind of materiality to Gyges' gaze, which can be "felt" on the naked back of the queen.[37] She sees him, after all, without ever turning around, suggesting that she somehow feels the touch of his look.

Thus, although what I have done in this essay is to focus on some of the places where the sense of touch is especially privileged over the sense of sight, it is worth stressing that these two stories that take place in the dark are also extreme cases. Perhaps their very oddness points to the unusual effect of isolating only one of the senses and separating it from the others, despite our own widespread use of this practice when reading ancient texts.

---

37. The eyes can either (or sometimes together) emit fiery or material rays on their object of sight or receive them back in from the object. Aristotle rejected both theories, but they can be found in early Greek poetry and philosophy, as in plenty of later sources. See further Simon (1988); Morales (2004: 130–35); Porter (2010: esp. 416–20); Cairns (2011); as well as Porter and Volk in this volume.

3

THE UNDERSTANDING EAR: SYNAESTHESIA, PARAESTHESIA AND TALKING ANIMALS

Mark Payne

WAGNER, POETRY AND THE EYE OF HEARING

Synaesthesia, as a goal for the arts, has meant the production of simultaneous aesthetic experiences in more than one of the senses, even if the artwork that aims at producing these experiences exists only in a single medium. Among nineteenth-century French poets, for example, Baudelaire, in his sonnet "Correspondances", spoke of equivalences between sound, smell and colour, such that the sound of poetry composed with these equivalences in mind might produce complementary olfactory or visual experiences in the listener. Rimbaud, in his sonnet "Voyelles", went so far as to offer a primer for this aesthetic labour by colouring in the vowels of the French language for future use: A is black, E white, I red, U green and O blue. In this version of synaesthesia, each of the senses is conceived as a single faculty, and the aesthetic experience it enables as unitary. A synaesthetic poem produces sounds for hearing, colours for seeing, and smells (fragrances, usually) for smelling, and these sensations are harmonious when they happen together because of a natural affinity between them.

From this perspective, the appeal of Richard Wagner's opera for French poetic theorists of synaesthesia is easy to understand. The idea that opera is a total work of art in which music, spectacle and libretto complement one another would seem to fully realize their ambitions for an artistic sensorium in which complementary aesthetic experiences happen simultaneously. Baudelaire, in fact, in his essay on *Tannhäuser*, claims that the real surprise of this opera is not that synaesthesia becomes a reality in it for the first time, but rather that it could be possible for sound not to suggest colour, for colours not to give the idea of a melody, and for sound and colour to be inappropriate to translate ideas. For the equivalence between them belong to God's utterance of the world as a complex, indivisible totality.[1] Baudelaire then cites his own poem "Correspondances" as an adumbration and

---

1. Baudelaire (1976: 784): "Ce qui serait vraiment surprenant, c'est que le son *ne pût pas* suggérer la couleur, que les couleurs *ne pussent pas* donner l'idée d'une mélodie, et que le son et la couleur fussent impropres

exposition of the composer's achievement in giving expression to the underlying unity of aesthetic experience in nature.

Baudelaire's praise of Wagner, and his conviction that his own work is based upon the same poetic principles, seem natural enough until you discover that Wagner himself thought that aesthetic experience was not a unitary phenomenon for the faculty of hearing. In *Opera and Drama*, he reflects on the nature of aesthetic conviction and what the production of such conviction in an audience demands of him as poet and musician:

> Just as that man alone can display himself in full persuasiveness, who announces himself to our ear and eye at once: so the message-bearer of the inner man cannot completely convince our Hearing, until it addresses itself with equal persuasiveness to both "eye and ear" of this Hearing. But this happens only through *Word-Tone-speech*, and poet and musician have hitherto addressed but half the man apiece: the poet turned towards this Hearing's eye alone, the musician only to its ear. Yet nothing but the whole seeing and hearing, – that is to say, the completely *understanding* Ear, can apprehend the inner man past all mistake.[2]

In contrast to Baudelaire, who believed Wagner's opera offered complementary, unitary satisfactions to the ear and the eye, Wagner imagines audition as a binary aesthetic experience accomplished by an "eye" and an "ear" of hearing. The composer of the total work of art must satisfy the "eye of hearing" in his capacity as a poet, and the "ear of hearing" in his capacity as a musician, and he does so with "Word-Tone-speech".

How, then, does the composer of Word-Tone-speech accomplish the twofold satisfaction he seeks with it? Wagner's poetry for the libretto of the *Ring* is composed in *Stabreim*, an assonant metre he adopted from early German verse. Examples of how to use it discussed in *Opera and Drama* are "Liebe giebt Lust zum Leben" and "Liebe bringt Lust und Lied". Both are good examples of *Stabreim* as far as the sound of the words is concerned, but there is a difference between them. The first is an emotionally consistent expression, and so requires music in a single key to accompany it if the Word-Tone-speech as a whole is to satisfy both the eye and the ear of hearing. The second, by contrast, is emotionally inconsistent and so requires variation.[3]

The task of the composer of Word-Tone-speech is twofold therefore: first, he must bring together speech-roots whose natural affinity has been sundered in ordinary language; second, he must match these roots with music according to whether their reunion in his lyrics is cognitively harmonious or dissonant. His task is further complicated by the fact that just as there is an ear of hearing that attends to the sounds of music, and an eye of hearing that attends to the sounds of poetry, so the eye of hearing attends differently to vowels and consonants. In Wagner's history of language, the first speakers of a language

---

à traduire des idées; les choses s'étant toujours exprimées par une analogie réciproque, depuis le jour où Dieu a proféré le monde comme une complexe et indivisible totalité."
2. Wagner (1995: 273–4). Original emphasis.
3. *Ibid.*: 227–9, 292.

produce vowels as unmediated emotional utterance; only later do they wrap these vowels in consonants so as to make their feelings intelligible to others as articulate discourse. In their naked vocalizations, human beings are no different from other animals. In this respect, the addition of consonants is analogous to the use of gestures, for both give semantic precision to the voice's intention. Even the wood-bird, "the animal which expresses its emotion the most melodiously", cannot easily make itself understood because it "lacks all power of accompanying its song by gestures".[4]

To summarize Wagner's theoretical position, then, we can say that just as Word-Tone-speech addresses music to the ear of hearing and poetry to the eye of hearing, so the *Stabreim* of which this poetry is composed addresses vowels to one part of the eye of hearing and consonants to another part. In keeping with Wagner's belief that vowels are the emotional body of lyric utterance and consonants its semantic clothing, we may call the faculty of the eye of hearing addressed by vowels its heart, and the faculty of the eye of hearing addressed by consonants its mind.

How does this theory work in practice? Consider the wood-bird's song in the second Act of *Siegfried*. At the moment when Siegfried licks his hands after killing the dragon Fafnir, he is able to understand the song of the wood-bird with whom he has been trying unsuccessfully to communicate since the beginning of the Act. Wagner rounds out their exchange by having the bird comment on the conditions for his being understood:

Lustig im Leid
sing' ich von Liebe;
wonnig aus Weh
web' ich mein Lied;
nur Sehnende kennen den Sinn!

Merry in grief I sing about love. Blissful, from pain I weave my song.
Only those who yearn understand its meaning.

The wood-bird's song deploys semantic clusters much like those Wagner refers to in his discussion of *Stabreim* in *Opera and Drama*: "Lustig, Leid, Liebe, Lied"; "Wonnig, Weh, weben".[5] Why is a bird's utterance the proving ground for the theory of Word-Tone-speech? Because for the clustering of these speech-roots to be properly appreciated, they must reach the heart and the mind of the eye of the audience's hearing, and a wood-bird – even one singing opera – is incapable of gestures that make its melodious expression semantically precise. The poetry has to work here without the additional expressive potential of a human actor's gestures, and its success or failure will be particularly noticeable given that the wood-bird is not only enacting inter-species communication but also reflecting on the conditions of its possibility. The performance seems to halt for a moment as

---

4. *Ibid.*: 224–5.
5. *Ibid.*: 270, 292.

communication itself – "the completely understanding ear"[6] that is the goal of all performance – plays out before the audience's ears in the staging of connectivity between human being and animal.

Hence the crucial encounter of *sehnen* and *Sinn* in the *Stabreim*. The wood-bird has nothing to say about dragon's blood or any other kind of magical hermeneutics. From his perspective, he has been expressing himself clearly all along. The audience likewise has always been privy to what Siegfried can only now understand. The second order awareness of a perceptual power coming online that the listener experiences in this scene is not therefore an awareness of cognition – of the mind of the eye of hearing in operation – but rather of understanding in a fuller sense – the "completely understanding Ear" in which music, and the vowels and consonants of poetry, are heard together as a kind of reattunement to animate being as a whole. The experience feels magical but its precondition is voluntary; Siegfried longs to communicate with the wood-bird when he first hears his melodious utterance but cannot understand it, and he makes a flute with which he tries unsuccessfully to communicate with him. It is this will to understand that emerges from desire that the wood-bird acknowledges when he recognizes Siegfried as one who, like himself, comes to understanding through yearning: *nur Sehnende kennen den Sinn*.

ANIMALS IN THE EYE OF HEARING

The performance of inter-species communication between Siegfried and the wood-bird is an aesthetic event that "addresses itself with equal persuasiveness to both 'eye and ear' of … Hearing".[7] As such, however, it is best described not as synaesthesia, but as par-aesthesia. The audience must feel the natural affinity between the speech-roots brought together in the *Stabreim*, and it must feel that the manner of their encounter there is properly expressed in the music that accompanies it. What the audience experiences, therefore, is not a plurality of unitary aesthetic experiences occurring together because of a natural equivalence between them (*syn*-aesthesia), but rather an unexpected fitness that emerges alongside the ordinary sense of words (*par*-aesthesia). The feeling that words have a natural aptitude for what they express is particularly intense in the scene between Siegfried and the wood-bird because the awakening of this feeling is thematized and staged as a reattunement to the sounds of the natural world. Hearing nature and hearing human language properly are one and the same experience.

I would like to turn now to two ancient attempts to communicate animal communication in human language – Aristophanes' *Birds* and the *Cynegetica* (*On Hunting*) attributed to Oppian – with Wagner's ambitions in mind. For it seems to me that Wagner's claim that, even within the eye of hearing addressed by poetry, there are two distinct faculties, a mind and a heart, and that both of these must be active if we are to speak of a completely

---

6. *Ibid.*: 274.
7. *Ibid.*: 273–4.

understanding Ear, is helpful for recognizing what is at stake in these ancient representations of inter-species communication.

I begin my approach to these ancient poetic endeavours with Aristotle, who, in *Parts of Animals*, suggests that human beings perceive a desire to make themselves understood in the songs of birds:

> All birds make use of their tongue to communicate with one another (πρὸς ἑρμηνείαν ἀλλήλοις) and some very much more so than others, so that with some there does indeed seem to be an exchange of knowledge among them (ὥστ' ἐπ' ἐνίων καὶ μάθησιν εἶναι δοκεῖν παρ' ἀλλήλων).[8]

Aristotle does not go beyond seeming here; a gap emerges between the observation on the basis of which one is likely to believe that birds exchange information with one another and what can legitimately be concluded from this observation. He does not suggest what would turn intimation into conviction, but there is a semantic deficit, as in Wagner's observations on birds' incapacity for gesture. Birdsong creates a cognitive desire it cannot fulfil because we cannot be sure whether what we hear in its mannered, patterned forms is really evidence of a desire to communicate or merely the externalization of an inner feeling without semantic conditioning: Wagner's wood-bird that "expresses its emotion the most melodiously", but whose utterance can only be felt as an intention to communicate, not understood as actual communication.

It is into this cognitive breach that Athenian Old Comedy boldly leaps. Its playwrights created a distinct subgenre in which encounters between human beings and other animals could be staged, as dialogue between them is made possible in a variety of ways.[9] Aristophanes' *Birds* belongs to this subgenre, although Aristophanes ups the tension in its opening scene by presenting the mutual incomprehensibility of human beings and birds as a dramatic problem that threatens to end the play before it has begun. Two Athenians in voluntary exile, Peisetairus and Euelpides, are lost and cannot understand the cawing of the corvids they have taken as their guides to the home of the tragic hero Tereus, who has been transformed into a hoopoe after his misadventures among humankind. It is only when Peisetairus suggests that, when calling upon a hoopoe, ἔποπα, one should shout not "Boy, boy (παῖ, παῖ)", but rather "oh hoopoe (ἐποποῖ)" (56–60), that they get a response from inside the stage building and the drama can go on.

ἐποποῖ is a sound that, in this play at least, is both a vocative of the noun hoopoe and evocative of the non-verbal exclamation of a tragic hero in pain, which is what Tereus had been before his transformation into a bird. The most ample examples of such cries are to be found in Sophocles' *Philoctetes*, where they extend to half lines and even, on one occasion, to a whole line of verse, the notorious ἀπαππαπαῖ, παπᾶ παπᾶ παπᾶ παπαῖ

---

8. Aristotle, *Parts of Animals* 2.17, 660a35–b3; cf. *History of Animals* 536b9–13, where he suggests that "one might call their voice [φωνή] a kind of speech" (ἢν ἄν τις ὥσπερ διάλεκτον εἴπειεν).
9. I discuss *Birds* more fully in relation to Aristotle's theories of nonhuman utterance and the subgenre of Old Comedy that staged encounters between human beings and other speaking animals in Payne (2010: 83–99).

(746). Philoctetes' cries are an indication of his suffering, much as the φωνή of non-human animals is, Aristotle claims in the *Politics*, a sign of their affective condition, without being language as such (1.1.10, 1253a11–13). And it is as such that these non-verbal utterances drive other human beings away, cutting Philoctetes off from human society. As H. P. Lovecraft observes in "The Call of Cthulhu", "there are vocal qualities peculiar to men, and vocal qualities peculiar to beasts; and it is terrible to hear the one when the source should yield the other".[10]

In *Birds*, however, the uttering by the human characters of a sound that is nominally a word within the fiction, but more familiarly a non-verbal indication outside of it, is a literal *open sesame*: it is the efficient cause that opens the doors of the house of Tereus that have hitherto been closed to them. The sufficient cause is desire: their yearning for a life unlike life at Athens that has brought them to the doors of Tereus' house and that will, in due course, induce Peisetairus to imagine a life for them among the birds.

Fortunately for Peisetairus, Tereus has taught birds the speech (φωνή) of human beings during his time with them, and he offers to gather them together to listen to Peisetairus' plan. He does so with an elaborate summoning song – a kletic hymn of sorts – in which he describes the various habitats in which birds of various kinds might be found pursuing their diverse feeding habits, from seed gatherers in sown fields, to meadow dwelling insect eaters and exotic oceanic kingfishers.

The summons weaves the sounds of bird song together with the sounds of human words that resemble them. A vocalization that sounds like an invocation at its outset – ἐποποποῖ – turns into pure sound – ποποποποῖ ποποῖ, | ἰὼ ἰὼ ἰτὼ ἰτὼ ἰτὼ ἰτὼ – only to have this sound morph seamlessly into its homophone, the imperative "come (ἴτω)", and conclude as a comprehensible request: "Let each of my wingmen put in an appearance" (227–9). This general summons is followed by a division into kinds: first, the invocation of seed eaters that ends τιο τιο τιο τιο τιο τιο τιο τιο; second, the call to berry feeders that ends τριοτό τριοτό τοτοβρίξ; third, the call to insectivores and sea birds that concludes with another general appeal and a final blend of human language and pure sound: δεῦρο δεῦρο δεῦρο δεῦρο | τορο τορο τορο τοροτίξ | κικκαβαῦ κικκαβαῦ | τορο τορο τορο τορο λιλιλίξ.

Given that the sound strings in the summoning song are prefaced by indications of lifestyle, it seems likely that Aristophanes is neither modelling the calls of particular species, nor imitating birdsong in general,[11] but rather representing kinds of birds, as Greek stylistic theory models kinds of human character – the smooth, the grand, the impressive, and so forth – on the basis of their characteristic forms of utterance. A relationship between lifestyle and phoneme inventory is articulated such that the audience perceives a fit between certain sound clusters in their own language and certain kinds of nonhuman lives. Indeed, it is this paraesthetic experience of their own language that opens up their hearing to the apprehension that the sounds of birdsong may encode the same kinds of information as they themselves exchange in their own everyday communication.

---

10. Lovecraft (2005b: 179).
11. For evidence in support of both claims, see Dunbar (1998: 155–66).

In addition, because of the way in which words of the Greek language are interwoven with sounds that are not, it becomes clear that what the audience is being invited to conceive are complete sentences in a variety of bird languages of which only parts are comprehensible to them. When δεῦρο δεῦρο δεῦρο δεῦρο is followed by τορο τορο τορο τοροτίξ, etc., the listener has, I think, to imagine that the latter somehow completes the request that is minimally present in the former by supplying additional information in the language of this particular group of birds. Dramatically, at least, this seems to be the case, since the various kinds of birds do in fact understand what is being asked of them and make their appearance shortly thereafter.

Did Aristophanes, as dramaturge, aim at a "completely understanding Ear" with musical accompaniment that would satisfy the ear of hearing as ambitiously as his text satisfies its eye? Or did the music deflate the pretensions of the mimetic event as the frequent reminders of the inadequacy of the actors' costumes do?[12] This is a question that cannot be answered. What can be said is that, in its address to the eye of hearing, Aristophanes' song produces conviction by giving pleasure, and that its way of giving pleasure turns tragic sound on its head.

The tragic hero in pain switches between rational discourse and nonverbal cries such that his expression of pure sound is an affective high point and an aesthetic low point: the thrill of hearing a human being fill the air with disquieting noise. In *Birds*, by contrast, the phonic blocks that instantiate these cries of pain are reused as elements of a nonhuman language. What in one discourse is an affective signal instantly productive of alienation in its auditors is in the other an index of sociality and an aesthetic climax: an occasion for metrical, vocal, and, surely, musical exuberance.

The joyous representation of nonhuman communication in *Birds* contrasts with tragedy's generally dismal conception of the lives of other animals as a wretched reduction from the blessed state of humanness. The play's address to the eye of hearing is upbeat about the conditions for communication. In contrast to the *Philoctetes*, in which to emit nonhuman sound is to forgo understanding even from one's own species, *Birds* offers a robust appraisal of the pragmatics of inter-species communication: one will not understand everything that is uttered in a foreign tongue but this is not an absolute barrier to understanding so long as one acknowledges an intention to communicate behind the alien physiognomy of the utterance.[13]

The *Cynegetica*, a third century CE Greek poem about hunting attributed to Oppian but dedicated to the emperor Caracalla, and so unlikely to be the work of the same Oppian who wrote a *Halieutica* dedicated to Marcus Aurelius that enjoyed wide appeal, assesses the conditions for acknowledgement and disavowal of this kind. The author of the *Cynegetica* appears to be less interested in how to catch animals than in dramatizing the suffering they endure in being hunted so as to suggest the continuity of their mental representations

---

12. See Foley (2000: 305).
13. Cf. Wagner (1995: 268): *Stabreim* makes the "physiognomic likeness" of root-words "swiftly recognizable" to the eye of hearing. Interestingly, given his friendship with Samuel Lehrs, an editor of Oppian, Wagner may well have known the *Cynegetica*; see Schadewalt (1999: 112).

with those of human beings.[14] When he comes to the hunting of wild goats, for example, he imagines the defensive behaviour of a mother goat towards her children to include explicit articulation of the death that threatens them (2.358–61):

τὴν μὲν γὰρ δοκέοις παῖδας μύθοισι δίεσθαι,
λισσομένην τοίοισιν ἀπόπροθι μηκηθμοῖσι·
φεύγετέ μοι, φίλα τέκνα, δυσαντέας ἀγρευτῆρας,
μή με λυγρὴν δμηθέντες ἀμήτορα μητέρα θῆτε.
τοῖα φάμεν δοκέοις.

You would think she was chasing away her children with words, begging them to go far away with her bleating: "Flee from the hard-hearted huntsmen, my dear children, lest by killing you they make me a grieving mother who is a mother no more". This is what you would think she said.

The poet puts his readers on the spot and tells them that, were they there, they might hear in the mother goat's voice not just an approximation of human lamentation, but articulate speech. The suggestion is keyed by the onomatopoeia in the last line of her address to her children: μή με λυγρὴν δμηθέντες ἀμήτορα μητέρα θῆτε. The *mus* and *etas* that not only compose human words but also reproduce the sound of bleating are drawn out of μυκηθμός, the noun for ruminant utterance that introduces her speech. The poet foregrounds the emotional core of the mother goat's utterance by stringing together a series of the vowels on which the ordinary language onomatopoeia of μυκηθμός depends. As parts of words in a human language, however, these vowel sounds come clothed in consonants that give them meaning as distinct semantic gestures. For the duration of a hexameter, we hear words in the mother goat's bleating, and bleating in our words. The paraesthetic experience of the Greek language opens the listener's ears to the possibility that goats have intentions in their voice, just as human beings do; in Wagner's terms, the poem appeals to the heart of the eye of hearing as well as to its mind.

By framing the mother goat's utterance with the repeated "you would think", δοκέοις, the poet invites his readers to consider what would be required on their part to hear it as speech and what would be involved in refusing it this status. If we think again of the *Philoctetes*, the mother goat's cries have the opposite effect to the hero's cries in that play, for they draw her children to her when she wishes they would flee, even as the poet is at pains to point out the scene's resemblance to the *mise-en-scène* of a classical tragedy (2.362–6):

---

14. Effe (1977: 174–84) notes the difficulty in identifying the point of view from which the poet of the *Cynegetica* approaches his material, and so has difficulty locating the poem within his typology of didactic poetry; Toohey (1996: 199–204) likewise points to a contrast between the poet's anthropomorphism and his "loathing of animal sexuality"; Whitby (2007: 125–6) suggests that the "rhetorical mannerisms and lexical novelties" of the *Cynegetica* proved less appealing to elite readers than the "Callimachean aesthetics and proportions" of the *Halieutica*, despite the popularity of hunting scenes in the plastic arts as "a symbol of wealth and power" (*ibid.*: 134).

τοὺς δ' ἑσταότας προπάροιθε
πρῶτα μὲν ἀείδειν στονόεν μέλος ἀμφὶ τεκούσῃ,
αὐτὰρ ἔπειτ' ἐνέπειν φαίης μεροπήιον ἠχήν,
ῥηξαμένους βληχήν, στομάτων τ' ἄπο τοῖον ἀυτεῖν,
φθεγγομένοις ἰκέλους καὶ λισσομένοισιν ὁμοίους.

Standing before her you would say that they first sang a mournful dirge for their begetter, then spoke the language of mortal men, breaking forth in bleating, and from their mouths uttered such words as this, like human speakers and resembling those who supplicate.

The young goats perform the parts of a tragedy, singing a mournful song like a chorus, then returning to the urgent task of dialogue with their pursuer. This time the poet puts his readers on the spot by framing his rendition of the young goats' utterance with verbs that typically introduce ecphrasis: φαίης (364) and τις ἄν δόξειε (373). In this case, however, the observer is asked to focus on auditory, rather visual phenomena. The invocation of ecphrasis reminds us that, as we always engage in interpretation, however minimal, when we look at what we recognize as a deliberately fashioned visual image, so the eye of the ear had also to be trained to find meaning in the sound even of other human beings, although this interpretive work is no longer before our eyes when we hear words in our own tongue.

The poet ends the scene by having the young goats ask the hunter if he too has an aged parent "left behind in his bright home" (2.367–72). The question recalls Priam's plea to Achilles in Book 24 of the *Iliad*, where the Trojan king's success in asking for the return of his son's body rests upon his ability to convince his fearsome adversary of the analogy between his father's situation and his own. As Priam's words have no power over Achilles until he allows them to be informed by an understanding of the paternal affects from which they emerge, so the bleating of the goats is imagined both as mere sound, and as what may be perceived as an entreaty if acknowledgement of an intention to communicate is allowed to enable semantic apprehension.

The outcome of neither encounter is a given. As Priam comes close to overtaxing Achilles' sympathy, so the hunter may be persuaded, but, if he has a heart that is entirely without pity, κραδίην παναμείλιχον, the young goats will follow their mother into bondage (2.374–6). In the *Cynegetica*, a single line of onomatopoeia stands for this critical moment of possibility and danger. For it is with this line, so jarringly alien to epic decorum, that the eye of hearing will either open or close and the imaginative superstructure that depends on it either stand or fall as a consequence.

ACOUSTIC FLESH, SEMANTIC SKIN, ANIMAL BONES

Paraesthesia, then, is something more than an aberration, a local effect or sideshow in the history of aestheticizing language. Recall Aristotle's description of the dubious sensation human beings experience when listening to birdsong. Is it what we think it is, and, if not, why do we experience it – dubiously – as such? Aristotle will elsewhere shoo away the questions raised by the haunting encounter with birds at the threshold of nonhuman utterance by invoking the metaphysics of *logos*. Human beings and birds may be similar in the manner of their vocal production in so far as both have a flexible tongue that divides their utterance into articulate units that sound remarkably alike, but this similarity is ultimately misleading: human beings alone among animals participate in the incorporeal reflective activity of the gods through the exercise of reason, and this participation makes their speech just as exceptional as an expression of this reasoning.[15]

We moderns, naturally, cannot so easily backstop our exceptionality with metaphysics and ontology; unless we simply stop our ears, there is no way for us to escape the connectivity with nonhuman lives our senses offer us. No contemporary thinker has attuned himself to this connectivity more profoundly than Michel Serres. Starting from where Aristotle ends up – reasoning human speech – Serres, rather than pulling the ladder up from below, attempts instead to climb down it, into that clamorous region from which human language emerged:

> Writing or speaking only have value if they suddenly capture, by dint of listening, that whole layer of language whose thickness is measured from the improbable meaning deposited, on top, over the acoustic flesh – vowels, rhythms, number and movement – down to the low base where this clamor touches the musical bole from which all languages bifurcate in branches.[16]

The human language tree has its roots in soil that supports growth of many kinds. When we attend to the sounds of our own language, we sense their divergence from the common stock of human utterance, and so in turn the rootedness of human utterance in the common ground of utterance as a whole, both human and nonhuman. From this perspective, paraesthesia is vital in bringing the connectivity of our senses online, in actualizing their potential to reattune us to nonhuman life. For paraesthesia is the aestheticization of dubiety, that feeling of a sudden strangeness in ordinary phenomena H. P. Lovecraft calls weirdness: "the suspension or defeat of those fixed laws of Nature which are our only safeguard against the assaults of chaos and the daemons of unplumbed space".[17] Our only safeguard, that is to say, against the reality of the other lives by which our own are constantly surrounded, and whose acknowledgement would make us something other than the human beings we know ourselves to be.

---

15. On the flexible tongue, see Aristotle, *History of Animals* 2.12, 504b1–3; 4.9, 535a28–536a22, and cf. *On the Soul* 3.4, 429a22–7: νοῦς is not present until the activity of thinking begins, is not mixed with the body, and, unlike perception, has no organ; for lengthier discussion in the context of Aristotle's treatment of nonhuman utterance in the zoological works, see Payne (2010: 87) and cf. Sorabji (1993) 12–16, 55–58; Heath (2005) 6–17.
16. Serres (2009: 265).
17. Lovecraft (2005a: 107).

4

ARISTOPHANES, CRATINUS AND THE SMELL OF COMEDY

Mario Telò

OLFACTION AND THE COMIC SELF

More than any other genre, comedy thrives on the representation of reality as an embodied experience involving the full spectrum of sensory perceptions and capitalizing on the synaesthetic effects entailed by their interactions.[1] The festive dialogue between multiple corporeal functions which lies at the root of the Bakhtinian idea of the grotesque body constitutes one of the distinctive features of ancient satiric discourse in all of its manifestations and, above all, in Old Comedy. Adopting a Bakhtinian viewpoint, one could say that the plays of Aristophanes and his rivals dramatize a transgression not only of social but also of sensory hierarchies.[2] The prominence accorded, in the surviving texts of Old Comedy, to the more sensuous and carnal senses of touch, taste and smell[3] seems, in fact, to call into question the epistemological centrality ascribed in ancient (as well as modern) times to sight and to foster an alternative aesthetic regime that enhances the inherently visual quality of theatrical performance. In this essay, I would like to illustrate the privileged position that Aristophanes affords to smell[4] by exploring the role of the olfactory experience in his articulation of his comic persona.

Studies on the psychology and sociology of the senses have indicated that smell functions as a favourite symbolic tool through which social actors construct the self versus other dichotomy.[5] The main contention of this essay is that, in *Knights*, Aristophanes'

---

1. By "synaesthesia" I define the process whereby a sensory experience is translated and assimilated into another. For an example, cf. Scarry (1999: 4): "a visual event may reproduce itself in the realm of touch (as when the seen face incites an ache of longing in the hand and the hand then presses pencil to paper)". See the Introduction of this volume.
2. On the Bakhtinian questioning of the ocularcentric bias, see Gardiner (1999: 60).
3. On Aristophanes' philosophy of multisensory perception, cf. Clements (2006) and in this volume.
4. Most recently, Tordoff (2011) has explored the centrality of the olfactory code in the thematic construct of *Peace*. For a survey of the various odours described in the Aristophanic corpus, cf. Thiercy (1993).
5. See especially Howes (2003: 54–6); Largey & Watson (2006); M. M. Smith (2007: 59–60, 66–74).

projection of his comic self is olfactorily coded. In particular, I maintain that, in this play, Aristophanes' depiction of the rivalry with his older competitor Cratinus follows an olfactory trajectory and fashions the confrontation between two opposed ideas of comedy as a conflict between two incompatible odours.

My journey through the smellscapes of Aristophanic comedy will touch upon another issue central to the semiotics of olfaction, namely the relationship between scent and memory.[6] Undoubtedly, "odours are unmatched in catalyzing the evocation of distant memories and places".[7] As has been observed, "the palimpsest is a particularly useful metaphor for smell":[8] both the literary palimpsest and the memory-inducing odour compress past and present into a unified plane of legibility. My analysis of *Knights* pushes this comparison further and suggests that, besides establishing links with past events and objects, smells can also act as triggers for intertextual recollection. As we shall see, the divine fragrance through which Aristophanes constructs his poetic identity in the finale of *Knights* allusively resonates (or, I should say, "re-olfactates") with a famous Odyssean scene. I hope to show that what is at stake in the olfactory struggle between Aristophanes and Cratinus that is staged in *Knights* is the styling of their comic personas after different literary forebears. Within this game of poetic affiliations, the Odyssean *essence* of Aristophanic comedy stands in stark contrast with the Archilochean one emanating from Cratinus' plays. As I argue, Aristophanes' nasal poetics as advertised in *Knights* amounts to a paradoxical attempt to rejuvenate comedy by re-connecting it to its Odyssean origins. Aristophanes' poetological discourse reaches far beyond the visual paradigm by shaping a smell-centered physiology that throws into relief conflicting generic genealogies as well as polarized models of comic reception. By constructing interpoetic rivalry through the olfactory sense, Aristophanes overcomes the material distance between performer and spectator that is inherent to theatrical vision, presenting the response to comedy as a "felt" experience, a form of contact affecting the bodies of the audience.

My argument is divided in three parts. In the first, I consider some of the strategies that, in *Knights*, Aristophanes deploys to map his rivalry with Cratinus onto the political contest between the Sausage Seller and Paphlagon. In particular, I call attention to Aristophanes' characterization of both Paphlagon and Cratinus as embodiments of olfactory badness. In the second part, I use the shared δυσοσμία of Paphlagon and Cratinus as a route into a broader exploration of the bearing that the olfactory code has on Aristophanes' definition of his generic affiliations and comic identity against his old rival's. The main outcome of this analysis is a new reading of the Sausage Seller's rejuvenation of Demos in the closing scene of *Knights* as a re-enactment of Athena's beautification of Odysseus through ambrosia in the *Odyssey*. As I detail in the third part, this connection with ambrosia aligns with Aristophanes' purported goal of restoring the comic self to its original Odyssean fragrance and rescuing the Athenian audience from the pungent aroma of Cratinus' Archilochean

---

6. On olfactory memory see, in particular, Corbin (1986: 82–3); Rindisbacher (1992: 14–15); Shulman (2006); Harris (2007: 469) (with further bibliography).
7. Drobnick (2006: 1).
8. Harris (2007: 472).

comedy. Whereas Cratinean comedy projects a hierarchical model of dramatist-audience relationship predicated upon the notion of comic reception as an overwhelming and intoxicating experience, Aristophanes views the same relationship in terms of an intellectual exchange replicating the collaboration between Odysseus and Athena in the *Odyssey*.

SNIFFING OUT INTERPOETIC RIVALRY IN *KNIGHTS*

In the parabasis of *Knights* Aristophanes outlines a chapter of "do-it-yourself literary history" by supplying a catalogue of his most illustrious predecessors (Magnes, Crates, Cratinus). Within this parade of comedy's greats, Cratinus occupies a central position. In lines 531–36, he is depicted as sexually as well as poetically impotent, a broken-down, babbling and, especially, drunken old man who has irremediably lost the river-like force (526–8) of his distinctive flooding satire:

> νυνὶ δ' ὑμεῖς αὐτὸν ὁρῶντες παραληροῦντ' οὐκ ἐλεεῖτε,
> ἐκπιπτουσῶν τῶν ἠλέκτρων καὶ τοῦ τόνου οὐκέτ' ἐνόντος
> τῶν θ' ἁρμονιῶν διαχασκουσῶν· ἀλλὰ γέρων ὢν περιέρρει,
> ὥσπερ Κοννᾶς, στέφανον μὲν ἔχων αὖον, δίψῃ δ' ἀπολωλώς,
> ὃν χρῆν διὰ τὰς προτέρας νίκας πίνειν ἐν τῷ πρυτανείῳ,   535
> καὶ μὴ ληρεῖν, ἀλλὰ θεᾶσθαι λιπαρὸν παρὰ τῷ Διονύσῳ

> But now you see him driveling around town, his frets falling out, his tuning gone and his shapeliness all disjointed, but you feel no pity; no, he's just an old man doddering about, like Conn-ass wearing a withered crown and perishing of thirst, who for his earlier victories should be getting free drinks in the Prytaneum, and instead of driveling should be sitting pretty in the front row next to Dionysus.[9]

Recent studies have demonstrated that the emphasis on alcoholic intoxication with which this portrait of Cratinus is suffused derisively distorts the old poet's self-styled affiliation with Dionysiac poetics as foregrounded in some openly self-reflexive moments of his plays and, in particular, in *Pytinē* ("Wineflask"). This play, which featured its author himself as the drunken husband of "Comedy", was performed the year after *Knights* (423BCE) with the purpose of reinvigorating Cratinus' image as a Dionysiac poet after Aristophanes' attacks and addressing, in programmatic terms, the relationship between the comic muse and alcohol.[10]

In setting himself up as a devotee of Dionysus, Cratinus deliberately proclaimed the generic kinship of his comic persona with the earlier iambic poet Archilochus, the archetype

---

9. Here and elsewhere I reproduce the translations of Aristophanes by Henderson (1998a & b); unless otherwise indicated, the translations of the other texts are my own.
10. Cf. R. M. Rosen (2000); Biles ([2002] 2011: 134–66); Ruffell (2002); Bakola (2010: 16–49, 56–72, 275–85).

of the "winestruck" satirist (cf. Callimachus, fr. 544 Pf. μεθυπλῆγος ... Ἀρχιλόχου). This poetic affiliation is brought into sharp focus in a fragment of *Pytinē* (fr. 199 KA.), where one of Cratinus' friends threatens to smite (συγκεραυνώσω) the poet's wine casks by re-employing the image of the dithyrambic thunder that marks Archilochus' famous fr. 120 W² : "I know how to initiate a fine song for Lord Dionysus, / a dithyramb, after my mind is struck (συγκεραυνωθείς) with wine".[11] But significant traces of this Archilochean self-presentation can also be retrieved in Cratinus' earlier poetry. Therefore, there is no doubt that Aristophanes' mockery of Cratinus' dipsomania is directed towards questioning his role as the prime inheritor of the iambic tradition in which, before the production of *Knights*, the older comedian had probably cast himself through the appropriation of Archilochus' Dionysiac self-fashioning.[12]

However, Aristophanes' dramatization of this interpoetic rivalry is not restricted within the parabasis, but subtly reverberates throughout the play, functioning as a secondary level of signification that overlays the plot with a metaliterary dimension.[13] The hallmarks of Cratinus' poetic identity are mapped onto the portrait of Paphlagon, the new tyrannical slave of Demos, obviously standing for the demagogue Cleon, who conflates greedy politicking, loud rhetoric and voracious hunger into a multisensory bestial physicality. What makes Paphlagon most similar to Cratinus is precisely the intimate connection between his flooding verbal excess, flagged by his *redende Name* ("Splutterer"), and his voraciousness.[14] Paphlagon's oral rapacity does not concern food only but alcohol as well. The prologic introduction of the demagogue provides the first report on his bibulousness (lines 103–4):

ἐπίπαστα λείξας δημιόπραθ' ὁ βάσκανος
ῥέγκει μεθύων ἐν ταῖσι βύρσαις ὕπτιος.

That devil's been licking the sauce off confiscated goodies, and now he's belly-up drunk on his hides, snoring away.

Later on, in the course of the *agon* with the Sausage Seller – the comic hero destined to win the competition – Paphlagon displays contempt for the rhetorical capacity of his opponent by lampooning his water-drinking habits (lines 349–50):

ὕδωρ τε πίνων κἀπιδεικνὺς τοὺς φίλους τ' ἀνιῶν,
ᾤου δυνατὸς εἶναι λέγειν. ὦ μῶρε, τῆς ἀνοίας.

---

11. On this Archilochean fragment, cf. Mendelsohn (1991–2). On Cratinus' appropriation of the Archilochean dithyrambic thundering, see R. M. Rosen (2000: 33); Biles (2002: 172–3); Bakola (2010: 17, 48).
12. Cf. esp. R. M. Rosen (2000: 26–35). On the poetic kinship between Cratinus and Archilochus, see, most recently, Bakola (2010), *passim* and below.
13. See Ruffell (2002); Biles (2011: 121–32); Telò (forthcoming a).
14. On Paphlagon's voracious orality see esp. Worman (2008: 88–92). On the resemblances between Cratinus' and Paphlagon's flooding voices, cf. Ruffell (2002: 144); Biles (2011: 122–3); Telò (forthcoming a).

Swearing off wine, and rehearsing with your friends till you got on their nerves, and then you started thinking you're a powerful speaker. You fool, what a delusion.

He thus echoes Cratinus' pronouncement on the paralyzing effects of ὕδωρ on comic creativity (fr. 203 KA ὕδωρ δὲ πίνων οὐδὲν ἂν τέκοις σοφόν, "by drinking water you would never create anything clever")[15] and subscribes to Cratinean poetics according to which Dionysiac intoxication is an essential recipe for success.[16] These and other passages debating the inspirational power of drunkenness posit a programmatic nexus between politics and comic performance and support the conclusion that the contest between Paphlagon and the Sausage Seller intersects with the interpoetic rivalry of Cratinean and Aristophanic comedy.[17]

What defines the multisensory quality of Paphlagon's all-consuming physicality is not only the encounter between sound and taste triggered by his mouth's compulsive expulsion of words and ingestion of alcohol and food, but also his enactment of the political metaphor of the "stink of corruption".[18] The relevance of smell to his embodied self becomes particularly evident in this passage, which draws attention to the odorous repercussions of Paphlagon's métier as a tanner of hides (lines 890–93):[19]

Πα. ἀλλ' οὐχ ὑπερβαλεῖ με θωπείαις· ἐγὼ γὰρ αὐτὸν
     προσαμφιῶ τοδί· σὺ δ' οἴμωζ', ὦ πόνηρ'.
Δημ.   ἰαιβοῖ.
     οὐκ ἐς κόρακας ἀποφθερεῖ βύρσης, κάκιστον ὄζων;
Αλ. καὶ τοῦτό ⟨γ'⟩ ἐπίτηδές σε περιήμπεσχ', ἵνα σ' ἀποπνίξῃ

PAPHLAGON Well, you can't outdo me when it comes to fawning. I'm going to put this [=a jacket] on him [= Demos] too, and you can eat your heart out, creep!
DEMOS Ugh! Get the hell away from me with your terrible stink of rawhide!
SAUSAGE SELLER And he tried to make you wear that thing deliberately, to suffocate you!

The stinky body ridiculed here for its suffocating and contaminating effects stands out as a key ingredient of the vitriolic invectives that, in other plays, Aristophanes launches

---

15. This statement, famously echoed by Horace, *Epistles* 1. 19. 1–3, has been traditionally assigned to *Pytinē*, but it "would be appropriate in any place where Cratinus clarified his poetics" (Biles 2002: 173).
16. Cf. lines 353–5: "I'll polish off a plateful of hot tuna right now, wash it down with a pitcher of neat wine, and then screw the generals at Pylos."
17. See Ruffell (2002: 148–50).
18. Miller (1998: 75, 77) notes that in the Western tradition "it is nearly impossible to keep bad smells out of the moral domain".
19. I follow the text of Henderson (1998a), who in line 892 prints the transmitted reading ὄζων. All the other editors instead accept Lenting's emendation ὄζον on the grounds that "the reading of the mss. would require us to suppose that the addressee was Paphlagon, but if Paphlagon himself had an objectionable smell Demos would be used to it by now" (Sommerstein 1981: 191). This argument, as recently observed by N. Wilson (2007: 56), is "overlogical".

against Cleon and his supposed occupation as a βυρσοπώλης ("tanner"). For example, in the parabasis of *Wasps* the comic poet fashions himself as a Herculean figure bravely rescuing humankind from the attacks of a repulsive Cleontic creature that embeds within itself several monsters of Greek mythology (lines 1029–35):[20]

οὐδ' ὅτε πρῶτόν γ' ἦρξε διδάσκειν, ἀνθρώποις φῄσ' ἐπιθέσθαι,
ἀλλ' Ἡρακλέους ὀργήν τιν' ἔχων τοῖσι μεγίστοις ἐπιχειρεῖν, 1030
θρασέως ξυστὰς εὐθὺς ἀπ' ἀρχῆς αὐτῷ τῷ καρχαρόδοντι,
οὗ δεινόταται μὲν ἀπ' ὀφθαλμῶν Κύννης ἀκτῖνες ἔλαμπον,
ἑκατὸν δὲ κύκλῳ κεφαλαὶ κολάκων οἰμωξομένων ἐλιχμῶντο
περὶ τὴν κεφαλήν, φωνὴν δ' εἶχεν χαράδρας ὄλεθρον τετοκυίας,
φώκης δ' ὀσμήν, Λαμίας δ' ὄρχεις ἀπλύτους, πρωκτὸν δὲ καμήλου. 1035

And when he [Aristophanes] first began to produce, he says, he didn't attack ordinary people, but in the very spirit of Heracles he came to grips with the greatest monsters, boldly standing up right from the start to old Jagged Teeth himself, whose eyes like the bitch Cynna's flashed terrible beams, and all around his pate licked a hundred heads of damned flatterers; he had the voice of a death dealing torrent, the smell of a seal, the unwashed balls of a Lamia, and the arsehole of a camel.

After the reference to Cleon's torrential voice (1034), the account of Aristophanes' Herculean labour ventures into three olfactory comparisons that couple the monstrous body of his adversary with the "deadliest smell" (*Odyssey* 4. 442 ὀλοώτατος ὀδμή) of a seal, the testicles of the demon Lamia and the anus of a camel.[21]

In *Knights* Paphlagon's identity is inextricably commingled with the multifarious aromas of the marketplace and the cooking fragrances of festive food preparations but, first and foremost, with the less appealing odours emanating from animal bodies.[22] It is certainly significant that, in *Acharnians*, Aristophanes similarly depicts Cratinus as an embodiment of δυσοσμία ("malodorousness") absurdly testifying to his kinship with goats (lines 848–53):

οὐδ' ἐντυχὼν ἐν τἀγορᾷ πρόσεισί σοι βαδίζων
Κρατῖνος ἀποκεκαρμένος μοιχὸν μιᾷ μαχαίρᾳ,
ὁ περιπόνηρος Ἀρτέμων, 850

---

20. On these lines, repeated with small variations in *Peace* 752-8, see Mastromarco (1988, 1989); Sommerstein (2002: 19–25; also published as Sommerstein 2009b: 155–60); Worman (2008: 94).
21. Lamia frequently shows up in Old Comedy and satyr drama as an hermaphroditic monster capable of chasing away its enemies with its foul smell: see Sommerstein (2002: 24–5 = 2009b: 159–60).
22. The Sausage Seller – whose name, at the end of the play, is revealed to be Ἀγοράκριτος – is equally implicated in the multisensory world of the agora but is never presented as a symbol of olfactory badness. On differences between Paphlagon and the Sausage Seller with regard to physical, political and rhetorical characterization see Worman (2008: 107–10).

ὁ ταχὺς ἄγαν τὴν μουσικήν,
ὄζων κακὸν τῶν μασχαλῶν
πατρὸς Τραγασαίου

Nor in your market will you meet Cratinus strolling about with an adulterer's cut done with a straight razor, an Artemon "the miscarried", too hasty with his poetry, his armpits smelling nasty, son of a father from the Goat d'Azur.

Besides re-formulating the charge voiced in line 852 (ὄζων κακὸν μασχαλῶν, "his armpits smelling nasty"),[23] the unexpected disclosure of Cratinus' lineage from the animal that in antiquity was deemed a proverbial symbol of δυσοσμία (line 853 πατρὸς Τραγασαίου, "son of a father from the Goat d'Azur")[24] accords well with Aristophanes' parabatic (mis)portrayal of his competitor. In fact, the foul-smelling of goats is frequently evoked as a term of comparison for nasty breath,[25] a physiological condition that, in comic texts, is often associated with old men[26] and boozers.[27]

Does Cratinus' olfactory identity as delineated in *Acharnians* leave any trace in *Knights*? Or, to put it another way, can we perceive Cratinus' poetic stink lurking behind the δυσοσμία of Paphlagon, the political alter ego of Aristophanes' rival? In the following section I will address these questions by scrutinizing the intersensory texture of the finale of *Knights* and teasing out the allusive resonances of a crucial moment of the rhetorical duel between Paphlagon and the Sausage Seller.

DREAMS AS SHINY FRAGRANCES: ODYSSEAN AROMAS IN THE AGON

The finale of *Knights* celebrates the Sausage Seller's transformation of the cranky, half-deaf, old Demos introduced at the beginning of the play (lines 40–46) into a young, well-dressed, beautiful and powerful king rescuing Athens from the dangers of Cleontic demagoguery and restoring the city to the glorious days of Aristides and Miltiades (line 1325). When the beautified Demos makes his exit from the *skênê*, the audience is confronted with the political and aesthetic miracle heroically pulled off by the Sausage Seller (lines 1329–32):

---

23. Armpit stink is frequently associated with goats: cf. e.g. Aristophanes, *Peace* 811 and Eupolis, fr. 258 KA.
24. On the malodorousness of goats cf. Lilja (1972: 151–52). Τραγασαίου is a double pun on τράγος and the toponym Τραγασαί in the Troad. As Olson (2002: 285) points out, "that Cratinus' father is allegedly from Tragasai also amounts to an oblique claim that he is not a real Athenian".
25. Cf. in part. Eupolis, fr. 7 KA (from the play *Aiges* ["Goats"]) and Pherecrates, fr. 30 KA.
26. See Plautus, *The Merchant* 574–5. See also Franko (1999: 7–9) on the stinking breath of the old protagonist of *Casina*, who, in the course of the play, is significantly compared to a "toothless goat" (line 550).
27. Cf. esp. Menander, fr. 170 KA; Plautus, *Pseudolus* 1295; Afranius, frr. 405–6 R³.

Χο. ὦ ταὶ λιπαραὶ καὶ ἰοστέφανοι καὶ ἀριζήλωτοι Ἀθῆναι,
δείξατε τὸν τῆς Ἑλλάδος ἡμῖν καὶ τῆς γῆς τῆσδε μόναρχον.   1330
Αλ. ὅδ' ἐκεῖνος ὁρᾶν τεττιγοφόρας, τἀρχαίῳ σχήματι λαμπρός,
οὐ χοιρινῶν ὄζων, ἀλλὰ σπονδῶν, σμύρνῃ κατάλειπτος.

CHORUS Oh Athens the gleaming, the violet-crowned, the envy of all, show us the monarch of Greece and of this land!
SAUSAGE SELLER Here he is for all to see, wearing a golden cricket, resplendent in his old-time costume, smelling not of ballot shells but peace accords, and anointed with myrrh.

The effects of the metamorphosis undergone by Demos are visual as well as olfactory, but it is through smell that Aristophanes stages the transition between two antagonistic political temporalities – a present redolent with the stench of a repulsive tyranny and a new Golden Age materializing into the pleasant aromas of an idealized past. Anchored in the private, intimate and erotic realm of scented oil (1332 σμύρνῃ), shiny unguents (1329 λιπαραί) and violet wreaths (1329 ἰοστέφανοι),[28] the utopia established by the Sausage Seller figures as the sanitized version of a demagogic regime whose identifying scent is not only that of the mussel-shells used in the lawcourts (1332 χοιρινῶν). In fact, the punning resonance of χοιρινῶν with χοῖρος ("swine")[29] forges a supplementary connection between Cleon's judicial bribery, symbolized by mussel-shells, and the bestial stink of corruption that, as we have already seen, constitutes a hallmark of Paphlagon's character.

Demos' rejuvenation brings to a conclusion an exhilarating *agon* in which his political wooers, Paphlagon and the Sausage Seller, exhibit their mastery of the art of "demophilic" rhetoric.[30] This debate reaches a climactic point in lines 1090–95, where each contestant recites his dream-oracle of Athena:

ΠΑ. ἀλλ' ἐγὼ εἶδον ὄναρ, καὶ μοὐδόκει ἡ θεὸς αὐτὴ   1090
τοῦ δήμου καταχεῖν ἀρυταίνῃ πλουθουγίειαν.
ΑΛ. νὴ Δία καὶ γὰρ ἐγώ· καὶ μοὐδόκει ἡ θεὸς αὐτὴ
ἐκ πόλεως ἐλθεῖν καὶ γλαῦξ αὐτῇ 'πικαθῆσθαι·
εἶτα κατασπένδειν κατὰ τῆς κεφαλῆς ἀρυβάλλῳ
ἀμβροσίαν κατὰ σοῦ, κατὰ τούτου δὲ σκοροδάλμην   1095

PAPHLAGON Wait, I've had a dream: I saw the Goddess herself pouring healthy wealthiness over Demos with a big ladle.

---

28. Line 1329 is a quotation from Pindar, fr. 76 M. On the intersensory meaning of λιπαρός (conflating fragrance and luminosity) see Lilja (1972: 59–61, 83–4) and below.
29. The adjective χοίρινος ("of hog's skin" *LSJ* s.v.) occurs as an alternative form of χοίρειος in Lucian, *How to Write History* 23. Paphlagon is explicitly assimilated to a pig in lines 375–81 and 984–96: cf. Sommerstein (1981: 163).
30. The rhetorical strategies adopted by Paphlagon and the Sausage Seller to please Demos turn their contest into an erotic pursuit: see Wohl (2002: 86–8) and Scholtz (2004).

SAUSAGE SELLER By god I've had one too: I also saw the Goddess herself, coming from the Akropolis with an owl sitting on her helmet; then down she poured a pitcher of ambrosia over your [=Demos'] head, and over his a pitcher of garlic sauce.

The Sausage Seller's dream foreshadows the final beautification of Demos and Paphlagon's defeat. The κατασπονδή ("libation") of ambrosia, both a fragrant drink and a scented unguent,[31] that is performed by the Sausage Seller's Athena (lines 1094–5) raises the suspicion that even in Paphlagon's oracle the goddess may likewise be commingling libation and bathing into a unified metaphorical ritual. In fact, the capacious ladle designated by ἀρύταινα is employed in many contexts "to give the ancient equivalent of a shower",[32] but can also be used to serve a copious quantity of wine, as confirmed by a fragment of Timon of Phlius (*Supplementum Hellenisticum* 778.3), in which a mysterious philosopher is likened to Lykourgos violently casting away the "insatiate-in-wine ladles" (ἀπληστοίνους…ἀρυταίνας) served during a sympotic gathering of worshippers of Dionysos.[33]

One can, therefore, conclude that the term ἀρύταινα turns Paphlagon's dream-oracle into an oneiric representation of his obsessions: the offer of "healthy wealth" (πλουθουγίειαν) that he makes to Demos cannot but take the form of an abundant ladling out of wine. But there is more. The figurative language of this line, loaded with allusive overtones, prompts the spectator to sniff out another instance of the politician-as-poet conceit that, as we have previously seen, lies at the core of the Aristophanic construction of Paphlagon's character.

In the only extant fragment of Cratinus' *Didaskaliai* (fr. 38 KA) a female character probably personifying "Cratinus' poetry, his Muse or one of his productions"[34] is reminded of an occasion when her ladling out (ἀναρύτειν) of dithyrambs was badly received: ὅτε σὺ τοὺς καλοὺς θριάμβους ἀναρύτουσ' ἀπηχθάνου ("when you ladling out beautiful dithyrambs incurred hatred"). Biles has remarked that "if, as seems likely, this verse comments on how one of Cratinus' own plays fared in the contests, the poet here characterizes his own comedy as a Dionysian hymn".[35] Through the verb ἀναρύτειν Cratinus pairs comic performance with the central activity of Dionysiac ritual and poetry. Thus, he pushes the metaphorical possibilities of his self-imposed drunken persona to the extreme,

---

31. On ambrosia, see below, n. 39.
32. Sommerstein (1981: 203). Cf. Aristophanes, fr. * 450 KA; Antiphanes, fr. 25 KA; Theophrastus, *Characters* 9. 8. Anderson (1991: 151) has drawn the conclusion that Paphlagon's dream "casts Athena in the role of a bath-attendant" and prefigures the image of the demagogue "drinking used bath-water and holding shouting matches with prostitutes and bathmen" that is provided at the end of the play (1398–1401). However, this reading does not capture the polyvalent figurative potential with which the term ἀρύταινα is charged.
33. Athenaeus 10.424b–c, who quotes the fragment, equates ἀρύταινα with κύαθος, a ladle used for "drawing wine out of the κρατήρ" (*LSJ* s.v.). Cf. Di Marco (1989: 120–22).
34. Bakola (2010: 49).
35. Biles (2002: 174). On θρίαμβος as a synonym of dithyrambic composition see Hesychius θ 746 L.

gesturing towards the Archilochean matrix of his poetry and identifying iambic aggressiveness with dithyrambic boozing.[36] In *Birds* 729–32 the Chorus of birds fancies itself as a community of bounty-giving gods and juxtaposes "healthy wealthiness" (πλουθυγίεια) with χοροί ("dances") and θαλίαι ("festivities"): "ever at hand we'll bestow on you, your children, and your children's children healthy wealthiness, happiness, prosperity, peace, youth, hilarity, dances, festivities". If we look at Paphlagon's dream-oracle through the lens of this passage, we see grounds for positing a connection between his promise of πλουθυγίεια ("healthy wealthiness") and Cratinus' overflowing display of Dionysiac art. Paphlagon's Athena seems thus to re-perform the plentiful libation of Dionysiac poetry overseen, in Cratinus' fragment, by the female subject who "ladeled out" (ἀναρύτουσα) his dithyrambs and to condemn the Sausage Seller's adversary to the same failure that Aristophanes' rival Cratinus experienced (ἀπηχθάνου). If placed against this background, the Sausage Seller's prefigured overthrow of Paphlagon replays and merges with Cratinus' poetic fiasco.

Let us now consider the dream of the Sausage Seller, which features Athena descending from the Akropolis to pour a libation of ambrosia over the head of Demos. This bathing / libation rite orchestrated by the goddess adheres to the narrative and ideological configuration of a famous Odyssean scene, where Athena's κατασπονδή ("libation") over Odysseus' head brings into play the same nexus between rejuvenation and political utopia that shapes the semantic texture of the finale of *Knights*. The transitional ritual that, in Book 23, paves the way for Odysseus' full re-integration into his οἶκος is a bath arranged by Eurynome, but secretly supervised by Athena (lines 153–63):[37]

αὐτὰρ Ὀδυσσῆα μεγαλήτορα ᾧ ἐνὶ οἴκῳ
Εὐρυνόμη ταμίη λοῦσεν καὶ χρῖσεν ἐλαίῳ,
ἀμφὶ δέ μιν φᾶρος καλὸν βάλεν ἠδὲ χιτῶνα·   155
αὐτὰρ κὰκ κεφαλῆς χεῦεν πολὺ κάλλος Ἀθήνη
μείζονά τ' εἰσιδέειν καὶ πάσσονα· κὰδ δὲ κάρητος
οὔλας ἧκε κόμας, ὑακινθίνῳ ἄνθει ὁμοίας.
ὡς δ' ὅτε τις χρυσὸν περιχεύεται ἀργύρῳ ἀνὴρ
ἴδρις, ὃν Ἥφαιστος δέδαεν καὶ Παλλὰς Ἀθήνη   160
τέχνην παντοίην, χαρίεντα δὲ ἔργα τελείει,
ὡς ἄρα τῷ κατέχευε χάριν κεφαλῇ τε καὶ ὤμοις.
ἐκ δ' ἀσαμίνθου βῆ δέμας ἀθανάτοισιν ὁμοῖος·

Now the housekeeper Eurynome bathed great-hearted
Odysseus in his own house, and anointed him with olive oil,

---

36. Cf. Biles (2002: 175).
37. Montiglio (2005: 59) claims that Odysseus "is beautified but not rejuvenated". But that Athena "reveals in the grizzled warrior the young husband who left twenty years before" (C. Segal 2001: 75) is guaranteed by the parallel scene in 24. 365-72, where the similar metamorphosis that Athena arranges for Laertes is presented as a restoration to his past military prowess. Cf. Heubeck in Russo *et al.* (1992: 401).

and threw a beautiful mantle and a tunic about him;
and over his head Athene suffused a great beauty, to make him
taller to behold and thicker, and on his head she arranged
the curling locks that hung down like hyacinthine petals.
And as when a master craftsman overlays gold on silver,
and he is one who was taught by Hephaistos and Pallas Athene
in art complete, and grace is on every work he finishes
so Athene gilded with grace his head and his shoulders.
Then, looking like an immortal, he strode forth from the bath.
(Trans. Lattimore 1965)

What is Athena's recipe for bringing about the physical rejuvenation of Odysseus? Critics have long discussed the nature of the liquid, subsumed under the metonymic rubrics of κάλλος ("beauty", 156) and χάρις ("grace", 162), that, in this and similar passages (especially the mirror scene of 6. 223–37), Athena pours upon Odysseus' head in order to effect the process of beautification.[38] A revealing clue is supplied by the expression ἀθανάτοισιν ὁμοῖος ("looking like an immortal") in line 163, which forges a close connection between Athena's action and scenes of the conferral of immortality through ambrosia such as the *Homeric Hymn to Demeter* 235–38, where Demeter is depicted making Demophon grow "like a god" (δαίμονι ἴσος) by anointing him with the fragrant nourishment of the gods:

ὁ δ'ἀέξετο δαίμονι ἴσος
οὔτ'οὖν σῖτον ἔδων, οὐ θησάμενος ⟨γάλα μητρός⟩
                         Δημήτηρ
χρίεσκ' ἀμβροσίῃ ὡς εἰ θεοῦ ἐκγεγαῶτα,
ἡδὺ καταπνείουσα καὶ ἐν κόλποισιν ἔχουσα

he grew like a diving being
though he ate no food and sucked no ⟨mother's milk⟩.
                         Demeter
anointed him with ambrosia, as if he were the son of a god,
breathing her sweet breath over him as she held him in her bosom.
(Trans. M. L. West 2003, adapted)

It is thus evident that based as it is on the bestowal of ambrosia, Athena's beautification of Odysseus reads as a supernatural supplement to the unguent that Eurynome uses to cleanse Odysseus' body (*Odyssey* 23.154 χρῖσεν ἐλαίῳ, "[she] anointed him with olive oil"). Notwithstanding the emphasis laid by the Homeric narrator upon the visual consequences of Odysseus' rejuvenation, it is an eminently olfactory process that engenders

---

38. Cf. Heubeck in Russo *et al.* (1992: 329). For example, Latacz (1966: 84) understands χάρις as an "ausstrahlende Patina, die die Krönung äusserer Schönheit, des κάλλος, bildet".

his metamorphosis, for not only is fragrance ambrosia's chief characteristic but ambrosia was also originally assimilated to pure odour "as the only thing good enough for gods".[39]

Cleansing Odysseus' body with the supernatural scent of ambrosia results in the expansion of his presence and visibility (line 157 μείζονά τ' εἰσιδέειν καὶ πάσσονα, "taller to behold and thicker")[40] "through diffusing a pleasing aroma".[41] In other words, Athena poses as a synaesthetic demiurge transmuting one sense into another – a scrubbing into smell, a scent into a sight – and suffusing this key moment of her protégé's *nostos* with the beneficial effects of a shiny fragrance or a fragrant sight. If it is true that "odors are perceived not only by the nose, but they constitute an element of communication which somehow involves the whole body",[42] it comes as no surprise that the hero's rebirth is engineered as a transgression of sensory boundaries and an exchange between alternative perceptual models.

A similar intersensory transposition underlies the fulfilment of the Sausage Seller's dream-oracle in the concluding scene of the play, which re-stages the Odyssean prodigy of a rejuvenation brought into view by means of a libation of perfume and unguents (lines 1331–2 "here he is for all to see, wearing a golden cricket, resplendent in his old-time costume, smelling not of ballot shells but peace accords, and anointed with myrrh"). In line 1332 the punning word σπονδῶν (meaning both "libations" and "armistice") conjoins the fragrant metamorphosis of Demos with the Odyssean κατασπονδή of ambrosia promised by the Sausage Seller in line 1091.

In the Sausage Seller's dream not only Demos but also Paphlagon benefits from Athena's κατασπονδή. The garlic sauce (line 1095 σκοροδάλμη) that the goddess pours over the head of Paphlagon encapsulates another trait of Cratinus' poetic personality. In antiquity, garlic's most distinctive quality was held to be its smell.[43] What is most noteworthy is that garlic's sharp odour – placed "at the opposed extreme from sweet perfume"[44] – and garlicky breath are figuratively exploited in satiric texts as self-reflexive emblems of dyspeptic invective, iambic anger and Archilochean aggressiveness,[45] that is, the salient

---

39. See e.g. Homer, *Odyssey* 4. 445–6 ἀμβροσίην ὑπὸ ῥῖνα ἑκάστῳ θῆκε φέρουσα / ἡδὺ μάλα πνείουσαν ("she [= Eidothea] brought ambrosia, and put it under the nose of each man, / and it smelled very sweet") and Aristophanes, *Acharnians* 196 ὄζουσ' ἀμβροσίας καὶ νέκταρος ("they smell ambrosia and nectar"). On the primarily olfactory quality of ambrosia cf. Lilja (1972: 19–25), from whom the quotation is taken (20).
40. In the *Homeric Hymn to Demeter* the perfume of ambrosia produces "a miraculous growth, underlined by the alliteration of *k* in l.238, ἡδὺ καταπνείουσα καὶ ἐν κόλποισιν ἔχουσα" (Foley 1994: 48). This description of Demeter's sweet breath is very similar to the definition of ambrosia's fragrance in Homer, *Odyssey* 4. 446, quoted above (n. 39). On ambrosia in epic scenes of beautification and/or immortalization, cf. J. S. Clay (1981–2).
41. The quotation is taken from Howes (2003: 76–7), who, in exploring the synaesthetic dynamics at work in Melanesian magic rites, observes: "in each of these rites, smell both complements sight and is transposed or transmuted into sight. ... Cleansing and odorizing the body also contributes to the intensification and expansion of a person's presence through diffusing a pleasing aroma".
42. Reichel-Dolmatoff (1978: 271).
43. On the olfactory dimension underpinning the opposition between the Skirophoria and the Adonia, two festivals dedicated, respectively, to garlic and perfume, see Detienne (1994: 80, 94).
44. Gowers (1993: 290).
45. Cf. *ibid.*: 280–310. On Cratinus' use of garlic sauce (σκοροδάλμη) as a symbol of his comic poetics, cf. Telò (forthcoming b).

characteristics of Cratinus' techniques of comic abuse, as recognized by ancient critics and, in particular, Platonius in his treatise *On the Differences in Character of the Comedians* (Περὶ διαφορᾶς χαρακτήρων, p. 6. 1–4 K):

> Κρατῖνος ὁ τῆς παλαιᾶς κωμῳδίας ποιητής, ἅτε δὴ κατὰ τὰς Ἀρχιλόχου ζηλώσεις αὐστηρὸς μὲν ταῖς λοιδορίαις ἐστίν· οὐ γάρ, ὥσπερ ὁ Ἀριστοφάνης, ἐπιτρέχειν τὴν χάριν τοῖς σκώμμασι ποιεῖ τὸ φορτικὸν τῆς ἐπιτιμήσεως διὰ ταύτης ἀναιρῶν.

> Cratinus, the poet of Old Comedy, in accordance with his emulative attitude towards Archilochus, is harsh in his abuse. For, differently from Aristophanes, he does not let grace flow upon his invectives in order to temper the vulgarity of his blame.

In this passage, Platonius defines the terms of Cratinus' Archilochean ζήλωσις ("emulation") through the adjective αὐστηρός, a fitting label for pungent tastes and odours like garlic.[46] In the same treatise (p. 7. 15 K), Cratinus is presented as a practitioner of iambic πικρία ("piquancy")[47] – another distinctive property of garlic, which equally applies to the contiguous spheres of taste and smell.[48] In other words, Platonius' sensitized dichotomy between Cratinean αὐστηρότης ("pungency") and Aristophanic χάρις ("grace") seems to re-configure the garlic versus ambrosia opposition to which the rivalry of Paphlagon and the Sausage Seller is symbolically attached.[49] Platonios is picking up on a feature of Cratinus' Archilochean self-portrait that comes to the fore in one of the extant fragments of the play *Archilochoi* (fr. 6.1 KA): εἶδες τὴν Θασίαν ἅλμην, οἶ' ἄττα βαΰζει; ("did you see what things the brine of Thasos is barking?"). In this line from the *agon*, which probably sanctioned the victory of Archilochus' supporters over Homer's and Hesiod's,[50] Cratinus assimilated the acerbity of his iambic forebear Archilochus and that of his own comic self to the synaesthetic πικρία ("piquancy") of a visually perceptible (εἶδες, "have you seen") barking spicy sauce,[51] thereby embracing the same garlicky persona that, in the oneiric visions of the Sausage Seller, Athena bestows upon Paphlagon.

It is thus evident that Cratinus' comic persona creeps into Paphlagon's characterization and brings the demagogue's drunkenness into the territory of olfactory badness. Cratinus'

---

46. For the use of αὐστηρός in relation to olfactory sensations, cf. e.g. Aristotle, *On the Soul* 412a, ὁμοίως δὲ καὶ δριμεῖα καὶ αὐστηρὰ καὶ ὀξεῖα καὶ λιπαρά ἐστιν ὀσμή.
47. The relevant sources on iambic and, especially, Archilochean πικρία are discussed by Bramble (1974: 190–204); Gowers (1993: 283–4); R. M. Rosen (2007b: 464–7).
48. On the πικρία of garlic, cf. e.g. scholium to Aristophanes' *Knights* 199a MJ. On the contiguity between taste and smell in the ancient theory of the senses, see Sharples (1985: 192) and Clements in this volume (on Aristophanes).
49. As we have seen, in the Odyssean subtext of this scene χάρις is the term that designates ambrosia.
50. Cf. Bakola (2010: 71–9).
51. Θασία ἅλμη ("Thasian sauce") indicates a kind of spicy dipping sauce for fish. Cf. Pretagostini (1982); R. M. Rosen (1988: 42–3); Telò (forthcoming b).

self-constructed Dionysiac voice is, as it were, degraded to the garlicky (or goaty)[52] breath caused by customary and prolonged hangovers.[53] Building on the connection between Archilochus' iambic virulence and his dithyrambic boozing, Aristophanes pairs Cratinus' intoxication with the satiric malodorousness conjured by garlic and thus turns ambrosia and the abuse of wine into the poles of a metapoetic conflict. Demos' rejuvenation at the end of the play can thus be sensed as the resolution of such a conflict. But how does this final outcome affect Aristophanes' articulation of his generic self in *Knights*? The dreams of Paphlagon and the Sausage Seller translate oneiric vision into an olfactory revelation of competing literary genealogies. Which idea of comedy does the Odyssean fragrance revived by the Sausage Seller reflect? To answer these questions, in the next section I will attempt to show that Aristophanes designs his appropriation of Odyssean ambrosia as a poetic antidote to Cratinus' foul-smelling and intoxicated comedy.

AROMATHERAPY: ARISTOPHANES' AMBROSIAL REGENERATION OF COMEDY

From the treatise *On perfumes and wreaths* of the Hellenistic medical writer Philonides we learn that perfumes were employed in sympotic contexts to temper the violence of wine and, in particular, to relieve headaches induced by excessive assumption of alcohol. The following excerpt from his work, preserved by Athenaeus, 15. 691f-92b, eloquently illustrates the rationale for this practice:[54]

> For Philonides in his work *On Perfumes and Wreaths* says: "The practice of oiling (λιπαίνειν) the head in drinking-parties arose from the following cause: when, namely, the head is dry, whatever is taken into the stomach is drawn upward; for this reason, as the fevers inflame their bodies, men moisten the head with lotions to prevent the partly burned elements from getting a start toward the part that is dry (πρὸς τὸ ξηρόν) and is moreover most empty. And so, taking this fact into account, and suspecting that during the drinking-bout the course of the wine is upward to the top, men were induced to oil the head (κεφαλὴν λιπαίνειν), believing that the violence of the wine would be abated if they moistened the head

---

52. In Plautus, *Mostellaria* 38–41, the urban and perfumed slave Tranio uses *hircus* ("he-goat") as a derogatory nickname for his rustic, smelly and garlic-eating colleague Grumio: cf. Lilja (1972: 127, 152).
53. Similarly, in Horace, *Epistles* 1.19, which pits the old "boozers" (Homer, Ennius and Cratinus) against their modern successors, who act out Dionysiac inspiration as mere drunkenness, "the strong verb *putere* (l. 11), effectively conveying the awful reek of the following day due to an excessive quantity of wine, forms a sharp contrast to the mild expression *vina fere dulces oluerunt Camenae* (5) which refers to the moderate drinking old poets" (Feeney 2009: 21).
54. On this passage cf. Classen *et al.* (1994: 40–41); Potter (2002: 177). The *Corpus Hippocraticum* similarly identifies the head as the primary bodily part beset by the effects of drunkenness: cf. Jouanna (1996: 415–17).

beforehand. And since life always adds to the useful some of those things which are conducive to amusement and luxury it leans towards the use of perfumes."

(Trans. Gulick 1941)

Scholars have pointed out that the trajectory of the Sausage Seller's victory at the end of *Knights* can be charted as a process of sympotic education, converting an initial water-drinker (cf. line 349 quoted above) into an experienced symposiast.[55] In fact, in the very last stage of the match between the two contenders Paphlagon "does not really share his food with Demos as he would be supposed to do at a symposium, but keeps most of it for himself"; by contrast, "the Sausage Seller ... wins because of this proper conduct of sympotic conventions"[56] and is accorded the permission to dine in the Prytaneum.

Viewed from this angle, the application of Athena's ambrosial unguent to Demos' head, which is oneirically announced at lines 1094–5, comes to represent the final and decisive step of the Sausage Seller's strategy to re-establish sympotic norms in opposition to the attempts of hard-boozing, Cratinean Paphlagon to draw his old master into his distorted practice of conviviality.[57] Whereas the drunk Cratinus of the parabasis wanders around "wearing a dry wreath, and all but dead with thirst" (line 534 στέφανον μὲν ἔχων αὖον, δίψῃ δ' ἀπολωλώς),[58] Demos – both a character and an allegorical stand-in for the Athenian audience – will have his head fragrantly refreshed thanks to the Odyssean treatment of the Sausage Seller and will lead Athens to a "gleaming" (λιπαραί) and "violet-crowned" (ἰοστέφανοι) future (line 1329 "Oh Athens the gleaming, the violet-crowned, the envy of all"). Both adjectives underscore the new sympotic status that Demos achieves at the end of the play.[59]

It is thus possible to conclude that, by aligning his demagogic art with Athena's libation of ambrosia, the Sausage Seller is purporting to alleviate the intoxicating effects imposed upon the Athenian audience by Cratinean poetics disguised as Paphlagonian politics. On these grounds, Demos' rejuvenation is to be read as the result of the Sausage Seller's therapeutic endeavours to rescue the Athenian audience from its subjugation to the tyranny of Cratinean drunkenness.

Aristophanes' olfactory therapy ultimately results in a contest of generic affiliations, fostering the transition from an Archilochean to an Odyssean idea of comedy. If it is true that

---

55. Cf. Bowie (1997: 6–8) and Pütz (2003: 134–44).
56. Pütz (2003: 141–2).
57. The solitary symposium of lines 50–52 exemplifies the influence exerted by Paphlagon's distorted idea of conviviality on Demos.
58. Sommerstein (1981: 172) and Biles (2011: 106) explain the reference to Cratinus' "dry wreath" as an allusion to the very few victories recently obtained by Aristophanes' rival, but the second part of the line supports the possibility of a sympotic garland. Cf. Ruffell (2002: 145). Cratinus' "dry wreath" may represent a paradoxical and humorous distortion of the customary scented wreaths.
59. On the use of flowery wreaths to control the intoxicating effects of alcohol, see Philonides, Περὶ μύρων καὶ στεφάνων ("On Perfumes and Wreaths"), quoted in Athenaeus, *Learned Banqueters* 15.674b–c. The adjective λιπαρός significantly occurs in *Odyssey* 15. 332 (λιπαροὶ κεφαλάς) to qualify the "neatly oiled heads" of the suitors' attendants whose appearance is contrasted with that of the old and not-yet-beautified Odysseus.

iambus holds a prominent position among the ancestors of Old Comedy,[60] the *Odyssey*, on the other hand, undoubtedly lends comedy a "spirit of consummate, individual, and perhaps rascally cleverness"[61] which finds one of its most eloquent incarnations in the Sausage Seller. The *Odyssey* also provides the poetry of Archilochus and Hipponax with a broad range of rhetorical gestures and situations that the poets of Old Comedy often adopt to construct their satiric personas.[62] In the finale of *Knights* Aristophanes stage-manages his triumph over the Archilochean persona of Cratinus by transmuting the traditions of Odyssean and iambic poetry into two competing prototypes of comedy and annexing his generic self with a symbolic return to the origins. Modeled as it is upon Athena's ambrosial beautification of Odysseus, the sensory utopia staged at the end of *Knights* purports not only to reinstate the Golden Age of Miltiades and Aristides, but also to re-define the identity of comedy in the terms of a literal "re-embodiment" of its Odyssean past.

It is not by chance that the Aristophanic reinvention of comedy takes shape through the mediation of smell, a sense that is able to recapture an otherwise unattainable past and import it into the present with exceptional vividness.[63] In the final scene of *Knights*, the refashioning of Athena's ambrosia as a heavenly mix of flowery aromas and ointments applied to the rejuvenated Demos causes the Odyssean past and Aristophanic present to merge into comedy's renovated generic form. One could say that the odorous strife between Cratinus and Aristophanes set up in *Knights* pits two temporal configurations against each other. Whereas the residue of ingested wine is redolent of the past,[64] the fragrance of unguents and *a fortiori* ambrosia palpably conjures a reassuring future of full vitality. Consequently, if the wine ladle used by Paphlagon-as-Cratinus in his libation over Demos consigns comedy to the decaying and stale aroma of an out-of-date Archilochean inspiration, the ambrosia of the Sausage Seller-as-Aristophanes sets in motion a generic rebirth by re-creating the same beneficial blend of temporalities – past morphed into future – which, in Book 23 of the *Odyssey*, frames Odysseus' re-entrance into the fullness of life.

This reading of Aristophanes' rivalry with Cratinus also brings out the antithetic modes of constructing the poet–audience relationship to which the two comedians attach their strategies of literary self-presentation. Cratinus' self-association with the intoxicated poetics of Archilochus couples comedy with a Dionysiac ritual that forces the audience into an ecstatic condition of sensory confusion and casts the comic poet in the role of an inspired and tyrannical performer. Cratinus is, in other words, constructed as a comic version of the Aeschylus of *Frogs*,[65] who establishes an unbridgeable hierarchical distance

---

60. On this much-discussed topic see, especially, R. M. Rosen (1988, 2013).
61. Whitman (1964: 28).
62. On Odysseus as a satirist, cf. R. M. Rosen (2007a: 67–116, 117–41). For specific connections between the *Odyssey* and iambus, see Seidensticker (1978) and R. M. Rosen (1990). On Aristophanes' dramatization of his comedy's generic kinship with the *Odyssey* through iambus, cf. Telò (2013).
63. Cf. Harris (2007: 467).
64. Wine usually only smells on a person some time after the drinking is over – making the wine-smelling Cratinus always yesterday's news (thanks to Alex Purves for this observation).
65. In this play Euripides' main charge is that "Aeschylus deliberately obfuscated meaning by presenting the audience with something fixed and unapproachable" (R. M. Rosen 2008: 159). On Cratinus as a comic

between the poet and the audience by self-consciously embodying the poetry of the past.[66] In the *Odyssey*, Athena's fragrant intensification of Odysseus' presence instantiates the *mētis*-based elective affinities between the goddess and the hero. As a result, Aristophanes' re-enactment of Athena's synaesthetic beautification of Odysseus epitomizes a mode of comic reception that rests upon the comedian's production and the audience's appreciation of poetic σοφία ("wisdom").[67] The Odyssean palingenesis that comedy undergoes in *Knights* seems thus to anticipate the collaborative relationship between poet and audience with which, in *Frogs*, the character of Euripides associates his own style of tragedy.[68]

In his famous essay "Cézanne's Doubt", M. Merleau Ponty asserted that "we *see* the depth, the smoothness, the softness, the hardness of objects; Cézanne even claimed that we see their odor".[69] In *Knights* Aristophanes suggests that in the comic theatre what one takes in through the eye also belongs to the domain of the nose. Thus, he lets us see the odours of different comic objects. By transforming the visual experience of comedy into an olfactory one, Aristophanes construes Cratinus' and his own comic modes as opposed objects that put the comic poet in touch with the bodies of the audience. If Cratinean comedy makes spectators feel the stale matter of the past and, thus, ultimately estranges them from itself, the fragrance of Aristophanic comedy affords them sensuous contact with the refreshing force of poetic origins. Thus, the incursion of smell into the visual field of the comic theatre turns interpoetic rivalry into the competition between conflicting paradigms of corporeal engagement between comic poet and spectators.

Aeschylus cf., most recently, Foley (2008: 27) and Porter (2010: 262–75); on Cratinus' Aeschylean self-fashioning, cf. Bakola (2010: 24–9).
66. Cf., esp., R. M. Rosen (2008: 159–62) and Ruffell (2008: 54).
67. On the relevance of poetic σοφία to Aristophanes' relationship with his audience as depicted in the parabases of his plays, see especially Silk (2000: 46–8).
68. Cf., in particular, R. M. Rosen (2008: 159, 163–6). On the Aeschylus versus Euripides dichotomy as an opposition between polarized audience responses (emotion and cognition respectively), cf. Lada Richards (1993). On the points of connection between the Sausage Seller and the character of Euripides in *Frogs*, cf. Worman (2008: 109).
69. Merleau-Ponty (1964: 15). For an approach to ancient aesthetics through Merleau-Ponty's synaesthetic perspective, see Porter (2010: 416–17).

5

"LOOKING MUSTARD": GREEK POPULAR EPISTEMOLOGY AND THE MEANING OF ΔΡΙΜΥΣ

Ashley Clements

WHAT THE SAUSAGE SELLER SAW

Picture the scene, or rather, try to picture *what* was seen. The play is *Knights*, Aristophanes' biting political satire on the corruption of late fifth-century BCE Athenian demagoguery and the complacency of its audiences, first performed in 424 BCE, and a character called the Sausage Seller is describing to the Chorus his recent contest with his political rival, Paphlagon, before the Athenian Council. Arriving at the Council chamber just as the Councillors' ears were resounding with Paphlagon's false accusations of conspiracy against the richest class of Athenian citizens, the eponymous Knights, he relates the strangely spicy response that spread through the Council as he watched, 629–31:

> … ἡ βουλὴ δ᾽ ἅπασ᾽ ἀκροωμένη
> ἐγένεθ᾽ ὑπ᾽ αὐτοῦ ψευδατραφάξυος πλέα,   630
> κἄβλεψε νᾶπυ καὶ τὰ μέτωπ᾽ ἀνέσπασεν.

> … as they were hearing this, the whole Council
> became full of false-orach,
> looked mustard and knit its brows.

For the political performers of the scene, the demagogues, this response signals that the Council is too readily swallowing the lies it is being fed (cf. 632–3). And so in the next fifty lines, the spectators of *Knights* are treated to a feast of culinary demagoguery as both political rivals muster ever more tasty treats to curry political favour, until, finally, a triumphant Sausage Seller calms the Councillors with the promise of delicious sprats, coriander and leeks (644–7, 676–9).[1] But for later audiences the blend of politics, physiognomy and

---

1. For the image of the comic play as itself a feast (δαίς) of words served up to the consuming spectators, see Lada Richards (1999: 139–41); Bramble (1974: 50–4, esp. 51 n. 1); cf. Gowers (1993).

food so evocatively cast out to the theatre here is difficult. At some cultural remove from *Knights'* comic world of competing cookery and flavoured rhetoric, we are left wondering what exactly was seen in the faces of the Council as its members sat as spectators to Paphlagon's tirade.

Consider the image at line 630, for instance, where we are told that the Council suddenly "became full of false-orach" (ἐγένεθ' ὑπ' αὐτοῦ ψευδατραφάξυος πλέα). The Scholia suggest that the comic compound ψευδατράφαξυς alludes to the lies that spread through the Council chamber as if shoots of fertile seeds springing up to overtake the Councillors' ears.[2] But the ancient physicians also tell us the fast-growing potherb ἀτράφαξυς, orach, was notoriously volatile, and if eaten by itself, apparently the cause of all sorts of maladies.[3] In fact, according to Pliny, its eaters took on a particular look, suffering an experience liable to drain all blood from the cheeks.[4] So what is likely evoked in line 630, then, is the Council paling as it digests lies whose disturbing (and falsely elicited, ψευδ-) effects are also those of the staple Mediterranean potherb.[5]

But if this beginning is difficult, then the expression that follows at 631, κἄβλεψε νᾶπυ, is more so. Here, we are told that, as (or perhaps before) its Councillors "drew up" (ἀνασπάω) their brows,[6] the entire Council "looked *mustard*".

Such an abrupt jump from sight to taste (or vice versa) in the midst of this comic evocation of political and culinary competition elicits a uniform response from critics: here, presented with typically concrete hyperbole, is a comic confusion of things that should remain separate.[7] It is a poetic shock tactic, some say – comparable to a jump from abstract to concrete, and intended to violate expectation and temporarily dislocate

---

2. Σ^Lh; see Theophrastus, *Enquiry into Plants* 7.1.3; see also Rogers (1930: *ad loc.*); Neil (1901: *ad loc.*); cf. Henderson (trans.1998a).
3. Galen advised eating ἀτράφαξυς with olive oil, fish-sauce and vinegar, or to risk suffering a bad stomach (*On the Properties of Foodstuffs* 2.45); Diocles and Dionysus held that it made its eater susceptible to many diseases. Pliny, *Natural History* 20.219, lists dropsy, jaundice, paleness of complexion and indigestion. On the identification of the plant, see Andrews (1948: 170).
4. See Pliny, *Natural History* 20.219; cf. Rogers (1930: *ad loc.*); Sommerstein (1981: *ad loc.*).
5. Merry (1895: *ad loc.*) suggests that the Council is also "heated" with Paphlagon's biting and pungent lies. On pallor in general, see Lateiner (1998: esp. 169–73).
6. On the puckered up brow, elsewhere a marker of seriousness, but not necessarily anger, see Rogers (1930: *ad loc.*) citing Aristophanes, *Acharnians* 1069.
7. Underlying this intuition is a set of basic assumptions regarding the *a priori* segregation of the senses. Contrast the reaction of the anthropologist Seremetakis (1994: 40 n. 7) to comparable culinary idioms found today in rural regions of the Greek mainland, which draw upon the language of audition (e.g. ἄκου σκόρδο, "hear the garlic"): "This metonymic displacement [of hearing into other senses such as taste and vision] violates any segmentation of the senses as discrete perceptual organs". Cf. Sutton (2001: 99) on the phrase δεν ἀκούγεται ("it is not hearable"), used to indicate one's inability to taste an ingredient of a dish, and ἄκου μυρωδιά ("listen to that smell"); and note the demotic language of the fifteenth-century Ἐρωτοπαίγνια 157, wherein sight, hearing and smell are similarly interwoven (Hesseling & Pernot 1913) with Politis (1973: 39) on the demotic style of the poet. As Seremetakis (1994: 126) has shown, at issue in such interweaving of perceptual experiences is not simply "poetic wordplay", but rather, the existence of regional epistemologies.

its listening audience with the disruptive "intrusion" of a strong taste;[8] or else, it is just a peculiar way of evoking a mass of risible winces and grimaces, a multitude of sour or bitter faces, as English-speakers would say, and therefore, simply a hyperbolic equivalent of the sort of English idiom Shakespeare extrapolates in his more colourful expression "of vinegar aspect".[9]

But quite aside from the twisted sense such analogies make of the visual dimension of the Sausage Seller's words, familiarizing Aristophanes' odd expression by transposing it into English like this is to make an illegitimate step: it is to suppose that this mustard, that is, νᾶπυ, can simply be glossed as a metonym that points to the same general field of meaning in Greek language and experience as do English "metaphorical" applications of the terms "bitter" and "sour"[10] – and that, of course, allows little space for the cultural particularity of Greek tastes or for any poetic elaboration of the basic taste-terms that might variously differentiate them,[11] and instead wriggles away from the real issue of what it is that is funny and meaningful in Greek about this particular collocation.

So what I want to do in this essay is to start again: my question is what possible comic and sensory logic might motivate Aristophanes at *Knights* 631 to connect the eyes that had witnessed the Council's look, the ears of the Council that heard the lies by which it was (falsely) elicited, and the nose and tongue to which mustard and its effects would

---

8. A poetic shock tactic, one of a series of synaesthetic jumps from taste to sight, all of which enact a "different version of, or relative of, intrusion [and are designed to] convey a sense of sudden but temporary dislocation"; see Silk (2000: 148).
9. Shakespeare, *Merchant of Venice* I.i, the stylistic equivalent cited by Silk (*ibid.*: 148, n.109).
10. The popular (and scholarly) assumption that the English terms "bitter" and "sour" are applied outside the domain of taste only metaphorically, where they register only vague negative evaluations, has been challenged by Rakova (2003: esp. 139–49). *Pace* Lehrer (1978: 98); Osgood (1963: 346–7) and Catrein (2003: 32); see also Phillips & Heining (2002) for recent evidence from neurophysiology revealing that co-implicated regions of the brain process the perception both of distinct flavours and of distinct emotions, encoding tastes "to a large extent in terms of their emotional component" and the fascinating finding that when a facial expression is perceived part of the emotion it expresses, processed via those neural regions co-implicated in the coding of tastes, is actually felt too. As Rakova (2003: esp. 34–47) has argued, such findings should prompt theorists of conceptual metaphor of the Lakoff & Johnson (1980, 1999) school to reconsider their model of metaphorical transference in order to explain everyday judgements of similarity across the sensory modalities; there are good neurophysiological reasons for English speakers' use of words like "hot" or "bitter" of certain (extra-gustatory) experiences, and their use of these words for other people's faces may be no exception. *Pace* popular and scholarly assumptions of analogy and metaphor, a process of conscious inference may well play no part in what motivates us to reach for such words; the perception of a physiognomony as "bitter" may be as direct and immediate as the perception of a bitter taste.
11. For the cultural particularity of experience see Sahlins (1995: 148–9, 155); for taste-experience (the "cultural sense *par excellence*"), see Backhouse (1994: 13). For one cultural elaboration of the taste-terms "bitter" and "sweet" (among the Cashinahua of Amazonia) which stands in significant contrast to associations carried by these terms in English, see Lagrou (2000: 156–7); and Asch (1958: esp. 89–90), who demonstrates that to assume a universal vague evaluative meaning when such terms are applied to persons is entirely wrong-headed: "*Sweet* does not just stand for any positive psychological quality; it is not employed … to describe courage or honesty … Similarly, *bitter* and *sour* are not synonymous with any negative quality. Our records do not contain reference to *bitter* or *sour* fear".

ordinarily seem to belong? And my approach to answering it will be simple: I shall try to unpick Aristophanes' interweaving of senses, first clarifying the sense of βλέπω, then addressing the meaning of νᾶπυ, before finally, reuniting these words to suggest against orthodox interpretations that their comic charge derives from an experiential communality that seeing and tasting in Greek share.

"LOOKING MUSTARD"

Aristophanes' use of the looking verb, βλέπω, is perhaps the least difficult of our two words to explain. The active construction with an internal accusative is used already by Aeschylus at line 498 of *Seven against Thebes* (φόβον βλέπων), where the poet exploits the familiar Greek conceptual model of emotions-as-external-objects transmitted in the crossing of glances to evoke the terror-inducing look of Hippomedon:[12]

> MESSENGER The man [sc. Hippomedon] himself raised a great war-cry; he is possessed by Ares,
> and he rages for a fight like a Bacchant, looking terror (φόβον βλέπων).

During the late fifth century, the comic poets extrapolate the same colloquial idiom frequently for various effect, with characters casting hyperbolic looks of all kinds, "hostile, nautical looks" (ναύφρακτον βλέπων, *Acharnians* 95), looks of a "war-dance" (πυρρίχην βλέπων, *Birds* 1169), looks of "lightning-bolts" (βλέπων ἀστραπάς, *Acharnians* 566), or even just "glaring whips" (σκύτη βλέπειν, *Wasps* 643).[13]

Such examples help clarify the active sense of βλέπω operative here with its conceptual model of a look as something thrown, but, of course, still leave us with the problem of how

---

12. Aeschylus' φόβον βλέπων develops the syntactically parallel usages of looking verbs in Homer echoed earlier in the play at line 53 (Ἄρη δεδορκότων, cf. *Odyssey* 19.446); see Kerr Borthwick (2001: 298). On βλέπω see Prévot (1935: 258–63). For the general principle that when followed by a noun βλέπω takes an active meaning see Kerr Borthwick (2001: 297–9); *pace* Thordarson (1971: 113), who argues that with cognate objects (or adverbs) it means "to have the look or appearance of, to look like". For the reciprocity of vision and the "two-way traffic" of emotion in which the eyes are implicated, common both to literary evocations and philosophical explanations of vision, see Goldhill (2000: 169–70); Pearson (1909); Padel (1992: 60–63); Allen (2000: 79–80), citing Aristotle, *On Dreams* 459b25–35; Cairns (2011).
13. On the "presumably colloquial" form of βλέπω with an internal accusative, see Willi (2003: 252). On Aristophanes, *Acharnians* 95 ναύφρακτον βλέπων, "a hostile, nautical look", see Olson (2002: *ad loc.*), lit. "looking (a) ship-fenced (look)"; *LSJ*: "looking like a warship", where *LSJ*'s "like" effects a comparison between sorts of ocular activity (not appearance *per se*), i.e. "looking in the manner of, or, the looks of …"; cf. Aveline (2000: 500) on the gigantic eye costume likely worn by the actor; on *Birds* 1169 πυρρίχην βλέπων *LSJ*: "looking like a war-dancer", i.e. "looking (the looks of) a war-dance", cf. Kerr Borthwick (1970: 321) and Ceccarelli (2004: 106), for the backward head turns of the dancer; for further examples of the idiom, see Kerr Borthwick (2001: 298) and Blaydes (1887) at *Acharnians* 95.

to construe the very inanimate νᾶπυ.[14] Placing it in a more specific series is one way to start, because the shock of something tasty in the air at *Knights* 631 is not an isolated joke; it recurs several times throughout our extant plays. If mustard is not to your taste, there are characters that look savoury-taste (βλέπουσα θυμβροφάγον, *Acharnians* 253–4)[15] or cress (βλεπόντων κάρδαμα, *Wasps* 455) or fig-juice (βλέπων ὀπόν, *Peace* 1184), others with eyes sending forth oregano (βλέπουτ' ὀρίγανον, *Frogs* 603), and still others that look a savoury sauce, *hupotrimma* (βλέπων ὑπότριμμα, *Ecclesiazusae* 292).

For one school of Aristophanic criticism, it is enough simply to invoke Aristophanes' fondness for the sudden dislocation of his audience to explain the poet's selection of such a disparate cluster of air-sent vegetables, juices and foods to spice up his characters' eyes.[16] In late fifth-century comedy, the βλέπω idiom is picked up, stretched to comic extremes, and then kept novel in subsequent airings with fresh substitutions of strong-tasting substances (which is likely to be exactly what the poet does in order to keep this series of jokes zestful). But to depend entirely upon this discontinuity-as-comic-logic here is to come close to eliding cultural knowledge altogether; most worryingly, it is to allow our own failure to register anything but striking incongruity at these moments to be rationalized as their "comic" success, even their principal connective, in the absence of any attempt to enter into the original audience's worldview.[17] But to settle for that is simply to allow these moments to sit undigested; we do better by turning back to the gustatory world of Aristophanes' spectators.

Here, in fact, as Taillardat (1965: 216–18) notes, a cultural logic can readily be found for Aristophanes' taste-full glances, albeit preserved in the later botanical treatises of Aristotle's pupil, Theophrastus.[18] For as Theophrastus sets about cataloguing the tastes of various fruits in his *Enquiry into Plants* at 1.12.1, he provides glimpses of the most culturally salient plant-members of several distinct perceptual categories. And here we find grouped the majority of our Aristophanic foods.

> Of juices some are wine-like, just as are those of vine, mulberry and myrtle; some are olive-oil-like, just as are olive, bay, hazel, almond fir, Aleppo pine, silver fir; some are honey-like, such as are fig, date, chestnut; some are δριμύς, such as are

---

14. For the conceptual model of visuality active here, see J. Chadwick (1996: 76–7) (on the Homeric verb βλεμεαίνω "to dart fierce looks"), who associates βλέπω with the family of βάλλω rendering *βλέμος ("a look") as "something you throw" and citing βλέπειν νᾶπυ at *Knights* 631 as one example. See also Smyth (1920: §1570) and Cooper & Krüger (2002: §2.46.6.10) on the status of the objects concerned: "the substantive is almost entirely a product of the internal object activity of the verb".
15. For θυμβροφάγος as "an adjective that adds an idea of penetration to the glance or gaze expressed" see Cooper & Krüger (2002: §2.46.6.3). *Pace* Olson (2002: *ad loc.*) who reads an expression "in which the lips are pursed up as if in anger or hostility so as to create a proleptic appearance of profound hostility to verbal or physical advances of any sort"; so Henderson (1998a) trans.: "keep a lemon-sucking look on your face".
16. See Silk (2000: 136–59, esp. 136).
17. Silk's (*ibid.*: 148 n. 109) concerns lie elsewhere, but he notes the discussion of Taillardat (1965: 216–18).
18. So also Sommerstein (1980) on *Acharnians* 254.

oregano (ὀρίγανον), savory (θύμβρα), cress (κάρδαμον), mustard (νᾶπυ); some are bitter, just as are wormwood centaury. (Trans. Hort 1916, modified)

In Theophrastus' *Enquiry*, such comparative illustrations of the perceptual qualities of plant-juices demonstrate the sorts of working equivalence that Theophrastus assumes to hold between the plant-members of each of the categories in his classificatory scheme (the "wine-like" (οἰνώδεις), the "olive-oil-like" (ἐλαώδεις), the "honey-like" (μελιτώδεις), the δριμεῖς, the "bitter" (πικροί)). But Theophrastus' illustrative lists of *taxa* also reciprocally serve to anchor those same categories by providing his audience with tangible instantiations of each one. And this is why his scientific classifications are so salient for our investigation; for both the plant-members that Theophrastus draws upon to communicate his findings, and the perceptual judgements of similarity and difference by which they are organized, originate from, and are still in part anchored to, a wider shared set of folk classifications (i.e. common linguistic and perceptual discriminations, cf. δριμεῖς, πικροί) shared also by Aristophanes.

Indeed, at the very heart of Theophrastus' categorizations, and integral to his practice of inquiry, is sense perception, and not least, distinctions of taste.[19] As Theophrastus continues at *Enquiry into Plants* 1.12.2, for instance, it is specifically the taste of the fruits that plants produce that is given as the εἶδος, or essential character, of each plant. This use of taste as a working category of inquiry, in turn, necessarily involves comparative discussions of the sort given at 1.12.1, since differences of taste are themselves delimited by reference to other, more familiar, plants, or taste-substances.[20] And this is what Theophrastus' lists of *taxa* inadvertently make explicit. For they expose the fact that underlying his empirical assessments of plants that are not known lies a scheme of taste-categorization anchored to the perceptual properties of those that are known. Hence just as Theophrastus uses the criterion of taste in order to differentiate new *taxa*, his own judgements of difference are already dependent upon the most perfectly developed plant examples (τελειότατα, 1.1.5) that he exploits as prototypical cases, or "focal exemplars" of particular physical properties (δυνάμεις) or perceptual attributes (πάθη, 1.1.1; 1.5.4) and which also serve to exemplify pre-existent shared taste discriminations.[21] Thus, just as taste-categories are drawn into Theophrastus' project in the process of defining new plants, so other plants are drawn into his discussion as the most salient points of reference for those perceptual categories.[22] And this is how *Enquiry into Plants* 1.12.1 may be read as inadvertently revealing the common linguistic and perceptual grouping (i.e. the folk categorization) of four of six of our comic

---

19. On the role of sensory perception as the indispensable starting point of Theophrastus' philosophy see Baltussen (2000: 83–4, cf. 143). For Theophrastus' treatment of taste in its own right, see Sharples (1985).
20. For this reason, Aristotle considers the investigation of tastes to fall within the bounds of the investigation of plants, see *Sense and Sensibilia* 4.442b23–6; cf. Theophrastus, *Causes of Plants* 6.1.1.
21. The quintessential plant, most perfect and best known, according to Theophrastus, is the tree, and it is this species that provides the most basic point of reference in his botanical studies. On Theophrastus' method in *Enquiry into Plants* see Wöhrle (1985: chs 4 and 5, esp. 149f).
22. See *Enquiry into Plants* 1.12.2 for the procedure of citing a series of category distinctions and then providing known *exempla* in order to anchor them.

food substances as focal exemplars of a single perceptual category: the δριμεῖς. The Scholia on our Aristophanic foods neatly supplement this inference, since all agree that what connects the plants cited by Theophrastus (ὀρίγανον, θύμβρα, κάρδαμον, νᾶπυ) and the Aristophanic foods that remain unlisted at *Enquiry into Plants* 1.12.1 (ὑπότριμμα, ὀπός), is that to a late fifth-century audience also, each one would similarly evoke the defining properties of the category δριμύς.[23]

ΔΡΙΜΥΣ FROM TASTE CATEGORY TO SYNAESTHETIC METAPHOR AND BEYOND

Yet making greater sense of that kernel of practical knowledge poses new problems. Firstly, our own familiarity with the majority of these taste-substances, of course, does not give us privileged access to the experience Aristophanes' audience may have perceived them to exemplify – as we shall shortly see; secondly, while a battery of English taste-terms are commonly used to translate the adjective δριμύς – these range from "bitter", to "pungent", to "acrid", to "sharp" – the lexical diversity they introduce to the category ought not to be misinterpreted as vagueness or confusion on its part; and not least on those frequent occasions where that misrepresentation is mostly easily made: that is, when the word is applied outside the domain of taste.[24] In fact, the barrier that this presents to understanding the conceptual organization of the word – and, by extension, grasping precisely what comic charge its concrete exemplars might detonate on stage – is perhaps no better illustrated than by considering usual scholarly approaches to it.

Here, Stanford's treatment of the word remains typical. As he catalogues it, δριμύς is simply dismissed as one of a range of adjectives "of loose sensory application γλυκύς, δριμύς, ὀξύς, βαρύς, ἀμβλύς, πικρός, τραχύς, which seem to have lost their precise sense-sphere (if they were ever thus precisely defined, *vide sub.*) long before even Homer's time (probably because they belonged to the lower senses of touch, taste and smell) …".[25]

---

23. For ὑπότριμμα see Σ^RA on *Ecclesiazusae*. 292: ἀντὶ τοῦ δριμύ. οἱ γὰρ δικάζοντες ὀφείλουσι δριμεῖς εἶναι (also noted by Taillardat 1965: 217). For ὀπός see Σ^V on *Peace* 1184: ἀντὶ τοῦ 'πικρίαν καὶ δριμύτητα ὁρῶν'; see also O'Brien (1984: 120–3), who suggests that Plato's account of the effects on the body of ὀπός in the *Timaeus* (at 60a3–8) echoes the effects caused by things that are δριμύς (at 65e6–7); both rise (65e6–7; cf. 66b4–5) and are "cutting". δριμύς taste-substances could appeal precisely for having these properties, see Archestratus fr. 46 l. 6–7 with Olson & Sens (2000) and cf. Xenocrates x (on deep-sea mullet). In linguistic terms, Theophrastus' plant exemplars represent taste axioms (foods that exemplify given taste qualities) whereas the observations of the Scholia draw upon taste norms (foods that usually taste a certain way). See Backhouse (1994: 16–18).
24. Translation words used include: "bitter": Rogers (1913) trans. of *Peace* 349; cf. Platnauer (1964: *ad loc.*); Olson (1998: *ad loc.*); "In a culinary context, pungent, with a bite": Olson & Sens (2000: 102, 5–6n.); O'Brien (1984: 120); "acrid": Schiefsky (2005: 245) on Hippocrates, *On the Diseases of Virgins* 14.4; "sharp": Dover (1993) *ad Frogs* 603; Sansone (1975: 11 n. 12) on *Iliad* 11.270; "severe": Henderson (1998b) trans. of *Peace* 349; "fierce": Henderson (1998b) trans. of *Wasps* 277; cf. Henderson (1998a) trans. of *Knights* 808.
25. Stanford (1936: 54).

Now, in saying this, Stanford is no doubt thinking of other poetic instances from the fifth-century stage such as Euripides' striking application of the term to the "rattling" sound of Odysseus at *Cyclops* 104:[26]

> SILENUS I know of the man, the δριμύς rattler, Sisyphus' son.

or Aristophanes' comical evocation of the smell of a fart at *Wealth* 689–93:

> CARIO [...] so then I hissed
> and grabbed [her hand] in my teeth, pretending to be a sacred snake.
> She instantly drew her hand back again,
> wrapped herself tight and lay there still,
> with terror farting [a smell] more δριμύς than a ferret.
> (Trans. Sommerstein 2001, modified)

or of Heracles' terrible glance at *Frogs* 562:

> INNKEEPER And then, when I asked him for payment,
> he gave me a δριμύς look and started bellowing.
> (Trans. Sommerstein 1996)

and lastly, perhaps also of more abstract examples, like Homer's earlier δριμύς battle at *Iliad* 15.696:[27]

> Now once again δριμύς battle was fought by the vessels.

A quick look at these examples may prompt us also to appeal to the sort of loose metaphorical transfer supposed by Stanford; that is, the sort of semantic extension by which

---

26. Euripides' usage here is a *hapax*, but analogous semantic stretches render it well within our comprehension, see Seaford (1984: *ad loc.*): "Nowhere else does δριμύς describe a sound, but there is no reason why it should not; cf. διαπρύσιος ("piercing") of the sound of κρόταλα at *Helen* 1308". Seaford suggests that the notion of a "piercing sound" may explain the hypothesis of Aristophanes Byzatius (*apud* Eustathius, *Commentarii ad Homeri Odysseam* 3.20) that Euripides used δριμύς at *Cyclops* 104 in order to evoke piercing intelligence (in place of συνετός). Such a sense is clearly within the range of usages of δριμύς; for use of the term to denote a psychological quality, reminiscent of the English use of the term "sharp" to denote intellectual acuity, cf. ὀξύς and a δριμύς taste used together of dicasts at *Wasps* 455 and the fact that from Aristophanes to Plato, jurors (who in Aristophanes are typically old and severe, if not outright fierce), are notoriously the most δριμύς group in Athenian society, see Σ^RA on *Ecclesiazusae*. 292; *Wasps* 277, *Knights* 808, *Peace* 349; cf. Plato, *Theaetetus* 173a, 175d-e. Σ^Va on *Clouds* 1176d assumed that an Ἀττικὸν βλέπος (a look which is taken by Strepsiades clearly to indicate that its wearer (Pheidippides) is both ἐξαρνητικὸς κἀντιλογικός) was typically δριμύς; cf. Plato, *Republic* 564c–e; *Statesman* 311a8; *Republic* 519a; and 535b4, where the ideal students of dialectic are those who meet the challenge of that intellectual pursuit with δριμύτης [or who] "... bring with them a piercing eye for their studies" (Davies & Vaughan 1879). For κρόταλον of the sound of clever or polished speech-making, see *Clouds* 260, 448.
27. Cf. Hesiod's μάχην δριμεῖαν at *Theogony* 713; *Scutum* 261, 411; cf. Theocritus 22.107.

```
                                    ┌──────────────────────────┐
                                    │                          ▲
                                    │                          │
       touch ───▶ taste ───▶ smell          dimension          │
                    │                          │               │
                    │                          ▼               │
                    └──────────────────────────────────▶ sound
```

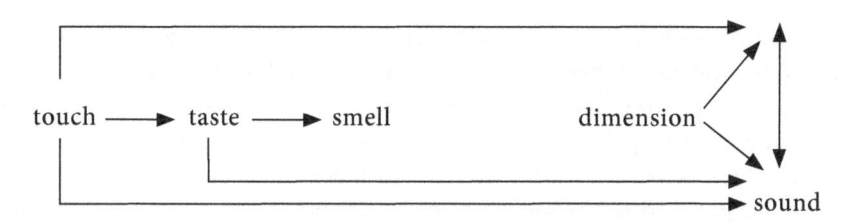

Figure 5.1 The direction of synaesthetic transfer of sensory adjectives between sense-domains. Redrawn from Williams (1976).

terms that are applied "basically" in one sense-domain, most often the domains of taste or touch, are further applied in others like sound or smell (or are even extended beyond these to more abstract domains, like disposition, appearance or behaviour). That response, as Stanford is aware, has its conceptual roots in the theorization of μεταφορά by Aristotle, for whom the application of δριμύς even to a certain sort of smell represents a "carrying over" from the domain in which it is used "properly" (taste), to another, in which it is not.[28]

In Figure 5.1, the historical linguist J. M. Williams plots the path of precisely this sort of poetic transfer according to his general pattern of synaesthetic extension extrapolated from a range of languages.[29] On this model, our examples from Euripides and Aristophanes would then seem simply to exemplify a universal tendency for taste adjectives to be transferred, on the basis of their affective values, into the domains of smell or sound, wherein they become only metaphorical.[30] But, in fact, Williams's diachronic schema tells a story only about (possible) origins; and the cognitive linguists tell us that the historical precedence of a term in one sense-domain is no determinant of its metaphorical meaning in any other domain in which it may subsequently appear. "Literal" meaning, if we choose to retain the problematic dichotomy that term implies, is determined in a synchronic frame by the current practice of speakers (which can admit all manner of "semantic stretches").[31] Indeed, even the synchronic model for determining literal versus

---

28. See Aristotle, *On the Soul* 420a29–b4 (on metaphorical transfers from touch to hearing) and esp. 421a26–b3 (on transfers from taste to smell, one of which is δριμύς), also cited by Stanford (1936: 49). See Johansen (1997: 227–37) on the judgements of similarity between sensory experiences (but not the "objects" of perception) underlying this passage. On Aristotle's definition of metaphor, see Kirby (1997); Silk (2003); with Lloyd (1987: 183–7; 2003) for the polemical agenda behind Aristotle's formulation of that category (anything but a "value-free" discovery) and a philosophical critique of the dichotomy of the literal and the metaphorical that Aristotle first theorizes.
29. Williams (1976: 463). The logic of this progression recapitulates that applied by Viberg (1983: 157–60), who, following Williams, compares (and conflates) the hierarchy of sensory modalities plotted by Ullman (1957) in the course of a literary study of the "synaesthetic transfer" of sensory adjectives in nineteenth-century poetry, with the hierarchy produced by Williams (1976).
30. I leave aside the apparently more abstract usage represented by Homer's δριμεῖα μάχη for the time being.
31. See Goodman (1968: 77), cited by Rakova (2003: 12–13), who exposes the fallacy of basing the metaphoricity of sensory adjectives upon historical primacy; see also 110–13 for a parallel case against the etymological arguments of Sweetser (1990: 32–44). See Lloyd (2003: 112–13) for the notion of "semantic stretch".

metaphorical status given by Aristotle, which is based upon the criterion of proper domain application, is problematic here too; because if we are faced with the current use of a sensory adjective in two different sensory domains, on what basis do we decide which usage is conceptually or perceptually "proper" and thus literal, and which is "improper", derivative, and thus metaphorical?[32] Historical primacy will not do;[33] and neither will the notion of conceptual primacy (implicit in Aristotle's model), for if we follow what most modern metaphor theorists say about this, that is, that the conceptual primacy of certain domains of experience over others is to be identified with their experiential primacy (the notion is that we encounter certain physical experiences first in the course of our lives, and then go on to model psychological or mental facets of experience in terms of them *via* conceptual metaphors), then it is by no means clear why the δριμύς-ness of a smell should be secondary to the δριμύς-ness of a taste (as Aristotle's theory proposes).[34] Nor, even, on that basis, is it clear why we should necessarily give primacy to the δριμύς-ness of a taste over the δριμύς-ness of a sound. How, after all, is the experience designated by δριμύς any more "basic" in one of these sensory domains than in any other?[35] Aristotle's influential diagnosis of one literal meaning, with all others as metaphorical derivatives, reduces to a claim about proper versus improper usage; and that proves neither to be theoretically compelling, nor, in any substantive sense, particularly elucidating.[36]

---

32. As Rakova (2003: 13, cf. 43), has asked in arguing a case for the non-metaphoricity of the term "hot" when used of gustatory-sensation as well as thermal temperature.
33. δριμύς in fact has no etymology, see Beekes (2010: 354), who offers instead only the translations "sharp, sour, bitter".
34. For the identification of conceptual primacy and experiential primacy, see the school founded by Lakoff & Johnson (1980, 1999). For forceful critiques of the theory of conceptual metaphor, see McGlone (2001) and Rakova (2003). Continuity between Aristotle's theory and Lakoff & Johnson's model of metaphor (both of which presuppose the notion of conceptual primacy): Kirby (1997). Marks *et al.* (1987, cited by Rakova 2003: 67) on the English word "bright" offers a significant corrective to the view that literalness is determined by conceptual primacy. Here, the understanding that "bright" applies to sounds only metaphorically is shown to emerge only when children have learned that "bright" has literal meaning in only the visual domain; at an earlier age than this, "bright" is treated as equally literal whether describing light or sound.
35. Cf. Rakova (2003: 43). As Rakova (2003: 114) points out: "The very claim that some sensory modalities are understood on the model of other sensory modalities is empty in the absence of any account of how the sensory modalities are understood on their own". Aristotle shows us the implicit basis of his theorization of proper meaning in attempting to theorize discrete and segregated sensory modalities, see *On the Soul* 418a12-3 (cf. Plato, *Theaetetus* 184e-85a3). Yet to authorize only this model of sensory experience by enforcing its concomitant, the strict compartmentalization of experience into mutually exclusive semantic domains, is to force issues that may distort the conceptual structures underlying evocations of sensory experience in Greek poetry. We are in danger of generalizing from the particular, and literary analyses of such evocations as "synaesthetic" metaphor (a category which assumes the *a priori* separation in *reality* of what is forged together in *language*) of the sort offered by Stanford (1936, 1942: 106–10), C. Segal (1977), and most recently, in Latin literature, by Catrein (2003), have not escaped the influence of Aristotle. See Ingold (2000: 268) for the potentially distorting assumptions brought by the notion of "synaesthesia".
36. Cf. Rakova (2003: 48–73, 142-3) on the English word "bright". The standard assumption is that only objects perceived visually can be labelled as literally "bright"; yet English speakers use "bright" to refer to a certain property in the domain of sound ("a bright voice") with consistency across speakers (cf. *ibid.*: 68, 147); and they do not do so "loosely", as if simply to impart intensity (i.e. as if brightness of sound

So what if we bracket for a moment the *a priori* assumption that the primary or "literal" sense of δριμύς denotes a discrete sensory quality belonging to a single, segregated domain of experience (i.e. taste)? Instead, let us consider the possibility that the semantic territory of this word should be plotted on some other aspect of sensory, or somatic, experience, conceptually salient qualities of which presented themselves to native speakers in a variety of different sensory contexts or domains. From this perspective, the, to us, disparate, range of referents that the word takes might no longer be taken as instances of "loose" or "vague" semantic extension. Rather, we would be forced to address the likelihood that for a Greek audience the various percepts described as δριμύς could all be intuitively felt to participate in a single conceptual field; and that each one registered within that field according to an internal logic of category membership, as one instantiation of a core concept at the centre of the word's range. On this model, we do not set out to reduce δριμύς to a single meaning; instead, our interpretative task lies in extrapolating from the various behaviour of the word the unifying concept that spans its range of application to apparently different properties across a variety of sensory domains.[37]

FROM WORD TO CONCEPT

I begin this investigation by discussing a selection of passages, ranging from Plato's account in the *Timaeus* of why his audience labels certain flavours as it does, to the Hippocratics' treatment of a head cold. My movement through them will be rapid because my claim

---

equals loudness, as Rakova (*ibid.*: 62), drawing upon Marks (1982: 184), shows), hence the basis of that assumption is not linguistic practice. Rather, as Rakova shows, it derives from a set of arbitrary claims about "proper meaning" that echo Aristotle's polemical dichotomizing of words between those used κυρίως and those used κατὰ μεταφοράν. As she argues (2003: 48–73) it makes much better sense of the linguistic data to work on the model that applications of "bright" in either sensory domain recognize two differing instantiations of a single supramodal concept. Here, the real-world physical properties depicted by "bright" in "bright light" and "bright" in "bright music" are not taken to be the same (one is a phenomenon of light and one is a phenomenon of sound); yet both applications of the word are nonetheless related in an un-arbitrary way on the basis that both are taken to map on to the same psychologically primitive concept, BRIGHT. That English speakers then use the word "bright" more frequently of their experience of light (where it seems to be more literal) than of sound is explained on the basis that we encounter its salient properties more frequently in certain sensory contexts than in the others. Rakova (2003: 34–47) explains that one basis for the perceived conceptual equivalence of different real-world properties in this way is neurophysiological: "the similarity of sensations [induced] mediated by the same neural mechanisms", where the sensations referred to are caused by two different stimuli, thermal heat and gustatory spiciness, both of which prompt speakers to reach for the word "hot" (*ibid.*: 44). This notion is forcefully argued by Rakova while discussing the "literality" of the words "hot" and "sharp" as used of spicy tastes. It has significant affinities with the argument I begin to develop here (indeed, Rakova includes δριμύς in her preliminary pool of linguistic data; *ibid.*: 39).

37. This is not to set out by conflating meanings and concepts, but rather to seek to uncover what underlying unity on a conceptual level connects the different meanings that δριμύς may take in relation to the different "real-world properties" of which it may be used. See *ibid.*: 149 on the ambiguity of "hot" in the phrase "hot soup", and my previous note.

here is very simple: in the various continuities identifiable between these writers, recurrent experiential aspects of the category δριμύς emerge – namely, volatile burning sensations, a quality of lightness (κουφότης), and a location for these experiences in a particular body-site, the sinuses, or nose.

In the *Timaeus*, Plato formulates an understanding of flavours as "affections peculiar to the tongue" (ἴδι᾽ ὄντα παθήματα περὶ τὴν γλῶτταν, 65c2–3) brought about by the contracting and dilating action on this sense-organ caused by all kinds of flavour particles.[38] The section of his account that interests us is at 65e4–66a2:

> And those which share in the heat of the mouth and are made smooth thereby, when they are fully inflamed and are themselves in turn burning the part which heated them, fly upwards because of their lightness towards the senses of the head, and cut all the parts on which they impinge; and because of these powers all such are called δριμύς. (Trans. Bury 1929, modified).

For the moment, we should just note that the point at which these flavour particles enter into the semantic range of δριμύς is when their behaviour inside the mouth causes a peculiar sort of physiological effect: it is when they become inflamed and fly upwards to the sinuses, there causing a volatile disturbance that Plato describes as "cutting" (τέμνοντα) that speakers are prompted to reach for the word.[39] Indeed, for Plato, when δριμύς particles cut our bodies, not only do we speak of ourselves as experiencing δριμύτης; we also speak of whatever causes us to feel that way as being δριμύς.[40]

In fact, Plato's formulation of a perceptual exchange between self and substance in these terms seems helpful also for understanding the application of the adjective in the Hippocratics. For the author of *Ancient Medicine* also has recourse to the term, this time in the context of a protracted discussion of the relationship of hot and cold to feverishness, as exemplified by the common cold (18.1–2):

> First let us take the most obvious cases, which we all often experience and will continue to experience in the future. In the first place, when we have caught a cold and there is a movement of flux through the nostrils, this is generally more δριμύς than what occurred before and passed from the nostrils every day, and it makes the nose swell and inflames it so that it is exceedingly hot and burning ... How does the burning heat in the nose come to an end? Not when the discharge takes place and the inflammation is present, but when the running is thicker and less δριμύς, ripe and more mixed than it was before – only then is the burning heat at an end.[41]

The sensations hinted at in this passage are essentially of the same sort as are those that Plato identifies as caused by the behaviour of a particular sort of flavour particle.

---

38. For the role of the tongue as arbiter of δριμύς foods, cf. Xenophon, *Memorabilia* 1.4.5.
39. Cf. Plato, *Timaeus* 61d5–62a5 with O'Brien (1984: 113–23).
40. Cf. Plato on trembling and shivering at *Timaeus* 62b4–6 again with O'Brien (1984: 150–51).
41. Text and trans. Schiefsky (2005).

Characterized by a feeling of intense congestion that inflames the sinuses, the cold that is δριμύτερος is, like the fever spoken of by the author of *Epidemics*, first particularly marked for its distinctive heat; for ἡ θερμότης δριμύτητος σημεῖον (*Ep.* 6. 6. 5).[42] But this flush of nasal agitation lasts only as long as the mucus (ῥεῦμα) that causes it continues to emanate from its point of origin at the back of the sufferer's stinging nose. When this flow matures, thickens and ceases to exert its volatile pressure on the sinuses (i.e. when it becomes less δριμύς), then this sensation passes, and the cold's fervour dissipates.

What emerges from the descriptions of Plato and the medical writers, then, is a sense that the meaning of the adjective here is tied to a localized set of sensations felt to rise to the face and pulse through a specific body-site, the nose. And precisely that impression is reiterated if we compare the word's use on the comic stage. Consider *Wasps* 146:

BDELYKLEON By Poseidon, why does the chimney make all that noise?
You in there! Who are you?
PHILOKLEON I'm smoke coming out!
BDELYKLEON Smoke? Smoke of what wood?
PHILOKLEON Of figwood (συκίνου)!
BDELYKLEON Of course! That's the most δριμύς of smoke!

Here Bdelycleon's invocation of δριμύς in response to his father's joke suddenly makes good sarcastic sense if we are supposed to imagine the rush of intense prickling, perhaps even tears, that the smoke of fig wood stirs up in the sinuses and brings to the eyes.[43] Likewise, returning to *Wealth* 693, we realize now just how much Aristophanes' parallel use of the adjective there milks the comedy of a pungent fart. What makes all of these things intuitive members of the δριμύς category is the fact that each one is experienced as instantiating a core concept in only very slightly differing ways. In fact, listening to Plato, and the Hippocratics, and Aristophanes, it seems quite plausible that its conceptual structure should be plotted not in a single perceptual domain, that is, taste (even if the reader is tempted to include, *contra* Aristotle, the olfactory in his definition of that domain), but as accommodating a much larger set of physiological sensations spanning a continuum of prickling, pangs and twinges, into which taste experience variously, but not exclusively, encroaches.

Yet for that very reason, we should not be surprised that it is possible only poorly to approximate in English what that central concept might be. The texts we have examined so far suggest a tentative working definition along the lines of *a flush of nasal irritation/heat/prickling pain, presaging tears*.[44] And proceeding on this basis, it turns out to be possible to understand most of the word's various referents by teasing out the relation of each one to such an organizing concept. So, for instance, Aristophanes' use of the term in the

---

42. Cf. Galen, *On Simple Drugs* 4.18 (Kühn 1821–1833: vol. 11, p. 679.9–16)
43. Note the pun here also in σύκινος (on συκοφάντης, malicious prosecutor); see MacDowell (1971: *ad loc.*).
44. This approximation is designed to be vague enough to accommodate the *range* of sensations from stinging pain to welling tears that we have encountered in the concept δριμύς.

exclamation δριμύς! at *Peace* 257 of a punch in the nose, and the allusion to garlic, a δριμύς taste, which it immediately elicits, suddenly makes good sense as a sort of physiological pun which plays upon the possibility of invoking in a single experience two differing instantiations of the same underlying concept.[45]

> War Boy! Boy! Uproar!
> Uproar Why are you calling me?
> War   You're really going to weep.
> Do you stand there idle? Here's some knuckles for you!
> Uproar Oh δριμύς! Woe is me oh Master.
> You didn't put any of that garlic into that blow did you?

Yet if that image is really accurate, we still need to explain why the adjective qualifies things that have no obvious relation to taste or smell, nor, at first blush, seem to fit at all into our tentative picture of its conceptual structure. If the concept that underlies the word's semantic range is activated by sensations associated most prominently with disturbances in the nose, how are we to relate to it such seemingly disparate sensory referents as the rattle of Odysseus' speech, or the weight of Herakles' glance, or the δριμύς-ness of Homeric battle?

In fact, perhaps we already have an answer to that dilemma. As peculiar as the connection of these things with, of all sensory organs, the nose, might sound, the problem here simply has to do with the deliberately abstract terms in which we have characterized our core concept. So far we have allowed our view of the sort of experience typically assimilated to it to be filtered through the objectifying lens of scientific language. What we have arrived at, then, are the broad brush-strokes of the physiology of that part of Greek experience that motivates speakers to reach for the word. The poets, by contrast, remind us that there remains a vitally important concomitant of that physiology yet to explore, and that is its emotionality.

REASONS TO BE TEARFUL

It is well known that outside of the medical writers, the same physical substances that participate in Hippocratic humoral theory take on further experiential aspects as at once both physical and expressly emotional forces that surge or ooze throughout the body. The imagery associated with Homer's usual word for anger, χόλος, for instance, illustrates that at key points it has a tangible existence as a bodily humour;[46] in such moments, it

---

45. Cf. Olson (1998: *ad loc.*) This allusion to δριμύς garlic reiterates the association made explicit by Trygaeus earlier at lines 248–9, as he watches War make a μυττωτός of the Greek States tearful by throwing Megarian garlic into the mix.
46. See Homer, *Iliad* 16.203; 22.93–5 (interestingly, a simile placing in causal sequence, the consumption of "bad" herbs, the invasion of the body by χόλος αἰνός, and a "terrible" glance, σμερδαλέον δὲ δέδορκεν).

is arguably best understood not in terms of a concrete physical substance or an abstract emotion-concept, but according to a set of poetic expectations that expressly draw upon the embodied nature of emotional experience.[47] Indeed, throughout the poetic corpus, thought, feeling and emotion are all tied to the ebb and flow of bodily sensations caused by substances that are at once psychological, physical and emotional. Examples of this in Greek poetry abound.[48] But I want to consider just two instances, one drawn from Homeric epic, the other, from later Hellenistic poetry. Together, they clearly illustrate the continuity of the basic associations carried by δριμύς in contexts of heightened emotion. First, the famous reunion of Odysseus and Laertes at *Odyssey* 24.315–9, a scene which enacts, with a nasal surge of δριμὺ μένος, the reciprocity of shared feeling that typifies moments of recognition in the epic.[49]

> So he spoke, and a black cloud of grief enwrapped
> Laertes, and with both his hands he took the sooty dust
> and poured it over his gray head, groaning without pause.
> And Odysseus' heart was stricken, and stabbing up through
> his nostrils surged δριμὺ μένος as he beheld his dear father.[50]

μένος referred to here is a difficult word: sometimes it can be the movement of breath; at others, it seems to behave with the physical, liquid qualities of vital fluids like mucus, or χολή, bile.[51] Second, Theocritus 1.18, where Pan is spoken of as "bitter, with δριμύς bile (δριμεῖα χολά) sitting ever on his nostril". Both passages, of course, describe intensely emotional contexts; Theocritus' description of Pan explains why shepherds dare not play their pipes at midday for fear of provoking the resting god's wrath.[52] But more importantly both texts present us with physical-emotion processes or substances, either μένος or bile (χολή), causing essentially the same sort of bodily disturbance as does the discharge (ῥεῦμα) of the Hippocratic head cold; the same disturbance, that is, which, Plato and our scientific texts, have characterized as δριμύς. That this is then differently interpreted

---

47. On the physical identification of χόλος with bile see Clarke (1999: 92–4, and n. 82) on the Myrmidons' story that Achilles was weaned on this substance instead of milk at *Iliad* 16.203: "uniquely vivid [in its emphasis on the physicality of χόλος but] consistent with what is said of [... it] throughout Homer" (*ibid.*: 93). For a different interpretation drawing upon Lakoff & Johnson's (1980) model of conceptual metaphor, and the work on metaphorical and metynomic structuring of emotion experience by Kövecses (2000), see Cairns (2003: 25–6). But see McGlone (2001) for research that challenges the orthodox view that speakers draw upon Lakoff's (1987) ontological anger metaphors in idiom comprehension, or in conceptualizing more abstract (i.e. pyschological-emotional) facets of experience. See Rakova (2003: 18–33).
48. See Padel (1992); Clarke (1999).
49. See Murnaghan (1987: 22).
50. On the meaning of μένος see Clarke (1999: 110–11).
51. Trans. Murray & Dimmock (1995), modified.
52. Cf. Verity's trans. of Theocritus 1. 18 "his lip is always curled in sour displeasure" (Verity & Hunter 2002), which makes use of precisely the same translation strategy seen earlier in scholarly evocations of our Aristophanic looks, turning what is genuinely a felt-experience into an aspect of appearance. For ἄχος similarly described, see Hesiod, *Scutum* 457.

or experienced in each text as a specific emotion, grief or anger, seems to be due to the particular context in which it is felt.[53]

It is precisely this folk-physiology of emotion, featuring emotional experience that registers physiologically in the nose, that holds the key to the examples we have yet to explain. What, for instance, if we think about the "rattling" speech of Odysseus at *Cyclops* 104 in terms of the emotional response described at Herodas 6.37? There, Koritto's presumed natural response to unsettling words is given precisely in terms of a surge of nasal sensation and affect: "Don't get bile (χολή) in your nose, Koritto, / as soon as you hear an unwise word". That remark suggests there is no problem at all with the idea that the sounds of certain sorts of speech might elicit a bodily disturbance in the nose.[54] Similarly, we might take the emotional events of *Odyssey* 24 to suggest that equivalent experiences of affect might be set in motion just as easily by emotive sights: for there a surge of δριμύ μένος is felt by Odysseus at exactly the moment of visual perception (εἰσορόωντι, 24.319) in which he recognizes the distress of his father.[55] Here, also, is a suggestive explanation for the δριμύς-ness of Herakles' glance at *Frogs* 562. In fact, in light of the model of visual and emotional reciprocity underlying the βλέπω idiom at lines 497–8 of Aeschylus' *Seven Against Thebes*, where the φόβος experienced on seeing the terrifying Hippomedon is said to be thrown from his eyes into those of his Theban viewers, the words of the unfortunate recipient of Herakles' look might well be taken to suggest that this sort of perceptual exchange is exactly what the comic speaker there has in mind: ἔβλεψεν εἴς με δριμύ ("he looked a δριμύς look at", or perhaps just "δριμύτης into, me" as if to say by his look he threw δριμύτης into my nostrils).

To follow this path of inquiry, then, is to arrive at an understanding of δριμύς as a physiological/affective state which can both be engendered through a variety of different senses and sensory contexts, but also transmitted to its recipients from those who inspire it exactly in accordance with the flow elsewhere in Greek thought of affective states like desire or fear. Against this characterization of the adjective nestle the kindred images of emotional experience contained in our poetic texts – those moments we have glimpsed from the *Odyssey*, Herodas, Theocritus, and to which we might add the explicitly martial imagery of *Anacreontea* 31, there recalling Homer's δριμύς battle[56] – each with their popular conception of violent emotion as affect-in-the-nose:[57]

---

53. Cf. Gow (1951: 81). For the μάλα ... δριμύς χόλος felt by Achilles after a night of weeping at the death of Patroclus, see Homer, *Iliad* 18.322.
54. Cf. Aristotle's use of δριμύς of those arguments that cause the greatest *aporia*, *On Sophistical Refutations* 182b32.
55. Note that emotive sights, sounds and smells are explicitly among those things that have an affect on the temperature and balance of bile and phlegm according to the Hippocratic writers also, see *On Diseases* I 23 (6.188.12–13); *On Affections* I (6.208.12–13) with Gundert (2000: 29–31).
56. For the Anacreontic portrayal of battles between Eros and the victims of love on the model of Homeric battle (cf. *Iliad.* 5.796–7; 21.51–2), see Rosenmeyer (1992: 103–4); cf. *Anacreontea* 28.5–7 on Eros' χολή-soaked arrows.
57. Cf. Csordas's (1993) notion of culturally significant "somatic modes of attention".

Love, beating me cruelly with a rod tied around with
hyacinths, ordered me to run by his side; and as I ran through
fierce torrents and thickets and gullies the sweat distressed me,
my heart climbed to my nose and I might have perished;
but Love fanned my brow with his tender wings and said,
"Can't you love, then?"[58]

TASTE-FULL GLANCES, TEARFUL FOODS: LOOKING AGAIN AT *KNIGHTS* 631

We have strayed far from Aristophanes, and it is time to return to the comic world of *Knights*, and the peculiar moment with which we began – the problem of κἄβλεψε νᾶπυ, the mustard those Athenian Councillors looked. For we can now see that Aristophanes there exploits the basic constellation of ideas and associations that structure the behaviour of the word δριμύς in a variety of other contexts. Like the δριμύς punch on the nose at *Peace* 257, that is, the logic of a mustard glance lies in the poet's use of the capacity of marked foods to instantiate, as focal exemplars of the sensation-affect at its centre, all the embodied qualities of δριμύς in its most immediate and concrete form.[59] That, in fact, is precisely the hyperbole of Xanthias' cry at *Frogs* 602-3: "... I'll show myself to be brave in spirit / and looking *oregano* (βλέποντ' ὀρίγανον)!": the point of this boast being that unlike Dionysus' pathetic attempts at mimicry, his comic version of Herakles will be so mindful of the god whose semblance he is adopting – characterized at 592, as we saw, by those δριμύτης-inspiring glances – that he'll go one better, and send forth looks more Heraklean than Herakles himself. (That what his audience get, however, is *oregano* and not, for instance, a more striking dose of mustard, clearly makes all the comic difference: δριμύς-ness, that is, comes in degrees; even with spiced-up eyes, Xanthias is not much of a Herakles.) Even so, the effect of his boast is to invite his audience to reflect upon the continuity of experience between what is felt in the context of one sensory exchange, the παθήματα of a δριμύς look seen, with what is experienced in the context of another, the παθήματα transferred from a δριμύς food tasted.[60] In this way, for those in the theatre, getting Aristophanes' joke is not to understand one sensory experience, a sight, in terms of another, a taste, as the model of synaesthetic metaphor would suggest; rather it is to recognize intuitively the way in which the two experiences of sensory exchange are already conceptually conjoined.

And this leads me to my larger – and final – methodological point: for the essential fallacy of metaphor in this context is that it simply assumes *a priori*, as an unproblematic fact, the existence of a familiarly segregated world. It recognizes only one (essentially

---

58. Trans. Campbell (1988). For the δριμύτης of love, see Plato, *Republic* 458d6.
59. Cf. Taillardat (1965: 17, 216–18).
60. For taste-experience as an emotional exchange between self and substance, see Seremetakis (1994: 28–9).

Aristotelian) account of sensory experience, even though at the base of this lies the very theoretical objectifications that are flouted by the comic language it would explain. Indeed, by authorizing this segregation of experience into specialized semantic domains as the only valid account of sensory perceptions, it entirely denies the existence of any other popular epistemologies at a time when the evidence of the comic stage suggests a flourishing rival poetic discourse of sensory relations. Herein lies the delimitation of the category δριμύς to proper meaning in only one sensory domain, the absolute segregation of experiences of seeing and tasting, and the scholarly assumption, when faced with our comic images, of ridiculous jumps between things that are essentially separate.

This is a start from which we can only go wrong; for the logic of Aristophanes' strategy of invoking δριμύς foods in order to evoke the weight of a glance lies not primarily in creating a moment of striking discontinuity; rather, its slide between the eye and the tongue exploits in the glimpse of a taste his audience's recognition of an inherent unity between those things. Against those who would partition off the visual – delimit what it means to see – what is to be experienced in a glance of mustard is a reawakening of knowledge every Athenian already knows: the "inner commotion" felt upon catching a δριμύς eye is a matter of παθήματα, not optics, and the worst kind of looks are those that you feel, most unambiguously, at the back of your nose.[61]

---

61. I borrow the phenomenological point and the phrase "inner commotion" from Rée (1999: 344). This essay has had an embarrassingly long gestation and leaves me with a plethora of debts to friends, colleagues and seminar audiences in the UK and USA whose thoughtful responses to its past incarnations have challenged and advanced my thinking. I am extremely grateful in particular to Robin Osborne (to whom I owe the phrase "Greek popular epistemology"), Paul Cartledge, Liz Irwin, Douglas Cairns, Michael Clarke, Yannis Hamilakis, Charles Stewart, Anna Chahoud and Tim Hill, and to Shane Butler, Alex Purves and Mario Telò.

6

PLATO, BEAUTY AND "PHILOSOPHICAL SYNAESTHESIA"

Ralph M. Rosen

When you listen to "Ecstasy", look straight into the eye of the Sun.[1]

If we are to believe Plato, it was common enough to see around the streets of Athens of his day people whom a later age might call – and with a suspicion shared by Plato – "aesthetes". Plato has Socrates call them at *Republic* 5.476b "lovers of sounds and sights", people who "like beautiful sounds, colours, shapes and everything fashioned out of them" (φιλήκοοι καὶ φιλοθεάμονες τάς τε καλὰς φωνὰς ἀσπάζονται καὶ χρόας καὶ σχήματα καὶ πάντα τὰ ἐκ τῶν τοιούτων δημιουργούμενα). A little earlier (476d1–5), Glaucon had spoken of the φιλοθεάμονες as "very strange" people (ἀτοπώτατοί) to include as philosophers, people who, while avoiding philosophical conversation, "rush off to all the Dionysiac festivals … as if their ears were hired out to listen to every chorus" (ὥσπερ δὲ ἀπομεμισθωκότες τὰ ὦτα ἐπακοῦσαι πάντων χορῶν περιθέουσι τοῖς Διονυσίοις). We might today more charitably refer to such people as fans; fans of music or art or literature, for example, or of other activities that bring pleasure through sensual experiences.[2] Plato of course famously disapproved of all obsessive devotion to the senses, and regarded such behaviour as inherently anti-philosophical in so far as it ascribed inordinate value to the acquisition of pleasures, which were transitory, often deceptive and stubbornly resistant to reason (*logos*). What Plato especially mocked in his "lovers of sounds and sights" was their manic attachment to *ta kala*, manifestations of beauty in the human arts: they lived firmly in the material world constantly in search of aesthetic experience, but their aesthetic appetites seemed insatiable, as they flitted from event to event, always with an eye

---

1. The composer Alexander Scriabin in a conversation about his work, "The Poem of Ecstasy", quoted in Bowers (1996: vol. 2, 135).
2. Both "aesthete" and "fan" are, of course, anachronistic terms when applied to Platonic characters, each with its own, largely post-Enlightenment, lexical history. But while they are not precisely synonymous, especially at the extremes (the fandom of a football hooligan, for example, is a long remove from the connoisseurship of an art-collector), they can often each be used to describe the kind of person who is both emotionally and intellectually devoted to a particular sensory phenomenon.

to new, future experiences. As Plato saw it, these aesthetic connoisseurs gratified their love of beautiful things to no great purpose. Their enthusiastic, erratic behavior was almost by definition anti-philosophical, and when he says at *Republic* 475 that they would be reluctant to engage in discussion (πρὸς μὲν λόγους καὶ τοιαύτην διατριβὴν ἑκόντες οὐκ ἂν ἐθέλοιεν ἐλθεῖν) he implies that whatever intellectual reflection such people could apply to their aesthetic experiences, they ultimately lacked the patience for anything resembling systematic thought and what we might call critical assessment.[3] If these people liked what they saw or heard, after all, they would hardly be eager to seek out someone who tried, in the name of rational inquiry, to second-guess their aesthetic values, and indeed their foundational premise that sensual pleasure was a good in itself.

Plato's lovers of sights and sounds are something of a parody and, as such, drawn out to extremes. They remind us, perhaps, of the disreputable rabble, described at Aristophanes' *Frogs* 771–8, who greeted Euripides in Hades as soon as he died and went to join them below – a crazed bunch of fanatics, who apparently hung on his every word while they were all alive and attended the dramatic festivals (ὑπερεμάνησαν κἀνόμισαν σοφώτατον). Plato's distorted portrait of such people lays out what he sees as the dangers inherent in a life devoted exclusively to the senses,[4] but it is hardly to be taken as his final word on aesthetics, beauty or pleasure. We have caught him here, as it seems, in one of his more austere moments, fretting about the arts as a potential distraction from living a moral life, and a genuine threat to one's psychological equilibrium. There is plenty of evidence elsewhere in Plato, however, that he was not entirely hostile to, or unappreciative of aesthetic pleasure. Even apart from the commonly noted fact that he was a great literary artist himself, he made at least some space in several dialogues for the role of the senses, and the pursuit of beauty and pleasure through them, within a systematically philosophical life.

Plato's attitude toward the senses, in short, is fraught with ambivalence, and nowhere is this more apparent than in his *Symposium*, a work suffused with anxiety and exhilaration about this area of human experience. Socrates' own attitude, within the great speech he imputes to Diotima, is also complicated: it takes a reasonably straightforward position – gratifying our senses with *ta kala* is, at best, trivial, at worst, base (cf. *Symposium* 210b5, 210e) – but also articulates a kind of *askēsis* ("practice, training") that presses the sensory experiences of the everyday world into the service of, finally, *transcending* them. This paradoxical move has generated surprisingly little attention from scholars, who tend to be more interested in the moment of transcendence itself, when the successful initiate will have attained the final vision of absolute beauty, than in the stage immediately preceding, when the initiate's mind is still embroiled in the material world of differentiated, multiple

---

3. At *Republic* 476b6 and c3–4, Socrates describes the lovers of sounds and sights as "incapable" of contemplating "beauty in itself"; presumably he means by this that their intransigent devotion to the sensory pleasures is incompatible with a desire to move their thoughts to more abstract realms.
4. On Plato's anxiety about the senses, see Porter (2010: 87): "Platonic aesthetics is … grounded in the most intense perception of the least amount of variability and fluctuation (or becoming) and in the greatest degree of changeless, unwavering, and unadulterated essences. As a consequence, it is unfriendly to the senses: it strives for an apprehension that is least contaminated by sensory interference."

kala. What Plato's Diotima recommends here, as I will suggest, amounts to a form of "synaesthesia" in which normally *differentiated* sensory experiences are conceptually *unified*, in the hope that the differentiated pleasures normally associated with each experience will be abandoned for the increasingly non-sensory, non-differentiated pleasures that arise from the experience of absolute beauty. For Plato, in other words, all the objects of the senses at this stage become indistinguishable from one another as individual examples of beauty, and appreciated as participating in a higher, more abstract conception of beauty. Synaesthesia occurs, then, as the penultimate step before the complete, intellectual experience of pure Beauty in its unalloyed totality.

What I would like to argue here is that this "synaesthesia" described in the *Symposium* was not the chaotic philosophical obstacle that we might expect it to be in Plato, but rather an aesthetic of multiplicity prerequisite for understanding Beauty as an immaterial unity. I would also like to consider what bearing this aesthetic might have had on Plato's attitudes towards everyday experiences of *ta kala* – whether, for example, he might have allowed his lovers of sights and sounds any legitimacy as philosophical individuals, and what kind of pleasures, exactly, he imagined emanating from the synaesthesia he seems to be recommending as a desirable state of mind. In short, did this stage of what I would call "philosophical" synaesthesia involve any actual aesthetic experience, any genuine engagement with the senses and sensual pleasure, or did Plato imply that one could will oneself, intellectually, into a communion with absolute beauty that bypassed altogether an appreciation of the differentiated *kala* of the real world? In what follows I will argue that the synaesthetic moment in Diotima's ascent, when the initiate comes to regard all sensory *phainomena* as, in some sense, equivalent, does, in fact, presuppose aesthetic experience, but at the same time highlights precisely what Plato objected to in such experience, namely, the inability of his aesthetes to articulate the "meaning" in their experiences. It is the movement up the ladder from *aesthesis* to *synaesthesis* – from bodily sensation to the intellectual understanding of the senses – that corresponds, I propose, to the process by which, for Plato, aesthetic *meaning* is created. And for Plato, as we will see, the ability to locate meaning in the things we perceive and to which we are drawn by virtue of their beauty, helps to lead the "lovers of sights and sounds" out of that nebulous space between not-being and being where Plato imagines them to be constantly "rolling around".

Before we turn to the *Symposium*, where Plato has Socrates describe the mental process I have called philosophical synaesthesia, it will be useful to examine in greater detail the passage in the *Republic* where Plato first lays out at length exactly what he sees as the problem with the "lovers of sights and sounds". The passage occurs at the end of Book 5 (475d–480), where Socrates sets out to define the term "philosopher" (φιλόσοφος) as a defensive strategy against the many people Glaucon supposes would object to their notion of the philosopher–ruler. The discussion begins by drawing a simple linguistic analogy with a variety of other compound words that begin with φιλο-. As a guiding principle, Socrates reminds Glaucon (474c8) of an earlier conversation in the work (438), where they had agreed that any person who can be said to "desire something" (φιλεῖν), desires (or "loves" here) not a part of it, but all of it (οὐ τὸ μὲν φιλοῦντα ἐκείνου, τὸ δὲ μή, ἀλλὰ πᾶν στέργοντα). The examples he gives are a remarkable prelude or allusion to Diotima's speech in the *Symposium* (depending on which we regard as prior) – the φιλόπαις ("lover of boys", 474d2), the φίλοινος ("lover of wine", 475a5) and the φιλοτίμος ("lover of honour", 475a9). The point Socrates wants to make is that all these people *love* more or less indiscriminately the many examples of their particular obsession. As he says of the wine-lover (475a5), that person loves *all kinds of* wine, and will drink it on any pretext.[5] This observation is meant simply to lead to the conclusion that, similarly, the φιλόσοφος will desire[6] "all of wisdom", not just a part of it (475b8). The philosopher turns out to be the one who always wants to get a "taste of learning" and has an "insatiable" appetite for it.[7] Socrates' conclusion here is what leads Glaucon to observe that, if this is this case, "A lot of strange people will end up being considered philosophers" (475d), since the people around town he sees as insatiable and curious in the same way are the theatre-and-arts fanatics, who can never seem to get enough of it. And presumably, the same could be said for Socrates' other examples in this passage, the lovers of beautiful boys and wine-lovers, who likewise are not especially easy to regard as "philosophical". Socrates, therefore, has to refine his definition of the philosopher: all the "lovers of X" he has been speaking of are *like* (e2: ὁμοίους) philosophers in their irrepressible devotion to the objects of their desire, but philosophers are different from all the others in that their object of desire is "truth" (ἀλήθεια). In fact, Socrates calls them – playing off of Glaucon's mention of theatre fans – "the sight-lovers of truth" (τοὺς τῆς ἀληθείας ... **φιλοθεάμονας**). At 476b5, then, the difference for Socrates between the true philosopher and the "lovers of sights, lovers of the arts [or crafts], and practical people" is that while the philosopher is after truth itself, all these lovers who live out their lives in constant search of beauty in the material world are incapable of "seeing or embracing" in thought (διάνοια) "the nature of beauty in itself" (αὐτοῦ δὲ τοῦ καλοῦ ἀδύνατος αὐτῶν ἡ διάνοια τὴν φύσιν ἰδεῖν τε καὶ ἀσπάσασθαι.). What is more, as he continues at 476c, the person who "believes in" (νομίζων) "beautiful things" (καλὰ πράγματα), but not beauty in itself (here αὐτὸ δὲ κάλλος) is living as if in a dream, because he confuses all the instantiations of beauty with beauty itself. As Socrates puts it, such a person thinks that "a likeness is not a likeness, but rather *is* the thing it's like" (τὸ ὅμοιόν τῳ μὴ ὅμοιον ἀλλ' αὐτὸ ἡγῆται εἶναι). This is the way the world mostly is, Socrates realizes, full of people who cannot bear being told that "beauty is a single thing" (ἓν τὸ καλὸν ... εἶναι, 479a4), and whose conventional thinking about beauty in the world (νόμιμα), as he says, rolls around somewhere in between not-being and pure being (μεταξύ που κυλινδεῖται τοῦ τε μὴ ὄντος καὶ τοῦ ὄντος εἰλικρινῶς, 479d5). Such people, he concludes at 480a6 are φιλόδοξοι, lovers of opinion, not φιλόσοφοι, lovers of wisdom.

---

5. Τί δέ; ἦν δ' ἐγώ· τοὺς φιλοίνους οὐ τὰ αὐτὰ ταῦτα ποιοῦντας ὁρᾷς; πάντα οἶνον ἐπὶ πάσης προφάσεως ἀσπαζομένους; (*Republic* 475a5). It should be noted that Plato is not describing here mere alcoholism or any other kind of clinical addiction. His wine-lovers care about the quality and hedonic experience of the wine they drink, even if Plato finds their devotion to "all kinds" of wine excessive.
6. It is noteworthy that Plato subtly shifts from φιλέω ("love") to ἐπιθυμέω ("desire") in this passage.
7. τὸν δὲ δὴ εὐχερῶς ἐθέλοντα παντὸς **μαθήματος** γεύεσθαι καὶ ἀσμένως ἐπὶ τὸ **μανθάνειν** ἰόντα καὶ ἀπλήστως ἔχοντα, τοῦτον δ' ἐν δίκῃ φήσομεν φιλόσοφον· (*Republic* 475c).

This passage does not present one of Plato's most elegant or lucid arguments, as others have occasionally noted;[8] in fact, it is difficult to decide if he is actually *praising* the fanatical "lovers" of things because they are something "like" philosophers in their passion and curiosity, or condemning them because they never want to be told to shift their attention from the visible, palpable world of the senses. But this difficulty, I think, is itself revealing because it shows Plato thinking, if somewhat obliquely, about that fraught juncture between pure aesthetic experience and one's *contemplation* of it – that moment where some kind of *meaning* emerges which identifies that experience as something beyond mere sensation. One of Plato's pedestrian examples might make this clearer: what he admires in his wine-lover or sight-lover is the fact that each of them likes all aspects of the things that they find beautiful and good in each; he would demote from this group, it seems, any of those who, for example, just liked one bottle of wine, or one production at the theatre. True "lovers of X" are smitten by the pleasure they derive from their objects of desire, and crave more experiences of them. Plato admires this, it seems, because it inspires them to think more broadly about their aesthetic experiences; put more concretely: if a wine-lover can begin to articulate *why* his experience of a California Zinfandel makes him want to try an Oregon Pinot, or even a French Sauternes, this is at least the first step in a more abstract consideration of the beautiful things that bring him so much pleasure.

This passage from *Republic* book 5 sets the stage, in a sense, for the more elaborate discussion of beauty and desire in the *Symposium*, almost as if Plato realized that a step was missing in getting his wine-lover or sight-lover to understand beauty as a purely intellectual concept. The fact that Socrates conceded to Glaucon that the lovers of sounds and sights were "like philosophers" in their ability to appreciate one compendious category of the beautiful (*all* music, or *all* theatrical spectacle) is a clear start on the path to a more abstract aesthetics, but as the *Symposium* suggests, Plato seems to have realized that a further level of abstraction is necessary – a stage I have called synaesthetic – where worldly aesthetes understand not only that the beauty they pursue encompasses far more than its individual instantiations, but also that it is akin as well to the beauty of *all* aesthetic phenomena, even those they have no particular passion for themselves. Plato is, in fact, emphatic about this point, and has Socrates articulate it at several different points in his speech at *Symposium* 210–11, as if to say that it is impossible to experience and understand absolute beauty without having first managed to blend the disparate forms of worldy beauty – material *and* abstract – into a conceptual whole.

Diotima, as Socrates relates it, is quite specific about what she has in mind here: at 210a5, she details a path that would doubtless appear counterintuitive to one of the "lovers of X" in *Republic* 5. First the initiate will begin, when young, by turning "to beautiful bodies"; he must first "fall in love with a single beautiful body, give birth to beautiful words, and then realize for himself that the beauty that there is in any body whatever is related to [lit: brother of] any other".[9] This lover of bodies will realize that if one is going

---

8. E.g., Halliwell (1993: 201).
9. καὶ πρῶτον μέν, ἐὰν ὀρθῶς ἡγῆται ὁ ἡγούμενος, ἑνὸς αὐτὸν σώματος ἐρᾶν καὶ ἐνταῦθα γεννᾶν λόγους καλούς, ἔπειτα δὲ αὐτὸν κατανοῆσαι ὅτι τὸ κάλλος τὸ ἐπὶ ὁτῳοῦν σώματι τῷ ἐπὶ ἑτέρῳ σώματι ἀδελφόν ἐστι … (*Symposium* 210a5–b1)

to pursue beauty in bodily form (τὸ ἐπ' εἴδει καλόν), it would be crazy (ἄνοια) not to think of all such formal beauty as "one and the same". The paradox that follows is less heartening, however: "he must become a lover of all beautiful bodies (πάντων τῶν καλῶν σωμάτων ἐραστήν), and relax this passionate love for one body, despising it and considering it a light thing". This is a distinct change from the process imagined in *Republic* 5, where one's ability to appreciate beauty in an increasingly abstract way does not explicitly imply that one should repudiate the concrete pleasure one experiences from the objects of one's desires – loving all kinds of art, for a φιλοθεάμων ("lover of spectacles") just increases the pleasure one takes in its many material examples. As many have often complained, in the *Symposium* "ascent", the higher one climbs on the ladder the more one is expected to repudiate any form of actual beauty in the real world. The details of this ascent are familiar: from the beauty of bodies one turns to, and privileges, the beauty of souls; from souls to "activities and laws, in order to observe that all of this is related to itself, in order that he think that the beauty of body is a slight thing – a young boy, some individual human being, or one kind of activity". The culmination for the successful initiate is his ability to look upon the "great sea of beauty" (ἐπὶ τὸ πολὺ πέλαγος τετραμμένος τοῦ καλοῦ, 210d3), an experience that will allow him to procreate, but now completely in the non-physical, discursive and noetic realm of beautiful *logoi* and *dianoēmata* (211d).

The details Plato offers of that final vision of absolute beauty constitute one of the most famous attempts in antiquity to describe an experience of the sublime *avant la lettre*,[10] but the passage most relevant for our interests here occurs just after that, at 211d5. This is where Diotima tells Socrates that life is most worth living for a human when he is able to contemplate "beauty in itself" (βιωτὸν ἀνθρώπῳ, θεωμένῳ αὐτὸ τὸ καλόν, 211d2):

ὃ ἐάν ποτε ἴδῃς, οὐ **κατὰ χρυσίον τε καὶ ἐσθῆτα καὶ τοὺς καλοὺς παῖδάς τε καὶ νεανίσκους** δόξει σοι εἶναι, οὓς νῦν ὁρῶν **ἐκπέπληξαι** καὶ ἕτοιμος εἶ καὶ σὺ καὶ ἄλλοι πολλοί, ὁρῶντες τὰ παιδικὰ καὶ συνόντες ἀεὶ αὐτοῖς, εἴ πως οἷόν τ' ἦν, μήτ' ἐσθίειν μήτε πίνειν, ἀλλὰ θεᾶσθαι μόνον καὶ συνεῖναι. τί δῆτα, ἔφη, οἰόμεθα, εἴ τῳ γένοιτο **αὐτὸ τὸ καλὸν ἰδεῖν** εἰλικρινές, **καθαρόν**, ἄμεικτον, ἀλλὰ μὴ ἀνάπλεων σαρκῶν τε ἀνθρωπίνων καὶ χρωμάτων καὶ ἄλλης πολλῆς φλυαρίας θνητῆς, ἀλλ' αὐτὸ τὸ θεῖον καλὸν δύναιτο μονοειδὲς κατιδεῖν; (*Symposium* 211d3–e4)

"That, if you ever see it, will not seem to you to be of the same order as gold, and clothes, and the beautiful boys and young men that now drive you out of your mind (ἐκπέπληξαι) when you see them, so that both you and many others (καὶ σὺ καὶ ἄλλοι πολλοί) are ready, so long as you can *see* your beloveds and be with them always, if that were somehow possible, to stop eating and drinking, and just gaze at them and be with them. What then", she said, "do we suppose it would be like if someone succeeded in seeing beauty itself, pure, clean, unmixed, and not

---

10. On Presocratic adumbrations of an aesthetic category of the "sublime" see Porter (2010: 137–47, 158–65).

contaminated with things like human flesh, and colour, and much other mortal nonsense (φλυαρίας θνητῆς)…" (Trans. Rowe 1988).

There are several striking aspects of this passage. It offers, first of all, a reprise, but with more detail, of Plato's various "lovers of X" in *Republic* 5. Here, no doubt with a touch of ironic banter, Diotima is addressing and mildly chiding Socrates himself (καὶ σὺ καὶ ἄλλοι πολλοί): Socrates, that is, is like the lover of sights; he appreciates aesthetic qualities of things in the material world, such as "gold, and clothes, and beautiful boys and young men".[11] Diotima describes here, moreover, not just casual viewing, but *obsessive* gazing, like that of Glaucon's theatre fan in *Republic* 5, who cannot get enough of dramatic performances. And like those obsessive aesthetes of *Republic* 5, the ones mentioned here by Diotima – and which include Socrates – are actually imagined to occupy an important step in the philosophical ascent to higher states of aesthetic (and in Plato's world, moral and epistemological) awareness. Starving oneself of food and drink in order to contemplate the beauty of boys may be, for Diotima, a bit ridiculous (as she presents it), but it is also, paradoxically, an *essential* state of mind to experience prerequisite to the attempt to transcend what Plato sees as the unproductive, stultifying grip of the physical senses.

I say that this is a "prerequisite" state of mind for psychic growth in Plato's view because the leap he advocates from the physico-material world to the purely noetic is utterly pivotal, and cannot possibly occur (as he seems to imply) in the absence of an already profound commitment to aesthetics in the real world. Indeed, this is perhaps the most difficult problem to confront in his entire notion of an ascent to absolute beauty – namely, how someone who loves worldly beauty can pry him/herself away from these pleasures – to abandon them, in fact – and transfer one's sense of aesthetic value from the material to the intellectual. What I think this passage in *Symposium* suggests is that this move from the material to the intellectual worlds requires a particular form of synaesthesia that for a time, at least, manages to straddle both worlds, while it stages the soul for its final embrace of a unified, non-material, beauty. This is a different sort of synaesthesia than the kind psychologists study: actual synaesthetes almost always experience an amalgamation of two senses or sensory phenomena.[12] Sometimes the combinations involve different senses (colours and sounds, for example), but often they involve different phenomena within the same sensory realm (as, for example, when letters suggest colours, and vice versa). When compared to clinical synaesthesia, then, the Platonic form I am suggesting here, is, in fact, far more radical, in that it involves *all* the senses: the initiate needs to reach the point where he can assimilate all aesthetic experiences into a unified whole, abandoning, as Diotima says, all the sensory noise of the world that we find so attractive, things which

---

11. This is probably not meant to imply that Socrates is obsessed with money and fashion, but simply that he can appreciate the *beauty* of gold or of fine clothing, regardless of how much *value* he would allot to them.
12. There has been much interest, both scientific and popular, in synaesthesia as a neurological condition over the past two decades. See, for example, Dann (1998), Cytowic (2002), Campen (2008), Ward (2008), Cytowic & Eagleman (2009).

Diotima refers to as the "mortal nonsense" (φλυαρία θνητή) of the senses. Everything in the world needs to blend in one's mind, so it can then become (again, in Diotima's words) "unmixed" (ἄμεικτον), pure and clean, and without form or colour.[13]

Plato is clearly after something here a little different from the experience of clinical synaesthetes, who, when they see colours and hear music at the same time, are not necessarily seeking to transcend their experiences. But I would suggest that even that kind of synaesthetic experience resembles Plato's "philosophical" synaesthesia in one important way: they each exist simultaneously in the material and intellectual world. What I mean by this is that when a synaesthete hears sounds but also sees colours, only the ears – of all the bodily senses – are involved; the experience of *colours* – a visual phenomenon – is purely in the mind, or as we would say, in the mind's eye. One *hears* sounds, but *visualizes* colours. And as the clinical discussions reveal, synaesthetes generally regard their experiences as a gift, a heightened state that separates them from all others who must be content with discrete, rather than blended and simultaneous, sensory experiences. Similarly, in Plato: the lovers of sights and sounds, lovers of beautiful bodies, of form and colours, all experience the objects of their fascination through one of their senses; but as Plato believes, it takes a mental, synaesthetic action to move beyond this state. It is not just that the aesthete should understand that beautiful music is "like" beautiful painting;[14] but rather that the beauty in each case is all, as Diotima would say, of a piece with one another, one and the same thing.

The main difference, then, between the clinical and the Platonic synaesthete is that the former has no choice about how one experiences the blending of senses – synaesthesia is a neurological condition that has nothing to do with an individual's aesthetic or moral choices – whereas the latter achieves his state of "philosophical synaesthesia" only by an

---

13. Throughout her description of the ascent to the form of beauty Diotima often uses the language of sight to describe even the final stages of the process, although she never says exactly how the initiate is perceiving what he is perceiving at the latest stages. When she says, for example, at 210d3 that the initiate at this point "turns to (τετραμμένος) the huge sea of the beautiful, and is contemplating it (θεωρῶν)", the metaphors are visual, but the process is by now thoroughly intellectual. The point of this contemplation, she continues, is to give birth to "many fine and lofty discourses and thought, out of ungrudging philosophia …", so that he will "look at (κατίδῃ) a certain single knowledge of the sort which is of this kind of beauty". We are here, it seems, well beyond the material world, and all these processes seem to be taking place completely in the mind. At 212a, Plato shows Diotima to be sensitive to the problem of using visual metaphors to describe what is ultimately a noetic experience. There she speaks of the successful initiate as someone who has "looked at" (βλέπω) the form of beauty "*by means of the faculty that he should use*" (ᾧ δεῖ), and who sees the beautiful "*by which means the beautiful is visible*" (ὁρῶντι ᾧ ὁρατὸν τὸ καλόν). As Dover (1980: 159, *ad loc.*) notes, this refers to Plato's notion of the "eye of the soul", which appears explicitly at *Republic* 533d, also in the context where he struggles to describe exactly what it would mean to contemplate the forms. Corporeal eyes and vision, in short, have nothing to do with this kind of noetic sight. See further Dancy (2004: 286–7) on the philosophical difficulties that arise from Diotima's implication that even beautiful thoughts can be contemplated somehow as "objects".
14. As Porter's discussion suggests (2010: 156–8), it may well be that Plato was influenced in this direction by Empedoclean cosmology (cf. the astonishing Empedocles. fr. B35, with Porter's discussion, p. 156: "each individual act of perception, by virtue of its combining the manifold of sensory appearances into a graspable unity, rehearses the world's first synthesis"). See also Laks (1999: 267), who describes every individual sensation for Empedocles as an "anticipation of the ultimate fusion of the elements in the unity of the divine Sphere".

act of the will, as a function of the kind of psychological *askēsis* ("practice, training") that Plato continually urges. Plato is not especially interested, in short, in what it *feels* like to amalgamate the many aesthetic experiences of beauty in the world, but in what the *intellectual* consequences are; what happens, when one *reasons* about aesthetic experience. Plato complains, as we saw, that the lovers of sights and sounds are "like" philosophers, but are not themselves philosophical. This is largely because, as I understand Plato's account of their behaviour, their experience of beautiful things is emotional, a function of the pleasure they *feel* in the presence of beauty – but these experiences, for Plato, lead nowhere except to a sense of physical gratification. Plato seems to want people to ask the most basic questions of their aesthetic experiences, such as *why* they find that this poem or that musical performance is so moving. And once one begins to answer such questions, one is on the path towards a more abstracted understanding of beauty. Determining, after all, what many beautiful poems have in common with each other as instantiations of beauty, and in what sense beautiful poems, in turn, are of a piece with beautiful images or sounds, requires the mental superimposition of all forms of beauty that I have been calling here philosophical synaesthesia; it derives from logos about beauty, a logos that leads towards understanding – *noēsis, epistēmē* – and away from sensation and affective experience more generally.

What we will ultimately want to know, of course, is how Plato really thought this was all supposed to play out. Even allowing for the fact that he is talking about only a select privileged few who would have the will and intelligence to transcend the sensory pleasures in favour of an intellectual apprehension of more stable abstractions, one still wonders how, in practice, Plato might have imagined a person making this monumental leap from the worldly to the noetic, especially in the particularly powerful realm of the senses? Can one who begins as a lover of sight or sound, who performs the act of synaesthesia recommended by Plato and apprehends absolute, unified beauty, ever regain an appreciation of the differentiated pleasures of worldly beauty? Are we really supposed to conclude that Plato had, in the end, only disdain for aesthetic pleasures, and no confidence that they could have anything positive to offer a human being? Between the ridicule of the lovers of sights and sounds in *Republic* 5 and the explicit contempt for material beauty in the *Symposium*, this seems a likely conclusion. But Plato takes up the issue of sensory pleasures again later in *Philebus*, and his angle there may add some useful nuance to the aesthetics of the earlier works we have been considering.

Philebus is a difficult work, concerned largely with the nature of pleasure in its relation to living a "good" life, but towards the end a few things appear to fall into place. One is a notion that there is such a thing as "true" pleasures, defined as pleasures that exist independently of whether or not they relieve pain. At 51b, Socrates includes in this category the pleasures that come from "so-called pure colours, shapes, most smells and sounds and … all those [pleasures] that are based on imperceptibles and painless lacks". A few lines later, he clarifies:

σχημάτων τε γὰρ κάλλος οὐχ ὅπερ ἂν ὑπολάβοιεν οἱ πολλοὶ πειρῶμαι νῦν λέγειν, ἢ ζῴων ἤ τινων ζωγραφημάτων, ἀλλ' εὐθύ τι λέγω, φησὶν ὁ λόγος, καὶ περιφερὲς καὶ ἀπὸ τούτων δὴ τά τε τοῖς τόρνοις γιγνόμενα ἐπίπεδά τε καὶ στερεὰ καὶ τὰ τοῖς κανόσι καὶ γωνίαις, εἴ μου μανθάνεις. ταῦτα γὰρ οὐκ εἶναι πρός τι καλὰ λέγω, καθάπερ ἄλλα, ἀλλ' ἀεὶ καλὰ καθ' αὑτὰ πεφυκέναι καί τινας ἡδονὰς οἰκείας ἔχειν, οὐδὲν ταῖς τῶν κνήσεων προσφερεῖς· καὶ χρώματα δὴ τοῦτον τὸν τύπον ἔχοντα [καλὰ καὶ ἡδονάς].

By the beauty of shape, I do not mean what the many presuppose, namely that of a living being or of a picture. What I mean is rather ... something straight or round and what is constructed out of these with a compass, rule, and square, such as plane figures and solids. Those things I take it are not beautiful in a relative sense, as others are, but are by their very nature forever beautiful by themselves. They provide their own specific pleasures that are not at all comparable to those of scratching. And colors are beautiful in an analogous way and import their own kinds of pleasures. (Trans. Frede 1997b)

We see here, then, a category of actual sensory experiences that seem to lie somewhere between the ephemeral instability of the sensory realm and the purely noetic counterparts to sensation. Plato does seem here to come close to entertaining the idea – even if this is not explicitly his purpose in this passage – that sensory experiences can carry with them the possibility of some sort of transcendence, and so bring a person closer to a higher plane of understanding.[15] Such a person *can* experience colours and sounds and smells that are in some sense both *phainomena* of the real world *and* noetic. Understanding what is true and pure among the *phainomena*, and then blending them all in a synaesthetic stroke makes for a somewhat more practicable philosophical regimen for the lovers of sights and sounds, and restores to the senses a degree of legitimacy that was muted, at best, in the *Republic* and *Symposium* passages. As Plato makes clear in the subsequent discussion between Socrates and Protarchus in *Philebus*, pleasures are not intrinsic goods, but always a process of generation (*genesis*) (53c5–54c)[16] that exists "for the sake of a kind of being/reality" (ἕνεκά τινος οὐσίας, 53c7). But the pleasures he regards as "true" or "pure", in so far as they are

---

[15]. See Gosling (1975: 122, *ad loc.*), who thinks Plato is trying to distinguish these "pure pleasures" in colour and sound from the kinds of pleasure "most people" experience: "[p]ictures and music imitate real life, and the form appreciation takes there indicates the form it takes in real life ... In no case is the shape, color, or sound isolated for appreciation." This is probably true for "most people", although for Plato's lovers of sounds and sights, who already have a heightened aesthetic sensibility, it seems likely that the contemplation of these "pure pleasures" in the phenomenal world could be appreciated in isolation from objects that exist in this world; indeed this seems to be the mental state that initiates would attain just before the final epiphany of absolute beauty in the *Symposium* ascent passage (e.g., 211b–212a). For Plato it has to be said that pleasure is never an intrinsic good, even if he is able to speak of some pleasure as "truer" than others (see n. 17 below).

[16]. Cf. his conclusion at 54d (a question posed by Socrates and answered affirmatively by Protarchus): "And so if in fact pleasure is a form of generation, will we be right to put it in a category different from the good?" (Ἆρ' οὖν ἡδονή γε εἴπερ γένεσίς ἐστιν, εἰς ἄλλην ἢ τὴν τοῦ ἀγαθοῦ μοῖραν αὐτὴν τιθέντες ὀρθῶς θήσομεν;). See Frede (1992: 454): "Even the true and pure pleasures remain processes that lead to the restoration of being (*ousia*), but they never have being in themselves nor a permanent immutable

painless and less acutely implicated in the processes of replenishment or restoration (cf., e.g., 33e), do rank separately from, and higher than, the other, more precarious, pleasures of human life. Pure colour or line, for example, does not restore a lack, so we experience pleasure in such phenomena differently from our experience of pleasures that correct an imbalance or deficiency (e.g., the pleasures of eating, drinking, money-making, and so on). Plato has Socrates hold up "pure whiteness" as a paradigm of a true pleasure (53a–b), and concludes from this exemplum that, by analogy, "all pleasure that is small or in small amounts, if untainted by pain, would be sweeter, truer and finer than pleasure that is large or in large amounts [but tainted by pain]" (σύμπασα ἡδονὴ σμικρὰ μεγάλης καὶ ὀλίγη πολλῆς, καθαρὰ λύπης, ἡδίων καὶ ἀληθεστέρα καὶ καλλίων γίγνοιτ' ἄν, 53c).

Socrates never returns in *Philebus* to a fuller discussion of these "true pleasures", probably because he understood them to be far rarer and less accessible than the kinds of pleasures most people confront in their daily lives – those that arise from redressing antecedent pain and lack. But there seems little question that he regards the true pleasures as "better" in so far as they are less wedded to the sensory and veer more towards the abstract.[17] It is revealing, for example, that at 52a1, Socrates makes sure to add to his list of true pleasures those pleasures that come from intellectual activity (τὰ μαθήματα). At 52b5, Socrates concludes that these intellectual pleasures are "unmixed with pain" (τὰς τῶν μαθημάτων ἡδονὰς ἀμείκτους ... λύπαις) and not available to many men (οὐδαμῶς τῶν πολλῶν ἀνθρώπων).[18] Plato aligns his colours, shapes, sounds and smells with *mathēmata* explicitly because they are all pleasures that do not, for the most part,[19] imply antecedent pain. But the main reason why none of these pleasures implies such pain in the first place is precisely because they are increasingly distanced from the sensory world, which Plato sees as chaotic and distracting under the normal conditions of life (63d-e). Socrates is aware at 53a5 how odd it is to contemplate pure colour divorced from a material instantiation of colour accessible to sight ("How can there be purity in the case of whiteness, and what sort of thing is it?", Πῶς οὖν ἂν λευκοῦ καὶ τίς καθαρότης ἡμῖν εἴη;), and he seems to be grasping for a notion of colour in the abstract. In the subsequent lines Protarchus notes that pure whiteness must be something "unadulterated" (εἰλικρινές, 53a8), and Socrates immediately adds that it will also be "truest" and "most beautiful" (ἀληθέστατον, κάλλιστον, 53b1).

---

nature ... Even the best kind of generation is only good relative to the being that is its end, but it is not desirable in and for itself."

17. See Hampton (1990: 70–71), who notes how Plato's description of true pleasures uses language he elsewhere uses to describe the Forms. Things such as colour or geometrical shape, that is, occur in the sensible world in many ways and always owe something of their reality to participation in the Forms, but in their purest, unmixed form, they map on even more closely to the Forms, and and so the pleasure they give would be the more pure. See Porter (2010: 87–9): The "true pleasures" are "beautiful, but only in a manner of speaking (τὰ καλὰ λεγόμενα). They are glimpses of Forms."
18. See discussion in Frede (1997a: 301–2).
19. Protarchus does worry a little, at 52a, that forgetting a thought and then desiring it might cause pain, but Socrates sets this aside as not quite relevant to their argument (52b). He is interested in whether intellectual pleasures are *intrinsically* painless, not whether they can become so if people start reflecting on them (νῦν γε ἡμεῖς αὐτὰ τὰ τῆς φύσεως μόνον παθήματα χωρὶς τοῦ λογισμοῦ διαπεραίνομεν).

Plato has his characters here describe the experience of pure whiteness (and colour, more generally, by extension; cf. 51b2) in terms that recall Diotima's description of the initiate's final ascent to absolute beauty at *Symposium* 211d5–e1 that we cited earlier (see above, p. 94). "Pure", "unmixed", "beautiful", "true" … such are Diotima's terms for the final vision of beauty – an experience that takes place, as she says, entirely apart from the material world – and they correspond strikingly to the language Plato uses to describe the pure colour and sounds of *Philebus*.[20] The state of mind that Diotima imagines here does not disassemble the unity of beauty (καλὸν…μονοειδές) into any differentiated components – even purified ones – such as colour, sound or shapes, and so it is placed at the top of the ladder of ascent. But the "true pleasures" discussed in *Philebus* are not far behind, and represent a largely noetic exercise that can propel even an aesthete closer to Plato's ideal of a rational understanding of the good, beautiful and true.

From a practical, protreptic point of view, we might infer that Plato in fact held out some hope for the sight- and sound-lovers he so much enjoyed mocking. Their problem, according to Plato, is not so much that they are devoted to the arts *tout court*, but that, they tend to like them indiscriminately and do not generally cultivate their aesthetic pleasures as they would intellectual pleasures. Plato, however, as I have suggested, developed a corrective path for the aesthete, one that exchanges the volatile, disorderly pleasures of the bodily senses for the more systematic, rational pleasures of aesthetic meaning. Meaning arises from that synaesthetic moment, when the aesthete processes intellectually the evidence of the senses and shapes them into a logos that requires increasingly synthetic and abstract thought. The goal, in Plato's view, may well be to elide and efface the senses altogether, but along the way, aesthetic pleasures are seen to play essential part. This is why Plato can speak of pure colours and sounds (etc.) in the same breath as he speaks of *mathēmata*; for we can only know pure colour, and then "all colour", if we have first experienced – and taken pleasure in – the many impure colours that the material world offers.

The perennial problem with Plato's aesthetics of the intellect remains the inability for him, or anyone, it seems, to explain fully what the experience of absolute, non-material, synaestheticized beauty really is. I would like to conclude, however, with one man's attempt (which is not to say a necessarily *successful* attempt) not only to explain, but even to realize such an experience. I refer to the composer Alexander Scriabin's several forays into synaesthetic music, matching sounds with colours, and then later even, imagining ways in which he could fuse all the senses in a performance that would enable all participants to transcend their reality and become one with the Cosmos.

Scriabin's 1910 work *Prometheus: the Poem of Fire* (Op. 60), in fact, featured a crude synaesthetic machine that projected colours on to a screen that the composer supposedly heard in his mind as he heard the specific tones of the work.[21] For a long time even

---

20. See now Castelnérac (2010: 141), who also notes the parallel between *Symposium* and *Philebus*.
21. For a contemporary critique of the use of the colour organ, or the "tastiera per luce" ("keyboard for light") as Scriabin called it, in a New York performance of *Prometheus*, see *Musical World* vol. 4.9, May 1915. One of the critics concluded it was at best a "diverting novelty". A remarkable version of the piece was performed February 2010 at Yale University, using an updated "tastiera per luce" and modern lighting

before this, however, Scriabin had been contemplating a far grander work that he called *Mysterium*, which has been described as follows:

> The performance was to be held for seven days and nights in India, during which time Scriabin planned to remove the barrier separating audience and performers and to create conditions favorable for spiritual communion ... and all-unity ... He imagined that the *Mysterium* would involve all people as votaries in a ritual enacting the miracle of terrestrial and cosmic transformation.[22]

And:

> It was to be the history of the universe ... of the human race ... of the individual soul. The *Mysterium* must transfigure and accomplish all the macrocosmic and microcosmic processes of our era ... Not a musical drama, not an oratorio neither presentation nor re-presentation, but a "direct experience". The universe would be completely destroyed by it, and mankind plunged into the holocaust of finality. But in this act of unity, the sons would become the father. Soul and matter would separate under the highest tension induced by the music's vibration, and man would be transfigured into an endlessness deeper than the deepest ocean. Male and female would vanish in a trice. All of us would be immersed as Scriabin said another time, "into an ecstatic abyss of sunshine ..."[23]

Scriabin was clearly swept away by the various esoteric movements of the day: Symbolist poetry, Theosophy, with its own amalgamations of Platonism and Eastern spirituality, Nietzschean and Wagnerian aesthetic ideology.[24] The composer died in 1915 at a period when he had renewed his interest in this unrealizable project, and all that survives is a libretto with some musical sketches he called the "Preparatory Act". As one scholar has described it, the "Preparatory Act" "imagined that the synesthetic stimulation of a sense (sight) other than the sense being directly stimulated (hearing) would offer a vision of the reality underlying reality".[25]

Like Plato, Scriabin was interested in a very specific problem, how one could make the transition from the material sensory world, messy and differentiated as it is, to a realm of transcendent unity, and so, of absolute knowledge. Neither solved the problem in the end, but both understood that the transition would have to involve some form of synaesthesia,[26]

---

techniques: see http://opac.yale.edu/news/article.aspx?id=7211, and for the performance itself, http://www.youtube.com/watch?v=V3B7uQ5K0IU.
22. Morrison (1998: 284).
23. Bowers (1996: 254).
24. Discussed by Morrison (1998) and Dann (1998: 71-6).
25. Morrison (1998: 305).
26. It is unlikely that Scriabin was actually a *clinical* synaesthete, as is often popularly claimed, but his system of "colour hearing", as he called it, was not something he regarded as a special gift idiosyncratic to himself. Most would now regard Scriabin's synaesthesia more accurately as associative or symbolic. See, for example, Dann (1998: 71): "There is actually no evidence that Scriabin was a synesthete, and

some mechanism at work partly within the body itself, and partly in the mind. From the vantage point of someone who is imagined to have experienced absolute beauty, it may well be (as Plato's Diotima claims) that the beauty of the material world is, by comparison, contemptible. But, as Plato also seems to have understood, and Scriabin even attempted to realize, a synaesthetic aesthetic of multiplicity is prerequisite for understanding Beauty as an immaterial unity.[27]

---

considerable evidence to the contrary. Scriabin's equivalences of colour and tones rather too neatly follow a circle of fifths ... No true chromesthete has such a systematic arrangement of color-tone equivalences." As Dann points out (*ibid.*: 71–5), Scriabin's reputation as an actual synaesthete was a function of the "mythical lineage of synaesthesia as a higher form of consciousness" (*ibid.*: 75) that so interested spirtualists and occultists in the early decades of the twentieth century. See also, Galeyev & Vanechkina (2001). Morrison (1998) describes Scriabin's synaesthesia more as a technique, an *askēsis*, that can transform a listener, than as a neurological condition: "For the *Preparatory Act*, [Scriabin] imagined that the synesthetic stimulation of a sense (sight) other than the sense being directly stimulated (hearing) would offer a vision of the reality underlying reality' (Morrison 1998: 305). Galeyev & Vanechkina (2001: 358) quote Scriabin on his belief that colour-hearing was universally accessible: "It cannot be personal ... There must be a principle, must be oneness. A freak of chance – is a ripple on the surface, and the essential must be common". Scriabin elsewhere said (also quoted in *ibid.*) that some of the colours he associated with tones were derived "theoretically". See also Cytowic (2002: 319), for other examples of artists (visual as well as musical) whose forays into synaesthesia he categorizes as "deliberate contrivances".

27. I wish to thank Dr Frederick Arends for his acute and stimulating critique of an earlier version of this chapter.

7

MANILIUS' COSMOS OF THE SENSES

Katharina Volk

The *Astronomica* of Marcus Manilius, a Latin didactic poem in five books composed in the early second decade CE, is our earliest extant comprehensive treatment of horoscopic astrology, containing highly technical discussions of such matters as the characteristics, divisions and influences of the signs of the zodiac, the computation of the ascendant and the significance of extrazodiacal constellations. However, despite its (pseudo-)scientific subject matter, the work is far more than a compendium of "sums in verse" (to use the derisive words of Manilius' famous editor A. E. Housman[1]): it is what is sometimes referred to as a *Weltgedicht*, a poem that projects a larger vision of the nature of the universe and man's place in it.[2] The cosmos that Manilius' text presents is indeed a *kosmos*, a realm of order and beauty that is governed by fate, the nexus of cause and effect that the astrologer attempts to uncover through observation and interpretation of the heavenly bodies.[3] Painting an image of the universe as a living and divine organism in which all parts are interconnected, the *Astronomica* shows great affinities to Stoic physics, which views the world as a corporeal continuum informed by the *sympatheia* ("feeling together") of its constituents.[4] It is this underlying cosmology that enables the poet's claim that the stars are capable of causing events on earth and that humans are at all times affected by and, to some extent, able to affect their cosmic surroundings. As I shall attempt to show in what follows, this intimate interaction with the universe is one that engages human beings through all their senses.

---

1. Housman (1903–30: 2.xiii).
2. The term "Weltgedicht" was coined by Zinn (1956) and applied to Manilius by Lühr (1969: 5–8) and Hübner (1984: 227–42). On the cosmic vision of the *Astronomica*, see also Volk (2009) and D. F. Kennedy (2011).
3. On the idea of the *kosmos* and its role in Manilius, see Volk (2009: 18–23).
4. On Manilius' Stoicism, see esp. Salemme (2000: 9–74), as well as Volk (2009: 226–34; with further references in 226 n. 13). The corporealism of the poet's universe is discussed in Habinek (2007; 2011).

THE COSMOS OF THE SENSES

The proem to the first book of the *Astronomica* presents an excellent starting point for our investigation of the sensuality of Manilius' cosmos. Didactic poems typically have lengthy introductions in which the poet reflects on his topic and his own task as teacher, and Manilius is especially fond of such programmatic expositions, using highly elevated and metaphorical language to describe his role as a divinely sanctioned *uates* ("prophet, poet", 1.23) charged with revealing the secrets of the universe. His initial announcement of his topic is rendered in riddling fashion:

> carmine diuinas artes et conscia fati
> sidera diuersos hominum uariantia casus,
> caelestis rationis opus, deducere mundo
> aggredior.   (*Astronomica* 1.1–4)

> By song I undertake to draw down from heaven the divine arts and the stars, knowledgeable of fate, which govern the diverse fortunes of men, a work of divine reason.[5]

The poet prepares to treat the "divine arts" (i.e. astrology) and the "stars", described as *diuersos hominum uariantia casus* (2). At the very beginning of the poem, then, we have a clear declaration of Manilius' cosmological and astrological creed: it is the stars that make human life into the complex series of events that it is. Note the participle *uariantia*, which immediately introduces an element of sense perception: the first meaning of this verb, according to the *Oxford Latin Dictionary*, is to "mark or adorn with contrasting colours" (s.v. *uariō* 1). The stars "colour", that is, crucially influence life on earth, but what is remarkable is that in the very same sentence, Manilius proposes to affect the stars in turn by "drawing [them] down from heaven by means of [his] song" (*carmine ... deducere mundo*, 1–3). The verb *deducere* is a metapoetic buzzword that, in the wake of a famous programmatic passage in Vergil's sixth *Eclogue*,[6] cannot fail to be read as a pledge of allegiance to the refined style of works in the Callimachean tradition.[7] In this passage, however, the main operative metaphor appears to be one from magic, a reference to the notion that witches are able to remove heavenly bodies – in particular, the moon – from the sky by means of spells, also called *carmina* in Latin. Manilius is here specifically alluding to another Vergilian line, *carmina*

---

5. All translations from Greek and Latin are my own.
6. Vergil, *Eclogue* 6.5: *deductum dicere carmen* ("[the shepherd ought to] sing a finely spun-out poem"). The image is that of drawing out a thread in spinning (*OLD* s.v. 4); as is well known, Vergil is creatively adapting the injunction of Callimachus' Apollo to "keep the Muse slender" (*Aetia* prologue, fr. 1.24). Compare also the well-known injunction *deducite ... carmen* of Manilius' contemporary Ovid, addressed to the gods of poetry at the beginning of the *Metamorphoses* (1.4).
7. On Manilius' Callimacheanism, see Volk (2009: 197–215). The poet likes to play with different connotations of the verb *deducere* in the context of metapoetic discussions: on 2.10 (*deducere* as "channeling water"), see Volk (2010b); on 2.128 (*deducere* as "leading captives in a triumph"), see Volk (2001, esp. 97–100).

uel caelo possunt deducere lunam ("songs/spells can even draw down the moon from the sky", *Eclogues* 8.69).[8] What this metaphor ultimately means, of course, is that Manilius is going to treat the stars in his poem, but the image is one of intense and immediate mutual interaction between the poet and the stars, an interaction that involves the senses of sight (*uariantia*), sound (*carmine*) and potentially touch (*deducere*) and one that conjures up a vivid dynamic between the heavens above and human beings, including the poet, below.

Despite the connotations of impiety carried by the allusion to magical practices, it turns out in what follows that the universe, viewed as alive and divine, invites human beings in general, and the poet in particular, to research its workings and make them known through song (cf. esp. 11–12: the *mundus* "favours" and "desires" human exploration).[9] Such cosmological research is repeatedly presented as some kind of physical interaction. Thus, in line 11, the cosmos appears as a body whose inner organs are scrutinized by the astrologer (*iam propiusque fauet mundus scrutantibus ipsum*, "now the universe is more favourably inclined to those investigating it"), an image that is taken up again a few lines later, when the poet expresses the desire to "know in depth the very heart of the universe" (*scire ... magni penitus praecordia mundi*, 17).[10] In a different metaphor, the poet describes himself as travelling through the heavens and observing up close the movement of the fixed stars and planets (13–15).[11]

The most sensual image occurs in lines 20–4, where Manilius appears in the role of a priest who worships at two altars, that of his song (*carminis*, 22) and that of his subject matter (*rerum*, 22). In doing so, he finds himself *duplici circumdatus aestu* ("surrounded by double *aestus*", 21), an evocative phrase of multilayered significance. The Latin noun *aestus* means primarily "heat" (*OLD* s.v. 1), including that of a fire (*OLD* s.v. 4), and thus refers to the metaphorical heat of Manilius' sacrificial offerings (cf. *bina mihi positis lucent altaria flammis*, "twin altars burn for me lit with flames", 20). It also denotes "love" or "passion" (*OLD* s.v. 5a), the poet's enthusiasm for his task. Finally, *aestus* refers to a "swell" or "surge" (*OLD* s.v. 7). What this movement is becomes clear in the next sentence, where the universe is said to "resound around the poet", that is, involve him in both motion and sound:

> certa cum lege canentem
> mundus et immenso uatem circumstrepit orbe.[12]   (22–3)

The universe resounds with its immense sphere around the poet who sings to a fixed measure.

---

8. See esp. A. M. Wilson (1985: 289–90).
9. On the motif of the self-revelation of the cosmos in Manilius, see Volk (2001; 2002: 209–24; 2009, Index s.v. "Universe, self-revelation").
10. On Manilius' concept of the *praecordia* ("entrails, vital organ") of the cosmos, see Schwarz (1972: 614) and Habinek (2007: 231–4).
11. On the motif of the heavenly journey in Manilius, see Landolfi (1999 = 2003: 11–28) and Volk (2001: 86–92; 2002: 225–34).
12. The phonetics of the two programmatic lines 22–3, which abound in nasals, liquids and velars, might be taken to echo the sound of universe: ca̱rmi̱nis et re̱rum. ce̱rta cu̱m lege ca̱ne̱ntem / mundus et i̱mme̱nso uate̱m ci̱rcumstrepit o̱rbe.

Manilius thus describes his poetic activity and its concomitant emotions as an intense physical experience: he is surrounded by surging heat as well as by the sound produced by the cosmos. The poet is here alluding to the Pythagorean concept of the Music of the Spheres, the sacred sound created by the revolutions of the firmament and the planets.[13] This music resounds around the poet as he himself is "singing" (*canentem*, 22); the descriptive *certa cum lege* ("to a fixed measure", 22) is best taken as referring to both Manilius" music and that of the heavens.[14] In Manilius' cosmos of the senses, the poet and the universe sing in unison.

ARATUS: THE VISUAL PARADIGM

Having preliminarily established Manilius' panaesthetic worldview, I shall now contrast his outlook with that of Aratus' *Phaenomena*, the famous Hellenistic poem about the constellations that throughout the Greco-Roman world came to be considered the classic treatment of the starry sky. Aratus inspired not only a rich commentary tradition but also numerous Latin translations and adaptations,[15] and Manilius himself is clearly indebted to his predecessor, especially in *Astronomica* 1, where his detailed catalogue of constellations is an example of creative imitation of the relevant section of the *Phaenomena*.[16] I am introducing Aratus as a foil to Manilius in order to show that the Roman poet's vision of sympathetic cosmic interaction was by no means the only possible way in antiquity of conceiving of man's relationship to the heavens. Unlike Manilius, Aratus presents the sky as something that is there primarily to be looked at, providing a prime example of what the editors of this volume refer to as the "visual paradigm".[17] The divergent ways in which these two great ancient poets of the heavens approach their topic is indicative of the different theoretical frameworks that underlie their texts. In the ancient debate over whether the stars are mere signs of earthly events or indeed their causes, Aratus belongs to the camp of those who see the constellations as shining signifiers, while Manilius believes that they literally affect the fabric of the universe and the bodies of human beings.[18]

---

13. See esp. Schrijvers (1983: 148–50) and, more generally, Radici Colace (1995) on the idea of the sound of the stars in antiquity.
14. For this interpretation, see Schrijvers (1983: 150), Volk (2002: 235–6) and Habinek (2005: 92).
15. The *Phaenomena* was translated by Cicero, Varro of Atax (part), Ovid, Germanicus and Avienius (the last two versions survive, as do sizable fragments of Cicero's translation and meagre scraps of Varro's and Ovid's) and had substantial influence on Vergil's *Georgics*. On the fortunes of Aratus in antiquity, see Lewis (1992); for a general introduction to the *Phaenomena*, see Volk (2010a).
16. On Manilius' use of Aratus, see Romano (1979: 27–36), Salemme (2000: 79–90), Abry (2007) and Volk (2009: 188–92).
17. Compare Butler (2010: 43–4). For a more detailed discussion of some of the issues raised in this section, see Volk 2012.
18. When Aratus was writing in the first half of the third century BCE, Stoic doctrine was still in the process of being developed (cf. Hunter 2008: 158) and astrology likewise had not yet become a dominant mode of thought in the Greco-Roman world. His ideas of the celestial bodies were thus developed in a different intellectual context from the one that shaped Manilius' poem.

We can discern the different mentality of Aratus vis-à-vis Manilius by taking a look at his proem, which takes the form of a hymn to Zeus. In a programmatic passage, the god is said to have created a stellar sign system for the benefit of human beings:

> αὐτὸς γὰρ τά γε σήματ' ἐν οὐρανῷ ἐστήριξεν
> ἄστρα διακρίνας, ἐσκέψατο δ' εἰς ἐνιαυτὸν
> ἀστέρας οἵ κε μάλιστα τετυγμένα σημαίνοιεν
> ἀνδράσιν ὡράων, ὄφρ' ἔμπεδα πάντα φύωνται.   (10–13)

> For he [Zeus] himself fastened the signs to the sky, distinguishing the constellations, and organized stars over the course of the year that might give to men most clearly established signs of the seasons, so that everything might grow without fail.

The establishment of the stars as signs is an expression of Zeus' providence and benevolence, a central idea of the poem. The basic situation Aratus envisages is that the stars are up there, while human beings down here can observe and interpret them. The only interactions between these clearly defined levels are signification and perception.

That this perception is exclusively visual is made clear again and again throughout the poem. The very title of the work, *Phaenomena*, points to the visual paradigm that underlies Aratus' worldview: *phainomena* (lit. "appearances") is the technical term for the observable heavenly phenomena (the revolutions of fixed stars and planets), where "observable" means "observable by sight". Fittingly, in my opinion, Aratus' commentator and translator Douglas Kidd even renders the poem's title *Visible Signs* (Kidd 1997). Manilius, by contrast, makes it quite clear that in his view, dealing only with the *phainomena* is not a satisfactory method of gaining knowledge of the universe. He stresses that an understanding of astrology moves beyond the outward appearance of the cosmos to a perception of its power:

> et ueneranda [sc. foret]
> non species tantum sed et ipsa potentia rerum,
> sentirentque deum gentes qua maximus esset.   (*Astronomica* 1.35–7)

> [The science of astrology as revealed by Mercury brought it about] that not only the appearance, but the very force of nature would be an object of veneration, and people would experience the god [i.e. the universe] at his most powerful.

Unlike Aratus' stargazers, Manilius' human beings do not just "look" at the sky (cf. *species*, 36) but "feel" it (*sentirent*, 37). Of course, Aratus treats only the outlines, positions and risings and settings of the constellations, while Manilius discusses their effects on human beings; whereas the astronomer sticks to appearances, the astrologer posits influences.

As a cursory reading of Aratus' poem shows, terms of vision abound in his description of the constellations, which are not only said to be "shining" or "bright", but are also often described specifically as easily visible. Note such terms as εἰσωπός (79; cf. 122), ἐπίοπτος (25), ἐπόψιος (81, 258), περίσκεπτος (213) and πολύσκεπτος (136). Conversely, human beings are depicted in the process of viewing or are specifically exhorted to look; verbs of vision occur repeatedly, including ὁράω/ὄψομαι/εἶδον, σκέπτομαι/σκοπέω and compounds and θεάομαι.[19]

Most of Aratus' poem consists of a description of the shapes and relative positions of the constellations, an extended passage that is by definition visual and that has been compared to the ecphrasis of a work of art.[20] Indeed, it is quite likely that Aratus was working with a star map or possibly even globe in hand and was thus actually describing a representation of the sky rather than the sky itself. This kind of slippage between model and copy comes to the fore in the extraordinary simile of *Phaenomena* 529–33, where Aratus compares the system of heavenly circles to an armillary sphere fashioned by a craftsman – that is, the kind of human artefact that represents these circles.[21] Heaven looks just like its image.

Of course, the craftsman simile at the same time points to the fact that the universe is itself a kind of artefact, one specifically designed by benevolent Zeus for the purpose of communicating with human beings by sending them signs. The language of signification is pervasive in the *Phaenomena*, with the noun σῆμα ("sign") appearing forty-seven times and forms of the verb σημαίνω ("signal, signify") eleven times. These signs are a way for Zeus, or more generally the gods and the stars themselves, to speak to us, a kind of visual language that replaces actual speech. Quintilian deplored the supposed lifelessness of the *Phaenomena*, pointing out that "the subject matter of Aratus is without movement since it contains no variety, no emotions, no characters and not a single speech" (*The Orator's Education* 10.1.55). The last observation is actually incorrect since in *Phaenomena* 123–6, the goddess Dike delivers a short rebuke to the deteriorating human beings of the Silver Age. Still, Quintilian has a point, in that this speech marks the end of the unmediated communication between gods and humans, a break symbolized by Dike's ultimate departure from earth and taking position in the sky as the constellation Virgo. However, even in the heavens she remains visible – ἔτι φαίνεται (135) – to human beings. Divine-to-human communication still takes place, though no longer in audible speech, but rather through *phainomena*, visible signs.[22]

Throughout the poem, the signs themselves (or otherwise the gods responsible for them) are repeatedly said to speak, teach or signal to human beings.[23] Interestingly, the humans talk back, by verbalizing the signs they perceive, and in particular by naming the

---

19. ὁράω/ὄψομαι/εἶδον: 78, 93, 142, 199, 223, 430, 456, 563, 573, 710, 727, 733, 756, 828, 957, 996, 1042; σκέπτομαι/σκοπέω and compounds: 75, 96, 157, 159, 199, 229, 256, 428, 435, 464, 474, 560, 729, 778, 799, 832, 852, 880, 892, 925, 987, 994, 1143, 1153; θεάομαι: 224, 325, 451, 618. There are also many occasions where Aratus points out that a constellation or individual star is *not* particularly easy to see. Though this is obviously a fact, it also seems to be the case that the poet has a special interest in hard-to-discern phenomena; see Volk (2010a: 205–8) for further discussion.
20. On the ecphrastic character of the *Phaenomena*, see e.g. Kaibel (1894: 87–92), Erren (1967 *passim*), Lombardo (1983: Introduction) and Fakas (2001: 197–203).
21. On the simile, see Erren (1967: 166–75), Gee (2000: 87–90) and Schindler (2000: 62–4).
22. For the emblematic role of Dike in Aratus' history of signification, see esp. Van Noorden (2009).
23. Verbs of speaking used for the signs: (ἀπ-)ἀγγέλλω (731, 1056), διδάσκω (734, 793), εἴρω (739), ἐξεῖπον (741), ἐρέω (773), λέγω (1048, 1071, 1148), (ἐπι-)σημαίνω (12, 248, 267, 381, 757, 808, 873, 891, 904); verbs of speaking used for the communicating gods: λέγω (7, 8, 732), σημαίνω (6, 420).

stars and constellations.[24] The poet views himself as being in the business of "speaking the stars": ἐμοί γε μὲν ἀστέρας εἰπεῖν / ᾗ θέμις εὐχομένῳ ("me, praying to speak of the stars as it is right", 17–18) and, with the famous pun on his own name in the second line of the poem, signals that he, Ἄρατος, is not one to leave things "unmentioned", ἄρρητον: ἐκ Διὸς ἀρχώμεσθα, τὸν δ' οὐδέποτ' ἄνδρες ἐῶμεν / ἄρρητον ("Let us begin from Zeus, whom we men never leave unmentioned", 1–2).[25]

This notion of the stars as signs in the communication between Zeus and mankind, signs that are perceived by sight but that occasion verbalization in human language, is highly suggestive of a kind of sign system with which we are all familiar: writing.[26] That Aratus may have viewed the sky as a kind of book or, in fact, poem is suggested by one of the most famous features of the *Phaenomena*, the acrostic in 783–7, where the first letters of the five lines in question are signs that signal the word λεπτή ("slender") – a term that plays an important role in the passage and, as I have argued elsewhere, in the *Phaenomena* as a whole.[27] It is attractive to consider this sophisticated word game – one perceived solely by vision – as programmatic for the visual paradigm of the *Phaenomena* as whole. Just like the poem that is its representation, the universe is a system of visible signs, a meaningful text to be deciphered by human readers.

To return to Manilius, the ability to correctly interpret the positions of the heavenly bodies is of course of central importance to the astrologer as well. However, the *Astronomica* is not so much concerned with the exegetical skills we might employ to make sense of the situation in the sky, but rather with the ways in which we are implicated in this situation. We are not so much reading a cosmic text as being inextricably woven into it. To illustrate further the kinds of manifold interactions that take place in Manilius' universe, I turn now to a detailed discussion of two passages, the poet's treatment of the relationships of the signs of the zodiac in Book 2 and his exhortation to the student at the end of Book 4.

CONSENTING STARS

An especially important feature of astrology is that the signs of the zodiac are significant not only on their own (e.g. when they are in the ascendant, or house the Sun or a planet), but also in relationship to one another, a topic Manilius discusses in *Astronomica* 2.270–692. What happens in one sign can affect or be affected by what happens in others, depending on how the signs are situated or otherwise relate to one another. Since the

---

24. On naming in the *Phaenomena*, see Cusset (2002). Aratus uses the verb καλέω and derivatives sixteen times in the context of naming the constellations.
25. On ἄρρητον, see Levitan (1979: 68 n. 18), Kidd (1981: 355) and esp. Bing (1990; 1993: 105–8).
26. I discuss Aratus' "heavenly writing" in greater detail in Volk (2012).
27. On the significance of the term λεπτός in the *Phaenomena*, see Volk (2010a: 205–8); compare also Tsantsanoglou (2009), whose conclusions, however, I cannot accept. The classic discussion of the acrostic is by Jacques (1960).

signs are identified with their underlying constellations (Aries, Taurus, Gemini, etc.), Manilius virtually personifies them, depicting them as members of a cosmic society who have their likes and dislikes, entering, as people do, into friendships, enmities, love affairs and plots. In an economic metaphor, their constant interactions are repeatedly referred to as *commercia*, literally "commerce".[28] The signs engage in exchange with one another, an exchange that is frequently depicted as a kind of sense perception. The classic form of such intrazodiacal relationship is what is known in astrology as "aspect" (discussed by Manilius in 2.270–432). As is clear from the term itself, the idea is that particular signs are, as it were, looking at each other. This kind of vision is especially effective among signs that are located at certain angles from one another: astrologers imagine the zodiac as a circle in which one can inscribe various geometric figures; thus, for example, the three signs situated at the points of an equilateral triangle form a so-called trigon, which means that they look at one another particularly intensely, exhibiting the powerful "trine" aspect. Signs at the corners of squares and hexagons likewise find themselves in significant aspect, as do those in diametrical opposition.

In addition to aspect, Manilius mentions four further types of relationship among zodiacal signs, two of which also involve sense perception (2.466–519): certain signs are such that they "see" or "hear" other signs, or (and these last two types are ones that are not found in any astrological sources aside from Manilius) they may "love" or, conversely, "trick" them.[29] We here see personification in full force: every sign is like a person caught in a web of interpersonal relationships, perceiving other signs and emotionally reacting to them. To explore how this works, let us consider the beginning of Manilius' description of these seeing, hearing, loving and tricking relationships. The poet goes through the signs one by one, starting with Aries, the constellation of the spring equinox, which was often considered the beginning of the zodiac:

> consilium ipse suum est Aries, ut principe dignum est,
> audit se Libramque uidet, frustratur amando
> Taurum; Lanigero qui fraudem nectit et ultra
> fulgentis geminos audit per sidera Pisces,
> Virgine mens capitur uisa. (2.485–9)

As is fitting for the leader, Aries keeps his own counsel: he hears himself and sees Libra and loves Taurus without success; Taurus weaves trickery against the woolly one [Aries] and hears through the stars twin Pisces that shine beyond [i.e. on the other side of Aries], and his mind is captured by the sight of Virgo.

And so on and so forth. The signs are not isolated but connected to one another through their senses and emotions, a state of cosmic interaction that Manilius a number of times

---

28. On the image of celestial *commercia* (in our passage: 2.346, 358, 382, 467), see Glauthier (2011).
29. These relationships, too, are predicated on the location of the individual signs within the circle of the zodiac and their geometrical positions vis-à-vis one another; see Goold (1992: xlvi–xlix) for a concise explanation, with diagrams.

refers to with the noun *consensus*, literally "feeling together" (2.63, 271, 345, 359, 386). As Michael Lapidge has shown, Latin compounds with *con-* (often calques on similar Greek compounds with *syn-*) are frequently used by Latin authors with a Stoic bent to express the fundamental interconnectedness of the Stoic universe with its uninterrupted corporeality.[30] We have already seen Manilius' *commercia*, and his *consensus* does in fact appear to be an actual translation of the central Stoic term *sympatheia*. This use goes back to Cicero, who refers to *iste quasi consensus, quam* συμπάθειαν *Graeci uocant* ("that concord which the Greeks call 'sympathy'", *On the Nature of the Gods* 3.28). Manilius has revived what in most Stoic texts is a rather muted metaphor by presenting his cosmic citizens, the stars, as literally "feeling" together and engaging one another's senses.

As the reader may have noticed, despite my talk about different senses, it is still the visual that plays the most important role in Manilius' interstellar perception. All aspect, for example, works via sight. However, we must keep in mind that in the belief of the ancients, vision itself ultimately involved touch: nearly all Greco-Roman theories of vision are predicated on the idea that some physical substance enters and/or leaves the eye in the act of viewing.[31] Manilius' seeing stars, too, have a more tangible effect, which explains why their gaze can be astrologically effective in the first place. Consider the following passage, where the poet makes the point that the force of vision and, thus, influences among signs in a trigon are greater than among those in a square:

> sed longe maior uis est per signa trigoni
> quam quibus est titulus sub quarto quoque quadratis.
> altior est horum summoto linea templo,
> illa magis uicina meat caeloque recedit
> et propius terras accedit uisus eorum
> aeraque infectum nostras demittit ad auras.   (2.352–7)

> But the power of the trigon is much greater among the signs than that of those that are called squares, which involve each fourth [i.e. third, by our non-inclusive reckoning] sign. Their line [i.e. of the quartile signs] runs higher up in a removed part of heaven, while that one [i.e. of the trine signs] comes closer, and their vision leaves behind the sky and approaches the earth and sends infected air down to our atmosphere.

The reason why the trine aspect is more powerful than the quartile (exhibited by signs in a square) is that the lines of vision in an inscribed triangle pass closer to the centre of the circle – and this centre is where the earth is situated and, on it, the people who experience this type of stellar influence. Because the *uisus* of the trine signs comes closer to the terrestrial realm, it "sends infected air down to our atmosphere" (357). However we are to

---

30. See Lapidge (1989: 1383–4, 1388, 1395).
31. See Dörrie (1965: 120–1, 123–4), Simon (1988: 21–56), Rakoczy (1996, esp. 19–37 and 236 with n. 40) and Park (1997).

imagine the physical details, it is clear that vision for Manilius is not something intangible, but a physical force that literally infects the air, which in turn powerfully affects the senses of human beings.[32]

TRANSCENDING THE VISUAL

I conclude my discussion of Manilius' cosmos of the senses by turning from the consenting stars to the human beings who attempt to make sense of the sky, in particular, to Manilius' long-suffering student, a generic second-person didactic addressee who, after listening patiently to all this talk about the influence of the stars, in Book 4 finally gets a word in himself, complaining that he finds his teacher's exposition difficult to follow.[33] There are two such interventions; I concentrate here on the second one, at the very end of the book (4.866–935). Manilius first reports the student's complaint verbatim:

> "conditur en" inquit "uasto natura recessu
> mortalisque fugit uisus et pectora nostra,
> nec prodesse potest quod fatis cuncta reguntur,
> cum fatum nulla posset ratione uideri".   (869–72)

> "Look", he says, "nature is hidden in a deep chasm and escapes from our mortal gaze and intellect. The fact that everything is ruled by fate is of no use if fate cannot in any way be seen".

The student employs the language of vision (cf. *uisus*, 870; *uideri*, 872) to make his point that the workings of the universe and thus of fate cannot be seen, that is, are impossible for human beings to know. It is now the teacher's job to convince him that insight into the cosmos is possible after all, an argument to which Manilius devotes 73 lines and one that culminates in a rapturous celebration of man's intellect and the fundamental intelligibility of the universe.

The poet begins by picking up on the student's vocabulary of vision (873–6): the god (i.e. the divine cosmos) does not begrudge (*inuidet*, 874) human beings knowledge of himself, but has instead provided them with the eyes (*oculos*, 875) of the mind. We are able to see (*perspicere*, 876) the sky, so why not also its further gifts to mankind? At this

---

32. See also 2.375–8 and 385–6 and compare 4.742–3. It is in such passages that Manilius comes closest to formulating a theory of how astrology is actually supposed to work, a topic on which he is otherwise quite vague (see Volk 2009: 59–67). The idea that the stars influence life on earth by sending forth some actual substance is also reported in e.g. Geminus 2.14; 17.16, 33 and 34 and Sextus Empiricus, *Against the Mathematicians* 5.4–5; see Dörrie (1965: 124) and Alesse (2003).
33. On Manilius' interaction with his student, see Neuburg (1993), Volk (2002: 198–209) and Green (2011) (the last argues provocatively that the student's professed difficulties indicate that Manilius does not actually wish to impart astrological information and that the poem's obscurity is thus deliberate).

point, Manilius switches from the language of sight to the imagery of cosmic travel that we know already from the first proem (877–81): in addition to simply looking at the universe, human beings are able to descend into its depths and become a physical part of it – indeed, are already a part by virtue of being themselves the offspring of heaven (*partum caeli*, 879). Contradicting the student's assertion that nature is hidden, Manilius contends that it lies fully revealed: *iam nusquam natura latet, peruidimus omnem* ("nature is no longer hidden anywhere: we have thoroughly seen it all", 883). Again we find the language of vision, but again the poet in the very next lines transcends it, maintaining that we not only "see" the universe, but actually "take possession" of it and ourselves rise to the stars:

> et capto potimur mundo nostrumque parentem
> pars sua perspicimus genitique accedimus astris. (884–5)

And we take possession of the captured universe, view our parent, of whom we are part, and rise to the stars, from which we were born.

Manilius' point is that visual perception of the universe is not merely possible: it is just the beginning. What we see – the *phainomena* as described by Aratus – is only the first step to a proper understanding of the cosmos, an understanding that is not a mediated reading of signs, but an immediate immersion. After celebrating the abilities of man, the only animal with the gift of divine reason (896–906), Manilius sums up the pinnacle of human achievement, the exploration of the sky (906–10). First, man only looks at the heavens (*ad sidera mittit / sidereos oculos*, "he directs his starry eyes to the stars", 906–7). In a second step, though, he does not remain satisfied with the outer appearance of the divine universe but digs deeper into the body of the heavens, a body that is related to him and one in which he is ultimately searching for none other than himself:

> nec sola fronte deorum
> contentus manet, et caelum scrutatur in aluo
> cognatumque sequens corpus se quaerit in astris. (908–10)

He does not remain satisfied with the outer appearance of the gods and searches the womb of heaven; pursuing a related body, he is looking for himself in the stars.

As the poet goes on to show (915–22), the fact that we have the *phainomena*, that the universe offers itself to our vision, is an indication that it wants us to go further, calling our minds to the stars:

> atque ideo faciem caeli non inuidet orbi
> ipse deus uultusque suos corpusque recludit
> uoluendo semper seque ipsum inculcat et offert,
> ut bene cognosci possit doceatque uidentis,
> qualis eat, cogatque suas attendere leges.

> ipse uocat nostros animos ad sidera mundus
> nec patitur, quia non condit, sua iura latere. (915–21)

> God himself does not begrudge his appearance to the earth and reveals his face and body through constant revolution and impresses and offers himself to his viewers in order that he might be well understood and teach them his nature and compel them to heed his laws. The universe itself calls our minds to the stars and, not hiding its laws, does not allow them to be hidden.

The visibility of the cosmos thus acts as a guarantee that we are not only able but indeed called upon to engage with it more deeply: "Who", Manilius asks, "would deem it wrong to understand what it is right to see?" (*quis putet esse nefas nosci, quod cernere fas est?*, 922). Seeing the universe is not enough: in order to properly comprehend it, we must learn to use more than our eyes.

Ultimately, of course, what makes us fathom the cosmos is not sense perception of any kind, but reason, *ratio*, which in the famous axiom that caps the argument really does conquer all: *ratio omnia uincit* (932). However, Manilius' reason is not some kind of immaterial capacity removed from the physicality of the world of perception. For the Stoics, everything is corporeal, and reason – both the reason of the ensouled universe as a whole and the reason of individual human beings – is ultimately a physical entity as well, interacting with the other parts of the wholly corporeal cosmos. As we have seen, Manilius envisages reason as digging into the entrails of the universe and travelling among the stars. Man's highest capacity thus remains an integral part of the cosmos of the senses.[34]

---

34. Many thanks to Shane Butler, Alex Purves and Mario Telò, the organizers of the splendid UCLA conference where I presented an oral version of this paper.

8

READING DEATH AND THE SENSES IN LUCAN AND LUCRETIUS

Brian Walters

The dead man has poetry in his stomach, bowels and genitals.
In the dead man's inner organs, poems are born, mate, change and die.
(Marvin Bell, *The Book of the Dead Man*, 1994: #10)

People have been dying since long before we were even really people, yet none of us knows how it feels to die, or what death ultimately means for our senses. Does it erase them? Or do they live on? And if the latter, at what intensity and for how long? In general, modern science says that death is the end: on dying our senses are snuffed out, and in a surprisingly consistent order.[1] But what happens to us after we die is an intensely personal question, and many of us – a shocking majority it seems – do not believe what our science has to say.[2] Instead, by some twist of fate death's blank silences make poets of us all. And for those who were already poets, its impulses, we are assured, sing with violent metapoetic possibility. For the Roman poets Lucan and Lucretius, death, poetry and the senses are intimately – and inextricably – connected. Exactly how, and what this means for our own experiences of their texts are the questions that frame the rest of this inquiry.

We start with a particularly violent episode. In 82BCE the city of Rome was filled with death and terror as a result of Sulla's proscriptions. According at least to the most vivid

---

1. The most common order given by various pamphlets and books devoted to caring for the dying is: taste (including hunger, thirst and the ability to speak), smell, vision, and finally hearing and touch, cf. Hallenbeck (2003).
2. As A. F. Segal 2009 suggests, among Americans, even those with no obvious religious affiliation, belief in some form of afterlife is on the rise. Perhaps unexpectedly, this increased belief in post mortem existence has, except among fundamentalists and evangelicals, been accompanied by a growing disbelief in the horrors and torments of hell – a species of skepticism that, according to Cicero, *Tusculan Disputations* 1.10, at least, many Romans would almost certainly understand (cf., e.g., Cicero, *On the Nature of the Gods* 2.5; Sallust, *War with Catiline* 51.20, 52.13). Lucretius, of course, offers a different perspective on Roman fears of the torments of hell, which, although frequently met with skepticism by scholars in the past, is perhaps not as misguided as seems: cf. the interesting remarks of Wiseman (1994) and, on Roman beliefs about the afterlife more generally, Hope (2009: 97–119).

accounts of the period, dead bodies were everywhere, piled headless in the Forum and in the streets, choking the sewers and the flow of the Tiber.[3] Sulla had put a price on the lives of his enemies and as a result, not just in Rome, but throughout all Italy, violence reigned supreme as heads were hacked off and sent back to the capital to be put on display. For those who lived through the nightmare, mere mention of this blood-stained chapter of Rome's history was enough to evoke a shudder of horror. But its countless atrocities also proved inescapably alluring for survivors and later generations alike, and its brutalities were constantly revisited in the subsequent pages of Latin literature.[4] Among the many murders of this period, however, one stands out as especially violent and favoured in our sources: the horrific end of Marius Gratidianus.

Descriptions of Gratidianus' mutilation appear in extant Roman sources starting in the 60s BCE – that is, in the lifetime of those who had, or at least could have, witnessed it first hand. Cicero, in fact, in a passage from a now-fragmentary speech whose scattered pieces have come to resemble Gratidianus' own, calls explicit attention to the cruel spectacle it provided the people of Rome, who watched on and groaned as Catiline hacked their hero apart one limb at a time, and carried his still warm and living head across the city to Sulla.[5] The historian Sallust, whose (also now-fragmentary) version in the *Histories* seems to have directly inspired many of our later sources, describes his body being torn apart in such a way that he died one limb at a time.[6] The younger Seneca in his work *On Anger* echoes Sallust's description, verbatim at times, and amplifies it, virtually making each and every wound deal its own individual death.[7] His remarks, moreover, make it clear that Gratidianus was seen as a sort of stand-in for the Republic, and his mutilation was symbolic of the dismemberment of the Roman state,[8] a fact that perhaps accounts for some of the popularity of the *topos* and explains why it continued to be repeated in Latin literature for hundreds of years.[9]

But Gratidianus' gradual death, limb by limb, has a more immediate relevance. From the beginning it forced the Romans to reflect on the nebulous divide between life and death, and what happened within this space to the senses. There are hints of this already in Cicero[10] and tantalizing glimpses in Sallust and Seneca as well. But this brutal murder's

---

3. Cf. Lucan 2.134–220. For the proscriptions under Sulla and their subsequent revival in the Triumviral period, Hinard (1985) is the definitive study. On the abuse of dead bodies and their disposal in the Tiber more generally: Kyle (1998: 213–54) and Hope (2000: 111–19).
4. Roman enthusiasm for this gruesome subject extended to, and cannot be separated from, the wider fascination with the horrors of Civil War, for which see Jal (1963).
5. Cicero, *In toga candida*, frr. 5, 14, 15 Crawford (= Asconius 87.16c, 89.25c, 90.3c). [Cicero], *Handbook of Electioneering* 3.1–2, another work from the 60s (assuming the text is authentic, cf. now Fedeli 2006), also mentions Gratidianus' murder.
6. Sallust, *Histories* 1.44.
7. Seneca, *On Anger* 3.18.2.
8. In this respect, Gratidianus was not alone. For the wider implications of this and similar metaphorical visions of late Republican history, see Walters (2011).
9. Other accounts of the mutilation of Gratidianus not already mentioned include: Livy, *Epitome* 88; Valerius Maximus 9.2.1; Plutarch, *Sulla* 32.4; Florus 2.9.26; Firmicius Maternus, *Math.* 1.7.31; Orosius 5.21.7.
10. Cf. Cicero, *In toga candida*, fr. 15 Crawford (= Asconius 90.3c): *caput etiam tum plenum animae et spiritus* ("the head, even then full of spirit and life").

description and its meaning for Gratidianus' senses receives its most morbidly baroque elaboration in Book 2 of Lucan's *Civil War*, where the chilling moment of dismemberment is spread out over nearly 15 hexameter lines describing in order the removal of his arms, his tongue, his ears, his nose, and – only after having witnessed the fate of the rest of these limbs – finally his eyes (2.173–85):

> Why tell of Catulus' ghost placated with blood? – when Marius, as victim, made unspeakable sacrifice to an insatiable tomb, grim offerings even the dead perhaps disliked; when we saw lacerated limbs, every part wounded, and although the whole body was butchered, no death-blow dealt to the soul; we saw a terrible act of unspeakable savagery – a dying man not allowed to die. Torn off, his hands fell to the ground, and his tongue, cut out, quivered and beat the empty air with a silent spasm (*palpitat et muto vacuum ferit aera motu*). One man cuts off his ears, another his curved nose's nostrils (*hic aures, alius spiramina naris aduncae / amputat*), a third rips his eyes from their empty sockets, and after they have seen the rest of the body, finally gouges them out (*ille cavis evolvit sedibus orbes / ultimaque effodit spectatis lumina membris*).

By turning Gratidianus' into a witness of his mutilation, Lucan both plays on a common trope of Roman literature, according to which dying is figured as a sort of spectator sport, and simultaneously perverts earlier accounts, like Cicero's, of the murder.[11] But Gratidianus' experience of his death here also gives us pause and forces us to linger a moment with the poet among the carnage, wondering about his other final perceptions. Lucan, in his characteristically grotesque way, makes us contemplate the almost unthinkable. Did Gratidianus' ears hear the vain smacking of his tongue against the empty air before they were removed? The passage, it is true, calls explicit attention to the tongue's *muto motu* (silent spasm), but the onomatopoetic character of this phrase, like the *palpitat* with which the line begins, is aurally suggestive. Was his tongue's final taste that of the bloody earth? Was the last thing he smelled the metallic sharpness of the knife as it cut through the *spiramina* of his nose – or the notoriously heavy perfume that Cicero elsewhere ascribes to his killer(s)?[12] Again the passage's language turns our attention to the senses: *spiramina* can signify both breathing holes (more specifically here: nostrils) and the breathing that takes place through them. Moreover, to borrow a common Roman metaphor, the line on the nose's amputation is not without further olfactory associations, giving off as it does a strong scent of Ennius;[13] just as we might note, too, that the line describing

---

11. On Roman death as something that demands spectators, see Edwards (2007: 1–11 and 46–77).
12. Catiline's heavily perfumed entourage comes under attack, for example, at Cicero, *In Catilinam* 2.5 and 23.
13. The Ennian line in question, *Annales* fr. 222 Skutsch, reads: *sulpureas posuit **spiramina Naris ad undas*** (with the specific borrowing in bold); cf. the comments of Skutsch (1985: *ad loc.*). For this kind of olfactory metaphor in Latin, see, e.g. Cicero, *On the Nature of the Gods* 1.72. Cf. Telò (this volume) on the notion of olfactory intertexts.

Gratidianus' severed tongue has a distinctly Ovidian flavour.[14] I return to the implications of these intertexts later. For now, let us just say that Lucan draws our attention to each of Gratidianus' senses, bringing it momentarily alive before violently snuffing it out for ever.

In an article exploring the meanings of dismemberment in Neronian literature, Glenn Most has suggested that (regarding other scenes of amputation in the poem) such speculations on the senses of the dying are not misplaced. Looking to the Stoic belief in a soul that extends, as it is sometimes described, like an octopus stretching its tentacles through the entire body and equipping it with sensation,[15] Most notes that "dismemberment posed disturbing questions ... [especially] if the amputation was sudden and particularly violent".[16] The mutilation of Marius Gratidianus provides a case in point, a space for the poet and his audience to reflect on the limits of sensory experience, to ponder what happens when body parts are cut off before the bits of soul they contain can be withdrawn. Do they still, at least momentarily, function? If an amputated hand can continue to grasp (as it does, for example, at Lucan 3.612–13), shouldn't eyes see, ears hear, noses smell and tongues taste?

One does not need to be a Stoic, of course, to ask these questions.[17] Lucan, at any rate, seems to be simply amplifying what is already present in the earlier accounts of the death. The emphasis in this passage is not really on what happens to the senses while dying; instead, the senses become the field on which life's final moments – and, just as importantly, Lucan's stunningly grotesque poetics[18] – are acted out. Only once Gratidianus has experienced his mutilation to the fullest are his eyes dug from his head, and though the poem continues, for our victim there is only darkness and the grave.

LUCRETIUS

The space for the senses that Lucan opens like a wound between life and death was something that his poetic predecessor, the Epicurean Lucretius, had emphatically tried to close. The shift from Lucan's account of Gratidianus' mutilation to Lucretius' earlier poem bent on eradicating the fear of death is not as drastic as it might seem.[19] Though we know little

---

14. Ovid, *Metamorphosis* 6.560: ***palpitat et moriens dominae vestigia quaerit***. Ambühl (2010: 27–8) notes additional Vergilian intertexts for this passage.
15. For this image of the soul, see Long & Sedley (1987), passage 53H (= Aetius 4.21.2-3).
16. Most (1992: 406).
17. Lucan is clearly and intimately familiar with the tenants of Stoicism (see, e.g., the discussions of Lapidge 1979, with additional bibliography on 344, and Braund 1992: xxiii–xxv), but it is important to remember that he was first and foremost a poet, not a philosopher.
18. Hömke (2010: 98–104) also discusses the aesthetic importance of dying in Lucan's poem (and briefly mentions Gratidianus' mutilation on 99), though with a different emphasis. Most relevant for our purposes is her discussion of Lucan's "expansion of the interval between life and death".
19. Despite their differences, both poets share an elemental antagonism that informs the whole of their works: Lucretius posits atoms and void; Lucan, in turn, evokes the clash between liberty and Caesar (7.696). These fundamental oppositions, which perhaps shape the more complex connections traced between Lucan and Lucretius below, contrast sharply with the ideologies of recurrence and change that, respectively, underscore the actions of Vergil's *Aeneid* and Ovid's *Metamorphoses*.

for certain about Lucretius' life, other than its approximate dates and a few odd details that we can glean from the poem itself, it is enough to assume (as most scholars do) a first-hand experience of the horrors of the proscriptions, of which Gratidianus' murder was just one.[20] In this regard it is no wonder that Lucretius' poem – whose catalogues of people's anxieties about death provide an extensive map of bodily experience – is filled with scenes of dismemberment, putrefaction and horrific pain. What is remarkable, however, is the way that Lucretius works constantly to separate sensation from these experiences,[21] a tactic that reaches almost ridiculous proportions in a famous passage from book 3 that claims that when bodies are cut in half, the soul within them is severed too. His proof that follows might profitably be read as a poetic forebear of the Lucan passage above (3.642–56):

> They say that blade-bearing chariots, warm with indiscriminate slaughter, often cut off limbs so fast that the severed part is seen trembling on the ground, although the injured man's force of mind cannot sense the pain because of the swiftness of the trauma (*mobilitate mali non quit sentire dolorem*) and because his mind is, at the same time, totally absorbed in the fight: with what remains of his body he charges back into the fight and slaughter, not perceiving his lost left arm and shield have been swept away among the horses, wheels, and snatching blades; nor does another realize his right arm has come off when he climbs up and threatens. Another attempts to rise on a leg no longer present, while his dying foot twitches its toes on the ground nearby (*cum digitos agitat propter moribundus humi pes*). Even a severed head, its body still warm and living, maintains a semblance of life on the ground and staring eyes (*et caput abscisum calido viventeque trunco / servat humi voltum vitalem oculosque patentis*) until it gives up the ghost entirely.

Even though severed limbs and toes continue to twitch, and lopped off heads still maintain a semblance of life, Lucretius denies that there is any sensation of pain because of the swiftness of the trauma (*mobilitate mali*). It is unclear as to whether the staring eyes (*oculos patentis*) still briefly see until the remaining soul pours out, but it seems unlikely. At a number of other places in the poem this problem is addressed explicitly, and there is no question, as there was in Lucan's text, of a severed nose, for example, continuing to smell for even a second: Lucretius assures us that once removed from the rest of our body, not any of our sense organs continues to work (3.551–3): "hands and eyes or noses, apart, and separate from us, cannot sense or even exist, but rot away in however short a time" (*manus atque oculus naresve seorsum / secreta ab nobis nequeunt sentire neque esse, / sed tamen in parvo liquuntur tempore tabe*). And we can compare with this, for example, another

---

20. Facts from antiquity about Lucretius' life are slim and controversial, and have been discussed by many before. Rough dates can be gleaned from Jerome's *Chronicon*, which gives a lifespan from about 96–51 BCE (readings vary and dates have been tweaked one way or another by different scholars); readers are referred to Bailey (1947: 1.1–21) (especially 14 for Lucretius' first-hand experience of the proscriptions) and the judicial discussion of Conte (1994: 155–6).
21. Warren (2002) and (2004 *passim*) both comment on this aspect of Lucretius' art; cf. C. Segal (1990) for Lucretius' strategies for getting these experiences back in.

passage that comes just a few lines later (3.563–4): "It is obvious: an eye, torn out by the roots, and separate from the whole body, can see nothing by itself" (*scilicet avolsus radicibus ut nequit ullam / dispicere ipse oculus rem seorsum corpore toto*). For the Epicurean Lucretius, sensation is only possible as a joint function of body and the super-fine mixture of soul;[22] and the bits of soul suffused through our sense organs do not survive the act of severing, but are dispersed instead, leaving what used to be seeing eyes, touching hands and smelling noses to rot, now nothing more than inanimate flesh.

The relevance this has for an individual's senses after death (rather than just the death of individual senses) is perhaps already clear, but, in any event, Lucretius spells it out for us a little later in a passage castigating those well-worn depictions of sentient spirits in the underworld that Cicero in the *Tusculan Disputations* dubs "monstrosities of poets and painters".[23] Later still in book 3, Lucretius will argue that the sensuous horrors of the underworld – the sweating Sisyphus, thirsty Tantalus and the like – are all merely projections of the mental torments of our day-to-day life (cf. 3.978–1023), but at present his interest is, instead, on the impossibility of the dead enjoying or suffering from sense perception (3.624–33):

> Moreover, if the nature of the soul is immortal, and sentient when separate from our body, it would have to be endowed, I think, with five senses. How else could we imagine ourselves wandering as shades in the Underworld? Thus painters and generations of writers have brought before us souls endowed with senses. But neither eyes nor noses nor hands can exist for bodiless souls, nor tongues nor ears: thus, souls cannot sense on their own nor even exist.

Just as the body is an insensate corpse without the soul, for Lucretius, the soul sees and feels nothing without the body.

DYING AND READING

If our treatment of the senses has so far frequently elided the process of dying, it is only because Lucretius tends to do the same. As numerous scholars have noted, the perceptibility of the process of dying is something that our Republican poet, like all good Epicureans, tends to de-emphasize, placing a sharp and swift break between being alive, of which we are aware, and being dead, which is literally "nothing to us" (*nihil ad nos* or οὐδὲν πρὸς ἡμᾶς, according to Epicurean doctrine) because in death we are literally nothing.[24] Death, like the dismemberments examined above, is for Lucretius a truly alienating experience because it makes us – or a severed part of us – something entirely alien, entirely other.

---

22. Long & Sedley (1987), section 14 provides a convenient overview of the soul in Epicureanism.
23. Cicero, *Tusculan Disputations* 11: *haec poetarum et pictorum portenta*.
24. Warren (2002: 199; 2004: 16) and Furley (2007).

This alienating effect is especially pronounced in passages that emphasize the sudden separation of body and soul as a result of violent trauma, but is equally present in the few passages that focus on the sensations of gradual death as well, like 3.526–30, whose immediate point is to show the interconnectedness of a person's body and soul: "We often see (*saepe ... cernimus*) people gradually die, and lose their vital sense one limb at a time: on the feet, first toes and nails go livid, then the feet and legs die, and later still, in a drawn out manner, the footsteps of icy death (*gelidi vestigia leti*) move through the remaining limbs". Lucretius describes the process of dying in great detail: as chill death creeps over the body, life fades away little by little, and sensation is lost one limb at a time. Death leaves the body cold and discoloured as it spreads from the tips of the toes, through the feet, then the legs and upwards through the rest. It is tempting to impart some awareness of the *gelidi vestigia leti* to the dying individual, but ultimately this temptation is false. Lucretius' language makes clear that the limbs that have gone cold and turned blue are, in fact, already dead; and nothing that is dead can have sensation. It is only as a spectator of his death, however slight the remove, that the individual can experience it: his still-living eyes can note the change of colour in his already-dead toes; his hands, before they die, can apprehend the cold in his legs. But in this way, at least, he is more like us than himself – we, inside the poem, who have often seen (*saepe cernimus*) the onset of death, and we, readers of the poem as well, who are seeing it now – because, in being dead, the parts of his dead body are no longer his. This is truly an alienating experience if ever there was one.

Importantly, for us, this passage finds a striking corollary in Lucan's account of the drawn-out dismemberment of Marius Gratidianus considered above, another description of death involving an uncomfortable confrontation with otherness. To appreciate the passage fully, however, literary-critical rather than philosophical notions must be invoked. For our ancient authors, we need remember, the language of the body provided much of their critical vocabulary. Texts were not only analysed and conceived of in bodily terms, but were also – like bodies – described as being composed of heads (*capita*), feet (*pedes*), limbs (*membra, artus*) and other organs.[25] It is precisely in this regard that Lucan's description of Gratidianus' death comes off as so devastatingly unnerving for its victim – and, ultimately, for us as well. Like the dying man in Lucretius, Gratidianus, too, is forced to experience his last moments at something of a remove, watching them unfold and realizing only too late that his severed limbs – licking and sniffing and grasping for their final sensations – are not really his own, but *membra* borrowed from Ovid and Ennius instead. Inasmuch as Lucan's account literalizes the metaphor found, for example, in Horace's famous *disiecti membra poetae* (at *Satires* 1.4.62), we might be tempted to take these lines as providing little more than a playful commentary on the process of poetic allusion, here metaphorized as an act of dismemberment.[26] But such a reading (although surely in part

---

25. Informative on this point are Van Hook (1905: 18–20), Most (1992: 407–9, with specific examples in n. 116), and Farrell (1999; 2007: 184–5). For further references, see note 28 below.
26. On dismemberment and intertextuality more generally, cf. the remarks of Butler (2011: 23–4) on Orpheus' dismemberment, to whose already elaborate "intertextual (and intratextual) nest" we can add the following telling detail: not only is Orpheus' *caput a cervice revulsum* ("head torn from his neck") at Vergil

true) falls short at exactly the point with which we are currently concerned by failing to explain the broader similarities in Lucan and Lucretius' texts – similarities that, as we shall soon discover, are not only greater than they first appear, but, more importantly, have as much to tell us about poetics as they do about dying.

With regard to both subjects, the shift from philosophical to literary preoccupations just made is crucial for pointing the way. Lucretius, after all, only foregrounds philosophy in his description of dying if we read from a strictly narrative perspective. If we pause to consider the broader texture of his passage – and, indeed, his poem at large – we are immediately presented with a different picture. In fact, once we are willing to turn our attention away from what Lucretius purports to be telling us about Epicureanism and focus instead on the manner in which it is told, we are confronted with a number of fascinating revelations. To consider a more general point first: although we are assured that for the dying the separation of soul from body happens in such a way as to be imperceptible, for readers of the poem death is accompanied by changes of colour and temperature, taste and smell. We have already considered Lucretius' claims about the non-perception of eyes ripped out by their roots, but his picture is made more sensually interesting by the comparison at 3.325–30, for example, where the destructive separation of soul from body is described in similar language, but ultimately likened to the violent extraction of scent from incense (*e thuris glaebis evellere odorem / haud facile est*). Elsewhere, at 3.221–3, the soul departing from the body is compared successively to the way in which a wine's bouquet vanishes, the sweet scent of perfume diffuses into the air, and the juice of a piece of fruit disappears with time.[27] In other words, for Lucretius' readers, dying, far from snuffing out the senses, actually opens doors onto a larger sensual world – a world in which poetic metaphor casts the otherwise imperceptible process as a truly synaesthetic experience.[28]

To appreciate the implications of this point, we need only return to Lucretius' account of death's deprivations at 3.526–30, this time focusing on our poet's Latin:

denique saepe hominem paulatim cernimus ire
et **membratim** vitalem deperdere sensum:
in pedibus primum **digitos** livescere et unguis;
inde **pedes** et crura mori; post inde **per artus**
ire alios tractim gelidi vestigia Leti.

    Georgics 4.523, a reprise of the same phrase at Ennius, *Annales* fr. 483 Skutsch, but Ennius' line itself, as Leonard & Smith (1942: 479) note, seems to prefigure Lucretius' *caput abscisum* at 3.654–5 (discussed above). For a detailed discussion of various self-reflexive intertextual strategies, see Hinds (1998: 1–16).

27. According to C. Segal (1990: 54), such comparisons don't just draw a connection between the fragility of these scents, flavours and life, but, in fact, count such scents and flavours "among the pleasures of being alive". Metaphors like these, then, allow the poet to confront the loss of sensation that accompanies dying from multiple perspectives, throwing into sharp focus the sensuous divide between the world of the living and the bleak nothingness of being dead.

28. Catrein (2003: *passim*) discusses the synaesthetic texture of Lucretius' poem; the sections on vision (51–8) and touch (155–99) are particularly interesting.

The changes of colour and temperature in this morbid vignette reinforce our claims about death's sensual aspects in Lucretian epic. But it is the rendering of dying as poetry – or, to be more specific, the way that Lucretian *ars* inextricably merges the subjects of dying and poetry here – that demands our attention. Given what we saw with regard to Gratidianus above, the metapoetic charge of these verses, with their repeated mentions of *pedes, membra, digiti*, and *artus*, requires little explication.[29] Rather, it is more important to note simply the way that death's slow creep through the dying man's limbs is, by virtue of these terms' double meanings, inscribed on the very fabric of Lucretius' poem. More important still is the way that death's movements perfectly mirror our own forward movement as readers through the text – each of us progressing one dactyl (*digitus*), foot (*pes*), and line (*membratim, artus*) at a time. And this, in fact, is the point toward which we have been heading all along, the ultimate revelation for which our inquiry into death and the senses has set the stage: that according to our Roman poets reading and dying overlap in remarkable ways.

Lest we imagine Lucretius to be alone in this regard, we need only recall Gratidianus' "reading" of his own intertextual death in Lucan. Indeed, the Neronian epicist's treatment of this episode is nothing if not a perverted and elaborated echo of our above Lucretian scene. To be sure, there is in Lucan's restaging of the dying reader within the medium of Gratidianus' mutilated body a certain comic grotesquery entirely absent from Lucretius' text. (Lucan, after all, aligns our act of reading not only with that of the dying popular statesman, but also with that of one of his killers, who "unwinds", *evolvit*, his victim's eyes like a book roll – and, indeed, perhaps with the actions of poet himself, if there is any further meaning to be found in his *effodit spectatis lumina membris*, something like "erases the highlights after the other *membra* have been scrutinized".[30]) But this is hardly surprising; such morbidly rhetorical flourishes, after all, are what we have been taught to expect from the precocious poet who, we might mention, only a handful of verses before those on Gratidianus embeds another gruesome tale of reading, this time cast as digging through piles of rotting cadavers "in search of *notae*".[31] Here, too, dying is implied by the entire surrounding context, inasmuch as the story (along with that about Gratidianus) is embedded within a reminiscence of the past intended to show the horrors that loom in the future for everyone.

---

29. Many of these terms are mentioned by Most (1992: 407–9, n. 116). For the metapoetics of *artus*, see Peirano (2009: 195, with n. 48); for *digitus* as a gloss for δάκτυλος, see *Thesaurus Linguae Latinae* 5.1122.77–9.
30. Given the range of possible meanings of *effodio* (*OLD* 2b) and *lumen* (*OLD* 11b), the phrase might be taken as metapoetically implying a sort of "wiping out" of Lucan's predecessors' choice phrases by the act of appropriating them, thereby bringing the poet's intertextual engagements in line with his larger treatment of the epic tradition as it is astutely presented by Hardie (1993: 109): "Violence and death characterize Lucan's dealings with the past ... Lucan takes control of his predecessors' material not as a respectful son entering into a father's inheritance, but as a rebel, yet unable to escape from the paradigms and values of his society, which he angrily seizes for his own and reverses into a negative parody of themselves, galvanizing the words and forms of the past into a furious appearance of life whose subsidence leaves, apparently, only death."
31. This point is owed to Butler (2002: 8).

DEATH AND THE END

For both Lucan and Lucretius, death's end for our senses is final. But as our discussion has shown, according to both poets, death's finality awaits us not so much at the edges of those last-grasped sensuous spaces that we have been exploring so far, but, rather, in that truly alien space beyond them all where their texts fall silent once and forever. Reading is dying, they assure us, and the silence of the grave, in other words, is really just that: the inevitable quiet that comes when our poems finally end. And end they must – though, to be sure, only after the numerous digressions and delays that give meaning to literature no less than life itself, delays that we find pointedly mirrored in death's gradual creep through the limbs in Lucretius' epic, or in the drawn-out deferment of Lucan's mutilation of Gratidianus (where we are told, "although the whole body was butchered, no death-blow was dealt to the soul", *et toto quamvis in corpore caeso / nil animae letale datum*). And soon, too, this essay must end. But before it does, let us turn at last to a brief look at the deaths that frame the finales of our two poet's texts.

In fact, for Lucan this is hard to do with much certainty, as there is no clear consensus as to where his text was meant to end.[32] As it stands, the poem's narrative cuts out too much in the middle of things, with the plot having reached no conclusion – or perhaps having gone on too long. Caesar is in a tight spot in Alexandria, and the action freezes as Scaeva appears. To be sure, the marks of death are everywhere on the episode, but few would maintain that they are intentional. Instead, if any design is to be found, it is surely to be located alongside the fact that every aspect of Lucan's poem is tinged with death. Nevertheless, we might note that the *Civil War*'s truncated form – usually explained with recourse to Lucan's own cut-short life – is strikingly emblematic of its similarly truncated hero, Pompey, whose headless corpse provides a paradigm for Lucan's decapitated epic. Even more relevant is the sudden presence of Scaeva himself, the Caesarian super-soldier whose wounding in Book 6 (spread out over lines 140–262) makes even Gratidianus' mutilation pale in comparison.[33] Scaeva's reintroduction in the final lines of Lucan's text stands as a reminder of the prolonged dying that has everywhere accompanied our progress through the preceding poem. A similar reminder would likely have also been present in the epic's intended end, which most (though not all) scholars agree would have treated Cato's suicide[34] in all its morbid glory – a death, we might note, already prefigured in the poem's opening image of the Roman populace eagerly disemboweling itself (1.2–3:

---

32. The problem of Lucan's end has been much discussed, most controversially by Masters (1992: 216–59), who discusses all the evidence and claims that the poem actually ends where it was intended. Stover (2008: 571, n. 1) provides a recent response to Masters. Both treatments contain ample references to further bibliography.
33. See Hömke (2010) for an intriguing discussion of Lucan's aesthetic treatment of Scaeva's mutilation.
34. The most recent arguments for this endpoint are made by Stover (2008). Cato's drawn-out attempts to disembowel himself – first with a sword and then, after the wound had been stitched shut, with his hands – are most memorably related at Plutarch, *Cato the Younger* 66–73.

populumque potentem / in sua victrici conversum viscera dextra).[35] If this really was the ending Lucan had in mind for his epic, Cato would provide the perfect emblem of an individual slowly dying across the poem's entire span, a drawn-out death mirroring that of the reader, spread from the *Civil War*'s opening to closing lines. But, again, we are only speculating.

Luckily, the problems posed by Lucretius' ending are less severe, and the conclusions to be drawn immediately more rewarding. The poem's final scene depicts in gruelling detail the effects of the Athenian plague of 430BCE and includes among its descriptions of heaps of corpses gradually disintegrating a vivid evocation of not only this sight, but also of the sounds of wailing survivors and the smells of sick and decaying bodies. Other than a few mutilated and transposed lines, the episode comes down to us essentially whole[36] and is, in fact, one of the most frequently imitated episodes in all of Latin literature. (Among its imitators, we might note, is included Lucan himself, who reworks this grim Lucretian scene at 6.80–117.)[37] Lucretius' motives for ending his poem on such a black note have often been scrutinized, and his horrifying account of death has, perhaps most famously, been explained as a sort of philosophical test that the (newly converted Epicurean) reader supposedly passes by remaining undisturbed.[38] But as our own account has suggested, philosophical exposition is only one of Lucretius' concerns – and not always the foremost. Indeed, from the perspective uncovered in this essay an entirely different conclusion suggests itself: Lucretius' text disintegrates into plague not so much to teach us some abstract lesson to take with us into our life beyond the *flammantia moenia* of his poem's world, but rather to show us that there is no life beyond.[39] Death closes in around us. And then the text simply ends.[40]

---

35. Quint (1993: 141–2) is one of the few scholars to explicitly draw a connection between this opening image and Cato's suicide.
36. A few dissenters, such as Kenney (1977: 22–3), maintain that Lucretius' poem is incomplete and would have had a different ending had Lucretius lived to complete it.
37. For a list of Lucretius' other imitators and a compelling account of the reason for this episode's popularity among later poets, see Butler (2011: 59–62).
38. The standard account for this reading is found in D. Clay (1983: 257–66). Butler (2011: 37–62), focusing on issues of poetic composition, provides a rare and refreshing divergence from such readings, while offering a slightly different take on decomposition than mine below.
39. The connections drawn here between plague, death, poetry and the end of Lucretius' epic perhaps receive further support from Fowler (1997), who, following Bockenmueller, suggests that the lines traditionally numbered 6.1250–51 have been transposed and were originally the poem's final lines. If Fowler is correct, then Lucretius' ending, through both language and sentiment, would have made my point incontrovertibly clear. For, with the lines placed back at the end, as death closes in on the reader, language in the poem breaks down (as noted by Fowler 1997: 135–6, building on the observations of Friedländer 1969) and words decompose into syllables and sounds, and the poem ends: *Nec poterat quisquam reperiri, quem neque morbus / nec mors nec luctus temptaret tempore tali*, "And no one could be found at such a time untouched by sickness or grieving or death".
40. For suggestions or inspiration many thanks go to Alex Purves, Julia Hawthorne, Anne Hawthorne, Kathryn Morgan, Jason Mitchell and the two anonymous readers from the press. Most of all a special debt of gratitude is owed to Shane Butler for his constant support and encouragement.

9

COLOUR AS SYNAESTHETIC EXPERIENCE IN ANTIQUITY

Mark Bradley

INTRODUCTION

In 1858, William Gladstone, British Prime Minister-to-be and a proficient Homeric scholar, famously argued that Homer's colour system was founded exclusively upon light and darkness, and that the organ of vision "was but partially developed among Greeks".[1] He was not the first to make such a claim about defective Greek colour vision: a generation before, the German polymath Goethe had made similar claims about ancient art, and others had drawn attention to the material poverty of colour in the ancient Mediterranean environment – the scarcity of dyes, paints and flower varieties, as well as the relative uniformity of ancient body colours. In the nineteenth century, these ideas chimed well with some of Darwin's theories about human evolution and the development of civilization, and some even invoked the newly-discovered phenomenon of colour-blindness to explain ancient insensitivities to colours.[2] The question about the poverty and imprecision of ancient colour vocabulary has been hotly debated by philologists and anthropologists ever since, and studies of ancient colour vision across the last hundred years have been dominated by efforts to demonstrate that the ancients in fact employed a highly sophisticated colour system. This system operated, the argument goes, along somewhat different parameters from our own: rather than hue, the ancients were sensitive primarily to such things as luminosity, saturation and texture, or even less obvious variables such as smell, agitation and liquidity.[3]

The ancients of course were certainly not "colour-blind", and we must be just as careful about using the term "synaesthesia" to describe ancient experiences. As we know,

---

1. Gladstone (1858: 488): "Homer's perceptions and uses of colour", discussed in Irwin (1974: 6–7).
2. See esp. Schultz (1904: 187–8).
3. The nature of the ancient colour system is still very much up for debate. For further detail, see Bradley (2009), esp. 12–17. For a detailed study of two particularly problematic Greek colour categories (although with some short-sighted conclusions), see Maxwell-Stuart (1981).

synaesthesia is a complicated neurological condition in which stimulation of one sensory pathway leads to automatic, involuntary experiences in a second sensory pathway.[4] In these terms, the ancients were not synaesthetic any more than they were colour-blind. However, this does not mean that we should not think about how and why associations between the different senses were taking place in ancient thought, or indeed revisit the distinction between the five senses that most of us now take for granted.

This essay will explore approaches to colour beyond the visual paradigm by examining a range of ancient colour experiences that may appear to be "synaesthetic". One approach might be to focus on a set of ancient contexts where colour appears to be used metaphorically to refer to other sensory experiences: early Greek musical theory, for example, with its "chromatic" scales, or the *colores* of Roman oratory.[5] There is a way of feeding these experiences into a story about synaesthesia: for experts trained in musical harmony, certain chords corresponded to colour experiences in a way that might be compared to the correlation of music and colours in the minds of genuine synaesthetes in the modern West (see Rosen, this volume, p. 96); and Roman orators from the late Republic onwards developed discourses in which their rhetorical style, arguments and embellishments were intimately connected to innate and artificial colours on the body. However, there is a more direct argument that can help us to connect colours to other sensory experiences in antiquity, and this involves redirecting our attention to some very basic questions: What did the ancients think a colour was? What part did colour play in the relationship between the viewer and the world around? And how was colour experienced and evaluated?

COLOUR AND CULTURE

There are two reasons why the study of colour in antiquity merits scholarly attention. The first is that many ancient colour terms are notoriously difficult to translate: there is a long list of terms in Greek and Latin that do not map straightforwardly onto English, and furthermore there are a number of basic colours that we use that appear to have no equivalent in antiquity. Classical colours, then, do not always make sense in our own sensory repertoires. We need to work towards a more sophisticated understanding of the ways in which poets, artists, orators, philosophers and historians deployed colour categories and formulated the relationship between their art or text, and the world it described. The second reason why colour is important is that it is formulated and packaged by the communities that use it.

In an engaging article published in 1985 titled "How Culture Conditions the Colours We See", Umberto Eco produced a diagram illustrating how differently English, Latin and Hanunóo colours work. The Hanunóo, a set of communities in a region of the Philippines,

---

4. On various artistic and scientific approaches to the subject, see Campen (2008).
5. On Greek musical colour, see Landels (1999: 90–92); Barker (1984), esp. 225–7; on Latin rhetorical *color*, see Bradley (2009: ch. 4); cf. *ibid.*: 69–70 on Greek concepts of colour (*chrōma*) in oratory.

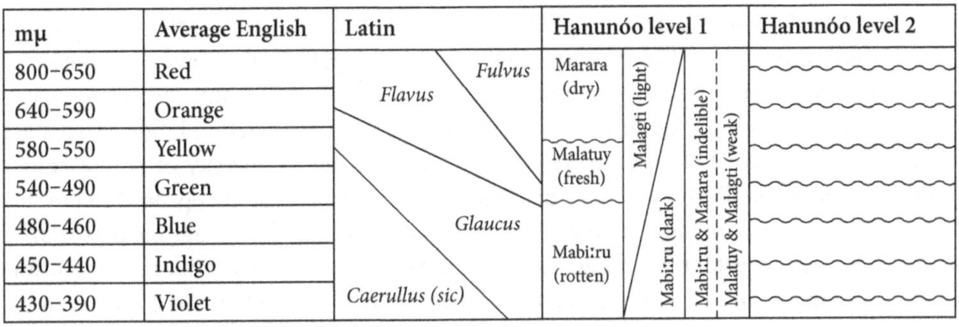

mμ	Average English	Latin	Hanunóo level 1	Hanunóo level 2
800–650	Red	*Fulvus* / *Flavus*	Marara (dry)	Malagti (light) / Malagti (indelible) / Malagti (weak)
640–590	Orange			
580–550	Yellow		Malatuy (fresh)	
540–490	Green			
480–460	Blue	*Glaucus*	Mabi:ru (rotten)	Mabi:ru (dark) / Mabi:ru & Marara / Malatuy & Malagti
450–440	Indigo	*Caerullus (sic)*		
430–390	Violet			

Figure 9.1 A comparative diagram of colour categories in English, Latin and Hanunóo, with light-wave estimates (after Eco 1985, discussed in Bradley 2009: 25). Redrawn from the original.

have long been recognized to use a complex system of colour terms that not only overlap and incorporate qualities of moisture, texture and shine, but also operate at two distinct levels depending on the type of communication being used.[6] Although this kind of diagram, which sets out to measure colour experiences against wavelengths, is of limited use (its interpretation of Latin colours is demonstrably misguided), it does show us how colour in different cultures can tap into a very different set of aesthetics.

Colour, then, is a basic cultural building block by which we can gauge how people see the world around them, and it is about much more than just lightwaves hitting the retina. It is well known that different cultures can discriminate and describe colours differently, and there are many examples of languages that employ unusual patterns of colour usage: Russian has two distinct terms for our colour blue; the Japanese category *ao* cuts across blue and green. Various African, South American and Asian communities employ what are to us very strange systems of colour usage, incorporating properties and qualities that cross into the domains of smell, taste, touch and even sound: the Hanunóo are one well-known example of such communities. In South Sudan, a nomadic tribe called the Dinka have captured the attention of anthropologists and sociologists for their unusual employment of colour: it used to be claimed that this community's rich repertoire of colour categories included dozens of terms within the yellow-brown range, perhaps due to the arid environment within which they lived (much like Eskimos with their versatile vocabulary for snowflakes).[7] In fact, recent research has tied the perception of many of these colours not to particular points on our colour charts, but unequivocally to the shades, patterns and markings of the cows that performed such a critical role in the Dinka's lives. What this means is that the world perceived by the Dinka, at least the world of the tribal song in which these colours are most conspicuous, is reformulated so that its various objects are intimately connected to the living, breathing, pungent, bellowing creatures which the

---

6. See Conklin (1955).
7. For this myth, see Lienhardt (1960: 12–16); Beard (2002: 47).

community values so highly.[8] It is telling that Berlin and Kay's influential (though now largely discredited) *Basic Color Terms* (1969), which proposed an evolutionary system of colour discrimination based on cultural progression – placing many "primitive" tribal communities at stage I, Homeric Greek at stage IIIb, and (predictably) English, Japanese and Russian at stage VII – completely misunderstood the complexity of Dinka colour language and ranked it in the dizzy heights of stage VII because it appeared to employ colours that mapped on those used by the developed West. Like Eco's diagram, then, Berlin and Kay have inadvertently exposed the limitations of assuming that colour is straightforwardly a visual phenomenon that can be systematically measured on our colour charts.

In fact, as the Dinka demonstrate (as do the Eskimos with their snowflakes), communities distinguish colours that are important or significant to them. Often these colours are grounded in the sensible, tangible material world rather than just what they happen to look like. Studies of primate colour vision have demonstrated that primates distinguish between yellow, green and red, corresponding to ripe, unripe and poisonous fruits: for them, colour is intimately connected to the world of taste and smell. Colour, then, is not an objective phenomenon: these same studies sometimes preface their work with the Cartesian principle that colour is in the mind, not in the physical world.[9]

This essay is not going to argue that we can be as schematic about colour in antiquity as we might be about the Dinka or fruit-seeking monkeys, but it is nonetheless axiomatic that we can learn a great deal about ancient values and priorities by looking at how contemporaries perceived, described and talked about colours. We will begin by thinking about what ancient thinkers considered a colour to be. How we define a colour in the modern West is hardly straightforward, but on the whole it is agreed that we operate using a predominantly abstract system of colours. We can conceive a colour as something detached from the people, objects and landscapes it coloured: we can picture "yellow" in our minds and transfer it straightforwardly from blond hair, to straw, to sulphur, to synthetic dyes and felt-tip pens; our "green" can describe plants, parrots, emeralds, sick faces; and so on. Ancient colours appear to have worked rather differently.

APPROACHING ANCIENT COLOUR

One of the most sensitive and successful recent studies of Greek colour terminology is Michael Clarke's "The Semantics of Colour in the Early Greek Word Hoard" (2004). This essay argues that there was a linguistic prototype at the bottom of ancient colour experiences: these were pivots or "cognitive reference points" around which various Greek experiences of colour fluctuated in concentric circles. Clarke's study focused on four complex

---

8. On Dinka bovine chromatography, see Coote (1992: 250). For a critical response to Coote's approach, see Gell (1995), who situates this colour repertoire in the competitive discourse of the Dinka poet, rather than the community at large. See also Bradley (2009: 29–30).
9. See for example Regan *et al.* (2001).

A. Plant
B. Dew
C. Cheese
D. River water
E. Tears

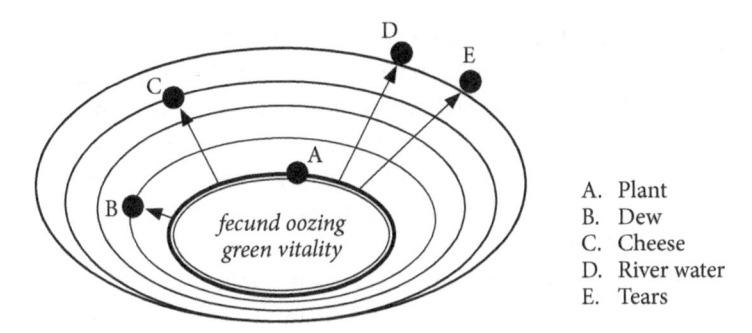

Figure 9.2 "Fecund oozing green vitality", from Clarke (2004: fig. 2). Redrawn from the original.

Greek colour terms: *chlōros* (interpreted as "green"/ "fecund"/ "oozing"); *argos* ("gleaming white"/ "nimble"); *porphureos* ("purple"/ "heaving"); and *oinops* ("wine-dark"/ "frenzied"/ "Dionysiac").

Figure 9.2 shows what Clarke believes happened with early Greek uses of *chlōros*: this category, which in essence evokes the abstract qualities implied by "fecund oozing green vitality", was applied to a range of objects or phenomena in the environment that approximate to those qualities; across time, these associations generally become looser, so that what began primarily as a descriptive category of plants could later be extended to such loosely-connected phenomena as river water or tears. Michael Clarke's approach provides us with a sophisticated model at the cutting edge of modern linguistics: the idea that ancient colour "prototypes" were often at "the meeting point of several cognitive domains" which the modern West usually keeps distinct – colour, light, movement, texture, mental states, and so on – offers a persuasive solution to understanding some of the more troublesome colour categories of antiquity.

The research presented in this essay has certain things in common with Clarke's approach. It argues that early categories of colour are tied to primary experiences and are then applied more loosely and creatively to other phenomena across time. However, rather than thinking in terms of an abstract prototype at the centre of ancient colour experiences, it contests that colours were associated primarily with specific, distinct objects, so that *chlōros* refers not to abstract green, fecund, oozing, but essentially means "verdant" or "plant-coloured"; *oinops* directly evokes wine and then (by extension) its colour, flavour, effects and association; and so on. The ramifications of this approach for the present volume, then, are self-evident: an object-centred experience of colour can also help us to understand why we find so many multi-sensory uses of colour in antiquity.

So when Romans think of *uiridis* (or *chloros*), they picture plants and verdure rather than just abstract green: this is why Columella can talk of the "green taste" (*uiridis sapor*) of olives, Horace can picture "green flames" (*uirens flamma*) spouting out of Mt Etna, and Aulus Gellius can describe a strong and vigorous sound, such as the letter "H", as *uiridis*.[10]

---

10. Columella, *On Agriculture* 12.49.8; Horace, *Epodes* 17.33; Aulus Gellius, *Attic Nights* 2.3.1. For a full discussion of *uiridis*, see Bradley (2009: 7–9).

Once we accept that Latin "*flauus*" primarily means "blond" rather than yellow, we can better understand why Latin poets might imaginatively describe billowing cornfields and olive-leaf garlands as "*flauus*": they might share similar wavelengths, but they also share similar tactile qualities and associations.[11] And when we recognize that *caeruleus* does not just mean "blue" but evokes the watery depths, we can better explain why storm clouds are often "*caeruleus*", but the clear blue sky is not, and why "*caerulea Crete*" is not a blue island, but one surrounded by and associated with deep waters.[12]

This idea of colour as an object-centred experience tallies well with various philosophical approaches to perception. Greek and Roman thinkers across a range of philosophical schools frequently described colour (*chrōma* or *color*) as the surface or outside skin of an object, what defined that object and made it visible. In *On the Soul* (2.132), Aristotle pointed out that colour exists only at the surface of an object (ἤπερ καὶ ἔξω χρωματίζεται); for Lucretius (*On the Nature of Things* 4.97), colour lies "in front and on the very outside (*in promptu quoniam est in prima fronte locata*)". The Greek words *chrōma*, *chroia* and *chrōs* appear to have approximated to our sense of "colour" through primary reference to surface, particularly the skin of the body or face, although they were sometimes extended to describe paints, dyes and cosmetics. The Latin word *color* carried similar connotations. The qualities to which these words referred, then, were inextricably bound up with the external and the superficial – the "surface" – and it is here that we can best situate an argument about the synaesthetic properties of ancient colours.[13] Colour in ancient thought operated as a basic index of the world around. It was sometimes described in philosophical circles as the primary object of vision;[14] however, because it was attached so closely to actual *things* in the world, it could mobilize the full range of senses, and this essay will now explore several contexts in which this object-centred experience plays out.

THE WINE-DARK SEA

Homer's wine-dark sea (*oinops pontos*) is perhaps antiquity's best-known colour problem.[15] This is the sea at which the grieving Achilles gazes at the funeral of Patroclus (*Iliad* 23.143), and the sea in which Odysseus loses his ship and men after the killing of the cattle of the sun (*Odyssey* 5.132; 5.221; 7.250; 12.388), and is an epithet used several other times in Homeric verse. Because many of these instances appear to occur at or around sunset, one explanation that has won favour in recent years is that it refers to "sunset-red", but this stubbornly visual interpretation assumes that "red" is straightforwardly transferable from wine (which might be one of several colours) to fiery sunsets. Other interpretations

---

11. On *flauus*, see Bradley (2009: 1–6). *Flauus* cornfields: Tibullus 2.1.48 *deponit flauas annua terra comas*; *flauus* olive leaves: Vergil, *Aeneid* 5.309.
12. Bradley (2009: 9–11). On *caerulea Crete*, see Seneca, *Hercules on Oeta* 1874.
13. For an extended discussion of philosophical definitions of colour, see Bradley (2009: ch. 2).
14. See for example Plato, *Charmides* 167c–d; Aristotle, *On the Soul* 418a27.
15. For a history of this problem, see Rutherford-Dyer (1983).

include the bubbling of fermentation, a shimmering surface similar to that evoked by the equally complex term *porphureos* (see below, pp. 135–8), or even a type of cheap bluish wine akin to the obsolete French "*petit bleu*"/ "*gros bleu*".[16] But all these again rely doggedly on a set of abstract sensory associations. More recently, as discussed above, Michael Clarke has suggested that *oinops* in fact referred to abstract concepts of "wine-dark", "frenzied" or "Dionysiac", and the category's more direct associations with the properties of wine (not just its visual appearance, but also its taste, smell, effects and dangers) contribute a great deal more to the semantics of the lines in which this colour is used than a straightforwardly chromatic interpretation. Achilles is intoxicated with grief and revenge; Odysseus is shipwrecked in waters that are as deep, intense, and treacherous as wine (and that might, at certain times of day, share similar wavelengths); and so on. *Oinops*, inasmuch as we can call it a "colour", appealed to the object as much as what it looked like.

MEDICAL COLOURS

There has been some important work done in recent years, particularly in French scholarship, on the use of colour classification in medical texts from the Hippocratic corpus through to Galen.[17] As well as drawing upon colour terms employed in Greek verse, medical experts would typically use categories derived from everyday objects, such as milk, metals, flower petals, lentils or bran in order to diagnose symptoms and describe the colour of patients' skin, eyes and secretions. Skin that was the colour of whey (*orōdēs*), to take one example, was not only yellowish-white in appearance, but also conjured up the idea of a bumpy texture and perhaps also the characteristic odour of pus.[18] There are also instances of men and women described as having "the colour of a sardine" (τὸ χρῶμα ἀφυῶδες), and the synaesthetic qualities of this category leave little to the imagination.[19] Ancient medical writers in fact plotted out a close relationship between the colours of the human body and the four humours: blood, phlegm, yellow bile and black bile, which for Galen corresponded to the four basic body colours – red, white, yellow and black; these were also, as it happens, characterized by properties of touch (hot–cold, wet–dry), as well as smell.[20]

PHYSIOGNOMIC COLOURS

Third, in a connected branch of science, physiognomic thinkers also drew upon some of these ideas to explain the appearance, character and behaviour of different ethnic

---

16. See Christol (2002).
17. See Villard (2002), esp. chapters by Villard, Boudon and Boehm. I have discussed some aspects of the relationship between medicine and colour in Bradley (2009: 130–5).
18. Hippocrates, *Epidemics* 7.5.9; 7.35.2.
19. See Hippocrates, *De mulierum affectibus* 2.110; 2.116, with Villard (2002: 63).
20. For the complexities of sense perception in Galen, see also Siegel (1970).

types.[21] The effects of physical environment on bodily appearance, and consequently on behaviour, had already been explored in medical texts such as the Hippocratic *Airs, Waters, Places*, and Galen is sometimes credited with integrating a theory of humours with physiognomic characteristics.[22] The category *Aethiops*, for example, described literally a "sun-darkened face" and was regularly used by Romans to evoke a sense of physical and cultural distance in the individuals to whom it was applied. Generally, such a face had been "coloured" (*coloratus*) or "burned" (*ustus*) by the heat of the nearby sun: as Pliny the Elder put it, these people were born with a scorched appearance and curly hair, compared to those in the opposite region of the world who have frosty skin and straight blond hair. Unsurprisingly, Pliny claimed that the Romans in the middle had a well-moderated complexion (*color temperies*).[23] Vitruvius noted the same polarities where colour was an indicator of various different qualities, both aesthetic and moral: the big well-watered northerners whose appearance (*color*) is not drained of moisture and so have a pale complexion, straight red hair and bright blue eyes and a lot of blood, versus the burnt and parched little southerners with their swarthy complexions, curly hair, black eyes and thin blood.[24] Seneca went as far as observing that people who are blond and ruddy-faced are particularly prone to anger, since their blood is thin and stirred up.[25] In these contexts, colour was not just part of the visual spectrum: it was an index of physiological make-up incorporating (as in ancient medical theory) a variety of sensory properties.

One physiognomic colouration that was not normally associated with race or origin, but which was a significant and recurring motif in Roman literature, was the blush. The Latin category "*rubor*", often translated as "redness", was a category of ancient experience inextricably connected to the blush, and all its physiological and moral connotations.[26] *Rubor* was felt as much as it was seen: whether we look at Lavinia's famous blush in the *Aeneid*, the *rubor* of embarrassed lovers in elegiac verse, or the emperor Domitian's *rubor* in the pages of Pliny or Tacitus, this colour is hot and flowing, tangible and uncontrollable.[27] One of Seneca's *Epistles* points out that youths are particularly affected by *rubor* because they have more body heat and a soft exterior; blood is stirred up (*incitatus*) and fluid (*mobilis*) and quickly rushes up into their face.[28] As with the other examples of somatic colour discussed above, *rubor* was imbued with sensory properties beyond the visual domain.

---

21. For an introduction to ancient physiognomy, see Barton (1994: ch. 2); on the relationship between medicine and physiognomy, see Sassi (1993).
22. On Galen and humoral theory in physiognomics, see Evans (1941: 287–96).
23. Pliny, *Natural History* 2.189. Generally on these categories, see Balsdon (1979).
24. Vitriuvius 6.1.3–4.
25. Seneca, *On Anger* 2.19.5.
26. I have discussed "the colour blush" in Bradley (2004).
27. Lavinia: Vergil, *Aeneid* 12.64–71; elegy: Ovid, *Amores* 2.4.33–50; Domitian: Pliny, *Panegyric* 48.4; Tacitus, *Agricola* 45.2.
28. Seneca, *Epistles* 11, with Bradley (2009: 153–4).

PURPLE

Dress was one of the most evocative means by which the ancient body utilized and exhibited colour.[29] By definition, costume colours were derived from synthetic dyes, and so we might perhaps expect that this experience of colour operated exclusively in the visual domain. However, the very dyes and pigments that were used often had olfactory and tactile properties that made the clothes on which they were used part of a versatile multi-sensory experience. Ancient thinkers such as Theophrastus, Vitruvius and Pliny the Elder lay great emphasis on the idea that dyes and pigments, like perfumes, were inherently objects with a range of aesthetic properties and associations, rather than just straightforwardly colours: the author of the *De coloribus* (*On Colours*), for example, made the fundamental claim that all dyed things take their colour from the object that dyes them.[30]

When ancients wore saffron robes (*crocotae*), for instance, they were doing so as much for their smell as for their distinctive colour, and accordingly ancient writers lost no opportunity to flag up associations with flowers and femininity: effeminate Roman noblemen in Ciceronian invective, fragrant women in Ovid's *Art of Love*, or the saffron costumes of the self-castrated eunuch priests of Magna Mater.[31] One of the most odorous of ancient costume-colours was that produced by sea-purple dye (Greek *porphura* or Latin *purpura*), a colour that distinguished the clothes of Persian monarchs, Hellenistic royalty and the formal trappings of Roman *imperium*. This dye, which came in many shades in the red-blue-black range, was well-known for its striking appearance, but also had an array of other properties that caught not only the eyes but also the noses of ancient observers.[32] And some of antiquity's thinkers contemplating "purple" were just as concerned as the authors within this volume about the limitations and ramifications of promoting the aesthetics of vision over all the other senses, and ignoring the manifold qualities and properties of the rich material culture of Greece and Rome.

Pliny the Elder, author of an encyclopedic natural history of the Roman world, provides perhaps the most striking case of this. He began his account of purple in the shoals off the Phoenician Coast in the mid-first century CE: this was where local fishermen made it their daily business to catch thousands of murex snails which made their homes in the shallow reefs off the shore of modern Syria and Lebanon. From the throats of each of these creatures, a small vein would disgorge tiny drops of fluid which for hundreds of

---

29. I thank Cambridge University Press for allowing me to reproduce parts of this section from ch. 7 of my book, *Colour and Meaning in Ancient Rome* (Bradley 2009).
30. *De coloribus* 4 (τὰ δὲ βαπτόμενα πάντα τὰς χρόας ἀπὸ τῶν βαπτόντων λαμβάνει). On the *De coloribus*, see Gottschalk (1964). On Theophrastus, see Baltussen (1998). On Vitruvius' interpretation of purple, see Bradley (2009: 192–3); on Pliny, see *ibid.*, ch. 3.
31. Cicero, *On the Responses of the Soothsayers* 21.44; Ovid, *Art of Love* 3.179; Apuleius, *Metamorphoses* 8.27; Vergil, *Aeneid* 11.762–77; cf. 9.614–7 (on effeminate Trojan invaders in *crocum* and *purpura*). Saffron continues to be a characteristic dress colour for Hare Krishna followers around the world. In general, on Hare Krishna traditions and rituals, see Dwyer & Cole (2007).
32. On the history of purple as a status symbol in antiquity, see Reinhold (1976). For various different approaches to the dye in a wider perspective, see Longo (1998). For its role in the Roman history of colour, see Bradley (2009: ch. 7).

years transformed the elite clothing of Babylonians, Egyptians, Persians, Macedonians and Romans. In spite of the dye's complex political history and deep-seated cultural narratives, Pliny preferred to get back to basics. His account of purple (*purpura* in Latin) forms part of a book of *Natural History* not on pigments or costume arts, but one which examines the sea, a catalogue of marine phenomena and all the ways Roman luxury had exploited them. Pliny's account of purple, then, was a potent reminder of precisely where it was that all those senatorial purple stripes, triumphal garbs and emperors' clothes – those hallmarks of Roman *spectacle* – came from.[33]

Pliny's purple-snail, sharing with the dye the name *purpura*, was an ugly and unpalatable lifeform, nurtured with mud, slime and algae. Pliny tells us (9.132) that fishermen trapped them by leaving baskets of cockles as bait, in which the snails would be snared by their greed (*auiditas*). Just a few sections earlier (9.104), Pliny had deplored the perils of the Roman appetite for seafood – the sea is most harmful to the stomach (*damnosissimum uentri mare est*) – but, he adds, that is nothing compared to the Roman greed for pearls and sea-purple dye. When it comes to greed, at least for Pliny, the purple snail and the purple Roman had much in common. Pliny's *purpura*, then, was a complex organic phenomenon with a life of its own, and a set of moral and behavioural tropes that matched the Romans who set it in such high aesthetic regard. Pliny then describes the production of the dye (133–4) in gruesome detail. The snail's vein was removed, mixed with salt, and boiled until most of the flesh had been deposited. Varying the mixtures and boiling times produced different shades of colour. The highest glory (*summa laus*) goes to that which resembled congealed blood. Another method diluted the dye with human urine to produce "that highly-praised paleness" (*ille laudatus pallor*), which meant the dyers could cheat the saturation process (*saturitas fraudata*) and save money. As an afterthought, Pliny adds that the fleeces devour (*esuriunt*, a particularly strong word) this diluted dye. The snail, the fleece, the dyer and the fashionable Roman – all shared this common greed (*auaritia*). Pliny goes to great lengths to demonstrate that purple was imbued with properties and characteristics that extended far beyond the chromatic.

Pliny interrupts his account of *purpura*, the eastern sea-snail, with an account of *purpura* the Roman colour:

> fasces huic [purpurae] securesque Romanae uiam faciunt, idemque pro maiestate pueritiae est; distinguit ab equite curiam, dis aduocatur placandis, omnemque uestem inluminat, in triumphali miscetur auro. quapropter excusata et purpurae sit insania; sed unde conchyliis pretia, quis uirus graue in fuco, color austerus in glauco et irascenti similis mari?

> [For *purpura*] the rods and axes of Rome clear it a path, and it likewise marks the dignity of boyhood; it distinguishes senator from equestrian and it is summoned to secure the favour of the gods. It illuminates every garment and on the triumphal

---

33. Cf. *De coloribus* 4, which attempts the same thing with "sea-purple" (τὸ ἁλουργές).

robe it is blended with gold. For this reason, even the craze for purpura might be excused – but why the price of purple-shells, with the unhealthy stench in their dye, and their grim colour which resembles a gloomy and angry sea?

(Pliny the Elder, *Natural History* 9.127)

Pliny provocatively alternates between using *purpura* to mean the dress-colour "purple", and *purpura* to mean the snail: to really appreciate the former, one must understand the latter. Earlier, he had prefaced his account of *purpura* (105) with an exclamation of his philosophical frustration: "What connection is there between the sea and our clothing, between the waves and waters and our woollen fabric?" The *Natural History* was a giant demonstration of how one could use perception and sensory categories to classify the world and derive knowledge. Ever since the Pre-Socratics, philosophers had wrangled over the difficult relationship between perception and knowledge – how far we can derive information about the physical world from what we see, hear, smell, taste and touch around us.[34] Some – like Plato – had argued that perception was a dim and unreliable measure of the world, others that perception and knowledge were inseparable (for Platonic "synaesthesia" as an ideal mode of perception, see Rosen, this volume). For Aristotle and the Peripatetics, colours were essentially real things that existed in the physical world. They were the fundamentals of sense perception, signposts containing crucial information about the environment. And it was the prerogative of the educated man to use all his faculties to make sense of that environment. This appears to have remained the dominant approach to perception through the Hellenistic era and into the Roman period, and is a theory deeply embedded in Stoic philosophy.

Pliny's angst, then, is not just that of a conservative on his moral high horse. One of his aims was to reassert and reinstate Aristotelian physics, to demonstrate that traditional epistemology was being undermined by the Roman habit of taking bits of the world – like *purpura* and colourful stones – entirely out of context, and deriving satisfaction from visual aesthetics alone. Just as the principles of food are grasped for eating, Pliny goes on, he will train his readers to have thorough knowledge of the objects that perform such an important aesthetic role in their lives. But *purpura* was dysfunctional: the snail was inedible, the cloth perishable (124), and the dye unpleasant and malodorous (127). Mobilizing taste, touch and smell, the argument goes, can teach you that. Pliny's fundamentalist assessment of purple posed to his elite Roman readers a pertinent rhetorical question: why the obsession? His mission was twofold: first, to reinstate *purpura* categorically as genus shellfish; secondly, to convince the reader that "purple" was not a particularly appropriate aesthetic experience for Roman indulgence.

Other early imperial writers, for similar reasons, were reinstating this connection between colour and shellfish, and the dye's smell was a potent reminder of where it came from. A generation later Martial, satirising contemporary fads for exotic luxuries, described mattresses dipped in strong-smelling Sidonian purple (2.16.3) and, among a

---

34. On the ancient philosophy of perception see Porter, this volume. Bradley (2009: ch. 2) discusses various philosophical approaches to colour perception.

list of typical urban nuisances, clothes smelling of murex dye (*olidae ... uestes murice*, 1.39.32); elsewhere (4.4.6) he ranks double-dyed purple among the foremost foul smells in the city, and one epigram (9.63) jokes that sweaty upper-class women wear purple-dyed garments for their concealing whiff, and not for their colour (*delectatur odore, non colore*). So Martial's witty repartees and Pliny's sharp cultural commentaries were doing the same thing with this dye: both recognized that in the rich material culture of first-century Rome, coloured objects and coloured surfaces were regularly taken out of context and paraded for their abstract visual properties alone.

CONCLUSION

One could point to many other categories of ancient colour that were used to evoke synaesthetic qualities. The category *marmoreus* ("marbled"), for example, was most often used in Latin elegy to describe the necks and limbs of beautiful girls, and evoked the cold, smooth, statuesque qualities of these females as much as it evoked the white colour of marble: so *Ciris* 256: *marmoreum tremebunda pedem ... rettulit intra* (All-trembling, [Scylla] withdrew her "marble-cold" foot within [the robe]).[35] In a different sensory domain, Martial creatively describes the consequences of culinary overindulgence (12.48): gout (*carnifices pedes*, "feet that eat flesh") and a *color sulphureus* (l. 10). The latter expression, where *color* best translates as "complexion", clearly evokes the unhealthy stench as well as the pale colour of sulphur, along with its traditional associations with death (for the relationship between the senses and death in Latin epic, see Walters, this volume). The multi-sensory uses of colour explored in this essay represent just the tip of the iceberg: classical literature contains countless further examples of colour usage, where literary *ekphrasis* playfully explores the connections between visual categories and the olfactory, tactile, gustatory and even auditory properties of the world they describe. This "synaesthetic" approach to ancient perception, then, provides an innovative and far-reaching argument against the traditional claims about the poverty of Greek and Roman colour vision.[36]

The implications of this complex sensory experience of the world are manifold. The ramifications it has for the ancient "spectacle", for example, are significant: whereas the experience of modern spectacles, such as Coronation ceremonies or the inauguration of Olympic Games, is normally dominated by the visual domain (just as our experience of music is increasingly confined to the auditory domain), the ancient spectacle, with its focus on the sophisticated aesthetics of the material world and the precise and systematic identification of features, objects, groups and individuals, was often a multi-sensory

---

35. On *marmoreus* as a category of colour, see Bradley (2006: 5–9).
36. The approach represented by this essay has been primarily literary and philological, although colour might also be explored as an index of materiality in art: see for example Rouveret *et al.* (2006). For a more recent wide-ranging set of approaches to ancient colour, see Carastro (2009).

experience (at least in the educated elite discourse which describes it).[37] In a brilliant description of the procession of new magistrates, senators and people on 1 January to the Temple of Jupiter Capitolinus, Ovid's *Fasti* employs the full range of senses – sight, hearing and smell – to evoke the annual renewal of Roman authority and the reassertion of Roman imperial superiority:

> A happy dawn arises: favour our thoughts and our hearts! Now must good words be spoken on a good day. Let our ears be free of lawsuits, and let mad disputes be banished forthwith; you malicious tongues, cease wagging! Do you see how the air shines with fragrant fires and how Cilician corn crackles on the kindled hearths? The flame with its own gleam beats on the gold of the temples and spreads a flickering light on the shrine's roof. In untouched garments there is a procession to the Tarpeian citadel, and the people themselves are the same colour as the festival. And now the new rods of office lead the way, fresh purple gleams, and the far-seen ivory chair feels new weights. Heifers, unbroken to the yoke, offer their necks to the axe, heifers that the Faliscan grass nourished on their plains. When from his citadel Jupiter looks down on the whole world, nothing that isn't Roman meets his eye. Hail, day of joy, and return forever happier still, day worthy to be cultivated by a people the masters of the world. (Ovid, *Fasti* 1.71–88)

What Ovid presents is a giant synaesthetic experience mobilizing sight, sounds, smells and touch in order to gain a full and complete appreciation of the spectacle (for synaesthetic approaches to the cosmos by a different Latin poet, see Volk, this volume). Alongside the visual – rising dawn, flames, golden temples, magisterial purple, ivory chair, and so on – Ovid integrates the full range of senses: words of cheer; fires that scent (*odoratis*) as well as light up the scene; corn crackling (*sonat*) on the hearths; the gleam (*nitor*) of the altar's flames *beating* (*uerberat*) on the temple's roof; white festival garments (the same colour, Ovid points out, as the lucky *dies candidus* of the 1st January) exhibiting their untouched (*intactis*) state; the ivory chair feeling (*sentit*) the weight of the new magistrates and the unbroken heifers exposing their necks to be struck (*ferienda*).[38] Clearly this is not (as we might have expected) just an assortment of abstract colours and experiences, but a rich and varied appreciation of the precise sights, sounds and smells that reaffirm the Roman people as masters of the world, of "stuff" (*res*), as Ovid puts it.

This essay has surveyed a range of material – from Homeric verse to Greek medicine to blushing brides and smelly clothes. Although it would be going too far to claim that ancient perception was in any technical sense "synaesthetic", we can identify a number of significant (and to us slightly unusual) examples of multi-sensory experience at work in Greco-Roman culture. Colour is something that those of us in the modern West normally attach to sight, but this essay has argued that, because of its close ties to objects in

---

37. I attempted a preliminary comparison of *ekphrasis* surrounding the Queen's Coronation of 1953 with descriptions of the Roman triumph in Bradley (2009: 212–20).
38. On comparable haptic approaches to geography in Herodotus, see Purves, this volume.

the environment rather simply to a part of the spectrum, the ancient colour experience could tap into smell, touch, taste and even sound. For Greeks and Romans, colour was a basic unit of perception, a source of information and knowledge, and a tool for accurately understanding the world around them. It was a primary index for describing an object, a person, a building or a landscape, as well as an evaluative category of "character" and personality. Using a single sense for all this was not always enough.

Although the model of five distinct senses is often credited to Aristotle, he would perhaps have been rather surprised by this accreditation. Aristotle himself developed a much more complex theory of the senses (and one that is not always consistent): at one point, he even suggested that all the senses can be reduced to touch because of the atomic films touching the eye.[39] And we certainly cannot assume in any case that Aristotle's view of the senses tallied with that of other ancient writers and thinkers; as Clements and Telò show in this volume, for example, the genre of ancient comedy represents a rather different approach to the senses. Even today, because it is so difficult to decide what we think a "sense" is, neurologists do not always agree about how many there are: claiming there are five senses is, one might argue, comparable to claiming there are seven colours in the rainbow.[40] The historian of the senses, then, needs to be open-minded and to accept when approaching the ancient world the possibility of system of perception, knowledge and understanding which could be very different from that which we employ in the modern West.

---

39. Aristotle's contribution to the five-sense model has been explored by Sorabji (1971); see also Johansen (1997). See also Porter, this volume.
40. The cultural development of a model of five senses has been explored by Vinge (1975); the ambiguities surrounded this model are persuasively examined by Classen (1993), esp. 2–11.

10

BLINDED BY THE LIGHT: ORATORICAL CLARITY AND POETIC OBSCURITY IN QUINTILIAN

Curtis Dozier

διὸ ποιητικῶς λέγοντες τῇ ἀπρεπείᾳ τὸ γελοῖον
καὶ τὸ ψυχρὸν ἐμποιοῦσι, καὶ τὸ ἀσαφὲς
διὰ τὴν ἀδολεσχίαν· ὅταν γὰρ γιγνώσκοντι
ἐπεμβάλλῃ, διαλύει τὸ σαφὲς τῷ ἐπισκοτεῖν.

Therefore, those who speak poetically in an inappropriate
way create absurdity, frigidity, and obscurity through excessive
long-windedness. For whenever one heaps words on someone
who understands, he destroys clarity by casting a shadow on it.
(Aristotle, *Rhetoric* 1406a32–4)

Que tout fût clair, tout vous semblerait vain.
(Paul Valéry, *Le Philosophe et la Jeune Parque*, 1917)[1]

These opposing attitudes toward poetry – Aristotle's claims that "those who speak poetically in an inappropriate way create ... obscurity" and that such a speaker "destroys clarity by casting a shadow on it", and Valéry's assertion that "if everything had been clear it would have seemed entirely empty to you" – mark out a familiar dichotomy between poetic and non-poetic discourse through visual metaphors (ἀσαφές, σαφές, ἐπισκοτεῖν, *clair*). This dichotomy between the "clear" and the "obscure" is a reflex of the hegemony of the visual in literary criticism that many of the essays in this collection resist. In antiquity this hegemony marked off oratory from poetry:[2] it was Aristotle who made σαφῆ εἶναι,

---

1. Cited by Lausberg (1998: 241, n. 1) in support of the idea that "a certain degree of *obscuritas* is necessary in poetry".
2. Philosophy was often also placed on the obscure side of the equation as Heraclitus' nickname, ὁ σκοτεινός, shows. For rhetorical writers' use of metaphors of darkness to describe philosophers, see Berti (2011). Quintilian also frames his critique of declamation in visual terms: students who "grow old in the shade

"being clear", the primary "virtue of style"[3] while declaring that "the poetic [style] is not appropriate for speech"[4] and rejecting the "excessively poetic" style of the sophists because it "destroys clarity by casting shadows on it" (διαλύει τὸ σαφὲς τῷ ἐπισκοτεῖν).[5] The association of poetry with riddling oracles in hexameters[6] and the allegorists' emphasis on opacity of meaning tended to bolster this divide.[7] If modern poets still feel the need to defend the obscurity of their work, it is in large part because Aristotle's insistence on clarity as a virtue has remained influential.

Yet, as Päivi Mehtonen's history of obscurity shows, the hegemony of the visual has always been partial: there have always been authors and even some critics that favoured obscurity over clarity, the deprivation of sight over visibility.[8] Taking a cue from these authors and critics, this essay examines the limits of the visual, investigating the realm of darkness and blindness in order to explore obscurity's function in ancient rhetorical theory, where the hegemony of the visual is not as complete as Aristotle's insistence on clarity might have us believe. Tracing visual metaphors that are so often taken for granted in rhetorical treatises allows us to see how the apparently simple dichotomies between light and darkness and poetry and oratory break down and blur. Orators whose allegiance to clarity might seem to imply a devotion to transparent transmission of facts must in fact rely as much on darkness as on light in order to win their cases, and the obscurity of poetry can be understood not as a failure of clarity, as the Aristotelian argument would have it, but as a characteristic, even celebrated, feature inherent in that discourse that responded to audiences' authentic desire for darkness.

My investigation focuses on Quintilian's account of clarity in the *The Orator's Education* (*Institutio Oratoria*), because Quintilian, more than perhaps any other ancient critic,[9]

(*umbra*)" of declamatory exercises may come to "fear true conflicts as if they were a kind of sunlight (*sicut quendam solem*)" (*The Orator's Education* 10.5.17).
3. Aristotle, *Rhetoric* 1404b1–2.
4. *Ibid*. 1404b4–5; cf. 1404a28–9: "The style of prose is not the same as that of poetry".
5. *Ibid*. 1406a34 (as quoted earlier); on the "poetic" nature of sophistry see 1406b1 (the styles of Alcidamas and Gorgias are "completely poetical", πάντως ποιητικόν) and 1407b8–11 (Gorgias' metaphors are ἀσαφεῖς and "excessively poetic", ποιητικῶς ἄγαν).
6. *Ibid*. 1407a39 gives the famous oracle that "Croesus, by crossing the river Halys, will destroy a great kingdom" as an example of poetic ἀμφιβολία, "ambiguity", which is a form of obscurity; Quintilian gives an Ennian example at *The Orator's Education* 7.9.6. Plato too may be regarded as, in a sense, treating poetry as obscure, even to the point of meaninglessness: see Porter (1995: 100) "Plato reduced poetry to its intelligibility as an idea and that idea to nothing".
7. On allegorical readings of poetry see Ford (2002: 68ff.) and Struck (2004), esp. 1–20 on the differences between allegorical and rhetorical criticism.
8. Mehtonen (2003). On criticism's ongoing resistance to obscurity, see de Man (1983: 170ff), especially 186: "To claim that modernity is a form of obscurity is to call the oldest, most ingrained characteristics of poetry modern". Alvarez (1961) is an example of a critic sympathetic to obscurity; Jarrell ([1951] 1999: 7–8) accuses an unambitious public of making the assumed obscurity of modern poets an excuse not to read them. Even in antiquity celebrations of obscurity were marginalized: an otherwise unknown Heracleodorus wrote a treatise "on behalf of obscurity" (ὑπὲρ τῆς ἀσαφείας), but the work is only mentioned by the apparently hostile Philodemus. See Porter (1995: 130–31) and Asmis (1995: 167–8, 176–7).
9. Assfahl (1932: 127ff) lists many metaphors of light and darkness in the *The Orator's Education*.

makes explicit the visuality of oratorical metaphors. Like Aristotle, Quintilian privileges clarity above all else, calling it "the highest virtue of oratory" and "the first virtue of eloquence".[10] But whereas Aristotle only rarely makes explicit the visual quality of his concept of clarity,[11] visual metaphors pervade Quintilian's account, as can be observed even in his choice of terms: Quintilian translates Aristotle's σαφηνεία with *perspicuitas*, noun form of a compound of *specio*, "I see", and the corresponding vice of τὸ ἀσαφές with *obscuritas*, which in Latin means "darkness".[12] And Quintilian develops these metaphors almost obsessively, advising, for example, that "it is a great virtue to express our subject clearly (*clare*) and in such a way that it seems to be seen (*cerni videantur*)".[13] He gives an explicitly visual treatment to *enargeia*: he endorses visual translations of the Greek term (*illustratio, evidentia*) while rejecting less visual possibilities (*repraesentatio*, ὑποτύπωσις),[14] and always invokes its visual dimension. Thus *enargeia* "makes us seem not so much to be talking about something as exhibiting it (*ostendere*)"; by *enargeia* "a whole scene is painted (*depingitur*), as it were, in words"; *enargeia* allows the orator to place his subject "before the eyes" (*ante oculos*) of his audience.[15] Quintilian even at times seems to elevate it above the clarity it serves, because while *perspicuitas* is only "plain to see" (*patet*), *enargeia* "shows itself off" (*se ostendit*).[16] When an orator succeeds in creating this vividness, his case "seems to be seen (*cerni*) rather than to be heard (*audiri*)".[17]

Good oratory, it seems, is inherently synaesthetic, because the orator, who in actuality can only make his audience "hear", must make his audience "see".[18] Quintilian insists that

---

10. Quintilian, *The Orator's Education* 1.6.41: [*orationis*] *summa virtus*; 2.3.8: *prima eloquentiae virtus*; cf. also 8.2.22: *nobis prima sit virtus perspicuitas*. Translations from Quintilian are taken, sometimes with modifications for emphasis, from Russell's Loeb edition (Russell 2001); other translations are my own. On Quintilian's somewhat haphazard Aristotelianism see G. A. Kennedy (1993). Quintilian was, of course, not alone in emphasizing the visual aspect of Aristotle's concept: other Latin translations included Cicero's *dilucidus* (Cicero, *On Oratory* 1.144, *Orator* 78) and, from the *Rhetorica ad Herennium*, *explanatio*, which is not itself visual but which is defined (4.17) as that which makes a speech *aperta* and *dilucida*.
11. My epigraph, in which the sophists "cast a shadow" on clarity, is one example. The other example I have found is Aristotle, *Poetics* 24 1460a2–4: "A highly brilliant diction (ἡ λίαν λαμπρὰ λέξις) obscures (ἀποκρύπτει) character and thought".
12. *Specio* is cognate with Greek σκέπτομαι and shares the same root as such visual words as *spectator, spectaculum, speculum*, and *species*. The etymology of *obscuritas* is, for lack of a better word, obscure, but de Vaan (2008) speculates that the Greek σκίρον (the canopy that shaded the priests in certain festivals of Athena) may be a cognate.
13. Quintilian, *The Orator's Education* 8.3.62.
14. Ibid. 6.2.32, endorsing Cicero's terminology. He records *repraesentatio* at 8.3.61 and the Greek term ὑποτύπωσις, with its sculptural metaphor, at 9.2.40. For a survey of ancient sources, see G. Zanker (1981). Birus (2003: 316) discusses the greater prominence of visual metaphors in Roman discussions of *enargeia* than in Greek ones.
15. *Ostendere*: Quintilian, *The Orator's Education* 6.2.32; *depingitur*: 8.3.63; *ante oculos* in the *narratio*: 8.3.81; in the *peroratio*: 6.1.1.
16. Ibid. 8.3.61.
17. Ibid. 9.2.40.
18. See the youthful Cicero's realization that "The ears of the Roman people are rather dull, but their eyes are sharp and keen" (Cicero *For Plancius* 66). It is the orator's job to speak to those eyes, as it were. Moretti (2010) analyses evidence for orators' use of visual props, but Quintilian's description of the orator's speech in visual terms shows that such aids were secondary, conceptually, to the vision of *enargeia*. Other

the sight made possible by *enargeia* is at least as keen that that of an eye-witness: "What more could anyone have seen who had entered the room?"[19] he asks in an analysis of one of Cicero's descriptions of the aftermath of a banquet. Indeed, the orator may even allow the audience to see more than they could had they been present: "Could anyone be so incapable of forming images of things (*concipiendis imaginibus rerum*)", asks Quintilian about one of Cicero's description of Verres, "so as not to feel that he is seeing the persons and the place and the dress and to add some unspoken (*non dicta*) details for himself?"[20] These *non dicta* are what make *enargeia* so powerful, because the orator does not produce them with the sound of his voice but instead leads the audience, who trusts their own perception, to produce them themselves. *Enargeia* can even engage the other senses, as when Cicero makes his audience see, among other things, the "silent loathing" (*tacita adversatio*) for Verres of the citizens of Sicily.[21] Such a detail, because it is *tacita*, cannot be conveyed by the orator's speech; only such vivid description can make an audience recognize it. Similarly Quintilian's example of a particularly vivid description of the sack of a city includes many sounds, including the *fragor* of falling roofs, the *sonus* of many *clamores*, and the *ploratus* of women and children.[22] It is not possible to "see" any of these sounds but, in Quintilian's view, the images the orator can create are the most effective means of conveying such aural experiences.

This is so because, as Quintilian recognizes, audiences equate sight with truth: "anything true (*quid veri*) requires not only to be told but in a sense to be shown" (*ostendendum*). Indeed, the images that the orator creates need not be factually exact: "we shall succeed in making the facts evident (*manifesta*) if they are plausible (*veri similia*); it will even be legitimate to invent (*fingere*) things of the kind that usually occur".[23] For these invented facts to persuade, they must be seen: "A speech does not adequately fulfil its purpose or attain the total domination (*plene dominatur*) it should have if it goes no further than the ears, and the judge feels that he is merely being told the story of the matters he has to decide without their being brought out (*exprimi*) and displayed to his mind's eye" (*oculis mentis ostendi*).[24] *Perspicuitas* is a virtue of style because the control of vision is the source of the orator's power.

Vision depends on light, and the orator's task is to provide his audience with the light to see things as he intends them to. Quintilian specifies the kind of light he expects the orator to provide in his account of how *sententiae* should be used. These pointed maxims were regarded by many ancient critics as a feature of a decadent style, but Quintilian recommends them as long as they are not given excessive prominence, because "they strike the mind, they often knock it over by a single stroke, their very brevity makes them more

---

synaesthetic dimensions of Quintilian's account oratory can be noted: B. Stevens (2008) discusses smell; *The Orator's Education* 12.2.4 refers to the "taste" (*degustarit*) of literature.
19. Quintilian, *The Orator's Education* 8.3.67.
20. Ibid. 8.3.64.
21. Ibid. 8.3.65.
22. Ibid. 8.3.68.
23. Ibid. 8.3.70.
24. Ibid. 8.3.62.

memorable, and the pleasure they give makes them more persuasive".[25] Quintilian distinguishes between the decadent and proper uses of these phrases in terms of the kind of clarity they produce in each case: "although [*sententiae*] seem to glitter and to some extent to stand out (*nitere et aliquatenus exstare videantur*), their brilliance (*lumina*) may be said to resemble not so much a flame as a few sparks flashing amid the smoke (*non flammae sed scintillis inter fumum emicantibus similia*), and indeed they are invisible (*ne apparent quidem*) when the whole speech is bright (*ubi tota lucet oratio*), just as stars cannot be seen in sunlight (*in sole*)".[26] The light that *sententiae* produce in moderation is of a specific type that is useful to the orator: not the overwhelming brilliance of the sun that illuminates everything or even the steady glow of a flame, but a more attenuated, shimmering light, like that of sparks, or, as Quintilian says elsewhere, like that of "certain little insects that look like sparks of fire (*igniculi*) in the dark (*in tenebris*), that shine when there is no sun (*lucent citra solem*)".[27] Such light may not be as strong as the sun but nevertheless has greater power to attract attention to itself, both because it "glitters", and because it "stands out" from the darkness surrounding it. Such glittering light is attractive because it avoids monotony, which is itself characterized as an improper use of vision: it arises when "everything is of one color" (*tota unius coloris*).[28]

The varied interplay of light and darkness that *sententiae* create confers a further benefit on a speech. Crucially, they do not illuminate all aspects of the case but leave some shrouded in "smoke" or in the darkness of night, and this is exactly as the orator wants it: he does not want his audience to see everything, only what he wants them to see. Thus when Quintilian calls these maxims *lumina*, "highlights", and praises them as "the eyes of eloquence" (*oculos eloquentiae*), he recognizes their power to provide the kind of limited light that the orator needs. He continues, "but I do not want there to be eyes all over the body, lest the other organs lose their function".[29] Too many eyes provide too many points of view; too many *lumina* illuminate aspects of the case that the orator would prefer to be left in darkness. The orator's task is not to eliminate all shadow or to illuminate everything but rather to manage what is illuminated and what is obscured. Quintilian compares this to the visual art of painting where "nothing stands out except against a surrounding background" and where figures must be separated "so that no shadows fall upon the bodies".[30] In such a painting shadows are present, even necessary, but are managed in a way that supports the speaker's argument. Oratorical clarity depends on the presence of darkness.

Indeed, the orator must be a master of light and vision because of the nature of his work. "When the facts are plain" (*in rebus apertis*), says Quintilian, there is no need for rhetoric

---

25. *Ibid.* 12.10.48; criticism of *sententiae*: Seneca, *Controversiae* 1.pr.10, 1.pr.22, Tacitus, *Dialogue on Orators* 35.5, Petronius 3 (this last probably parodying such authorities).
26. Quintilian, *The Orator's Education* 8.5.29. Tellegen-Couperus (2003) discusses the persuasive force of one of Quintilian's examples of a "sparkling" (*clarescit*) *sententiae* in the context of the case in which it was used.
27. Quintilian, *The Orator's Education* 12.10.76.
28. *Ibid.* 8.3.52. The Greek term for monotony is ὁμοείδεια.
29. *Ibid.* 8.5.34.
30. *Ibid.* 8.5.26.

any more than there is need "to bring a lamp into bright sunlight" (*in clarissimum solem mortale lumen inferre*).[31] In such situations there is an abundance of light and everyone sees things in the same way.[32] More often, however, the facts are not *aperta* and can be seen and interpreted in many different ways. It is in these cases, which Quintilian tellingly calls "obscure",[33] that oratory becomes necessary. The orator uses light in the way that he does because he works in the dark. Thus when Quintilian rejects the claim that "the truth" (*veritas*) must sometimes be "obscured" (*obscuranda*) and urges his students instead to make their case "as vivid as possible" (*quam evidentissima*),[34] he does not mean that they should allow their audiences to see everything. Rather, he means that the orator should shine a light on *veritas* as he wants them to see it and to leave everything else cloaked in shadow.[35]

The proper amount and type of light, applied in the proper places, ensures oratorical success. "If we say no less and no more than we ought, and avoid disorder and indistinctness (*inordinata aut indistincta*), things will be clear and obvious (*dilucida et aperta*) even to an inattentive audience."[36] Saying "less than we ought" means bringing insufficient light, saying "more" means revealing too much; the proper amount of light ensures that even those who are not paying attention see things as the orator wants them to. This is especially true of the judge, who Quintilian says should not be expected "to dispel obscurities (*obscuritatem discutiat*) by himself and bring light (*lumen*) from his own understanding (*sua intellegentia*) to bear on the dark places (*tenebris*) of a speech". These comments are directed at an inattentive judge, but in a sense the orator does not want any judge, attentive or negligent, to "dispel obscurities himself", because the judge who does so is shining his own *lumen* into the *tenebrae* that the orator aims to conceal; rather, Quintilian says, we want our case to be "so clear (*tam clara*) that our words (*verba*) make their way into his mind, like sunlight into the eyes (*ut sol in oculos*), without his attention being directed to them".[37] The sun is the source of all light, but also, if looked at directly, can blind the viewer, and both connotations are operative in Quintilian's comment. Just as the orator deploys *sententiae* in imitation of the stars rather than in imitation of the sun, the orator prefers limited vision to the all-encompassing light of broad daylight. It is, however, in his interest that the judge believe that he is seeing everything, because then he will not feel the need to direct his vision anywhere else. The judge is thus blinded to the limitations of his own sight. In the best case, Quintilian implies, the images presented by the orator are

---

31. Ibid. 5.12.8; Quintilian calls the lamp *mortale lumen*; perhaps calling the "light" of rhetoric *mortalis* (the expression is not easily paralleled) in contrast to the light of the sun conveys some recognition of the imperfect practicality that governs rhetorical "sight".
32. Cf. ibid. 7.2.4 where facts "perceived by the eyes, not by arguments" do not require the use of *coniecturae* and other techniques of *inventio*.
33. Ibid. 4.1.40; cf. 4.4.4.
34. Ibid. 4.2.64–65.
35. Cf. ibid. 2.1721: "When Cicero boasted that he had cast a cloud of darkness (*tenebras offudisse*) over the eyes of the jury, in the case of Cluentius, he saw clearly enough himself."
36. Ibid. 8.2.23
37. Ibid. 8.2.23.

so vivid and so apparently clear that the judge will not even recognize the language – the *verba* – out of which they are constructed.

By limiting the judge's sight, the orator limits his inclination and ability to "bring light from his own understanding (*sua intellegentia*) to bear on the dark places of a speech". A fragment from Suetonius' *Pratum* helps us understand why the orator wants to inhibit this "understanding". Suetonius, distinguishing *sensus* from *intellectus*, writes that "*sensus* is *naturalis* but *intellectus* relates to *obscuris rebus*".[38] That is, *intellectus* is the faculty that is useful in the dark, when *sensus* – which includes sight – fails. If the orator has accomplished his task, the judge does not know where light and obscurity lie but feels that he is seeing with the complete light of the sun even though he is surrounded by shadows; if he were to engage his *intellegentia* he might start discovering things that the orator wants to suppress. "The thing to aim at is not that he should be able to understand but that he should not at all be able not to understand" (*non ut intellegere possit sed ne omnino possit non intellegere*).[39] This is a subtle but crucial distinction: in the first half of Quintilian's *sententia* the judge, as the subject of *possit*, controls his *intellectus*, but in the second half the judge's sense of control is illusory: he is still the subject of *possit* but he is able to understand only what the orator wants him to understand. However many *obscuritates* a case might have, it is up to the orator to ensure that the judge does not see them and hence is not empowered to try to understand them.

The orator's tools for limiting his audience's *intellectus* are, in large part, the devices of poetry, which is potentially surprising in a text that declares that "the biggest mistake is made by those who believe that everything is appropriate in prose which is permitted to the poets".[40] This commonplace, found as early as Isocrates (*Evagoras* 9), seems to define a hard line between poetry and oratory, a line which derives from the orator's aim of clarity and poets' love of obscurity. Certainly Quintilian's caricatures of those who take *obscuritas* too far point towards the danger of using poetic devices in speeches. These include the man who, in his archaizing zeal, "hunts through the records of the *pontifices*, ancient treaties, and obsolete authors, deliberately seeking unintelligibility (*quod non intellegatur*)"[41] or those who imitate the *Saliorum carmina* that were so obscure that they were "adequately understood (*intellecta*) not even by their own priests".[42] The obscurity referred to here is the obscurity that is characteristic of poetry, whether explicitly, since the Salian hymn is a *carmen*, or implicitly, since the *exoleti auctores* of the past certainly included the early Latin poets.

Elsewhere Quintilian makes the connection between poetry and reduced *intellectus* even more explicit: "we borrow figures and metaphors from the most decadent (*corruptissimo*) of poets and take it that the unique sign of genius is needing a genius to understand

---

38. Suetonius, *Pratum* fr. 176, line 177 (ed. Reifferscheid); *sensum et intellectum: sensus naturalis est, intellectus <exercetur> in rebus obscuris* (*exercetur* is an editorial addition).
39. Quintilian, *The Orator's Education* 8.2.24
40. Ibid. 8.6.17; cf. 10.1.28: "The orator should not follow the poet in everything".
41. Ibid. 8.2.12.; at 8.3.25 Quintilian refers to archaic words taken *ex ultimis tenebris*.
42. Ibid. 1.6.40.

us (*ad intellegendos nos*)".⁴³ But in fact Quintilian's warnings against poetic devices need to be balanced against his endorsements of them. For example Quintilian recommends that his students use metaphors because they "often confer a great amount of light", "shine by their own light however splendid the context", and have the power "to place things before our eyes"; the most exemplary speeches of Demosthenes "sparkle" (*nitet*) with them.⁴⁴ *Nitere* is the same verb that Quintilian used to describe the "glitter" of *sententiae*; metaphors thus provide the kind of light the orator depends on, the kind that directs his audience's vision where he wants it to go. But Quintilian also warns that "while moderate and timely use of metaphor brightens (*inlustrat*) a style, frequent use of it leads to obscurity (*obscurat*) and tedium, and its continuous application ends up as allegory and *aenigma*".⁴⁵ Metaphors are a source of both light and darkness, and are thus perfect for use by orators who need to be able to control both. The same can be said of similes, which are "excellent for shedding light on facts" (*ad inferendam rebus lucem*) and "are devised for making pictures of things" (*ad exprimendam rerum imaginem compositae*), even though "we should leave to the poets" similes that "illustrate the obvious by the mysterious" (*occultis aperta demonstret*).⁴⁶ Quintilian urges his students to avoid archaic words taken "from the darkest recesses of the past" (*ex ultimis tenebris*)⁴⁷ but also sees a role for archaism in a speech, recommending words that "shine more pleasingly with age" (*vetustate ipsa gratius nitent*);⁴⁸ the orator should avoid words that "hide" (*latent*) in favour of those that are "discovered by their own light" (*cernuntur suo lumine*).⁴⁹ Just as the line between clarity and obscurity is not as sharp in oratory as is often assumed, the line between oratory itself and poetry admits, as it were, several shades of gray.

Quintilian's general term for poetic devices used in oratory is *lumina orationis*, "highlights of style", a metaphor that itself conveys his approval of their usefulness in controlling

---

43. Ibid. 8.pr.25
44. Ibid. 5.14.34, 8.6.4, 8.6.19, 12.10.24.
45. Ibid. 8.6.14. Quintilian elsewhere (8.6.52) defines these *aenigmata* as "too obscure (*obscurior*) an allegory" and declares that such riddling allegories are a fault in oratory, "but the poets use them". His example is Vergil *Eclogues* 3.104, which puzzled readers as early as Servius. For the rhetoricians' concept of allegory, which differed from that of the allegorists themselves, see Boys-Stones (2003).
46. Quintilian, *The Orator's Education* 8.3.73; such similes emphasize "any obscure (*obscurum*) or unknown (*ignotum*) feature in the subject chosen". This ambivalence between oratorical use and poetic use recurs in many places where Quintilian discusses poetic devices, and even though he does not use visual terminology we should probably see the same principle at work. 8.6.20: "poets have more scope for synecdoche than orators;" 8.6.24-25: Metonymies such as *Liber* for "wine" and *Ceres* for "bread" are "too bold for the seriousness of the courts"; the bold metonymy of Vergil *Aeneid* 2.311–12 (*iam proximus ardet Ucalegon*, where Ucalegon stands for his house) "would hardly be ventured except by a poet". 8.6.29–30: *antonomasia* (periphrastic description) is *frequentissima* in poets but has only *rarus usus* in orators. 8.6.34-5: the poets use *catachresis* (use of words far beyond their proper meanings) even when a perfectly good word is available.
47. Ibid. 8.3.25.
48. Ibid. 8.3.25.
49. Ibid. 8.pr.21.

light and vision.[50] Quintilian took this phrase from Cicero, who in his *Orator* declares that such *lumina* improve a speech because "they provide great *ornatus* to oratory".[51] *Ornatus*, which means something like "decoration" or "embellishment", is Cicero's translation of the fourth virtue of style that Aristotle's successor Theophrastus is supposed to have added to the list of the three other virtues implicit in Aristotle's *Rhetoric*: correctness, appropriateness and, of course, clarity.[52] We do not know what Theophrastus called this virtue,[53] but the Latin word *ornatus* itself contains a visual metaphor. It is derived from the verb *ornare*, whose meaning by Quintilian's time had narrowed from "to equip" to "to adorn".[54] This verb in turn is derived from *ordo*, "row", another visual word that often refers to "rows of plants or trees",[55] and Quintilian himself compares the proper use of stylistic *ornatus* to trees planted in a *quincunx* pattern: "whichever way you look (*spectaveris*), it is in straight lines".[56] His endorsement of *ornatus* is couched in visual terms: "I disagree with those who believe that arguments should always be expressed in language which is pure, lucid, and distinct (*purus, dilucidus, distinctus*) but not elevated or ornate (*minime elatus ornatoque*) … if the subject is a grander one I do not think that any ornament (*ornatus*), so long as it does not lead to obscurity (*obscuret*), should be denied it".[57] Language that is merely *purus* and *dilucidus* runs the risk of being *too* clear, of not allowing the orator to control what his audience sees; a clarity attenuated by *ornatus* is far more likely to result in the interplay of light and darkness that will enable him to win his case.

Ornatus is also, in a sense, the most "visible" aspect of oratory: while other aspects of rhetorical skill should, as Quintilian says, be "concealed" in order to be effective (*occultantur ut artes sint*), *ornatus* only functions if it is visible, that is, if its weapons "shine forth" (*[arma] fulgentia*).[58] All of this is in line with the orator's goal of controlling vision. Indeed the weaponry of *ornatus* provides precisely the kind of coercive light that the orator needs to win his case: the sword of *ornatus* is not only useful for cutting but "strikes terror also to the eye; even lightning would not dismay us so much if it was only the force we feared,

---

50. See, e.g. *ibid.* 9.2.2 "all *lumina* … are valuable features of oratory to the point that one cannot really conceive of oratory without them." At 8.6.7 Quintilian cites *lumina orationis* as a particularly effective metaphor.
51. Cicero, *Orator* 134, quoted by Quintilian at *The Orator's Education* 9.1.37.
52. Theophrastus' work is fragmentary; Cicero *Orator* 79 is our source for his canon of virtues and his addition of *ornatus* to Aristotle's three.
53. κόσμος and κατασκευή have both been suggested (Fortenbaugh 1995: 268). I would be inclined to favour the former given its more obviously visual nature. The term *ornatus* in its Theophrastan sense comes from Cicero *Orator* 79 where Theophrastus' canonization of the virtues is described.
54. De Vaan (2008) s.v. *ordo*.
55. *OLD* s.v. *ordo*.
56. Quintilian, *The Orator's Education* 8.3.9. Several ancient writers refer to the *ordines* of the *quincunx*.
57. *Ibid.* 5.14.33–4. The very structure of Quintilian's work reflects the tension between *perspicuitas* and *ornatus*: the former is treated in *The Orator's Education* 8.2 and the latter in 8.3; furthermore Quintilian explicitly likens his approach to *ornatus* to his approach to *perspicuitas*: *tam ornatus quam perspicuitas* (8.3.15).
58. *Ibid.* 8.3.2; elsewhere (8.pr.28) Quintilian advises the orator that practice is necessary to keep his skills "always ready at hand (*in promptu*) and in full view (*ante oculos*)".

and not the flash (*fulgor*) as well".⁵⁹ But *ornatus*' visibility also has another side which can undermine the orator's authority. In Roman elegy *ornatus* refers to the cosmetics and finery of the *puella*, and Quintilian invokes this metaphor when he warns that a speaker's stylistic *cultus*, which is a synonym for *ornatus*,⁶⁰ should not be *muliebris* or *luxuriosus*, "effeminate or indulgent", because such clothing does not "adorn" (*exornat*) its wearer but "uncovers" (*detegit*) him; he goes on to call such a style "translucent and multicolored" (*translucida et versicolor*).⁶¹ The effeminacy that Quintilian describes is entirely at odds with the autonomy required of Roman men,⁶² but the visual metaphors Quintilian uses give another dimension to this danger. If the orator aims to paint a picture for his audience that is so vivid that they do not realize what that same image conceals, the last thing he wants is to make that process "transparent" or to "uncover" his technique in the way that a woman's transparent and eye-catching attire attracts scrutiny to her: *occultae artes* are what win cases.⁶³ The proper use of *ornatus* directs the audience's gaze where the orator wants it to go; the improper use directs the audience's gaze onto the orator himself.

This self-display is connected to the kind of obscurity that Quintilian wants his orator to avoid. "Expressions which reveal the trouble they have cost (*curam fatentur*), and strive to seem artificial and contrived (*ficta atque composita videri etiam volunt*) fail to achieve elegance and at the same time lose credibility (*fides*), to say nothing of the fact that they cast a shadow over the sense (*sensus obumbrant*)."⁶⁴ Such a style does everything that the orator wants to avoid: it "confesses" its technique, the very thing the orator wants to conceal; it "wants" to appear to be *ficta* whereas the orator wants his *ficta* to appear plausible; the *fides* that such a style gives up is the very thing that the orator needs for persuasion. In this context "casting a shadow over the sense" means casting shadows haphazardly where they do not belong and where they work against the control of light and vision that is essential to the orator's success. Hence Quintilian's revulsion at the teacher who supposedly "told his pupils to obscure (*obscurare*) what they were saying" by exhorting them with the Greek imperative σκότισον, "Darken it!"⁶⁵ From Quintilian's point of view this teacher has fundamentally misunderstood the function of darkness in oratory: whereas Quintilian knows that the orator relies on darkness as a background against which he can highlight what he wants, this teacher has made darkness an end in itself. He and his students, in Quintilian's view, have been "seduced by the appearance of brilliance" (*ducti*

---

59. *Ibid.* 8.3.5. Elsewhere (10.1.30) this *fulgor* is said to apply to "the mind at the same time as the sight". The metaphor here is of a weapon grazing a foe (*mens simulque visus perstringitur*).
60. E.g. at *ibid.* 8.3.2 and 8.3.61. Further references at Lausberg (1998: §455). See also the similar sentiment at 8.3.7 where *ornatus* should not "favor the false coloring (*ementitus color*) of cosmetics but must shine (*niteat*) with health and vigor".
61. Quintilian, *The Orator's Education* 8.pr.20.
62. Gleason (1995), Richlin (1997), Gunderson (2000), and for a survey, J. Connolly (2007).
63. *Ibid.* 12.9.3 and 12.9.5: "artifices and stratagems, and anything that cannot survive discovery should be kept hidden (*lateant*)".
64. *Ibid.* 8.pr.23.
65. *Ibid.* 8.2.18.

specie nitoris);⁶⁶ their trust in their own powers of sight is misplaced, as they pursue not true clarity but a mere *species* of it in their belief that the orator's goal is merely to dazzle, not necessarily to win.

The poet's goal, however, is precisely this, to dazzle: Quintilian calls poetry a "type [of language] designed for display (*ostentatio*)".⁶⁷ The traditional dichotomy of oratory and poetry, clarity and obscurity, is thus further complicated because while oratory, in spite of its claimed commitment to clarity, attempts to conceal, poetry makes visible the very devices designed to impede critical sight. This paradoxical quality of poetry – that of making its obscurity visible – is implicit in Quintilian's critique of speakers' reasons for imitating "corrupt" poets: "they take it that the unique sign of genius is needing a genius to understand us (*ad intellegendos nos*)".⁶⁸ Such speakers strive to challenge their audience's *intellectus*, the very faculty that the orator, as I have shown, is trying to suppress. Quintilian objects to this kind of oratory because it invites an audience to do the very thing that the orator tries to stop them from doing, to "bring light (*lumen*) from their own understanding (*sua intellegentia*) to bear on the dark places (*tenebris*) of a speech".⁶⁹ But poets, with their unrestrained use of metaphor, simile, and all the other devices of obscurity, do this as a matter of course. And Quintilian implies that audiences were eager for this kind of challenge. Commenting on the *occulti sensus*, "hidden meanings" that some orators embed in their speeches, he laments that "the conviction has become widespread that nothing is elegant or refined unless it needs interpreting (*interpretandum*)" and expresses disdain for audiences who "enjoy these things because they delight in their own cleverness (*acumine suo delectantur*) when they understand (*intellexerunt*) them, and rejoice (*gaudent*) as if they had not so much heard them as thought of them for themselves".⁷⁰ This pleasure (*delectantur, gaudent*) invites audiences to engage their *intellectus* – again, the very faculty that orators are trying to suppress – and so puts such a style directly at odds with that which Quintilian advocates. This pleasurable style is a poetic style. Poetry is a discourse, Quintilian says, that aims "exclusively at pleasure",⁷¹ as well as one that "needs interpreting" (*interpretandum*): the *grammatici* who taught young Romans how to read poetry were known as *poetarum interpretes*⁷² and Quintilian has young students learn to "interpret" (*interpretari*) the words of poets before they paraphrase them in their *progymnasmata*.⁷³ "How faulty", exclaims Quintilian, "oratory would be (since its basic virtue is *perspicuitas*) if it needed an interpreter (*interpres*)!"⁷⁴ Such oratory is "faulty" in that it does the very

---

66. *Ibid.* 8.2.17.
67. *Ibid.* 10.1.28.
68. *Ibid.* 8.pr.25.
69. *Ibid.* 8.2.23, discussed above.
70. *Ibid.* 8.2.21.
71. *Ibid.* 10.1.28: *solam petit voluptatem*.
72. Suetonius, *Lives of Grammarians and Rhetoricians* 4.2; cf. Cicero, *On Oratory* 1.187: *in grammaticis ... verborum interpretatio*.
73. Quintilian, *The Orator's Education* 1.9.2. Cicero, *On Divination* 1.34 compares divination to *interpretatio poetarum*.
74. Quintilian, *The Orator's Education* 1.6.41.

things that poetry tries to do and that oratory tries to avoid, namely inviting interpretation and engaging *intellectus*.

Modern critics tend to call only certain ancient poets "obscure": in Greek, for example, Pindar and Lycophron; in Latin, Persius and Propertius.[75] But Quintilian's account of the obscurity of poets tells a different story, namely that ancient audiences expected obscurity in all their poets (at least, in any poet that employed metaphor or any other figured language), not just in a select few whom our critical assumptions deem obscure. In fact, many of his examples of obscurity are taken from Vergil, one of the poets least likely to be designated as such in modern times.[76] Writing about the kind of obscurity that can arise in "the structure and development of a sentence", that is, from syntax, Quintilian gives an example from the *Aeneid*, citing a description of the rocks on which the Trojan fleet is dashed, *saxa vocant Itali mediis quae in fluctibus aras*,[77] which he calls a "tangle of words" (*mixtura verborum*). He then turns to a passage from the *Georgics* where Vergil interrupts a description of a horse's response to noise with an evaluation of the different colours of horses;[78] when poets use such "parentheses", "*intellectus* is often impeded". In his study of the role of obscurity throughout the reception of Pindar, John Hamilton argues that obscurity needs to be seen as more than "merely a moment toward some elucidation or ultimate clarification".[79] This is true, in my view, of all ancient poets.

A further example from Quintilian gives some idea of what function unelucidated obscurity might have had for the ancient Romans. Drawing on the names and style of comic dialogue (rarely any critic's example of obscurity), Quintilian illustrates the *ambiguitas* possible in indirect statement: *Chremetem audivi percusisse Demean*, either "I heard that Chremes struck Demas", or "I heard that Demeas struck Chremes".[80] Like Vergil's aside about horse colouration, this kind of sentence "makes *intellectus* uncertain". This is not, however, the kind of obscurity that is useful for the orator because it results not in a vivid picture, however contrived, but in a multiplicity of possible interpretations of the very sort the orator wants to avoid: while leaving the audience in the dark about whether it was Chremes who struck Demeas or the other way around might be extremely useful for a comic poet seeking to play on such ambiguity, in a court of law it is imperative that the orator indicate clearly who struck first.

This difference between how orators and poets use darkness points to a fundamentally different conception of the role of the audience in the production of meaning. I would

---

75. On Pindaric obscurity, see Hamilton (2003). Lycophron's obscurity was first noted by Statius (*Silvae* 5.3.157, *latebrae Lycophronis atri*). For Persius, see Powell (1992), whose attempt to determine whether Persius was obscure to his original audience ignores, unlike Reckford (1962), the possibility that his original audience expected and enjoyed obscurity in Persius and all other poets. Butrica (1997: 178–81) shows how debates about how to edit Propertius turn on editors' positions on the poet's obscurity.
76. Ancient critics such as Servius were much more tuned into Vergilian obscurity. See Hexter (1990) and Starr (2001: 445 n.61).
77. Vergil, *Aeneid* 1.109.
78. Vergil, *Georgics* 3.79–84.
79. Hamilton (2003: 7).
80. Ribbeck makes this, and the similar example at 7.9.10, fragment 10 of the *fragmenta ex incertis incertorum fabulis* but comments (rightly, in my view) *fortasse fictum exemplum est*.

suggest, in fact, that the appeal of poetry to Roman audiences derived from the way its obscurity invites the audience to make up its own mind. Quintilian praises poetry because it has the power to "refresh the ears (*aures*) after the *asperitas* of the *forum*".[81] He focuses on the ears not because, as is often claimed, Latin poetry was composed to be heard,[82] but because in the *forum* one is always being told where and how to look; vision is the sense by which an orator dominates his audience. It is often argued that modern poets' penchant for obscurity derives from "the disintegration of the great (social, religious) systems of meaning and the increasing fragility of the *sensus communis*" in the modern period.[83] But in ancient Rome poetic obscurity found an audience not because the "great system of meaning" – oratory – disintegrated, but because oratory, and its meticulous control of vision, was so dominant. The pleasures of poetry in such a culture derive from the relief that eyes weary from orators' assault find in poetry's darkness, which, by making a multiplicity of interpretations possible, empowers, rather than dominates, the reader.[84]

---

81. Quintilian, *The Orator's Education* 1.8.11.
82. Parker (2009) offers a vigorous refutation of this commonly held view.
83. Mehtonen (2003: 22).
84. Thanks to Rob Brown, Shane Butler, Carolyn Dewald, Emily Dozier, Rachel Friedman, Sean Keilen, Rachel Kitzenger, Bert Lott, Barbara Olsen, Brian Walters, and the two anonymous readers for their assistance in revising this paper.

11

THE SENSE OF A POEM: *OVIDS BANQUET OF SENCE* (1595)

Sean Keilen

They will get it straight one day at the Sorbonne
We shall return at twilight from the lecture
Pleased that the irrational is rational,

Until flicked by feeling
        (W. Stevens 1990: "Notes toward a Supreme Fiction", III.x. 16–19)

Philosophy has always been ambivalent about the senses. Its doubts begin with Plato, who makes fun of people who take pleasure in the sound of music, or in the colours and shapes of spectacles, while failing to grasp the nature of beauty itself (Plato *Republic*[1] 474d–477b).[2] Plato's distinction between these *philodoxoi*, who relish appearances and love opinion, and philosophers, who go beyond perception in order to know the essence of things, lays some of the groundwork for the separation of rational minds and sensitive bodies in the pages of Descartes. The Cartesian argument that that we know that we exist because we think – and not because we see, hear, smell, taste and touch – is one of philosophy's most audacious efforts to establish that its methods for finding out the truth are intrinsically superior to the organs of perception that mediate experience and make life meaningful, whether one is a philosopher or not (Descartes 2008: 28). According to the tradition that starts with Plato and reaches a point of lasting influence in Descartes, sense perception is an obstacle that the intellect must remove in its quixotic pursuit of innocent knowledge.

Montaigne, ever mindful of the flaws and limits of his own body, argues in a similar vein that the senses are "the ultimate frontiers of our perception" and "the ultimate boundary of our faculty of knowledge", and furthermore, that it is in our nature that "nothing reaches us except as altered and falsified by [them]" (Montaigne 1991: 664–5, 678). Emerson

---

1. Griffith's translation of Plato's *Republic* (Griffith & Ferrari).
2. I am grateful to Ralph Rosen for alerting me these passages. For an extensive discussion of Plato's comparison of *philodoxoi* and philosophers, in relation to the senses, see Rosen's chapter in this volume.

concurs with Montaigne, writing that "inevitably does the universe wear our colour, and every object fall successively into the subject itself" (Emerson 2003: 307). But whereas Cartesian thought reacts to the intractability of the senses by renewing its commitment to free the thinking mind from the feeling body, Montaigne and Emerson embrace the senses as untranscendable contexts for all the experiences that we have and for every judgment that we make about their meaning. For Montaigne, every man "can see only with his own eyes, grip only with his own grasp", while for Emerson, "our constitutional necessity [to see] things under private aspects" is further evidence that we must accept our sense impressions in a spirit of "self-trust", "hold hard to this poverty, however scandalous" and "by more vigorous self-recoveries, after sallies of action, possess our axis more firmly" (Montaigne 1991: 683; Emerson 2003: 308). In other words, the only knowledge that we can have, about ourselves or anything else, comes through the senses that make us human rather than divine, and without them, we would not be who we are or understand anything at all. "[W]e do not see directly, but mediately", writes Emerson, and "we have no means of correcting these colored and distorting lenses which we are" (Emerson 2003: 304). What is true of life is also true of art. As Geoffrey Hartman puts it, writing specifically of literature: "Books are our second Fall, a reenactment of a seduction that it also a coming into knowledge" (Hartman 2007: 21).

Philosophy imparts its ancient ambivalence about the senses to the scholarly disciplines that take it as a model for inquiry, but suppose that Roland Barthes is right and knowledge is itself *"delicious"* (Barthes 1975: 23). The word "aesthetic" comes down to English from the Greek *aesthesis* (perception or sensation). Works of art, as collaborations between perception and matter, appeal directly to our sensitivities. In turn, their meaning depends upon our capacity to share the sensory experiences that they offer. It is therefore somewhat surprising that Susan Sontag should have written that "[w]hat is important now is to recover our senses ... We must learn to see more, to hear more, to *feel* more" (Sontag 2001: 14). Apart from becoming insensate, how could one see, hear or feel *less*?

A philosophical aversion to sensation would appear to frustrate the very discoveries that artworks allow us to make about ourselves, the world, and them, but for the disciplines that study art, this aversion is a bid for authority in academic institutions that value subjective experience less highly than objective knowledge, and the humanities and fine arts much less than the natural sciences. My discipline, English, tends to assume that the senses are too subjective to be objective, and that assumption goes hand in hand with the discipline's history of trying to persuade its critics that the study of English literature has more in common with science than with art; that it is scholarly, not amateurish; and that English professors are not merely imaginative or opinionated or sensitive, but knowledgeable. Writing of the relatively new discipline, during the period between the World Wars, Albert Feuillerat, a professor at Yale, explains that the status of English in Anglo-American universities is directly related to its success in distinguishing itself from impressionistic styles of interpretation, associated with Romantic poets, Oscar Wilde and Walter Pater. The "necessity of bringing criticism into closer contact with scientific methods of research", and of proving its superiority to "inductive analysis" and "the haphazard inspirations of mere subjectivism", means that English professors have been obliged to "refrain from enjoying [literary works]", to "break away from the literary attitude of mind" and to bring themselves to "the point of losing all contact with literary matter". The "beauty, the artistic value of the works, no longer appeal to us", writes Feuillerat; "in fact, those things have disappeared from our purview" (Feuillerat 1925: 312, 314–15).

Feuillerat's essay betrays a certain nostalgia for "aesthetic criticism", but it is not a plea that literary scholarship should be aestheticizing. On the contrary, although he regrets the discipline's deliberate insensitivity to literature, he doubts that feelings lead to knowledge: "There never was any school founded upon aesthetics which built safely and permanently, for the definitions of the beautiful and the artistic are too elusive and changeable" (*ibid.*: 319). Other writers in this period make a different case about the relationship between the senses and interpretation, a case drawn from the experience of literature itself. Joel Elias Spingarn, a professor at Columbia, argues that the function of literary critics is to "have sensations in the presence of a work of art and to express them" – making new works of art that take their place alongside their models (Spingarn 1917: 5). I. A. Richards announces a "theory of Beauty *par excellence*", called "Synaesthesis", according to which "we become more fully ourselves the more our impulses are engaged" by works of art ("impulse" is Richards's term of art for sense perceptions and the feelings that arise from them as they are incorporated into consciousness; Richards *et al.* 1925: 7, 78). Virginia Woolf echoes both Spingarn and Richards when she writes that every reader must seek "to receive impressions with the utmost understanding" before passing judgement on them (Woolf 1987). From her perspective, readers have to follow their own instincts with texts, because "even if the results are abhorrent and our judgments wrong, still our taste, the nerve of sensation that sends shocks through us, is our chief illuminant; we learn through feeling; we cannot suppress our own idiosyncrasy without impoverishing it" (Woolf 1986: 268).

It is perhaps unsurprising that none of these arguments succeeded in overcoming academic doubts about the senses, or the specific anxieties that English has about its stature among scientific disciplines. However, it does surprise me that the final defeat of aesthetic and impressionistic styles of criticism, as legitimate scholarly pursuits, came at the hands of the New Critics, for whom literature is, above all, an aesthetic object. "The report of some readers that a poem or story induces in them vivid images, intense feelings, or heightened consciousness is neither anything which can be refuted nor anything which it is possible for the objective critic to take into account." This essay, by W. K. Wimsatt, marks virtually the last time that anyone in an English department took the claims of subjective experience seriously enough to go to the trouble of refuting them. "The purely affective report is either too physiological or too vague" (Wimsatt 1954: 32). But whom, apart from English professors, did Wimsatt's argument persuade? Every other university department continued to regard literary studies as little more than rhetoric and much less than knowledge, a reality that the discipline's more recent preoccupations with history, politics, law, and science have done nothing to change. It has been more than forty years since Sontag exhorted us to come to our senses, but Michael Wood observes that even now, "we are trying to explain our unnatural science to the natural scientists and to all those who take the natural sciences as their model for the production of knowledge" (Wood 2009: 60).

Free from the pressures that literary scholars feel to emulate the sciences, poets teach different lessons about the senses and the access that they give to truth. This essay explores one poet's vision of the role they play in mediating the relationship between reading and writing, and between a work of art and a person who loves it. My text is *Ovids Banquet of Sence*, an erotic epyllion published by George Chapman in 1595, at the height of Ovid's popularity in England.[3] Ovid had many imitators during the 1590s,[4] but only Chapman seems to have entertained the idea that in order to understand Ovid's poems, and to write like Ovid in English, it is desirable to feel about beauty as he felt, and to see, hear, smell, taste and touch with Ovidian senses. The *Banquet* is a story about experiences with a beautiful woman, Julia, that moved Ovid to write the *Art of Love*. That story, which Chapman published with erudite marginal notes, is a critical hypothesis about the context in which the truth of Ovid's poem should be understood. On the other hand, the *Banquet* imitates the Ovidian text that it interprets, and thus forecloses the distance that the scholia create, as it approaches its model along an asymptote of similarity: the distance that makes interpretation possible.

The senses mediate every stage of two, interwoven movements that occur both between Ovid and Julia and between Chapman and the Ovidian poem that he would imitate and understand. First, there is the movement, along the relays of the senses, towards someone or something beautiful (Julia, the *Art of Love*). Chapman associates this movement – in which subjects and objects, as it were, engross each other through sense impressions – with reading. Then, there is a retreat from sensory experience, and a movement away from beauty, in order to interpret what experience means. This movement does not return to the way things were. On the contrary, it establishes new distinctions between subject and object and acknowledges that changes have occurred. For Chapman, it is associated with writing. And thus, according to the *Banquet*'s logic, which is entirely typical of Ovid's own verses, subjects of perception become objects of attention in order to understand and communicate what they have seen, heard, smelled, tasted and felt. Readers become writers in order to relate experience to others, but in the process of consigning their experience to language, they also become texts, which give rise to new readers, who will have new impressions of beauty and become writers and texts in their turn, in the endless interchange of subjects and objects. A tradition takes shape as a community of feeling as beauty extends and diversifies its meaning through countless subjective truths: from Julia's song about beauty's power to Ovid; from Ovid to the *Art of Love*; from that poem to Chapman; from Chapman to the text that expresses what it was like for him to read Ovid; from the *Banquet* to me; and from me to you, through the essay that you are reading now.

To what end? *Ovids Banquet of Sence* purports to explain what the *Art of Love* means by recreating the sensuous encounter with beauty in which that text originated. In that sense, its confidence in sensation as means to objective knowledge about Ovidian writing appears to be high. On the other hand, the neo-Platonic framework of Chapman's erotic

---

[3]. I use the edition of Chapman's poem in Donno (1963). Parenthetical references in the text are to stanza and line numbers.
[4]. H. James (2009) is an excellent introduction to Ovid's presence in Renaissance English literature.

poem dictates that truth always lies beyond our utmost knowing, and that it must do so, in order that we may keep wanting (and failing) to understand, and keep making the works of art in which our perceptions are preserved and shared. At the end of the *Banquet*, Ovid's encounter with Julia is interrupted before he can consummate the desires that his senses have excited. Because he cannot know her, he makes do with the incomplete experiences that his senses have afforded him, and with writing poetry instead of making love. Likewise Chapman, as an interpreter and imitator, contents himself with understanding Ovid imperfectly, and with writing in a way that only partly resembles his model. This outcome asserts the deep connection between physical sensation, poetic activity and the truth, even as it insists that there is so much more to truth than our senses and our poems will ever let us know. But there is at least one benefit to accepting the idea that poems are half-truths, fashioned from the error of the senses: Our every perception becomes a work of art.

Ovids Banquet of Sence takes place in a garden in Rome, sometime before the composition of the *Art of Love* in the first century BCE. Julia, the daughter of Augustus, whom Chapman calls "Corynna", is bathing in an arbour, when Ovid comes upon her and her beauty ravishes each of his five senses in succession. He hears her voice, then smells her breath, and these impressions stimulate appetites that only other senses can fulfill. The poet moves closer in order to see Corynna, at which point – some two-thirds of the way through a poem of roughly one thousand lines – she becomes aware of him, and they speak to each other for the first time. Ovid's gaze offends Corynna, and she makes a move to leave, but Ovid, calling her "great Goddesse" (75.7), professes love and promises, finally, to raise her to heaven in his verses: "thy perfections shall be to heaven Mused, / Deckt in bright verse, where Angels shall appeare / The praise of vertue, love, and beauty singing" (115.6–8). His arguments persuade Corynna to stay. She consents to let Ovid taste and touch her, and he does, but before things can go further than that, they are interrupted. The poem ends with Ovid's promise to "write the Art of love" hanging in the air (113.5).

I read *Ovids Banquet of Sence* as a parable about the way we stand in relation to literature through our senses and the way it stands in relation to us. It is a difficult and unfamiliar text, so let me repeat the story that I just sketched, in more detail. One day, at noontime, Ovid overhears Corynna playing a lute and singing while she bathes in a fountain; then he smells the odour of the words and notes that her breath carries to him on the wind. Corynna's song celebrates "beauties sorcerie" (12.10), and she relishes the idea that the more elusive a beautiful woman is, the more men will love her. The content of the song should be a warning to Ovid keep his distance, but he is unable to resist the way Corynna sounds and smells. Like a reader at the margins of a text, he spies on Corynna, "[m]askt in a Thicket neere her Bowre" (46.2). When, moving closer in order to find out more about her, Ovid sees her naked body for the first time, Corynna also sees him in the reflection of her mirror (74.1–2). Ovid's eye pierces through the arbor that hides Corynna from his view. Her naked body also reflects his gaze, "[s]triking him to the hart with exstasie" (49.2–3). "[T]hat looke" places Ovid in-between the myth of Actaeon and Diana and the myth of Narcissus and Echo, and a certain equilibrium is achieved (50.2). A subject looks, and an object looks back, as it were with the subject's own eyes. What separates the gaze from its reflection? Or a reader from the text in which he sees himself?

As Ovid changes from a subject of perception to an object of attention and back again, he speaks an eloquent discourse that imitates Corynna's disarming beauty. His speech is a second mirror, made of language, and meant to show Corynna to herself in a way that will change her along the lines that Ovid himself has been changed, by hearing her song, smelling her breath, and seeing her body.

> This motion of my soule, my fantasie
> Created by three sences put in act,
> Let justice nourish with thy simpathie,
> Putting my other sences into fact,
> If now thou grant not, now chandge to that offence;
> To suffer change, doth perfect sence compact:
> Change then, and suffer for the use of sence,
> Wee live not for our selves, the Eare, and Eye,
> And every sence, must serve societie.   (87.1–9)

In this passage, which explicitly identifies physical sensations as the source of poetic fantasy and of factual knowledge, Ovid appeals to Corynna for a love that's equal to the love that the sound, smell, and sight of her have created in him. He also expresses a desire to know her through his other senses. A moment later, Ovid will ask to taste Corynna's lips, then to touch her body. She obliges him: first, by imparting a kiss that "infused / Restoring syrrop" and "fild him with furious influence" (97.5–6, 9); later, by shifting her veil and revealing the body parts that Chapman archly calls "*Latonas* Twinns" (105.7). At this point, through the touch of his hand, "King of the King of Sences" (107.1), Ovid reaches for an ecstasy beyond articulation (112.8–9), "feeles … defied" by his sense-impressions working in concert with each other (113.2), and commits to write "the Art of love" (105.5).

Not until the late nineteenth century would the word "synaesthesia" refer explicitly to the "[a]greement of the feelings or emotions of different individuals, as a stage in the development of sympathy" (*OED* 1989: "synaesthia, *n*."). Here, however, in a striking anticipation of that later, technical usage, Chapman associates the "sympathie" that Ovid seeks from Corynna with the integration of all his sense impressions of her in "perfect sence compact". As each of Ovid's sense impressions is studied in turn, the *Banquet* explores what Chapman takes to be the source of the *Art of Love* and the basis for objective knowledge about Ovid's creativity. The synaesthetic passages suggest what our knowledge would be like were beauty able to lift the senses above the confusion in which they are ordinarily at odds and unite them in a perception of itself that was whole and impartial. But the *Banquet* also asks whether synaesthesia really is knowledge in this more perfect sense and whether sympathetic union is a better approach to understanding than approaches that establish themselves at a distance. For it is equally plausible that Ovid's synaesthesia and his sympathy are, as he himself says, "fantasy". Chapman keeps us poised between two different ideas about the relationship between the senses and knowledge, which Georges

Poulet discusses in "The Phenomenology of Reading". "Sensuous thought is privileged to move at once to the heart of the work [of art] and to share its own life"; however, this kind of thought – thinking with the senses, if you will – remains distinct from "clear thought", which "is privileged to confer on its objects the highest degree of intelligibility" (Poulet 1969: 63). As the *Banquet* moves toward its conclusion, where the interruption of the physical communion between Ovid and Corynna leads to the composition of the *Art of Love*, Chapman continues to suggest, in line with Ovid's seductive arguments, that sense perceptions provide clear knowledge, on which all poetic composition should be based. But several incidents in the poem suggest the contrary: that excited sense perception is far from objective knowledge. That would suggest that when we encounter something beautiful, and try to understand it, it is more likely that we face an unhappy choice between "a union without comprehension" and "a comprehension without union" (*ibid.*).

In order to bring this dilemma into clearer focus, consider the setting in which Chapman's meditation on the senses, and the relationship between what Ovid feels and what he knows, takes place. At the centre of the bower stands a fountain, and in the centre of the fountain, there stands what appears to be a statue of "*Niobe*, shedding teares" (2.9), faced by relief carvings of her fourteen children in their death throes, over which the sun, filtered through pyramids made of purple glass, casts a vivid light (2.4–6). I say "appears", because although Chapman tells us that "the Fountain [is] the eye of the Arbor" and "the Arbor sees with the Fountaine", he also says that "Stone *Niobe*" is an optical illusion, "[s]o cunningly to optick reason wrought, / That a farre of, it shewd a womans face, / Heavie, and weeping; but more neerely viewed, / Nor weeping, heavy, nor a woman shewed" (3.1, 6–9). The closer one comes to the statue, the less lifelike it appears to be. Consequently, the less conducive to sympathy it is, and the more resistant to the kind of understanding that Ovid tells Corynna that he wants. We are quick to associate proximity with a lack of clarity, and distance with a lack of feeling, but that is not how Chapman seems to see interpretation here. For him, somewhat obscurely, the problem is that if one stands too close to a work of art, one will not be able to respond to it aesthetically (with feeling); whereas if one stands too far away, it will be unclear that it is a work of art at all.

Presumably, the bower is a mirror in which the poem gazes at its own reflection, or an eye through which Chapman contemplates his efforts to bring into clear focus the sense perceptions that led to the composition of the *Art of Love*. But as a weeping eye that is bleary with illusions, the bower is also a lens that subjects every scene of sensuous understanding in the poem – in which a feeling subject merges with an object of perception, or one sense becomes another, in what appears to be a moment of sympathy and perfected knowledge – to scrutiny, scepticism, and distortion. For example: When Ovid hears Corynna singing, and smells the incense of the "Hecatombs of [her] notes" (21.2), he fancies that his body "fades, and into spirit turns" (22.9), in order that his life "might passe into my loves conceit, / Thus to be form'd in words, her tunes, and breath" (24.7–8). In this condition, fully inhabiting Corynna through his senses and identified with her thoughts, Ovid can claim to be "her notes", even "before they be" notes – that is, to be a truer expression of Corynna's own life than she herself is (26.5). But all of these things happen, if they can be said to happen at all, in the privacy of Ovid's mind, before he so much as speaks with, or even sees, the lady. Reading the lines in which Ovid's senses effect this miraculous communication, are we supposed to trust or to doubt the evidence of our own?

The process of spiritual transmission through sense impressions, on which the bower's eye casts a doubtful look, also works in the other direction, bringing Corynna into Ovid as a "furious influence". In the passage that I mentioned earlier, Chapman compares the taste of Corynna's kiss to the touch of a goddess, writing that Ovid "imaginde *Hebes* hand had brusde / A banquet of the Gods into his sence" (97.7–8). The forceful and bruising movement of Corynna's spirit into Ovid's body is one of two passages that occur here, at the transition between stanzas 97 and 98. At the same time that Corynna's kiss fills Ovid with her inspiring breath, Ovid appears to merge with Chapman, right before the reader's eyes. For a long moment, without any punctuation or speech tags in the text to mark the difference between them, Ovid and the narrator who has been telling his story speak in the same voice. Of Corynna's kiss, this composite person – a poetic subject formed by the kind of inter-subjectivity that imitation makes possible – says that the taste of her mouth strikes a chord in him, as though his skin vibrated with the percussion of the spheres: "With this sweete kisse in mee [the heavens] theyr tunes apply, / As if the best Musitians hands were striking: / This kisse in mee hath endlesse Musicke closed" (98.6–8).

Sounding deep within the self, these vibrations radiate outward, like ripples from a stone cast into water, "[o]ne forming another in theyre issuing" until "over all the Fount they circulize" (99.3–4). Just so, says the composite speaker of stanzas 98 and 99 – who calls to us from inside and outside the experience that the poem relates – just so "this perpetuall-motion-making kiss, / Is propagate through all my faculties, / And makes my breast a endless Fount of bliss" (99.4–7). A moment later, the kiss ends, the harmony of the senses is broken and the momentary fusion of different minds passes. Ovid, now clearly distinguished from Corynna and from Chapman, reflects, "I, alas, fair eccho of this kisse, / Onely reiterate a slender part / Of that high joy it worketh in my hart" (100.7–9). Able to perceive but not possess the object of his desire, he suffers a predicament that Poulet identified with the whole enterprise of criticism. "[W]hereas in the perfect identification of two consciousnesses, each sees itself reflected in the other, the critical consciousness can, at best, attempt but to draw closer to a reality which must remain forever veiled. In this attempt, it uses the only mediators available to it in this quest, that is the senses" (Poulet 1969: 60). This means that "the unfortunate critic is condemned never to fulfill adequately his role as reader" – namely, to participate in a "community of feeling" with the texts he that loves (*ibid.*: 59).

Poulet wonders whether literary critics will ever feel enough to understand the texts they read. Wimsatt worries that they may feel too much. T. S. Eliot, on the other hand, criticizes English poets of the later seventeenth century for the "dissociation of sensibility" that he detected in their work. Their tendency to separate thought from feeling, he argued, was the result of an inability "to feel ... thought as immediately as the odour of a rose" (Eliot 1975: 64). By contrast, Eliot praised earlier Renaissance writers, such as Chapman, Ben Jonson and John Donne, for "constantly amalgamating disparate experience" in their poems, and for having "a mechanism of sensibility [that] could devour any kind of experience". These were poets who "incorporated their erudition into their sensibility" and whose "mode of feeling was directly and freshly altered by their reading and thought" (*ibid.*: 63). Indeed, writes Eliot, "[i]n Chapman especially there is a direct sensuous apprehension of thought, or a recreation of thought into feeling" (*ibid.*). On the basis of *Ovids Banquet of Sence*, I wonder whether Chapman would feel the same way.

Certainly, the *Banquet* makes the argument, in favour of sense perception, that the very existence of the senses proves that they are to be employed in understanding the world and our experiences in it: "Nature dooth not sensuall gifts infuse / But that with sence, shee still intends their use" (62.8–9). Moreover, good judgment is said to depend on such pleasure as the senses afford, since "sence is given us to excite the minde, / And that can never be by sence exited / But first the sence must her contentment minde, / We therefore must procure the sence delighted, / That so the soul may use her faculty ..." (63.1–5). Whoever is not, or will not be, moved by the appeal that beauty makes to the senses, that person – in contrast to "[g]entle and noble" folk who "can be quickned with perfumes and sounds" – is "cripple-minded, Gowt-wit lamde", and like a block of wood that will not catch fire, "dead without wounds, / Stird up with nought ..." (35.1–5). Emphatic though these endorsements of sensitivity are, it is important to note that they are all made by Ovid, in the full flush of his desire and in the process of seducing Corynna (and himself). In a poem that is reluctant to say, finally and unequivocally, that sensuous thought is understanding or that sympathy is knowledge, we are obliged to consider possibilities that elude Eliot – among them, the difference between devouring an experience and digesting it.

Chapman asks that we dispose ourselves toward our senses in at least two ways that contradict each other. On the one hand, he prefers that we reject Ovid's example as a reader and conscientiously deny the evidence of our senses. On the other, he urges us to approach reading as an extension of the senses, rather than a purely intellectual activity. The instances of synaesthesia in the *Banquet* make this paradoxical request of us as well, by virtue of the fact that this phenomenon points both to an *objective knowledge* that is super-human in its clarity and innocence of desire and to a combination of *subjective perceptions* that are all-too-human in their tendency to approach the world from the blind self-interest of desire. For Chapman's period, Augustine may be said to represent the first of these possibilities, and Bottom the second.

"[W]hen I love you, what do I love?" Augustine asks God in his *Confessions*. "It is not physical beauty nor temporal glory nor the brightness of the light dear to earthly eyes, nor the sweet melodies of all kinds of songs, nor the gentle odour of flowers and ointments and perfumes; nor manna or honey, nor limbs welcoming the embraces of the flesh". Nevertheless, Augustine imagines that the love of God is synaesthesia, a plenitude of sense-impressions that perfects sensitivity itself.

> Yet there is a light I love, and a food, and a kind of embrace when I love my God – a light, voice, odour, food, embrace of my inner man, where my souls floodlit by light which space cannot contain, where there is sound that time cannot seize, where there is a perfume that no breeze disperses, where there is a taste for food no amount of eating can lessen, and where there is a bond of union that no satiety can part. (Augustine, *Confessions* 10.6.8; trans. H. Chadwick 1992)

In this context, synaesthesia is a perception of the truth, such as human beings have not known since the Fall and will only know again in Paradise.

By contrast, in *A Midsummer Night's Dream*, Bottom's experience in the forest outside Athens suggests that synaesthesia, far from giving access to a mode of perception that is above and superior to the senses, is a drowsy fantasy that waking makes incomprehensible. "I have had a most rare / vision", says Bottom to himself. "I have had a dream, past the wit of man to say what dream it was." This dream – a fantasy of sensory gratification, confused identities, and commingled pleasures – is the inspiration for a poem that is never written, a celebration of the self and its grandiose desires: "I will get Peter Quince to write a ballad of this dream: it shall be called 'Bottom's Dream', because it hath no bottom …". It is also an instance of the human mind's prodigious capacity for ignorance and self-delusion, even when confronted with clear evidence of its limited capacity to understand itself. "[M]an is but an ass, if he go about to expound this dream", says the man who just wore an ass's head. "Methought I was – there is no man can tell what. Methought I was, – and methought I had, – but man is but a patched fool, if he will offer to say what methought I had". Methought, methought, methought, methought: Bottom never scrutinizes himself more closely, nor understands less, and synaesthesia is the metaphor in which his folly is pronounced: "The eye of man hath not heard, the ear of man hath not seen, man's hand is not able to taste, his tongue to conceive, nor his heart to report, what my dream was" (Shakespeare 2006: 4.1.203–15).

Does Chapman adopt either of these stances as his own? It is precisely at the moment when Ovid has encountered Corynna in all five senses, feels deified by his experience and, in this godlike situation, prepares to create a poem, that he and Corynna are interrupted by a group of ladies. Ovid retreats from the arbour and does not put his sexual desires into effect. At the point of knowing that the *Art of Love* really began with a commingling of bodies, the reader is asked to contemplate instead "the curious frame" of Chapman's own text (117.7). The last stanza, comparing the poem with a painting of a "Monarchs royall hand / Holding a scepter", in which only half the fingers are revealed, concludes with the promise that "*Ovid* well knew there was much more intended, / With whose omission none must be offended" (117.2–3, 8–9). Such is the understanding that Chapman's sensational poem finally affords about Ovidian poetry. Neither godlike knowledge, unspoiled by the Fall, such as Augustine imagines, nor Bottom's unredeemable solipsism, Chapman's critical imitation of Ovid's creative experience yields the innocence of frustrated desires and the partial knowledge of unconsummated love.

At the end of Chapman's poem, Ovid is a ridiculous figure and, by virtue of the poem that he is about to write, a figure of authority as well. The yoking together of authority and folly is an opportunity to revisit an argument that I mentioned earlier. "There never was any school founded upon aesthetics which was built safely and permanently, for the definitions of the beautiful and the artistic are too elusive and changeable" (Feuillerat 1925: 319). Because Feuillerat's own discipline was founded upon literature, it is a curious thing for him to write; but presumably, it is only natural for scholars, including literary scholars, to be protective of their work and want it to last. The idea that scholarship should aspire to the kind of knowledge that does not change is deeply rooted in academic life, along with a conceptual framework that opposes the subject and the object of study, mind and body, reason and irrationality, truth and error. Yet, if Chapman's poem has anything to teach us about the way that we interpret texts, and imagine the meaning of our own writing, no perception of beauty is safe and permanent, no matter how objective, philosophical or scientific its foundations are said to be. Meaning is elusive because our capacity to understand is finite. By the same token, it is only because we ourselves are changeable, that works of art are capable of changing us.

Of course, we are free to reject our impressions about art. We may go on working towards a future when rational minds may contemplate eternal truths without the mediation of the senses, but that would be a future in which we would have little to gain from works of art, because we would have nothing to risk by encountering them, not even being wrong about their meaning. However, we are also free to set aside the long-standing fantasy of perfectibility at the heart of our scholarship, and make our error-prone experiences the basis for understanding the meaning of works of art. In *Ovids Banquet of Sence*, the senses lead to the ludicrous rather than the sublime, and the situation in which Chapman leaves Ovid, and himself, at the end of the poem – the imaginary ruler of a kingdom of partial truths and compelling illusions – is a playful acknowledgement that the propensity to find ourselves no matter where we look is the essence of our creativity and insight. "[S]ince our state makes things correspond to itself and transforms them in conformity with itself", writes Montaigne of the influence of the senses on judgement, "we can no longer claim to know what anything truly is" (Montaigne 1991: 678). A literary criticism that tuned itself to this music might not regard the senses as obstacles that must be overcome in pursuit of certain knowledge, but as phases in an intrinsically imperfect process of interpretation, leading to poetry and self-knowledge, which is to say a perception of the limitations, humanity, and folly of one's search for truth. The point of allowing our senses back into criticism is not, then, to surpass them, which we cannot do in any case, but to know and enjoy them for what they are.

12

SAUSSURE'S *ANAPHONIE* : SOUNDS ASUNDER

Joshua T. Katz

SOUND SOUND

When I was a senior in college, a classmate of mine, fresh from having been awarded a Rhodes Scholarship, stopped by my room one evening to ask for advice on a paper he was writing on Plato. A philosophy major who knew little Greek, he was planning to claim – and over my protestations I believe did in the end claim – that when Socrates said that someone or something was "sound", he was referring not solely to somatic and mental health but also to music, for (he earnestly explained to me) was it not the case that just as a beautiful piece of music is held together by the soundness of its sounds, so, too, was it with a beautiful person or thing? Putting on my linguistic hat, I explained to him that the Greek adjective ὑγιής "sound, healthy" and noun ὑγίεια "soundness, health", as well as the derived adjective ὑγιεινός "sound, healthy", which we have borrowed into English as *hygiene*, have nothing to do with music, and I remember all too well the time I spent trying to keep him from getting the wrong idea about the phrase ὑγιὲς φθέγγεσθαι in the *Theaetetus*, which the standard Greek lexicon of Liddell, Scott and Jones translates, perhaps unfortunately, as "ring *sound and clear*".[1] And that is not all, for I explained to him in addition that, as far as English is concerned, the *sound* in *sound of mind and body* is from a historical point of view a completely different word from the *sound* of Mozart, with the former a native word of good Germanic stock and the latter a borrowing from Romance descendants of the word classicists know as Latin *sonus*:

---

1. *LSJ* s.v. ὑγιής III notes "neut. as Adv., ὑγιὲς φθέγγεσθαι ring *sound and clear*, opp. σαθρόν, Pl. *Tht.* 179d" (italics in original). The phrase refers to "rapping" on the doctrine of motion as the fundamental essence to see "whether it rings sound or unsound" (εἴτε ὑγιὲς εἴτε σαθρὸν φθέγγεται).

sound "healthy" < Middle English *sund* < Old English *gesund* (cf. e.g. German *gesund* and Dutch *gezond*) < Proto-Indo-European **sun-tó-* "healthy", a derivative of a root (?) **su̯en-*²

≠

sound "sensation produced in the organs of hearing" ← Anglo-Norman *soun* / Old French *son* (cf. e.g. French *son* and Italian *suono*) < Latin *sonum*, acc. of *sonus* < Proto-Indo-European **su̯enH-* "make a sound".³

I can still see my classmate's shocked look. And I remember adding for good measure a snarky comment about the final sound of this latter word *sound*, that *-d*, conspicuously absent from its proximate source, *so(u)n*, as well as from Latin *sonus* and the like. Showing off a piece of recently acquired knowledge, I told him that it was an "excrescent stop", a consonant that was added (for reasons that are not entirely clear) once this Latinate monosyllable had become a true part of English vocabulary.⁴ Bottom line: not only did sounds not contribute to musical soundness, but "sound" itself not too long ago sounded rather like "soun".⁵

---

2. It would appear that **su̯(e)n-to-* is a rhyming variant of the form **k̂u̯én-to-* that is reflected in words for "holy" in Iranian (Avestan *spəṇta-*) and Balto-Slavic (e.g. Lithuanian *šveñtas* and Old Church Slavonic *svętŭ*), but what is the underlying root **su̯en-* (and **k̂u̯en-*, for that matter)? For a possible answer, see Cantera Glera (2000: 46–9 and *passim*), who tentatively suggests connecting it to Proto-Iranian **hu̯an-* "frisch, angenehm (sein)" (cf. e.g. Middle Persian *hunsand* "contented").
3. "Y < X" means that X develops into Y naturally (i.e. via normal parent-to-child communication over the generations, without external interference); "Y ← X" means that Y has been taken from an outside X (i.e. is a borrowing from another language); and an asterisk indicates that what follows is a so-called pre- or proto-form, i.e. a word (or morpheme or other bit of linguistic material) that is not actually attested but that linguists have reconstructed. For the phonological and semantic development of the two words *sound* in English, it is easiest to turn to the *Oxford English Dictionary* (s.vv. *sound*, adj[ective] and *sound*, n[oun]³); a convenient survey of their Proto-Indo-European background may be found in Watkins (2011 s.vv. *swen-to-* and *swen-*), with more detailed information on the latter in Th. Zehnder in Rix (2001 s.v. **su̯enh₂-*). Incidentally, the final aitch in **su̯enH-* (sometimes specified as **h₂*, but the evidence for this is inconclusive; compare Rix 2001 s.v. **su̯enh₂-*, n. 5) is a laryngeal, a category of sound in Proto-Indo-European discovered by Saussure (see below in the text).
4. "The form with excrescent *-d* finally established itself in the 16th cent., but is condemned by Stanyhurst as late as 1582" (*OED* s.v. *sound*, n.³). Luick (1940: 1038–43) provides a classic (but incomplete and in some ways contentious) survey of excrescent stops (not just *-d*) in English; a small amount of research suffices to show that there is no possibility of a unitary explanation for *betwixt* (Old English *betweoh(s)*), *thumb* (Old English *þúma*), *varmint* (cf. *vermin*), etc., not to mention such German words as *Obst* "fruit" (Old High German *obaz*).
5. In addition to the adjective and the noun under consideration here, the *OED* provides entries for five further nouns of the shape *sound*: aside from n.² (a long-obsolete alternative to *soundness*) and n.⁶ (an obscure seventeenth-century hapax for "cuttlefish"), they are n.¹ ("narrow channel of water (*vel sim.*)", as in Long Island Sound), n.⁵ ("act of or tool for sounding", a derivative of the more familiar *sound*, v[erb]² "measure, esp. a water's depth") and n.⁴ (a now-dialectal form of *swoon*). This footnote is obviously not the place to consider their histories, but the etymology of *swoon* and its variant *sound* – another form with an excrescent *-d* – is unknown, while the other two are derivatives of the Proto-Germanic root **su̯em(m)-* "move, stir, esp. swim" that also yields the verb *swim*: both n.¹ and n.⁵ go back to Old English/Old Norse

SOUND STRUCTURE, SOUND STRUCTURE

I felt very superior. Indeed, the argument my classmate wished to advance was in many ways a silly one, but had I been less of a snotty know-it-all myself, and in particular if I had known more about Saussure, I might have tempered my scorn. For Saussure was interested in every way in sound structure – I mean both "sound strúcture" and "sóund structure" – and he understood far better than I did back then the importance of perspective, the importance of recognizing that there are different ways of looking at and analysing just about every phenomenon. And that is why still today his name carries so much weight among general linguists, comparative philologists and lit-crit folks – three types of people who in the contemporary academy are not usually known for seeing eye to eye. Saussure knew and cared about the synchronic and diachronic; indeed, he more or less invented the distinction for language – I should say, for language (*langue*) and speech (*parole*) since this is yet another distinction for which he is responsible. Twentieth- and twenty-first-century thought owes a huge amount to the understanding of pairs such as synchrony ~ diachrony and *langue* ~ *parole*, pairs that Saussure began spelling out a hundred years ago and ones whose complex dances – since each half of what one might call Saussure's syzygies operates in interesting ways both on its own and jointly with its partner – provide language with its essential structure: phonology ~ semantics; ordinary language ~ poetry; internal psychology ~ external sociology; intention ~ unconsciousness; text ~ orality; and so on. All of these binary oppositions (generally speaking, the hard ~ the soft) characterize Saussure's work and come to the fore in the subject on which I focus in this necessarily somewhat impressionistic paper, namely his synaesthetic sense and idea of anagrammatism – or rather, to use the term that he should have preferred but felt he could not use (see below), *anaphonie* ("anaphony"[6]).[7]

Consider the following four big observations, all things about which Saussure's so sure.[8] He recognized that:

1. Synchronic and diachronic linguistic analyses are both important but do not always yield the same results.
2. Sounds hold language together as much as meaning does, with phonology and semantics operating both separately and together. Furthermore, the study of sound patterns is one of the more intriguing aspects of literary analysis, existing today as

---

sund "swimming; sea (*vel sim.*)", the former directly and the latter – an interesting case of reborrowing – via French. (The *OED* also lists the adverb *sound*, as in *sound asleep*, and four different verbs *sound*, but the histories of all of these – not just of $v.^2$ – are closely connected to other, non-verbal, forms already mentioned.)

6. Neither "anaphony" nor any related forms (e.g. "anaphone" and "anaphonic") appear in the *OED* or other standard dictionaries of English.
7. For some useful remarks on the relationship between such binary oppositions and Saussure's work on *anaphonie*, see Gordon & Schogt (1999).
8. Compare Bernstein (1999: 5: "Don't Be So Sure / (*Don't Be Saussure*)"), as well as Tallis (1995: *Not Saussure*) and Kretzschmar (2009: xi: "What makes Ferdinand so sure?").

a recognized discipline largely thanks to the expansion of Saussure's theories by his many epigones and acolytes.
3. Sounds are fickle. Understanding this contributed to Saussure's early and (see below) truly spectacular success as a diachronic linguist.
4. Language – and in particular its sound patterns – has embedded in its very fabric the element of play: sóund structure can play with (and thereby strain but never break) ordinary language's sound strúcture.

This last aspect is not unknown to scholarship, and yet Saussure's ludic pursuits receive so much less study than everything else he did that quite a few people who think they know their Saussure are not really aware of them. Because Saussure was Saussure rather than just anybody, because his anaphonic pursuits deserve greater attention from classicists and because these pursuits have, I believe, the potential for much wider application cross-linguistically and cross-culturally, for all these reasons I shall attempt in what follows not just to describe Saussure's play with phonic patterning but also to begin to come to terms with the unquestionably striking relationship between this play and everything else he believed, a subject that I find very intriguing as a matter of intellectual biography.[9]

The Swiss polymath Ferdinand de Saussure was born in Geneva in 1857 and died in Vufflens, a municipality in the nearby canton of Vaud, in 1913.[10] Recognized at a young age for his prodigious talents and renowned in his adult life as a philologist – he held professorships in Paris and Geneva – Saussure nevertheless published very little in his fifty-five years aside from the brilliant *Mémoire sur le système primitif des voyelles dans les langues indo-européennes*,[11] which came out just days past his twenty-first birthday and which many historical and comparative linguists regard as containing within its pages the single

---

9. The most comprehensive attempt at a synthesis so far appears to be Gandon (2006), though see also Johannes Fehr's book-length introduction to Saussure (1997) and Fehr (2000), both with bibliographies that are especially useful for tracking down Saussurean material published posthumously.
10. The bibliography on Saussure is enormous. For a good introduction to various aspects of his life and work, see the papers in Sanders (2004), among them Wunderli (2004) on anagrams (largely unchanged from Wunderli 1972c). The foundational books on the more ludic aspects of Saussure's researches are Starobinski (1971), Wunderli (1972b) and the English translation of the former, Starobinski (1979); further secondary literature may be found in Katz (2009: 90–98 and *passim*), as well as in two works that appeared too late for me to take them into account, Bravo (2011) and Bruzzese (2011). The most interesting studies of Saussure have for some years been coming from the pen of John E. Joseph (see www.ling.ed.ac.uk/~josephj/), some of whose publications I cite in the following pages; the appearance in 2012 of Joseph's biography of Saussure should make a splash.

    The first volume of Claudia Mejía Quijano's Lacanian psycho-sexual biography, covering Saussure's early years, has made a splash in its own right, as anything would that has such unlikely section headers as "La nasale sonante, ou de la bisexualité humaine" (Mejía Quijano 2008: 189); it will be interesting to learn what she makes of Saussure's anagrams (on which see for now *ibid.*: 100–103). I note that at least one other psychoanalyst, Izabel Vilela, has also been thinking about Saussure and has been writing articles about him and Lacan since the late 1990s (e.g. Vilela 1998 and 1999, in Portuguese); in Vilela (2008: 4) she promises an "essai biographique" titled *Le Désir de Saussure: des "Souvenirs d'enfance" à la recherche sur les anagrammes*.
11. Saussure (1879 = 1922: 1–268).

most remarkable achievement in the history of linguistics, namely the discovery literally *avant la lettre* of what would come to be called laryngeals. The details of the "laryngeal theory" are intricate and cannot reasonably be explored here, but the essential point is that laryngeals are sounds that do not appear as such in any Indo-European language that was known and understood during Saussure's lifetime.[12] (That's what I mean by *avant la lettre*.) And yet – and here comes the matter of sheer genius – Saussure pointed out that assuming that these sounds had once been there in Proto-Indo-European would explain a large set of hitherto inexplicable morphological features in such well-attested languages as Sanskrit and Greek (languages *après la lettre*, as it were). And lo and behold, Saussure's idea was proved right, soon after his death, when (to make a long story short) the cuneiform language Hittite was deciphered (by Bedřich Hrozný in 1915) and seen (by Jerzy Kuryłowicz in 1926/27) to have consonants in just the places where Saussure, on the basis of deep insight, had posited that the reconstructed proto-language did.

This spectacular example of structuralist thinking exhibits the first three of the four main strands of Saussurean sureness on which I am concentrating, that is, everything but the play:

1. The synchronic anomalies that Saussure noticed led him to form a diachronic hypothesis about the prior existence of a set of consonants.
2. These synchronic anomalies had to do with sounds that in some sense held the linguistic system together, keeping it sound, so to speak.
3. Yet the sounds in question were fickle, disappearing in almost all the Indo-European languages – but despite the strain of their loss, the system still held.

Clearly, language is resilient, is (in the famous words of Saussure's greatest student, Antoine Meillet) "un système où tout se tient"[13] – though the strain led to a split between synchrony and diachrony and, thus, to the puzzle that Saussure solved.

SAUSSURE 'N' STRUCTURE, SAUSSUREAN STRUCTURE

Structuralism is as closely associated with Saussure as the laryngeal theory, and I shall in what follows poke a bit at Saussure's structuralist program – no, not the way the bad old deconstructionists did in the bad old days in what was once the centre of the universe, Yale, where my possibly unsound classmate and I went to college – by pulling apart,

---

12. This is not in fact entirely true, for as Joseph (2009) beautifully demonstrates, Saussure's abiding interest in Lithuanian accentuation – arguably the single thorniest area in Indo-European linguistics today – was not a "one-off problem unconnected to his other linguistic concerns" (*ibid.*: 182) but held for him the possibility of demonstrating through a living language the validity of the hypothesis he had advanced in the *Mémoire*.
13. On the history of this phrase and its intimate connection to Saussure, see various papers by E. F. K. Koerner, especially Koerner (1999: 182–200).

sundering, the words of my paper's title. The first of these words is the phonologically and orthographically balanced name Saussure,[14] and my initial task will be to go somewhat more thoroughly through the four aspects of Saussure's thought that I have been discussing.

First, let us consider the Saussurean sign – the signifier (*signifiant*) and the signified (*signifié*) – and let us do so from both a synchronic and a diachronic point of view. If I say the word [kʰæts], this leads a certain group of speakers to think, by convention, of two or more felines. But if I say the word [saʊnd], what does this lead to? Here we have a fine example of how Saussure's sense of what would come to be called structuralism has substantially advanced our understanding of language: when I said to my classmate that of course English *sound* wasn't the same as English *sound* (or, for that matter, English *sound*; see n. 5 above), I was speaking as a historical linguist. But in his mind – that is to say, not diachronically, but synchronically in the English of at least one native speaker – they were the same, and how could one really blame him, for the signifiers are identical.[15] And the fact that they were (and, for all I know, still are) the same for him had real effects: at the very least, causing him to believe certain things about Plato and, as a result, write an uncompelling paper on ὑγίεια. This is, as it were, a personal folk etymology, and we are all guilty of harbouring such notions.[16] I myself, for example, despite knowing that it is only recently that their sound patterns have converged, find it impossible to think of ears of corn (German *Ähren*, cognate with Latin *acus, -eris* "chaff" and *acus, -ūs* "needle, pin"; < Proto-Indo-European *$*h_2ek̂$ - "(be) sharp") without thinking that they look like the ears (German *Ohren*, cognate with Latin *auris* "ear"; < Proto-Indo-European *$*h_2eus$-) with which the people who (h)ear(e)d the talk on which this paper is based took in my words.

This leads me to the second point, about sound patterns and the related matter of meaning.[17] Saussure separated[18] the pronunciation [kʰæts] from the semantic notion of the animals this series of sounds represents, but he was also well aware of the fact that it is a *series*, four ordered sounds and not just a single one. A hallmark of Saussureanism, it

---

14. More balanced, in any case, than Saulxures(-lès-Nancy), the village from which the Saussures came and took their name.
15. Note, by contrast, that the relationship between [kʰæts] and multiple instantiations of *Felis domesticus* is stable diachronically as well as synchronically since speakers of English have been talking about [kʰæts] throughout the history of the language. The precise etymology of the word *cat* is, however, almost certainly impossible to trace, for it seems to represent a widespread, long-standing *Wanderwort*.
16. Compare Katz (2010a: 345 and *passim* and esp. 2010c: 31–3, with notes on 40–42).
17. In the "Introduction" to the delightful recent collection of essays titled *The Sound of Poetry / The Poetry of Sound* (Perloff & Dworkin 2009), Craig Dworkin claims, with reference to the *OED*, that sound (i.e. n.³) is an "autantonym" since it refers to "'the audible articulation corresponding to a letter or word' … as distinct from linguistic meaning … [and] often … diametrically opposed to meaning … [but] can also denote precisely the signifying referent of language: 'import, sense, significance'" (*ibid.*: 9, with 292 n. 16); this second sense is, however, listed as obsolete. Although Perloff & Dworkin do not talk about the matters that occupy me here, anyone interested in them will want to look through the volume, perhaps especially at Hélène Aji's paper on Jackson Mac Low, Antonio Sergio Bessa's on Augusto de Campos and those by Johanna Drucker, Ming-Qian Ma and Brian M. Reed on the relationship between sound and shape.
18. Or, rather, would have separated – had he been writing in English and actually used this example (which is standard in introductions to structuralism).

is invariably said, is the essential linearity of language:[19] just as one word is pronounced before another in a given utterance, so too is there an internal structure to each word, with (in this case) the [k⁽ʰ⁾] coming before, that is, being pronounced before, the vowel, which is pronounced before the dental stop, which in turn is pronounced before the sibilant. In *cats*, the sounds more or less map onto letters – [k⁽ʰ⁾] ~ *c* + [æ] ~ *a* + [t] = *t* + [s] = *s* – but it is a matter of some interest (and one to which I shall briefly return) that this is quite unlike what happens in a word like *knight*, which is pronounced [naɪt]. On the topic of linearity in and other structural relationships inside larger chunks of language – in literature, say, whether written or oral – Saussure did not publish anything in his lifetime, and his reputation in literary studies is principally the result of the extension of his theories about little linguistic signs to larger ones. As we shall see, though, he was in fact himself very interested in how larger units of language – sentences, paragraphs, texts – hang together, in how sóund structures create sound strúctures.

But sounds (and this is now the third point) behave in ways that may plausibly be described as fickle, as we have already seen in the remarkable case of laryngeals, and it is because of sound change and semantic change – that is to say, alterations in both signifiers and signifieds – that we often find peculiarities in a system. An important linguistic mantra is, If you see a synchronic oddity, search for a diachronic explanation – an idea that explains why *knight* is spelled as it is, for once upon a time, in Old English, this word, whose meaning was something ordinary like "boy" or "lad", was in fact pronounced [knɪçt] (and written *cniht*), with the now extraneous consonants that hang on thanks to orthographic conservatism actually uttered. And, if I may return for a moment to the word ὑγίεια "health", it seems only right to point out both its conjectured prehistory and its known historical trajectory. According to the most plausible etymology, which rests on a passing observation by none other than Saussure, ὑγι-, which is clearly synchronically a single morpheme, means (or, rather, once did mean) something like "everlasting life" and goes back to *h_2iu-$g^{u}ih_3$-, a Proto-Indo-European compound (NB: two morphemes!) of "lifespan, age" and "live".[20] Furthermore, this phonologically cumbersome, laryngeal-heavy reconstruction, which (when supplemented with a nominalizing suffix) yields the normal Classical Greek word ὑγίεια, spelled with six letters plus a marker of rough breathing, exists still in Modern Greek today – where, however, it is pronounced [ja], as in the first word of the everyday greeting γεια σου / σας "hi!". Talk about linguistic fickleness!

And this brings me, finally, to the fourth point: play. The fact that sounds and meanings change is what gives to historical linguistics its special challenges and pleasures, especially to etymology, the science (Voltaire is supposed to have said, though he didn't, actually[21]) in which consonants count for little and vowels for nothing at all. Etymology is hard to practice well, for it requires an acute sensitivity to diachronic possibility: sounds do the

---

19. Joseph (2008: 170–72) has useful and unusually arch remarks on the subject.
20. See Saussure (1892: 89–90 = 1922: 457–8), though the heavy lifting on the etymology came only a century later, in Weiss (1994), who refers to Saussure on pp. 131 n. 1 and 149–51. Beekes (2010 s.v. ὑγιής) gives the Saussure–Weiss etymology his blessing.
21. See now Considine (2009).

damnedest things, and the shifts in signification can, if anything, be even more startling. For instance, *blessing* has to do with *blood*; a number of languages use the same word, or nearly so, for "caviar" and "calf (of the leg)" (e.g. Russian *ikra*); and the Greek negative particle οὐ happens to go back to the same word for "lifespan, age" mentioned in the previous paragraph in connection with sound health.[22] Good etymology, I suggest (and, indeed, have argued more formally in two recent publications[23]), calls for a sense of linguistic play, but play is not just for diachronists. For if language can tolerate such shifts in sound and meaning diachronically, then surely it can tolerate them synchronically as well. Literary theorists of various stripes regularly talk about layers of meaning in a text and sometimes (though this pursuit is unfortunately less common) they also point to layers of sound, as for example when a motif is driven by a homophone or a pun. But there is, perhaps, another layer to language as well, a mysterious, special, hidden level that links sound and meaning in a way separate from but parallel to the link between the two halves of the Saussurean sign in ordinary linguistic use. This is a layer that Saussure, himself working largely in secret, played with. This is *anaphonie*, the second word of my title.

NINETY-NINE NOTEBOOKS (~ CENT CAHIERS)

As already noted, Saussure did not publish much – the majority of his publications are between one paragraph and two pages long[24] – and he is most famous for the paradoxical achievement of not having written himself the foundational book of which he is the author: the posthumously and very messily published *Cours de linguistique générale*.[25] A veritable textual industry surrounds this work, thanks to the notes of the students, never many in number, who sat at the feet of the master in the three rounds of lectures that he delivered at the Université de Genève between 1907 and 1911[26] and thanks now also to the discovery of Saussure's own manuscript notes, which just a decade and a half ago were found to have spent the better part of a century lying unnoticed in the *orangerie* of the family home.[27] But at the same time as he was inventing structuralism, telling his students about the syntagmatic and paradigmatic (or associative) axes of language, distinguishing

---

22. The story of *bless* (Old English *blóedsian*), literally "to hallow with blood, i.e. consecrate", is a staple of first-year historical linguistics classes; the remarkable semantic association between "caviar" and "calf" is explored in various publications by Otto J. (von) Sadovszky, especially Sadovszky (1973 and 1995, esp. 1–17, both with important prior references in the first footnote – but the year of C. C. Uhlenbeck's paper is 1904, not 1874); and for οὐ, see above all Cowgill (1960).
23. See Katz (2010a and 2010c, the latter with a few further remarks on both Voltaire and οὐ).
24. See Saussure (1922), plus the material noted in Fehr (1996: 196 and 2000: 255) and Saussure (1997: 557).
25. So messy indeed that I refrain from citing an edition, for fear of incurring the wrath of the true Saussureans by choosing the wrong one.
26. Specifically, January–June 1907, October 1908–June 1909 and October 1910–July 1911.
27. Some phrases in this and other sections are lifted more or less verbatim from my programmatic paper "Wordplay" (Katz 2009), in which Saussure figures prominently.

between *langue* and *parole* and sundering *le signifiant* and *le signifié* while at the same time keeping them together to form the totality of *le signe* – indeed, at the very same time as he was promoting the idea of the essential linearity of language – he was more or less privately taking copious notes on what would seem to be very different things. For between December 1905/January 1906 and April 1909,[28] Saussure scribbled secretly, filling ninety-nine or more notebooks, now housed in the Bibliothèque de Genève, with thoughts and diagrams about, of all things, anagrams.[29]

Conventionally, anagrams involve the rearrangement of letters, as for example in *Alec Guinness ~ genuine class* and, with apologies to Lisa Simpson, *Jeremy Irons ~ Jeremy's iron*.[30] For Saussure, however, the matter was not so straightforward: he was investigating "les mots sous les mots",[31] that is, individual bits – and especially paired bits: so-called *diphones* or *polyphones* – scattered across a phrase (*mannequin*) that in his opinion could be recombined to reveal a key word (*mot-thème*), typically a name.[32] Such anagrams Saussure found (if that is the right verb; some might prefer "invented") in the first place in Latin Saturnians, but he quickly began to uncover them also in other kinds of poetry, in prose and in languages well outside Italy. The *Paradebeispiel*[33] is the secret Saturnian Scipio in *CIL* I^2 7.5 (see Figure 12.1). The claim that this verse hides the name of the person it celebrates would raise eyebrows under any circumstances, but it seems especially

---

28. See the "Journal des anagrammes" in Gandon (2002: 14–20) and the revised version ("Le 'journal' revisité") in Gandon (2006: 140–60), as well as Fehr (1996: 193–4 and 2000: 244–8) and Saussure (1997: 546–9).
29. The classic number ninety-nine (plus "dossier de tableaux sur grandes feuilles") goes back to Godel (1960: 11) and has been widely repeated, e.g. by Jean Starobinski at the start of his groundbreaking article (Starobinski 1964: 243) and by Francis Gandon in the opening sentence of the most detailed study of the anagrams to date (Gandon 2002: 3); Starobinski (1971: 7–8; trans. 1979: vii–viii) provides a basic inventory. Wunderli (1972b: 8 n. 20) counts "117 Hefte und 2 Umschläge mit losen Blättern" (compare Wunderli 1972a: 194), explains how one might add the loose sheets so as to arrive at the number 121 (Rossi 1968: 113: "22 + 99 quaderni") and states, "wieso dagegen Starobinski … von 99 Heften spricht, ist mir nicht klar". Dupuis (1977: 11–12), too, speaks of "117 cahiers d'écolier et de nombreuses feuilles indépendantes", noting correctly that "[l]a diversité des avis sur la somme totale des papiers consacrés aux anagrammes s'explique par le fait qu'on trouve des traces de ces recherches dans des manuscrits appartenant à d'autres travaux, ainsi dans les cahiers de métrique védique"; Gordon & Schogt (1999: 140) count 134. François Rastier (2009: 14) reports that there are "3700 feuillets consacrés pour partie aux anagrammes" (compare François Rastier 2010: 320).
30. See *The Simpsons*, episode "Lisa's Rival" (written by Mike Scully and originally aired on 11 September 1994). A transcript is available at www.snpp.com/episodes/1F17.html.
31. Thus Starobinski (1971).
32. This onomastic emphasis – which is by no means confined to Saussure – is no accident: names are cross-culturally imbued with power (in the context of Saussure, see e.g. the jargony paper of Kinser 1979: 1118–19 and *passim*), and authors frequently embed (consciously, as in a *sphragis*, or unconsciously; see below in the text) into the fabric of their works their own name, that of their patron or that of a pragmatically significant figure (e.g. a god, hero or friend). Of course, readers may also look for names that are not there. As Johannes Fehr writes at the end of his introduction to Saussure, "[W]er wollte wissen, ob aus dem, was er [sc. Ferdinand de Saussure] schrieb, nicht dereinst jemand F–e–r–d–i–n–a–n–d–u–s oder einen anderen Namen herauslesen sollte?" (Fehr 1997: 225; compare Fehr 2000: 202).
33. It is the first example in the account of Jean Starobinski that brought Saussure's secret work to a wider audience: Starobinski (1964: 245); compare Starobinski (1971: 29; trans. 1979: 16).

```
        Taurasia   Cīsauna   Samnĭo   cēpĭt
                      │
                      S────┼──C
                      │
                  CĪ──────────┼──── PĬ
                              │
                              ĬO
```

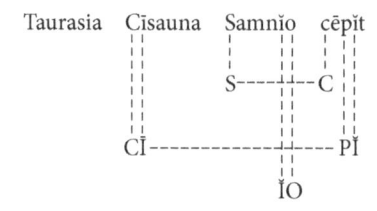

Figure 12.1 From Wunderli (1972b: 27). Redrawn from the original.

remarkable coming from Saussure: anagrams clearly overturn the notion of linearity, not to say wreak evident havoc, when things get the least bit complicated, with conventional notions of lexical meaning.[34]

What did Saussure think he was doing?[35] Could he really have been inventing post-structuralism at the same time as he was inventing structuralism?[36] These questions must remain open, but there is, I believe, a quite simple answer to why scholars have not paid more attention to Saussure's anagrammatic pursuits. Having seemingly decided that the phenomena he was researching were largely in the eye of the beholder and that examples could be multiplied indefinitely by anyone intent on "finding" them (kabbalism gone mad, as in the so-called Bible Code today), Saussure abruptly stopped searching for anagrams at the end of April 1909.[37] And since pondering the *mot-thème* SCIPIO in the *mannequin* (*Taurasia*) *Cisauna Samnio cepit* (i.e. "CI----- S---IO C-PI-") is not a normal activity even

---

34. Such anagrams as *Alec Guinness* ~ *genuine class* (first noted publicly by Dick Cavett) are of course striking for being semantically coherent in spite of it all. To some extent, the same can be said for Saussure's SCIPIO.
35. Some first answers can come from Saussure's own words, in the "1ᵉʳ Cahier à lire préliminairement", edited and introduced in exemplary fashion by Wunderli (1972a); for a German translation, see Saussure (1997: 446–54).
36. The presentation copy to Paul de Man of Starobinski (1971) happens to be in my possession (on the flyleaf: "pour Paul de Man / ces sub-positions sur le / processus de com-position / Très amicalement / Jean Starobinski"). Unfortunately, de Man (who discusses Saussure's anagrams in de Man 1981, to my mind obscurely) did not leave any especially interesting marginalia. (I take the opportunity to mention, in case anyone should ever wish to consult it, that I also own Rudolf Engler's somewhat marked-up presentation copy of Wunderli 1972b.)
37. In an article titled "Undangerous Fair-mindedness" – an anagram of Ferdinand-Mongin de Saussure – Joseph (2008: 173) writes reasonably that "more attention needs to go to the cardinal fact about the anagram research, which is not how much of it Saussure did (a great deal), but that *he gave it up*, without ever making any aspect of it public. In the end he was not sufficiently persuaded that the phenomenon could be proven to be real, non-accidental, for him to follow it through to a conclusion" (italics in original); this, he continues, "leaves the anagram research with a dubious, apocryphal status within the vast Saussurean corpus". Saussure's work on anagrams certainly overlapped temporally with his development of the ideas that would turn into the *Cours*; see e.g. Wunderli (1972b: 60–62, 70–74 and *passim*) and Gandon (2002: 3–5, as well as 2006: 131–3). Starobinski (1971: 9; trans. 1979: viii) protests too much when he writes at the end of his "Avant-propos", "Il convient ici de signaler que le *Cours de linguistique générale*, exposé entre 1907 et 1911, est, pour une bonne part, postérieur à la recherche sur les anagrammes."

in the postmodern academy, much less in Switzerland a century ago, it is not for nothing that some have regarded "les deux Saussure"[38] as they might the three faces of Eve and thus perhaps unsurprising that the guardians of Saussure's legacy sat on this potentially embarrassing material for many decades before daring to release it. Only in 1958 did his two sons begin to deposit notebooks and other materials on anagrams in the Bibliothèque publique et universitaire de Genève (as it was then called); only in 1960 did Robert Godel issue the first, and wholly guarded, announcement of their existence;[39] and only in 1964 did Émile Benveniste publish, apologetically, what was then known of the correspondence on the subject between his own teacher, Meillet, and Meillet's teacher, Saussure.[40] While Saussure's wayward anagrammatic musings have received a number of fine treatments in the past half-century, above all from the fancier French post-structuralists and their epigones,[41] this work has largely remained separate – in my view unsatisfyingly so – from the vast body of scholarship on mainstream Saussurean linguistics and has been considered at best a mild curiosity by classicists and most other literary scholars.[42] Whatever the heuristic value may be of Saussure's efforts in his "anagram notebooks", they need to be taken seriously as part of his thought; the fact that the vast majority are still unpublished means that there is much work to be done,[43] and some of it should be undertaken by *Altertumswissenschaftler*.[44]

---

38. See in the first place the influential journal volumes *Les deux Saussure* (*Recherches* 16, 1974 [= *Saussure's Anagrams* (*Semiotext(e)* 2(1), 1975)]) and *The Two Saussures* (*Semiotext(e)* 1(2), 1974). (It should be noted that the phrase "(les) deux Saussure" is also sometimes used in connection with an alleged split between the Saussure of the *Mémoire* and the Saussure of the *Cours*; see e.g. Redard 1978.)
39. Godel (1960: 11).
40. "Nous avons cependant hésité longtemps à les [sc. les lettres] faire connaître, à cause de la préoccupation singulière de l' 'anagramme' qui s'y fait jour, Saussure n'ayant rien voulu publier à ce sujet" (Benveniste 1964: 91).
41. *Prima inter pares* Julia Kristeva: see above all Kristeva (1967). Another well-known perspective comes from Baudrillard (1976: 285–308). Note, too, the prominent use by Milner (1978) of Saussure's anagrams as an example of Lacanian *lalangue*, on which see most recently Pluth (2010: 184–7). Further references to pertinent work by and about Lacan, de Man, Derrida and others may be found in Katz (2009: 91–2 n. 35) and nn. 10 and 36 above.
42. But see classicist Lowell Edmunds's discussion of (poetic) "text" from Saussure to Kristeva and Derrida in Edmunds (2001: 1–18, esp. 10–12).
43. In a brief but hard-hitting paper, Georges Mounin writes, "L'intérêt dont bénéficient actuellement les anagrammes saussuriens découle moins du désir de mieux connaître Saussure, ou du désir de résoudre le problème qu'il posait, que de leur utilisation pour justifier une théorie actuelle de la littérature" (Mounin 1974: 241). Sharply critical of "la transformation de la culture scientifique en quasi-culture journalistique, et la difficulté du travail inter-disciplinaire" (*ibid*.), he suggests, not unreasonably, that "il eût été plus sage de publier la matière des recherches de Saussure, sans interprétations philosophiques et littéraires conjecturales, et prématurées. Les problèmes posés restaient suffisament vastes" (*ibid.*: 237).
44. Françoise Rastier ends her skeptical account of Saussure's attempts to find anagrams in Saturnians with the sentence, "Dans l'attente d'un[e] publication plus complète des travaux de Saussure, on reste donc dans l'indécision" (Françoise Rastier 1970: 24). Over forty years later, the situation is better but still far from ideal.

ANAPHONIE: PHON(E)Y?

What is *anaphonie*? And what is the relationship between *anaphones* (same in quasi-English: "anaphones"[45]) and *anagrammes* (anagrams)? The latter, far more normal, term, which I have thus far been preferring for its recognition value, contains a *gram(me)* and thus refers to writing, discussion of which is surely discouraged in a volume based on a conference whose subtitle contained the words "beyond the visual paradigm". Now, Saussure himself employed plenty of gramm-atical terms to describe his findings – in addition to *anagrammes*, especially *hypogrammes*, but also *paragrammes*, *cryptogrammes* and others[46] – and yet he was, quite unusually, more interested in *phones* (cf. *diphones* and *polyphones*, mentioned above) than in *grammes*, and there was only an unfortunate, low-level reason why he chose to refer to the phenomenon that fascinated him largely as *anagrammes* rather than *anaphonie*.[47] In the words of Peter Wunderli,[48]

> Saussure considered for a moment replacing *anagramme* by *anaphonie*, in order to indicate that the element underlying the phenomenon that he was investigating was not graphic but phonic; but then he gave up on this choice of term since *anaphonie* seemed to him to be most suitable as a designation for the incomplete anagram.

Nonetheless, it is clear that Saussure to a remarkable extent privileged sound over writing in his anagrammatic studies. As Wunderli writes, "Der Primat der Lautung gegenüber der Schrift ist also ... in Saussures Beschäftigung mit den Anagrammen ganz eindeutig."[49]

It should be stressed that much of the literature in which Saussure searched for and found anagrammatic or anaphonic phenomena is at some level oral. If most surviving examples of the Saturnian in Latin are like the Scipionic epitaphs in not betraying the verse line's origin in preliterate *carmina*, still to be reckoned with are the Indic *Rigveda*, the Old High German *Hildebrandslied* and of course Homer (not for nothing was Milman Parry Saussure's "grandstudent", a student of Meillet).[50] Consider just one of Saussure's

---

45. See n. 6 above.
46. Wunderli (1972b: 42–54) has an excellent discussion of the various terms, and see also now the "Petit glossaire des anagrammes" in Gandon (2002: 381–93), as well as the "Glosario" of Rodríguez Ferrándiz (1998: 265–74). Further work on the matter is clearly called for, though it would not make sense to undertake it without a firm knowledge of all the unpublished material (compare nn. 43 and 44 above).
47. On Saussure's use and non-use of the term *anaphonie*, see Starobinski (1971: 27; trans. 1979: 14–15) and Wunderli (1972b: 13–14 and 53–4).
48. "[Saussure hat] sich ... einen Moment überlegt ..., Anagramm durch Anaphonie zu ersetzen, um so zu markieren, daß nicht das graphische, sondern das lautliche Element der von ihm untersuchten Erscheinung zugrundeliegt; auf diese Bezeichnungswahl hat er dann aber verzichtet, da ihm Anaphonie vor allem dazu geeignet schien, für das unvollständige Anagramm zu stehen" (Wunderli 1972b: 53). See also Rodríguez Ferrándiz (1998: 266) and Gandon (2002: 382).
49. Wunderli (1972b: 14).
50. The leading papers on both Saussure's Vedic and his Germanic studies are written by one and the same person, David Shepheard: see Shepheard (1982 and also 1983) on the former and Shepheard (1986), as well as Rodríguez Ferrándiz (2000), on the latter.

examples, *Odyssey* 11.400 (= 407), where Odysseus reports having suggested to the shade of Agamemnon that perhaps his demise came about as a result of Poseidon: ὄρσας ἀρχαλέων ἀνέμων ἀμέγαρτον ἀϋτμήν "rousing a wretched blast of destructive winds" – a verse in which Saussure decoded the name Ἀγαμέμνων.[51]

SAUSSURE'S SYNAESTHESIA

But there is another matter to consider aside from orality. The very distinction between sounds and letters – a distinction that is difficult for some people to fully appreciate but that all linguists view as critical – is in the case of Saussure made tremendously complicated by the fact that he apparently had synaesthesia. Individual human beings manifest many fascinating forms of this condition, as seen, for example, from the titles *The Man who Tasted Shapes* and *Wednesday is Indigo Blue*, two books by Richard E. Cytowic, the neuroscientist who thirty years ago convinced the medical profession that synaesthesia is a real phenomenon worth studying.[52] Curiously, at least to me, Cytowic does not mention Saussure in either of these, or in his third (chronologically first) book on synaesthesia, and neither do the authors of other good accounts from the past few years.[53] But a memorable account of Saussure's synaesthesia by the linguist and linguistic historian John E. Joseph appeared in the *Times Literary Supplement* in 2007, on the sesquicentenary of his birth: the title – "The Poet who Could Smell Vowels" – is, as far as I can tell, an example of sensationalism on the part of the *TLS*'s editorial team,[54] but what Joseph himself actually writes about Saussure's nuanced and idiosyncratic sense of "letter-sounds" is no less remarkable. It bears quoting, and at length.

---

51. This verse is highlighted in an important recent paper by Pierre-Yves Testenoire, who plausibly connects Saussure's search for anagrams with the twelfth-century Homeric commentator Eustathius' interest in parachesis (παρήχησις) – and, as a consequence, suggests that "Débarrassés des fantasmagories héritées de la réception des années 1970, les anagrammes saussuriens perdent ainsi de leur caractère aberrant. La dimension cryptique n'est pas essentielle au travail de Ferdinand de Saussure. Il ne s'agit pas tant pour lui de chercher des 'mots sous les mots', comme le veut Jean Starobinski, que de traquer des échos sonores sur l'axe syntagmatique des vers homériques" (Testenoire 2010: 230). The formal publication of Testenoire's doctoral thesis at the Université de Rouen, "Ferdinand de Saussure à la recherche des anagrammes: les cahiers homériques" (defended 3 December 2010), will be a major event. Incidentally, nearly every scholar of Saussure who mentions *Odyssey* 11.400 = 407 – from Starobinski (1964: 258 and 1971: 127; trans. 1979: 96) to Rodríguez Ferrándiz (1998: 53), via Rossi (1968: 118) and Wunderli (1972b: 58) – mis-cites it as ἄασεν ... ἀϋτμή; as I have learned from Testenoire (p.c.), this error goes back to Saussure himself, who quotes the verse in at least two of his notebooks, once correctly and once not (see Saussure 1997: 460).
52. Cytowic (2003) and Cytowic & Eagleman (2009).
53. See also Cytowic (2002, first publ. 1989), as well as Duffy (2001), Campen (2008) and Ward (2008). The readings collected in Baron-Cohen & Harrison (1997) – from Baudelaire and Luria to Baron-Cohen and Cytowic – provide essential background.
54. This is the title of the online version (http://entertainment.timesonline.co.uk/tol/arts_and_entertainment/the_tls/article2869724.ece). The cover of the issue of the *TLS* in which Joseph (2007) appears advertises "The Secret Saussure", while the title above the piece itself is "He was an Englishman"; I quote from the paper version.

Talking about the development of Saussure's important ideas about language in the mind of an individual and its relationship to language as a social institution, Joseph describes Saussure's interactions with the Genevan professor of psychology Théodore Flournoy:[55]

> [Saussure] became centrally involved when [matters relating to language and consciousness were] taken up in 1892 by his psychologist colleague Théodore Flournoy, the most regular European correspondent, confidant and intellectual soulmate of William James. In his review of Flournoy's book on "coloured hearing" (also called synopsia or photism or, more generally, synaesthesia), James underscores the vast range of individual peculiarities discovered in the research. "Sometimes", James notes, "it makes a difference how one imagines the sound to be written. The photism, e.g., of French *ou* may differ from the same individual's photism of German *u*, though the sounds are the same." The individual James was writing about – referred to by Flournoy as "the eminent linguist Mr X" – was Saussure.

Photism, a word James himself was the first to use in English, had been a popular subject in German and French psychological research since the start of the 1880s. None of the studies mentions the poem "Voyelles", written in 1871–2 by the young Rimbaud, even though these psychologists were scholar-scientists who kept up with literature. Of Flournoy's 700 anonymous subjects, Saussure was the only one to report that it made a difference to him how a sound was written:

> In French we write the same vowel four different ways in terrain, plein, matin, chien. Now when this vowel is written *ain*, I see it in pale yellow like an incompletely baked brick; when it is written *ein*, it strikes me as a network of purplish veins; when it is written *in*, I no longer know at all what colour sensation it evokes in my mind, and am inclined to believe that it evokes none.

When Saussure associated *ain* with an incompletely baked brick, it is hard not to think of the prototypical baked good, and one of the two most common French words to contain *ain*. Although *pain* (bread) is not mentioned, it too is a pale yellow when incompletely baked. When *ein* strikes him as a network of veins, this time the word used to identify the visual association is present – *veines* – though while the letters *ein* are there, in this word they are not pronounced with the vowel he is discussing. If *in* evokes nothing, could that have to do with *in-* being a negative prefix? Or with *in* being the stressed vowel of his given name, Mongin, which he never used? [Saussure] continued:

---

55. Joseph (2007). Incidentally, Théodore Flournoy's grandson, the psychoanalyst Olivier Flournoy, wrote the very interesting "Préface" to Mejía Quijano (2008), on which see n. 10 above. The Saussures and the Flournoys, both distinguished Genevan families, came to be linked by marriage: Théodore's youngest daughter, Ariane, married Ferdinand de Saussure's son Raymond (a psychoanalyst who studied under Théodore, whose only son, Henri, was likewise a psychoanalyst and psychiatrist).

So it does not seem to be the vowel as such – as it exists for the ear, that is – that calls forth a certain corresponding visual sensation. On the other hand, neither is it seeing a certain letter or group of letters that calls forth this sensation. Rather it is the vowel as it is contained in this written expression, it is the imaginary being formed by this first association of ideas which, through another association, appears to me as endowed with a certain consistency and a certain colour, sometimes also a certain shape and a certain smell.

The linguistic relationship between sight and sound, writing and spoken language, can never be straightforward in a literate society, and Saussure's exquisite sensibilities make his work on *anaphonie* even more interesting and difficult to assess.

ASSESSING SOUNDS ASUNDER

In my 2009 paper "Wordplay", directed at historical and comparative linguists, I discuss, among other things, Saussure's *anaphonie* and its influence on Indo-Europeanists and other linguists, especially Roman Jakobson, Vladimir Nikolayevich Toporov, Martin Schwartz, Françoise Bader and my own teacher Calvert Watkins, who is himself Saussure's intellectual great-grandson (via Meillet and Benveniste).[56] Although I cite plenty of examples of ludic phenomena, and from a number of languages, not many of them are Saussure's, and I am well aware that the present contribution, directed at classicists, is likewise light on Saussurean data. The reason is that when one thinks, reads and listens upside-down and backwards, around and about, as Saussure seems to have done, then multiplying examples does not really help: if you accept that the name SCIPIO lurks in *Taurasia Cisauna Samnio cepit* and that Homer is encoding Ἀγαμέμνων in ἀργαλέων ἀνέμων ἀμέγαρτον ἀϋτμήν, then more cases will make you happy; but if you do not immediately accept one or both of these – and I expect that more of my readers are skeptical than not – then being bombarded with further instances of such strangeness is likely just to be annoying.[57]

Whatever one may believe, engaging with Saussure's motivation and method is clearly important, and this requires taking the following two questions seriously. First, is it

---

56. See Katz (2009).
57. Shepheard (1990: 240) writes, "L'anagramme est un peu comme le yéti: comme le dit Mounin, tout le monde en parle mais personne n'en a jamais vu." Writing in 1974, Georges Mounin concluded the article cited in n. 43 above with the claim that the early studies of Saussure's notebooks, especially by Jean Starobinski, had led to "une nouvelle version de l'histoire de l'homme à la dent d'or, telle que la racontait Fontenelle: à force d'en parler tout le monde oublie qu'il n'y a pas d'anagrammes – sinon par une illusion d'optique statistique, dont on peut montrer comment Saussure s'y est, selon le mot de Starobinski, pris au piège" (Mounin 1974: 241).

actually plausible that – even in poetic language, never mind ordinary speech – there would be widespread polyphonic wordplay that, breaking all normal phonological conventions, enhances textual meaning by taking discontinuous bits from across lexemes? And second, if we decide that it is plausible, to what extent is such wordplay consciously engineered?

In answer to the first question, any claim that Saussure's SCIPIO is stunningly strange, as opposed to merely special, is, I believe, overstated, for in fact no one doubts that marked language regularly relies on the interactions of separated, discontinuous sounds across words, including for the purpose of enhancing meaning. Consider alliteration, which was probably one of the principal poetic devices in Proto-Indo-European verbal culture, to judge from the special fondness that many of the early languages have for it, including of course the Latin verses with which Saussure began his off-beat studies;[58] consider rhyme; and consider (more vaguely) consonantism/assonance – from #Μῆνιν ... #οὐλομένην (Homer, *Iliad* 1.1–2) and #Μοῦσαι ... ἐτήτυμα μυθησαίμην# (Hesiod, *Works & Days* 1–10)[59] right at the beginning of oral Greek literature through Gerard Manley Hopkins and up now to Paul Muldoon.[60] Effects such as these give language a sort of poetic bass line.[61] Is *anaphonie* really so different? If your ears are good enough to hear it, then you may find Saussure's scramble-phones to have a more thumping bass than some, but wordplay is universal – it transcends writing, age, education – and I know of no *a priori* reason why *anaphonie* should not belong on the list of real phonologico-semantic effects.

And then there is the matter of consciousness. Here Saussure probably made a mistake in assuming that the anaphonic effects were deliberate.[62] I do not have either space or gumption to tackle this big issue here, but it seems unlikely for oral poetry and certainly need not be the case for other forms of verbal art in which Saussure believed he found

---

58. Note that Saussure was explicitly interested in alliteration. For the clear connection between this interest and the beginnings of his researches into *anaphonie*, see the "1er Cahier à lire préliminairement" (references in n. 35 above) and Starobinski (1971: 28–9, 38–40 and *passim*; trans. 1979: 15–16, 24–6 and *passim*); see also e.g. Wunderli (1972b: 23–4 and 61), Lotringer (1973: 2–4) and Culler (1986: 125–6), as well as Shepheard (1982: 514 and 1986: 56) and now Testenoire (2010).

59. Watkins (1995: 100–101), referring to Saussure, writes of Hesiod's ten-verse proem that the "simple message [ἐτήτυμα μυθησαίμην ("I would speak true things")] is in fact *the poet's truth*, and it is cunningly hidden and cunningly unveiled. The poet's truth sees in two direction at once, forward and back; etĒTUMA MUTHĒsaimēn is an iconic palindrome of the elements of TRUE and SPEAK. This phonetic inversion finally calls attention to – perceptually cues – the hidden phonetic and semantic ring which frames the entire proem. The first word is Μοῦσαι, the Muses, the personified mind of the poet .... And the last word of the proem contains a Saussurian hypogram of the same word, to form a ring: MOUSAI -- MUthēSAImēn" (italics in original).

60. For an account of "inherited poetics" in Greek, see now Katz (2010b), with remarks on sound effects in *Iliad* 2.459–68 on p. 366; Le Feuvre (2009) offers an interesting perspective.

61. The BACH motif in Johann Sebastian's bass line is mentioned by many Saussureans, e.g. Jean Starobinski at the end of the final section ("Échos") of *Les Mots sous les mots*: Starobinski (1971: 159; trans. 1979: 128–9).

62. Compare Starobinski (1971: 151–4; trans. 1979: 120–23), as well as e.g. Christy (1999a and 1999b).

anaphonic instances: in Lucretius (e.g. AP(H)RODITE throughout the invocation to Venus that opens the *De rerum natura*),[63] Vergil (e.g. CAESAR in *caelestia dona / exsequar* [*Georgics* 4.1-2] and MAECENAS in *magnanimosque duces* [*Georgics* 4.4])[64] and Horace (PINDARUS and ANTONI in *Odes* 4.2.1-4[65]), for example, not to mention also in Cicero and Valerius Maximus.[66] Work by Jakobson in particular has shown that "subliminal verbal patterning"[67] is a very real and significant textual force and that all sorts of profound effects can come from what the poet and critic John Shoptaw calls "lyric cryptography",[68] a concept that Ellen Oliensis has recently given a boost in a classical context.[69]

In other words, Saussure's sundering of sounds may not be as remote from his broader theories about sound and meaning as most have thought it must be. But is it really, as he may have been so rash as to claim, the fundamental principle of Indo-European poetry?[70] And if so, what are the diachronic implications of this, given, after all, the level of linguistic fickleness that I have described? I leave such matters for the future – a future that will, I hope, include a trip of my own to the Saussure archives. For now, while I am acutely aware that my words have been more mood music than analytical argument, I hope that they will reach a wide-ranging audience and will stir up more people to investigate Saussure's anagram notebooks, the ways in which Saussurean *anaphonie* actually works (and doesn't), the role it plays in Saussure's intellectual biography and – aside from Saussure – the very idea of concealed words in oral and textual literature the world over. If I have managed in these pages both to tickle your senses and to begin to come to terms with reconciling "les deux Saussure" – the would-be opposition in the man himself

---

63. See Starobinski (1971: 79–100; trans. 1979: 57–74) for the classic account and especially Gandon (2002), so far the only large-scale study of *anaphonie*.
64. The joint issue of *Recherches/Semiotext(e)* mentioned in n. 38 above ends with the first reasonably extensive set of published facsimile pages from Saussure's anagram notebooks, including those that present his explication of the beginning of *Georgics* 4. (Some notes on APHRODITE in the *Aeneid* [compare immediately above in the text] are included in the selection as well.)
65. John Henderson *apud* R. F. Thomas (2011: 104) notes that "there seems to be play with names and partial acrostics: the opening PINDARUM begins to generate an acrostic (P I N ...), but instead creates incomplete P I N N-, an iconic image of what is going on in the lines, the crash of Icarus into the sea. *nititur pinnis* at the start of 3 descends in the next line to *nomina ponto*, with *nomina* drawing attention to the play"; Saussure goes unmentioned.
66. See for all this the summary account in Wunderli (1972b: 55–7).
67. Thus e.g. Jakobson (1980), which opens with an epigraph by Saussure. Compare Mikhail Gronas's excellent (and bibliographically valuable) paper (2009), inspired in large part by Saussure, on "mnemopoetics", his provisional term for a "subfield of literary scholarship ... that borders on both poetics and cognitive science ... [and] focuses on the mnemonic aspects of the creation, circulation, and reception of poetry" (*ibid.*: 156); see also now Gronas (2011: 97–129, with notes on 147–54). Barilli (1981) – an unusual reference I owe to Lowell Edmunds – deserves to be better known.
68. Shoptaw (2000).
69. See Oliensis (2009: 6–7, with nn. 12–13, and *passim*).
70. See Wunderli (1972c: 37 and 2004: 175); in the "1er Cahier à lire préliminairement" (see n. 35 above), Saussure mentions the "premier principe de la poésie indo-européenne, tel que je le conçois maintenant" (Wunderli 1972a: 212; compare Saussure 1997: 451).

between demand for linear order and the controlled chaos of the *anaphonie* he heard, saw and for all I know also touched, tasted and smelled – well, maybe that doesn't sound unsound.[71]

---

71. My thanks go to Shane Butler, Alex Purves and Mario Telò, the organizers of the wonderful synaesthesia conference at UCLA at which I delivered a version of this paper on 1 May 2010, and to Charles de Lamberterie, at whose invitation I had the privilege, just over a year later (well after the written paper had been submitted but not too late for some literature from late 2010 and 2011 still to be added), of leading a seminar on *anaphonie* at the École pratique des Hautes Études, where Saussure taught from 1881 to 1891. For comments and suggestions I am grateful to Françoise Bader, Ann Bergren, David Blank, Lowell Edmunds, Daniel Heller-Roazen, Charles de Lamberterie, Georges-Jean Pinault, Amy Richlin, Haun Saussy, Pierre-Yves Testenoire and my fellow synaesthetes, especially Shane Butler and Jim Porter. It is a pleasure to acknowledge the support I have received from All Souls College, Oxford, the EPHE, the John Simon Guggenheim Memorial Foundation, the Loeb Classical Library Foundation and my own university, Princeton.

13

BEYOND NARCISSUS

Shane Butler

A key text of twentieth-century thought went missing decades ago. More mysterious than the loss itself has been our indifference to it: the affair was never widely publicized, and even those in the know have tended to regard the disappearance as a bibliographic curiosity rather than as reason for serious regret. I am referring to Jacques Lacan, "The Mirror Stage". To be clear, I do not mean Jacques Lacan, "The Mirror Stage as Formative of the *I* Function as Revealed in Psychoanalytic Experience", delivered on 17 July 1949 to the Sixteenth International Psycho-Analytical Congress in Zurich and published the same year in the *Revue Française de Psychanalyse*.[1] I mean instead the earlier version with the shorter title, sometimes said to have been published in 1937, among the acts of the Fourteenth Annual Psycho-Analytical Congress in Marienbad, in *The International Journal of Psycho-Analysis*, vol. 18.[2] What one actually finds here, on page 78, sandwiched between summaries of papers on "The Dynamics of Puberty" and "The Early Diagnosis of Psychoses in Analysands", is only this brief notice: "2. Dr. J. Lacan (Paris). The Looking-Glass Phase". And that is all.

This part of the mystery, at least, is easily solved: Lacan himself, *en passant* in later writings, admits to being the immediate culprit, though he assigns ultimate blame to Ernest Jones, President of the Congress, "a position for which he was no doubt qualified by the fact that I have never encountered a single English colleague of his who didn't have something unpleasant to say about his character".[3] At the Congress's afternoon session on August 3, 1936, Lacan had begun his address, but when he ran overtime, Jones cut him off and would not let him finish. Annoyed, Lacan abandoned the meetings and went instead to Berlin to watch Hitler's Olympics. Naturally, wrote Lacan in 1946, "I did not submit

---

1. Lacan (1949).
2. Thus Sheridan in Lacan (1977: xiii): "An English translation of this version appeared in *The International Journal of Psychoanalysis*, vol. 18, part I, January, 1937, under the title, '*The Looking-glass Phase*'". The error has often been repeated.
3. Lacan (2006: 150–51 [184–5 in Paris: Éditions du Seuil, 1966]).

my paper for inclusion in the proceedings of the congress".[4] Three years later – twelve after its first, truncated delivery – the essay for which Lacan is best known (even by those who have never read him) finally saw print. Some have attempted to deduce what Lacan is likely to have revised, and Jane Gallop uses the missing original for some clever play on the question of when and where Lacan "begins".[5] But most have been content to look forwards rather than back.

Case closed? Or have we just fallen victim to the same sleight of hand that so captivated Lacan in Poe's "The Purloined Letter", on which he would give a famous seminar in 1955 and in which both villain and hero substitute for one text another that, at first glance, seems to be the same?[6] There are, as has been noticed, some important omissions from the 1949 publication, though it is generally assumed that they were missing all along: namely, Lacan's predecessors and sources, especially Henri Wallon, from whom Lacan borrowed the phrase *stade du miroir* but whose name "Lacan always tried to obliterate … so as to present himself as the inventor of the expression".[7] But I am more interested in how the substitution of the later paper and the revisions it embodies contribute to the extrication of Lacan's contribution from an even larger context and past. Some minimal recovery of these will lead us from the case of a misplaced text to the deeper mystery of a missing person. By the end I hope to suggest at least one reason why scholars of the last century seemed to lose touch with the non-visual senses – and what we must do to get them back.

We begin in Paris in the 1930s, where we find a Lacan we do not readily recognize, one arguably more a Surrealist than a psychoanalyst, often in the company of his closest Surrealist friend, Salvador Dalí. In 1936–7, while Lacan was not delivering and not publishing "The Mirror Stage", Dalí was painting *The Metamorphosis of Narcissus*, which he accompanied with a poem of the same title, simultaneously published in Paris and New York, his prologue to which trumpets the international debut of "the first poem and the first painting obtained entirely through the integral application of the paranoiac-critical method".[8] A few years earlier, in the inaugural issue (1933) of the Surrealist magazine *Minotaure*, Dalí had offered a "paranoiac critical interpretation" of a painting by Jean-François Millet in the course of which he enthusiastically cites Lacan's dissertation of the year before.[9] We turn the page of the same issue to find an article by Lacan himself on paranoia and "the problem of style" in art.[10] Writing decades later, Lacan would offer a rare mention of Dalí in order to take direct credit for having inspired the latter's "critical paranoia" by his own "paranoiac knowledge".[11] But he never comments on the coincidence

---

4. Lacan (2006: 151 [185]). Brief discussion of both passages and the "bibliographical riddle" in Ragland-Sullivan (1986: 27–8); much more in Roudienesco (2003).
5. Gallop (1982).
6. Lacan (2006: 6–48 [11–61]).
7. Roudinesco (2003: 27).
8. Dalí (1998: 324).
9. Dalí (1933: 66).
10. Lacan (1933).
11. Lacan (2006: 51 [65]).

that finds the two friends in Paris at the same time, reflecting on reflection, rewriting the same myth.[12]

Of course, in Surrealist Paris, Dalí and Lacan scarcely needed to look far to find still others pondering the interpenetration of mirrors and selves. Let us limit ourselves to just three examples. First, Jean Cocteau's 1930 film *The Blood of a Poet*, the opening sequence of which features a painter who is urged by a talking statue to enter a mirror and walk around. Second, Picasso's well-known 1932 *Girl Before a Mirror*, which has been said to play on the fact that this particular kind of dressing mirror is, in French, called a *psyché*.[13] Third, another Picasso: his cover for the same 1933 issue of *Minotaure* we have been flipping through (Figure 13.1).

Picasso depicts the journal's eponymous monster, holding a knife whose shape also suggests that of a pen, a brush, a phallus, but most of all, a mirror, into which he seems to gazes with more vanity than horror. He cannot otherwise see his own monstrous head; it is in the mirror, therefore, that he must come to terms with his own thingness, and thence, with his own hybridity. If all of Lacan can be said to be present in germ in "The Mirror Stage", then it is just as surely so here. There is, of course, the pen-like mirror that marks both word and image (*langue, Imaginaire, Symbolique*) but that is also a phallus and a "cut" (*coupure*). The scene is captioned with "the name of the father" (*le nom du père*), or rather, with the name that combines those of two fathers, Minos and the bull, the first of whom, who of course confines his beastly namesake to the Labyrinth, has already imposed his "no" (*le non du père*). Even the foil of the surrounding collage seems to anticipate the glittering sardine-can of the eleventh instalment of Lacan's *Seminar*.[14] Add to this the fact that, for the Picasso who figured his own Spanishness with bulls and bulls' heads, this Minotaur is looking at *his* own reflection; the ensemble thus offers a multiply self-conscious (and self-alienating) self-portrait. One could object that we would not see things precisely this way without Lacanian hindsight; still, when Lacan later insists, "Everyone knows that I entered psychoanalysis with the little brush that was called the 'mirror stage'",[15] it is difficult, in the face of this image, not to hear instead the confession (or repression) of a debt in the other direction. Whatever it may eventually become,

---

12. Roudinesco (1997: 55–6) argues that the suppression of Lacan's debt to Dalí and the Surrealists was there from the get-go: "[In 1931] his encounter with Dali began to have its effect. It soon led him to reject automatism and place the full anthropological significance of madness at the center of the human mind. Thus every so often the thesis on paranoia that he completed in the autumn of 1932 reveals a tendency to appropriate the positions of the surrealists. But he didn't breathe a word in avowal of this major influence. He was careful not to quote the relevant sources, never even mentioned any of the great surrealist texts that lay behind his own, and made no reference to Dali, Breton, or Eluard. He was anxious about his career and didn't want to offend either his masters in psychiatry, who rejected the literary avant-garde, or the supporters of orthodox Freudianims, of whom he was still a disciple. But he had guessed wrong: the first people to do him honor were those whose importance to himself he had disguised, and the first people to decry him were those he had tried to please." Already in 1930, she suggests (*ibid.*: 31–2), the impact of an article of Dalí's ("L'Âne pourri") had been decisive on Lacan's thought.
13. Gottlieb (1966: 510).
14. Lacan (1998b: 95).
15. Roudinesco (2003: 27).

Figure 13.1 Maquette for the cover of the journal "Minotaure" (1933), Pablo Picasso (1881–1973) 19⅛ × 16⅛ in. (48.5 × 41.0 cm). Gift of Mr and Mrs Alexandre P. Rosenberg. The Museum of Modern Art, New York. © 2012 Estate of Pablo Picasso / Artists Rights Society (ARS), New York. Digital image © The Museum of Modern Art; licensed by SCALA / Art Resource, New York.

Lacan's "mirror stage" is, in origin, one particular distillation of a Surrealist artistic and psychoanalytic *Zeitgeist*.

With that *Zeitgeist* our plot thickens. Let us return briefly to Dalí. Dalí's paintings often offer riffs on classic works; thus the very painting by Millet to which he applied critical paranoia would soon be transformed into his *Archeological Reminiscence of Millet's Angelus*, finished in 1935. A smaller citation in *The Metamorphosis of Narcissus* is seldom noticed but plain once you see it: Dalí closely echoes the general pose and, in particular, the form of the knee from the famous *Narcissus* attributed to Caravaggio.[16] Knowingly or not, Dalí thereby ties his painting to a tradition not only of painting Narcissus but of seeing Narcissus *as a painter* (and the painter's art as a search for self-in-image), a notion that in its simplest form goes back to the Renaissance classroom of Leon Battista Alberti[17]

---

16. Heyd (1984: 122).
17. Discussion in Baskins (1993).

but which has antecedents in ancient epigrams and the lost paintings they describe, in surviving Pompeian wall painting, and arguably, if implicitly, in our principal source for the story: Ovid's *Metamorphoses*. This particular thread twines with others of the whole Ovidian tradition, powered from the beginning by the reading of the poem as, above all, a long meditation on artmaking itself. It is precisely this reading that has allowed the poem a role in Western art that has been, on the one hand, nearly uninterrupted and, on the other, especially evident in ages that seem to be asking most insistently the question, "What is art?"

Little wonder, then, that Ovid seems to be everywhere in the first half of the twentieth century, especially in the 1920s and 1930s, which comprise an *aetas Ovidiana* ready to rival any other, driven, as Dore Ashton beautifully explains, by an abiding interest in "metamorphosis as an artistic principle".[18] Let us limit ourselves to the artists we already have seen. Cocteau's *Blood of a Poet*, which opens with the painter at work on a translucent canvas and which is constantly introducing the filmmaker himself as the poet's double, plays not only on Narcissus but also on Pygmalion and, eventually, on Daedalus and Icarus, all figures for the artist familiar to the Ovidian reader. Picasso, in addition to the Minotaur who, in Ovid, is both the product and the prisoner of Daedalus' *ars*, also produced the etchings for the illustrated *Metamorphoses* published by Albert Skira (publisher of *Minotaure*) in 1930; these anticipate the *Girl Before a Mirror* and offer a fugue of images that explore quite literally the *lines* between subject and object, implicating art both in creation (e.g. *Deucalion and Pyrrha Creating a New Human Race*, where lines are reproduced—and thus reproduce) and in death (e.g., *The Sacrifice of Polyxena*, whose blood is as much the product of the artist's tool as it is of Neoptolomus's dagger).[19]

Naturally, Ovid lurks behind Dalí's *Metamorphosis of Narcissus*, both poem and painting, details of which respond to (and transform) specific moments and elements in the Ovidian text.[20] Ovid, however, joins other miscellaneous sources: Caravaggio (as we have seen), illustrated alchemical texts, and, more personally, the elder brother who died before Dalí was born and for whom he was raised as a kind of substitute and double.[21] No source, however, is as important here as Freud, whose gigantic influence on Dalí's art is hard to miss. Dalí was scarcely alone in this: André Breton himself "had launched Surrealism as a quasi-Freudian movement", even though, when he met Freud in 1921, he was sorely disappointed by the master's disinterest.[22] Much later, in 1938, Dalí too met Freud, in Paris, bringing to the meeting his painting of Narcissus. As with Breton, Freud seems to have been perplexed, later confiding to the meeting's host that Dalí struck him as a "fanatic".[23]

---

18. Ashton (1969).
19. Extension discussion of the Ovid illustrations in Florman (2000: 14–69; reproductions of these particular images, 36, 58).
20. Heyd (1984: 125–7).
21. *Ibid.*: 122–31.
22. Rabaté (2003: 17).
23. Rojas (1993: 82 n. 33): "Dalí states that Freud knew very little about him, but that before knowing him he already admired his art. However, judging from Freud's letter to Stefan Zweig, it seems evident that he hadn't seen a single painting by Dalí before the latter visited him and showed him *The Metamorphosis of*

Lacan, by contrast, never met Freud, though he did send him a copy of his thesis, which Freud answered with only a curtly polite postcard of thanks.[24] Indeed, it is arguable that what Lacan and his Surrealist friends most had in common was their fraught relationship with the always authoritative, always aloof *Doktorvater* Freud.

These two influences, Freud and Ovid, intersect in the figure of Narcissus. Freud borrowed the psychoanalytic deployment of the myth from Paul Näcke and Havelock Ellis[25]; his first mention of "narcissism" in print was in a footnote added in 1910 to a second edition of his 1905 *Three Essays on the Theory of Sexuality*. A version of the concept is used later that same year in *Leonardo da Vinci and a Memory of His Childhood* to explain the attraction of an adult homosexual to "boys whom he loves in the way in which his mother loved *him* as a child. He finds the objects of his love along the path of *narcissism*, as we say; for Narcissus, according to the Greek legend, was a youth who preferred his own reflection to everything else and who was changed into the lovely flower of that name."[26] This is a rare direct reference by Freud to the myth and its hero, whom he never really regarded as more than the etymological origin of a technical term; indeed, Freud was so indifferent to this namesake that he even defended lopping off a syllable of his name for the sake of euphony in the resulting complex, which he called *Narzissmus* ("narcism") rather than *Narzissismus* ("narcissism").[27] By the time of Freud's major work on the subject, *On Narcissism: An Introduction* (1914), the title term needs no gloss and Narcissus himself is never named. Here Freud moves well beyond his earlier use of narcissism to account for homosexuality and turns instead to the universal role of "a primary and normal narcissism"[28] in the infantile origins of what he calls the "ego-ideal".

These concepts, together with their further elaboration in, for example, *Beyond the Pleasure Principle* (1920), provide the context in and against which Dalí and Lacan, in 1936, find their vision and voice regarding Narcissus. In his poem and the reading of the painting which it prescribes, Dalí zeroes in on the question of sexual object choice: Narcissus and his alienation from the "heterosexual" crowd are finally redeemed by the sprouting flower, which Dalí ends the poem by saluting with the name of his wife, Gala, "my narcissus". Despite the loss of Lacan's Marienbad paper, we know something of its shape from unpublished notes taken by Françoise Dolto, who attended a trial run of it in

---

Narcissus. On the day of their meeting, Dalí insisted so much on Freud's reading his article 'New General Considerations abut the Mechanism of the Parnoiac Phenomenon from the Surrealist Point of View,' that the old man exclaimed to Stefan Zweig: 'Have you ever seen such a full-blooded Spaniard? What a fanatic!'"

24. Roudinesco (1997: 58; 1990: 133–4).
25. For the basics, see Strachey's comments in Freud (1957b: 69–70, 73 n. 1), but for a fuller discussion of the antecedents, parallels, and influence of Freudian narcissism, see May-Tolzmann (1991), who also considers the role of Isidor Sadger, and Lock (2000), who follows the tradition forward to Lacan.
26. Freud (1957a: 100).
27. Early English translators initially followed his lead with *narcism* but soon switched to *narcissism*. The French say *narcissisme* but the Italians *narcismo*. Freud defends his form in Freud (1958: 60 n. 3); cf. Freud (1957b: 73 n. 1).
28. Freud (1957b: 74).

Paris shortly before.[29] These reveal that Lacan divided his argument into nine parts, the headings of which are enough to indicate direct engagement with Freudian intertexts and their terms (e.g., libido, Death Instinct, Oedipus Complex). Narcissism appears explicitly in two rubrics, including the final one, "The values of narcissistic symptoms: twins", which invites at least superficial comparison with the doubled Narcissus of Dalí's painting.

Freud inevitably looms large in Lacan's article on "La famille" for the *Encyclopédie Française* (specifically for the volume on *La vie mentale* edited by Henri Wallon), written two years later in 1938, into which he inserts a capsule explanation of his own theory of the mirror stage; in a sub-section on the "Structure narcissique du moi" he proclaims that "nous voulons aussi pénétrer sa structure mentale avec le plein sens du mythe de Narcisse".[30] With these words still ringing in our ears, we turn at last to the definitive 1949 version, delivered and published, of "The Mirror Stage". As has often been observed, and as we ourselves have already noted, Lacan fails here to acknowledge Wallon as the originator of the phrase. Less often noticed, though perhaps it should be, is the fact that Lacan mentions Freud only in a footnote. But none of this is as surprising as the fact that Lacan never once names Narcissus and invokes "the term 'primary narcissism'" only near the end of the essay in order to proclaim that his "conception" of the mirror stage has superseded it.[31] Thus does the mythic hero that had been good to think with for a half-century of sexologists, psychoanalysts and Surrealists finally vanish, without leaving his name on anything at all.[32] One could perhaps suppose that the name itself was, by this point, already implied and therefore superfluous; certainly its omission did not prevent contemporaries from receiving "The Mirror Stage" as a revisionist theory precisely of "primary narcissism". But both Freud and Lacan are always telling us to pay attention to tiny details, so let us subject this omission to a closer look.

Much, of course, had changed between 1936 and 1949. After Auschwitz, the Surrealists' nightmares began to seem puerile and self-indulgent, as did their long fights over what to do and think about Stalin and Hitler, however sincere the antifascism that had driven most of them.[33] Most but not all: there was the awkward matter of Lacan's friend Dalí, the odd man out who was somewhat perversely destined to be the best-remembered Surrealist of all. Back in the 1930s he had risked expulsion from the group for some ambiguous statements about Hitler, and precisely in 1949, he sparked outrage by moving back to Spain, where he would soon cozy up to Franco. If in 1936 Dalí and Lacan had shared a common interest in Narcissus, who had already emerged as a kind of Surrealist icon, then to invoke him in 1949 was to date oneself publicly to an era and privately to a friendship that were now distant and maybe more than a little discredited.

---

29. These are summarized by Roudinesco (2003: 26), whom I follow here.
30. Wallon (1938: 8.40.10).
31. Lacan (2006: 79 [98]).
32. Antigone, by contrast, keeps her name in Lacan, whose appropriaton of her is more fully his own. On Lacan's Antigone, see most recently Leonard 2006, with earlier bibliography (122–3).
33. The political struggles within the Surrealist group are carefully reconstructed by Durozoi (2002). Particularly revelatory is the defensiveness of André Breton's 1946 "Preface for the New Edition of the Second Manifesto", in Breton (1969: 113–15).

A more basic anxiety of influence, however, is also at work here. In his 1966 collection of *Écrits*, Lacan prefaces his second section of essays (among which appears "The Mirror Stage") with a long note "On My Antecedents", by which he means not "predecessors" (of whom he only really discusses Freud) but, rather, the beginnings of the thinking he means to vindicate as his own. Here Lacan looks back on his 1936 presentation in Marienbad as "my first pivotal intervention in psychoanalytic theory".[34] He can do so in part because, in 1949, he already had taken pains to edit out of this intervention the names that might make it seem too closely bound to the past. On the one hand, the excision of Narcissus completed a quiet Oedipal victory over the likewise excised Freud. On the other, with Lacan preparing to position himself as the very defender of authentic Freudianism, a change of vocabulary helped him to mark his distance from those he saw as Freud's banalizers. Already in Marienbad, Lacan had endured – assuming he stayed until the end of his own panel – an "Attempt to Explain the Enjoyment of Music" as a manifestation of narcissism, for example.

Here we add another consideration. "Narcissism" had begun, in Ellis and Näcke, as part of an effort to account for adult male homosexuality; Freud's earliest use of the term, in *Leonardo* and elsewhere, was directed toward the same end. As we have seen, Freud's eventual *On Narcissism* revises his subject into a universal part of human psychic development – "a primary and normal narcissism" – though Freud still finds this useful for accounting for adult homosexuality; at the same time, he links the "narcissistic libido" to another universal, the "homosexual libido".[35] Turning instead to the artists we have considered, Dalí's *Narcissus* aims to mythologize the poet-painter's own journey through and beyond homosexuality-as-narcissism. But even more striking is Cocteau, who arguably is unrivalled in the whole history of art in his exploitation of the homoerotic power of Narcissus's self-encounter. This is clear enough in the voyeurism of *The Blood of a Poet* (where, among other things, we are shown the moments just before and after our half-clothed hero's full enjoyment of the mouth that has grown in his own hand), which however is nothing compared to the frank pornography of *The White Book* (1930), in which a male narrator spies on showering sailors through a two-way mirror while they masturbate to the sight of their own reflection, staring, unknowingly, into his own eyes.[36] Cocteau never lost interest in the mirror, which would be central to his greatest film, *Orphée* (1950), in which the title character, played by Cocteau's own lover Jean Marais, meets and loves Death in and through the mirror's face.

By casting instead a fully anonymous infant in the starring role of the final version of "The Mirror Stage", Lacan takes Narcissus, gay icon, out of the picture. Perhaps we should lodge some small protest at this ironic sequence of events. Narcissus enters the twentieth century, especially in the work of Ellis, as a tool for gay emancipation, whence he is seized upon by Freud who, however, psycho-pathologizes homosexuality, albeit mildly and apologetically, only then to decide that narcissism is in fact a universal part of early human

---

34. Lacan (2006: 57 [72], n. 4).
35. Freud (1957b: 74, 96, 101–2).
36. Cocteau (2001: 50–53).

psychic development, an idea borrowed and adapted by Lacan who, in "The Mirror Stage", need finally make no mention of homosexuality at all. One cannot, however, accuse Freud or Lacan of homophobia without some heavy glossing, nor is heteronormativity really a sufficient explanation of what is going on here.

Rather, Narcissus's loss of a sexual orientation is part of his more general deracination, most conspicuously from his mythographic origins and their literary and artistic tradition. In the end, even his name must go, an erasure already begun, as we have seen, in Freud. But we would be wrong to think that nothing finally is left of Narcissus. On the contrary, the surprise ending of this vanishing act is an essay that, at times, seems to offer precisely a reading of Ovid's Latin. Both Lacan and Ovid offer a farce that we come to read as a tragedy. In Lacan we meet an ungainly infant blithely unaware that there is a place where he ends and the world begins; in front of the mirror, he begins to piece things together. The farce lies precisely in the fact that this new sense of self is reflective/reflexive: this subject emerges as an object; "I" depends on "me". Here we compare Ovid, where at the crucial moment, Narcissus cries to the lake, "That's me!", *iste ego sum*, Ovid's virtually untranslatable combination of the so-called second-person demonstrative pronoun with the first-person personal pronoun to produce something like "You, that one down there, I am", made even more remarkable by the fact that *iste* elides with *ego* (i.e., it is read *ist'ego*) as if imitating Narcissus's efforts to kiss his reflection: if they move any closer, they will annihilate one another. At the conclusion of "The Mirror Stage", Lacan seems to play on these very words, suggesting that "psychoanalysis may accompany the patient to the ecstatic limit of the '*Thou art that*' ('Tu es cela')". Naturally, one could object that I am reading Lacan through Ovid-coloured (looking) glasses. Most of us, in fact, read Lacan's notoriously sibylline texts with the help of what we already know; where I see Ovid, the philosopher will hear Hegel.[37] In any case, my purpose is hardly to demonstrate that Lacan is derivative of Ovid. Rather, I am trying to draw our attention towards the one thing they would seem most indisputably to have in common: the mirror. For I want to argue that this mirror, on inspection, fails to justify taking either as offering a parable of vision.

Literally speaking, Ovid gives us not a mirror (*speculum*) but a spring (*fons*). Here we should perhaps remind ourselves that the faithful illusion we expect from a mirror was not fully realized until the perfection of mirrored glass in the seventeenth century, nor were mirrors cheap and ubiquitous before the Industrial Revolution. Ancient mirrors were made of polished metal; this already would have made even simple ones costly; many that survive are unambiguously luxury items. Ovid's pond, however, is more than a primitive (or poor man's) mirror; indeed, it is not merely a mirror at all. Years ago, John Brenkman observed that the pond's reflection of "words not reaching our ears" offers an allegory of writing, and I myself have argued elsewhere that this pond, framed by a wood, "glittering with whitecapped ripples" and, having been disturbed, unable to reflect unless it has again been smoothed, figures the very waxed tablets in which Ovid's poem was first written.[38]

---

37. And just as with Ovid, this would be no accident: also in 1936, Lacan began attending Alexandre Kojeve's seminar on Hegel: Roudinesco (1997: 63–4).
38. Brenkman (1976: 317); Butler (2011: 77).

This textual surface can be analogized to an image, though not so much the image cast back by a mirror as the image that is captured and fixed in a work of art. *Ut pictura poesis*: Ovid's description of what Narcissus sees unfolds as an *ekphrasis*, while Narcissus himself freezes "like a statue shaped from Parian marble".[39] Ovid's episode, in this regard, tells a story of *mediation* (in the sense of artistic *media*): creation as alienation and loss. All poets and painters are narcissists, not because they love what they do, but because they are always looking down at their *tabulae* and saying, "That's me", i.e., that is no longer part of me, or perhaps more accurately, I am no longer part of it.

Lacan's mirror is no less elusive and complex. Lacan would soon come to regard the mirror stage as his key formulation of the relationship between the Imaginary, the realm emblematized by the mirror, the Symbolic, paradigmatically language but not limited to it, and the Real, all that escapes the Symbolic, a realm from which we are forever estranged by the mirror's intervention. These he would much later describe as being inseparably linked in a "Borromean knot",[40] but the encroachment of the Symbolic on the Imaginary began almost right away. Lacan soon revised the central scene of the mirror stage to require the presence of language and the (m)Other, who says, "That's you"; he sometimes treats the relationship between Symbolic and Imaginary as something like that between signifier and signified. One way or another, the Symbolic is Lacan's true purview (and that of psychoanalysis generally) and is read in relation to the Real; the Imaginary becomes, increasingly, the Holy Spirit of this trinity, difficult to describe on its own terms.

Why, then, does Lacan appeal to the mirror in 1936 and, more strikingly, stick to it throughout his career? Wouldn't the reflexive pronoun, for example, have served him better? In 1936 at least, part of the answer is that Lacan really is still thinking about vision and mirrors: he clearly understands the mirror stage as an actual event (both as a moment in human development and as a turning point in human evolution); he appeals to comparative evidence from the animal kingdom; he praises the visual experiments of Roger Caillois. But the mirror's persistence needs a deeper explanation. And I would suggest that, to find that explanation, we must do two things. The first is to recognize that the appeal of Lacan's mirror stage, and of Lacan generally, rests in no small part on the fact that *he confirms that we have lost something*. So anxious are we to have this confirmed that we are willing (indeed, especially eager) to hear it from someone who tells us that we cannot have what we have lost back. In Lacanian terms, this is the Real, that obscure object of our desire that is not an object at all but, rather, a realm free of mediation, of alienation, of Others. The second thing we must do is to restore Lacan, and psychoanalysis, to the world of literary and artistic metaphor from which they sometimes seem to emerge – not just Ovid's metaphors, but those of the Surrealists and, more generally, of an age to which we too still belong.

Had I introduced this essay as being about a major twentieth-century French thinker who explored the relationship between the image and loss, many readers would have

---

39. Ovid, *Metamorphoses* 3.419.
40. Thurston (1998).

expected Roland Barthes – that is, not the mirror, but the photograph.[41] The dead stare back at us from photographs, as does our own long-gone youth, and all manner of other things that, for better or for worse, we have left behind. The mirror can mark a similar kind of loss-in-time, but only when calibrated against memories that we arguably cannot help understanding in photographic terms and even reinforcing with actual photographic comparanda. I know I do not look like I used to, but I don't think I can fully recall what I looked like in the mirror; rather, I largely deduce this from what I know of myself from photographs. To be clear, the photographic loss-in-time is not the same as the instantaneous loss/gain of the mirror stage. But we should perhaps note that the fact that Lacan calls the latter a stage or phase does situate it in time and that, through photographs, we can in fact know what we looked like before we first saw, and found, ourselves.

Let us return for a moment to Cocteau. As we have seen, no mirror of his is merely such. In his films, they are patent – and deliciously ironic – stand-ins for the silver screen itself. Generally speaking, it is the connection of the photograph to loss and death that leads Cocteau to Orpheus, whom he has enter the Underworld through the filmic mirror and reflective screen. Cocteau, however, is no mere student observer of the photograph: he is its maestro, and the images *in* his films reflect the larger spectacle *of* his films as lavish meditations on art-making by this most Ovidian of filmmakers. As a result, we are always seeing the screen from both sides, that is, we see the film through both machines through which it passes, both camera and projector. Thus we see through the self-portrait at which the hero of *Blood of a Poet* is working as the first scene opens, just as we will soon see him face the mirror from both back and front, the latter of which transforms him into a reflection of ourselves as people out there, in the dark. These migrations, like those of the poet-hero Orpheus, are fantastic versions of Cocteau's own, as he watches his own immortalizing objectification and death through and as his art, a serious enough matter in these films, less so in the final installment of the trilogy, *The Testament of Orpheus*, Cocteau's narcissistic high-camp version of Ovid's final *vivam*, "I shall live".

One can argue that Lacan did not really know first-hand this kind of artistic vanity. He was not really a writer except of lectures (which comprise the bulk of his somewhat paradoxically named *Écrits*), and most of the rest of what we have from him are his "Seminars", transcribed from tape-recordings of his lessons. But he certainly knew of the artist's relationship with the art object from his time with Dalí, and it is hard not to hear this reflected in Lacan's description of the mirror stage as his own "little brush", object of a vanity that would, as we have seen, several times lead Lacan to assert, "That's me." You cannot sign a mirror, but you can, it seems, sign a mirror stage. For a text, like a photograph, but unlike a real mirror, remembers.

Ovid did not know the photograph, but he did know analogues like the ancestral portrait-masks (*imagines*) collected by Roman families. Nor, more broadly, was his age spared the "the power of images",[42] including ones that were not only reproduced (like statue-portraits of the emperor) but mass-produced (like the same on coins). Augustan

---

41. Barthes (1981).
42. P. Zanker (1988).

Rome provides a salutary reminder that tracking images is not the same as tracking the importance of ordinary vision: if there's one thing that the imperial imagery just evoked tells us, it is that the "face-to-face" Republic is over. One way or another, Ovid cannot speak of the mirror's fleeting *imago* without pointing as well toward *imagines* in more durable form. And ultimately, as I already have suggested, he is not thinking of pictures as much as he is thinking of the image that is the written text. One way or another, then, as now, (written) word and (pictorial) image compete and collaborate as dominant modes of mediation: both *record*.

The brain too is a recording device; so central is this fact to psychoanalysis from its beginnings that Thomas Elsaesser has recently argued, quite rightly, that we must recover Freud first and foremost as a media theorist.[43] For Freud, the core problem of the mind-as-media is that a unitary device cannot both transmit/process information (data come and go) and store information (data remain). Thus in "A Note Upon the 'Mystic Writing-Pad'" (1925), he famously analogizes the psychic apparatus to the *Wunderblock* of his title, a toy in which one writes with a stylus on a thin sheet of cellophane that is pressed into a tablet of black wax below, producing words that vanish from the cellophane when it is lifted but which remain inscribed in the wax; endless repetition of the act of writing and erasure would look something like the interaction of consciousness (what appears briefly on the cellophane) and the Unconscious (what lingers in the wax).[44] We focus now on the cellophane for its more than superficial resemblance to Lacan's mirror. For where Freud needs a fantasy of the unfixed, immaterial word, Lacan needs the same for the image. For the infant must not only recognize that what she sees is not another person (this, apparently, is the mistake that most other primates, save our close cousins the chimpanzees, make): she must also decide that it is not first and foremost a shiny object, just as, in order to read, we must avoid seeing books and pages, paper and ink, lines and shapes. In their respective efforts to precipitate consciousness and the I, Freud and Lacan quietly abstract word and image from the sensual world. We do the same in daily life, but not exclusively because of some primal event or neural configuration. Rather, we find ourselves under lifelong pressure from *regimes of legibility*, among which we may include psychoanalysis itself.

Every Freudian symptomatology reveals his stake in legibility, but the matter is thrown into particular relief precisely by his interest in narcissism. Freud pretends to come to Leonardo da Vinci as an ordinary case, in order to prove that "there is no one so great as to be disgraced by being subject to the laws which govern both normal and pathological activity with equal cogency".[45] But it is easy to illustrate what makes Leonardo special by asking a question: Have you seen the most famous Leonardo of all, in the Louvre? Most of my readers will understand my "Leonardo" to mean not Leonardo da Vinci the person but *Mona Lisa* the painting. Nor would be there any risk of misunderstanding if I were to ask: Have you read Freud? The elision of "the painting by" and "the works of" is perhaps

---

43. Elsaesser (2009).
44. Freud (1961).
45. Freud (1957a: 63).

easier posthumously, but artists and authors begin it themselves already in life: remember Dalí lugging his painting to his meeting with Freud, and Lacan introducing himself with a copy of his dissertation. If art is anything, it is a certain surrender to mediation. And the question is not whether we should take the art-object to be a substitute for the artist-subject (let us suppose this to be irresistible, with our without "The Death of the Author"); rather, it is on what terms we would go about doing so. For Freud, the legibility of the product presupposes the legibility of the producer, and vice versa. Leonardo paints Leonardo; by reading the latter, Freud reads the former. And this tyranny of the sign necessarily privileges the textual and the graphic, as Freud moves from Leonardo's writings to his drawings to, in passing, what actually makes him most famous, his paintings, without once mentioning colour.[46]

Leonardo paints Leonardo; Narcissus loves Narcissus. Lacan steps in, let us say, to remind us of our (Latin) grammar: properly speaking, Narcissus actually loves *Narcissum* (*Narcissus Narcissum amat*). If the mirror really were capable of teaching infants the difference between subject and object, we Latin teachers would not have such a hard time of it. We are only partially helped by the fact that someone else has already taught our students to say "He loves him" and even "He loves himself". Indeed, the very fact that such lessons must be repeated would seem to offer important evidence that our understanding of the relationship between subjects and objects is not the fruit of the activation of some cognitive birthright but, rather, something that we learn, expand, and reinforce over time. And we may hazard to suppose that not only every language we learn but every discursive system in which we are emplotted is forever reminding its forgetful students of these very rules. For grammars like these, we have been told, are society's most basic coin; without them, no complex economy of power – that is, no society at all – is possible.

But the notion that we are subjects so that we may become subjects of the regimes that regulate us ultimately banalizes the reasons for our complicity. For we first enter the semiotic realm neither to join society nor even, in simpler terms, to communicate. And this is what Lacan most surely gets right: we are led to signs first and foremost by our need for *self*-control. We do not, however, need to anticipate the social self in order to explain why this happens. Our first need is far more basic, and it lies in the very richness of the senses themselves and especially of the sensual world that stimulates them. This is a problem that already preoccupied Freud; its most pointed articulation comes in *Beyond the Pleasure Principle*, where he is describing the system of Perception-Consciousness (Pcpt.-Cs.) that he eventually will consolidate into his formulation of the ego. Here Freud describes evolution itself as a progressive retreat from the world's stimulation:

> Let us picture a living organism in its most simplified possible form as an undifferentiated vesicle of a substance that is susceptible to stimulation. Then the surface turned towards the external world will from its very situation be differentiated and will serve as an organ for receiving stimuli ... It would be easy to suppose, then, that

---

46. Except as a graphic device, in a footnote on the painting of Mary with child and St. Anne, where the former's blue drapery is read as demarcating the silhouette of a vulture (Freud 1957a: 115–16 n.).

as a result of the ceaseless impact of external stimuli on the surface of the vesicle, its substance to a certain depth may have become permanently modified, so that excitatory processes run a different course in it from what they run in the deeper layers. A crust would thus be formed which would at last have been so thoroughly "baked through" by stimulation that it would present the most favourable possible conditions for the reception of stimuli and become incapable of any further modification ... *Protection against* stimuli is an almost more important function for the living organism than *reception of* stimuli. The protective shield is supplied with its own store of energy and must above all endeavour to preserve the special modes of transformations of energy operating in it against the effects threatened by the enormous energies at work in the external world ... In highly developed organisms the receptive cortical layer of the former vesicle has been withdrawn into the depths of the interior of the body, though portions of it have been left on the surface immediately beneath the general shield against stimuli. These are the sense organs, which consist essentially of apparatus for the reception of certain specific effects of stimulation, but which also include special arrangements for further protection against excessive amounts of stimulation and for excluding unsuitable kinds of stimulation. It is characteristic of them that they deal only with very small quantities of external stimulation and only take in *samples* of the external world. They may perhaps be compared with feelers which are all the time making tentative advances toward the external world and then drawing back from it.[47]

The need to sample/protect is there for all the senses, but it is the visual version that has attracted the attention of a long series of Freud's heirs, from Gestalt psychologists, to Rudolf Arnheim and his studies of perception,[48] to cognitive scientists, to researchers of artificial intelligence and those who use their lessons to study the brain, to, as Thomas Elsaesser argues, systems and media theorists (among the latter of whom, as we have seen, he counts Freud himself). And it is by restoring Lacan to *this* context that we may most readily illuminate what "The Mirror Stage" obscures. The image, Lacan tells us, is needed to produce the I. But if the mirror thus cuts us down to size, we just as surely teach it the same lesson, eliminating its shining surface in its frame on its wall in its room and all that we could know about any of these until finally we have reduced it to an image that is not even its own. In this light, I would suggest, our discovery of ourselves seems a bit like one of Guildenstern by Rosencranz: a puppet show that is only incidental to the real drama, which lies instead in our endless struggle to make our whole world smaller.

This reduction eventually mingles with the play of language, which not only filters but itself emerges through filtering, as we learn to reduce the voices we both hear and produce down to the phonemes of our languages, just as we shall later learn to see not flecks of varied black on fibres of varied white, nor lines nor even letters, but words. Language is the social extension of our sensory "rind" and must therefore be first understood in relation

---

47. Freud (1955: 26–8); italics original.
48. See, for starters, Arnheim (1969: 13–53).

to its base, that is, not as that which enables us to communicate with one another but as that which aims to limit our contact with the world. Starting with its crude sensory palette, language hews everything down to this or that. It plays *alter ego* to all our senses, but it does so through the two particular senses through which we best know language itself, hearing and vision. And it is mostly in this latter form that we have enshrined language as our favourite self-reminder, ostensibly because writing is an image of speech but really because writing is an image of our image-making. Reading, like our vision, requires blindness: you must see words here, not paper or a screen, just as surely as Ovid must not see his wax; Narcissus, his lake.

But, of course, having been reminded of it, you do now see the page, just as Ovid saw the wax he worked into water. Even when we limit ourselves (as I have just done) to the question of writing materials *as images*, their occasional competition with words for our attention is a reminder of what should be obvious anyway: words too are images; strictly speaking, the page can "show" us nothing more. And while it is doubtless the case that the page is in part responsible for a certain domination of vision over our other senses in literature and thought, it is important to recognize that the page mirrors us because it is itself relatively insensate, just as we ourselves are to it and to our world, endlessly reducing the infinite variety of everything. This is the sensual world framed by Lacan's mirror, one that narrows our senses down to one and which then narrows that vision down to something as close as possible to reading, so that the world shows us mostly the only images that a text really can: words.

In this light, let us take one last look at Ovid's Narcissus. It probably should have begun to bother us long ago that the story we take as parable and paradigm of our visual existence begins with a blind man, the prophet who foretells the boy's doom. Even more worrying is our persistent deafness to Tiresias's exact words. We all remember that Narcissus will live to a ripe old age "provided that he not come to know himself". And no commentator fails to note that this prophecy parrots the *gnōthi seauton* inscribed over the entrance to the temple of Apollo at Delphi, just as the entire episode parodies the philosophical search for self-knowledge, Socratic or otherwise. But the Latin gives us something more: **si se non noverit**, the episode's first echo.[49] There she is – *Ecce Echo*, we might say – the one whose disappearance from the psychoanalyst's list of patients (though not from his couch) is even more conspicuous than that of Narcissus. Echo does come back, briefly and late, in Lacan's twentieth seminar, where he introduces the concept of *lalangue*, of which language is only a subset.[50] The term combines the French article with its noun and probably plays on the Greek verb *lalein*; it also echoes, narcissistically, Lacan's own name, even as it suppresses Echo's, for Lacan is refashioning an existing psychoanalytic term, *echolalia*, one which, by the way, had captured Breton's imagination in the first Surrealist manifesto.[51] Echolalia is a real condition in which questions are answered by being repeated, wholly or in part; it is especially common among blind children.

---

49. Ovid, *Metamorphoses* 3.348.
50. Lacan (1998a: 44 and *passim*). Cf. Certeau 1996.
51. Breton (1969: 34).

We begin our histories of classical literature with a blind man; then as now we have supposed that this makes sense because poets, like prophets (both *vates*), are set apart by a sixth sense and second sight. But Ovid's sonic high jinks, which begin with Tiresias and continue right through the episode, including but hardly limited to Echo herself, shout something simpler: poetry is sound as much as it is sense or sight. Technically speaking, we know this: we master metres and rhythms, learn to call this an alliteration and that an assonance. And then we turn right back to Narcissus, the Imaginary and the Symbolic. Indeed, we are unphased by his eventual disappearance; Ovid, expecting this, puts him in the Underworld, staring into the Styx, out of sight but not out of mind. But Echo, meanwhile, is still here with us, forever and everywhere. Prove it to yourself by reading the following aloud: *dixerat 'ecquis adest?' et 'adest' responderat Echo*.[52] Did you not hear her echo your voice?

Where does this leave us? Poetry by its very nature pushes beyond the Symbolic, away from language and toward what alone we have graced with the name "music". We do not even need to play Ovid's page to know this; indeed, even a Latinless "reader" will suspect that its words are arranged into more than syntax from its roughly consistent line-lengths, that its letters and syllables are arranged into more than just words from their dense repetitions. Our senses here do not always *make sense*: we see more, hear more, and since both the hand that wrote those words and any throat and mouth that pronounce them are also known haptically, we can add that we *feel* more, if only to add another suggestively ambiguous term to our vocabulary. The limit of sense is sense, and vice versa; Echo pulls word into sound and sound back into word and so on, endlessly.

The arts of all the Muses reflect *both* the Symbolic *and* its penumbra; even as they traffic in symbols, they are forever reminding us that we and our world and even our words are made of more than meaning. But what of psychoanalysis? That it walks a similar line is clear enough from its debt to the same traditions and from the resemblances that draw analysts and artists together, in mutual if not always exactly reciprocal admiration: Freud of Leonardo; Dalí of Freud. But psychonalysis in Lacan ultimately falls victim to its own less than poetic resilience, its excessive literalism. Lacan weds us to the image, the image to the Symbolic, the Symbolic to language, language to meaning; he then struggles, throughout the rest of his career, to name and describe our efforts to reach beyond, from his early comments on the Real to his later lectures on the *objet petit a*. While some have seen this struggle as our own, I would suggest that it exists more in theory than in practice, and that Lacan thus goes looking not for what we lose in the mirror but for what he has lost for us in "The Mirror Stage". In this sense, in these our senses, poets and other artists offer us better reflections on our embodied lives as we actually live them: forever deferring any definitive choice between sense and sensuous nonsense.[53]

---

52. Ovid, *Metamorphoses* 3.380.
53. On this last point, compare Merleau-Ponty on "Cézanne's Doubt", the essay that opens the collection he titled *Sense and Non-Sense* (Merleau-Ponty 1964: 9–25).

BIBLIOGRAPHY

Note: translations from Greek and Latin are by the contributors unless otherwise noted. Frequently used abbreviations are *LSJ* (*Liddell–Scott–Jones Greek–English Lexicon*), *OLD* (*Oxford Latin Dictionary*), and *OED* (*Oxford English Dictionary*). Other standard abbreviations are those listed by the *Oxford Classical Dictionary* (*OCD*).

Abry, J.-H. 2007. "Manilius and Aratus: Two Stoic Poets on Stars". *Leeds International Classical Studies* **6**(1), http://lics.leeds.ac.uk/2007/200701.pdf.

Ackerman, D. 1990. *A Natural History of the Senses*. New York: Random House.

Ahmed, S. 2010. "Orientations Matter". In Coole & Frost (2010), 234–57.

Alesse, F. 2003. "Il tema dell'emanazione (*aporroia*) nella letteratura astrologica e non astrologica tra I sec. a.C. e II d.C.". *MHNH. Revista Internacional de Investigación sobre Magia y Astrología Antiguas* **3**: 117–33.

Allen, D. S. 2000. *The World of Prometheus: The Politics of Punishing in Democratic Athens*. Princeton, NJ: Princeton University Press.

Alvarez, A. 1961. "English Poetry Today". *Commentary* **32**(3): 217–23.

Ambühl, A. 2010. "Lucan's 'Ilioupersis' – Narrative Patterns from the Fall of Troy in Book 2 of the *Bellum Civile*". In *Lucan's Bellum Civile: Between Epic Tradition and Aesthetic Innovation*, N. Hömke & C. Reitz (eds), 17–38. Berlin: De Gruyter.

Anderson, C. A. 1991. "The Dream-Oracles of Athena, *Knights* 1090–95". *Transactions of the American Philological Association* **121**: 149–55.

Andrews, A. C. 1948. "Orach as the Spinach of the Classical Period". *Isis* **39**(117): 169–72.

Arnheim, R. 1969. *Visual Thinking*. Berkeley, CA: University of California Press.

Asch, S. E. 1958. "The Metaphor: A Psychological Enquiry". In *Person, Perception and Interpersonal Behavior*, R. Tagiuri & L. Petrullo (eds), 86–94. Stanford, CA: Stanford University Press.

Ashton, D. 1969. "A Mobile Life in a Changing World: Metamorphosis as an Artistic Principle". In his *A Reading of Modern Art*, 69–79. Cleveland, OH: Press of Case Western Reserve University.

Asmis, E. 1995. "Philodemus on Censorship, Moral Utility, and Formalism in Poetry". In Obbink (1995), 148–77.

Assfahl, G. 1932. *Vergleich und Metapher bei Quintilian*. Stuttgart: W. Kohlhammer.

Aveline, J. 2000. "Aristophanes' *Acharnians* 95–7 and 100: Persians in the Athenian Assembly". *Hermes* **128**(4): 500–1.

Backhouse, A. E. 1994. *The Lexical Field of Taste: A Semantic Study of Japanese Taste-Terms*. Cambridge: Cambridge University Press.

Bahti, T. 1996. *Ends of the Lyric: Direction and Consequence in Western Poetry*. Baltimore, MD: Johns Hopkins University Press.

Bailey, C. 1947. *Lucretius: De Rerum Natura. Edited, with Prolegomena, Critical Apparatus, Translation and Commentary*, 3 vols. Oxford: Oxford University Press.
Bakker, E. J. 2002. "The Making of History: Herodotus' *Histories Apodexis*". In *Brill's Companion to Herodotus*, E. J. Bakker, I. J. F. De Jong & H. van Wees (eds), 3–32. Leiden: Brill.
Bakola, E. 2010. *Cratinus and the Art of Comedy*. Oxford: Oxford University Press.
Balsdon, J. 1979. *Romans and Aliens*. London: Duckworth.
Baltussen, H. 1998. "The Purpose of Theophrastus '*De sensibus*' reconsidered". *Apeiron* 31(2): 167–99.
Baltussen, H. 2000. *Theophrastus Against the Presocratics and Plato: Peripatetic Dialectic in the De Sensibus*. Leiden: Brill.
Barilli, R. 1981. *Viaggio al termine della parola: la ricerca intraverbale*. Milan: Feltrinelli. Published in English as *Voyage to the End of the Word*, T. Fiore & H. Polkinhorn (trans.) (San Diego, CA: San Diego State University Press, 1997).
Barker, A. 1984. *Greek Musical Writings Volume I: The Musician and his Art*. Cambridge: Cambridge University Press.
Baron-Cohen, S. & J. E. Harrison (eds) 1997. *Synaesthesia: Classic and Contemporary Readings*. Oxford: Blackwell.
Barthes, R. 1975. *The Pleasure of the Text*, R. Miller (trans.). New York: Hill & Wang.
Barthes, R. 1981. *Camera Lucida: Reflections on Photography*, R. Miller (trans.). New York: Hill & Wang.
Barton, T. 1994. *Power and Knowledge: Astrology, Physiognomics and Medicine under the Roman Empire*. Ann Arbor, MI: University of Michigan Press.
Baschet, F., & B. Baschet 1987. "Sound Sculpture: Sounds, Shapes, Public Participation, Education". *Leonardo* 20(2): 107–14.
Baskins, C. L. 1993. "Echoing Narcissus in Alberti's 'Della Pittura'". *Oxford Art Journal* 16(1): 25–33.
Baudelaire, C. 1976. *Oeuvres complètes*, vol. 2. Paris: Gallimard.
Baudelaire, C. 1982. *Les Fleurs du Mal: The Complete Text of The Flowers of Evil*, R. Howard (trans.). Boston, MA: D. R. Godine.
Baudrillard, J. 1976. *L'Échange symbolique et la mort*. Paris: Gallimard. Published in English as *Symbolic Exchange and Death*, I. H. Grant (trans.) (London: Sage, 1993).
Baumgarten, A. 1735. *Meditationes philosophicae de nonnullis ad poema pertinentibus*. Halle: J. H. Grunertus.
Baumgarten, A. 1750. *Aesthetica*. Frankfurt (Oder): J. C. Kleyb.
Beard, M. 2002. "Did Romans have Elbows? Or: Arms and the Romans". In *Corps Romains*, P. Moreau (ed.), 47–59. Grenoble: J. Millon.
Beekes, R. 2010. *Etymological Dictionary of Greek*, 2 vols. Leiden: Brill.
Bell, M. 1994. *The Book of the Dead Man*. Port Townsend, WA: Copper Canyon Press.
Benveniste, É. 1964. "Lettres de Ferdinand de Saussure à Antoine Meillet". *Cahiers Ferdinand de Saussure* 21: 89–130.
Benveniste, É. 1971. "The Notion of 'Rhythm' in its Linguistic Expression". In his *Problems in General Linguistics*, M. E. Meek (trans.), 281–313. Coral Gables, FL: University of Miami Press.
Berlin, B. & P. Kay 1969. *Basic Color Terms*. Berkeley, CA: University of California Press.
Bernstein, C. 1999. *My Way: Speeches and Poems*. Chicago, IL: University of Chicago Press.
Berti, E. 2011. "Platone, Demostene, e *L'Umbratilis Oratio*: A Proposito di Dion. Hal., *Dem*. 32 (I. p. 200, 21 ss. US.–R.)". *Parola del Passato* 66(1): 17–32.
Biles, Z. 2002. "Intertextual Biography in the Rivalry of Cratinus and Aristophanes". *American Journal of Philology* 123(2): 169–204.
Biles, Z. 2011. *Aristophanes and the Poetics of Competition*. Cambridge: Cambridge University Press.
Bing, P. 1990. "A Pun on Aratus' Name in Verse 2 of the *Phainomena*?". *Harvard Studies in Classical Philology* 93: 281–8.
Bing, P. 1993. "Aratus and his Audiences". In Schiesaro *et al.* (1993), 99–109.
Birus, H. 2003. "Picturing It: The Issue of Visuality in the Classical Theory of Metaphor". *Arcadia* 38(2): 314–22.
Blaydes, F. H. M. (ed.) 1887. *Aristophanis Acharnenses*. Halle: Orphanotrophei Libraria.
Bowers, F. 1996. *Scriabin: A Biography of the Russian Composer 1871–1915*, 2nd edn. Mineola, NY: Dover.
Bowie, A. M. 1997. "Thinking with Drinking: Wine and Symposium in Aristophanes". *Journal of Hellenic Studies* 117: 1–21.

Boys-Stones, G. R. 2003. "Introduction". In *Metaphor, Allegory, and the Classical Tradition*, G. R. Boys-Stones (ed.), 1–5. Oxford: Oxford University Press.
Bradley, M. 2004. "The Colour 'Blush' in Ancient Rome". In *Colours in the Ancient Mediterranean World*, L. Cleland & K. Stears (eds), 117–21. Oxford: John & Erica Hedges.
Bradley, M. 2006. "Colour and Marble in Early Imperial Rome". *Proceedings of the Cambridge Philological Society* **52**: 1–22.
Bradley, M. 2009. *Colour and Meaning in Ancient Rome*. Cambridge: Cambridge University Press.
Brague, R. 1988. *Aristote et la question du monde: Essai sur le contexte cosmologique et anthropologique de l'ontologie*. Paris: Presses universitaires de France.
Bramble, J. C. 1974. *Persius and the Programmatic Satire: A Study in Form and Imagery*. Cambridge: Cambridge University Press.
Braund, S. H. (trans.) 1992. *Lucan. Civil War*. Oxford: Oxford University Press.
Bravo, F. 2011. *Anagrammes: sur une hypothèse de Ferdinand de Saussure*. Limoges: Lambert-Lucas.
Brenkman, J. 1976. "Narcissus in the Text". *Georgia Review* **30**(2): 293–327.
Breton, A. 1969. *Manifestoes of Surrealism*, R. Seaver & H. R. Lane (trans.). Ann Arbor, MI: University of Michigan Press.
Bruzzese, D. 2011. "La ricerca anagrammatica di Ferdinand de Saussure: un'altra riflessione sul segno". In *Saussure, filosofo del linguaggio*, E. Fadda, G. Gallo & L. Cristaldi (eds), 119–37. Acireale: Bonanno.
Burnett, A. P. 1983. *Three Archaic Poets: Archilochus, Alcaeus, Sappho*. Cambridge, MA: Harvard University Press.
Bury, R. G. (trans., ed.) 1929. *Plato IX: Timaeus, Critias, Cleitophon, Menexenus, Epistles*. London: George Allen & Unwin.
Butler, S. 2002. *The Hand of Cicero*. London: Routledge.
Butler, S. 2011. *The Matter of the Page: Essays in Search of Ancient and Medieval Authors*. Madison, WI: University of Wisconsin Press.
Butrica, J. L. 1997. "Editing Propertius". *Classical Quarterly* **47**(1): 176–208.
Cairns, D. L. 2003. "Ethics, Ethology, Terminology: Iliadic Anger and the Cross–cultural Study of Emotion". In *Ancient Anger: Perspectives from Homer to Galen*, (Yale Classical Studies XXXII), S. Braund & G. Most (eds), 11–49. Cambridge: Cambridge University Press.
Cairns, D. L. 2011. "Looks of Love and Loathing: Cultural Models of Vision and Emotion in Ancient Greek Culture". *Métis* **9**: 37–50.
Campbell, D. A. (trans., ed.) 1988. *Greek Lyric: Anacreon, Anacreontea, Choral Lyric from Olympus to Alcman*. Cambridge, MA: Harvard University Press.
Campen, C. von 2008. *The Hidden Sense: Synesthesia in Art and Science*. Cambridge, MA: MIT Press.
Cantera Glera, N. A. 2000. "Urir. *hu̯an-, germ. *swinþa-: Die indogermanische Wurzel *su̯en-". In *Indoarisch, Iranisch und die Indogermanistik: Arbeitstagung der Indogermanischen Gesellschaft vom 2. bis 5. Oktober 1997 in Erlangen*, B. Forssman & R. Plath (eds), 37–50. Wiesbaden: Reichert.
Carastro, M. (ed.) 2009. *L'antiquité en couleurs: catégories, pratiques, représentations*. Grenoble: J. Millon.
Carson, A. 2002. *If Not, Winter. Fragments of Sappho*. New York: Vintage Books.
Castelnérac, B. 2010. "Plaisirs esthétiques et beauté dans le *Philèbe*: un essai de reconstruction du discours platonicien sur l'art". In *Plato's Philebus: Selected Papers From the Eighth Symposium Platonicum*, J. M. Dillon & L. Brisson (eds), 140–51. Sankt Augustin: Academia.
Catrein, C. 2003. *Vertauschte Sinne: Untersuchungen zur Synästhesie in der römischen Dichtung*. Munich: K. G. Saur.
Ceccarelli, P. 2004. "Dancing the *pyrrhikē* in Athens". In *Music and the Muses: The Culture of Mousikē in the Classical Athenian City*, P. Murray & P. Wilson (eds), 91–120. Oxford: Oxford University Press.
Certeau, M. de. 1996. "Vocal Utopias: Glossolalias". *Representations* **56**(1996): 29–47.
Chadwick, H. (trans.) 1992. *Saint Augustine: Confessions*. Oxford: Oxford University Press.
Chadwick, J. 1996. *Lexicographia Graeca: Contributions to the Lexicography of Ancient Greek*. Oxford: Oxford University Press.
Chantraine, P. 2009. *Dictionnaire étymologique de la langue grecque: Histoire des mots*, new edn. Paris: Klincksieck.
Chapman, G. 1963. "Ovids Banquet of Sence". In *Elizabethan Minor Epics*, E. Donno (ed.), 207–43. New York: Columbia University Press.

Christol, A. 2002. "Les couleurs de la mer". In *Couleurs et vision dans l'antiquité classique*, L. Villard (ed.), 29–44. Rouen: Publications de l'Université de Rouen.

Christy, T. C. 1999a. "Between Intellect and Intuition: Saussure's 'Anagrams' and the Calculus of the Auri-(ora-)cular". In *Interdigitations: Essays for Irmengard Rauch*, G. F. Carr, W. Harbert & L. Zhang (eds), 557–68. New York: Lang.

Christy, T. C. 1999b. "Saussure's 'Anagrams': Blunder or Paralanguage?". In *History of Linguistics 1996: Selected Papers from the Seventh International Conference on the History of the Language Sciences (ICHOLS VII), Oxford, 12–17 September 1996. Volume II: From Classical to Contemporary Linguistics*, D. Cram, A. Linn & E. Nowak (eds), 299–305. Amsterdam: Benjamins.

Clarke, M. J. 1999. *Flesh and Spirit in the Songs of Homer: A Study of Words and Myths*. Oxford: Oxford University Press.

Clarke, M. J. 2004. "The Semantics of Colour in the Early Greek Word Hoard". In *Colours in the Ancient Mediterranean World*, L. Cleland & K. Stears (eds), 131–39. Oxford: John & Erica Hedges.

Classen, C. 1993. *Worlds of Sense: Exploring the Senses in History and across Cultures*. London: Routledge.

Classen, C. 2005a. "Fingerprints: Writing about Touch". In Classen (2005b), 1–9.

Classen, C. (ed.) 2005b. *The Book of Touch*. Oxford: Berg.

Classen, C., D. Howes & A. Synnott 1994. *Aroma: The Cultural History of Smell*. London: Routledge.

Clay, D. 1983. *Lucretius and Epicurus*. Ithaca, NY: Cornell University Press.

Clay, J. S. 1981–2. "Immortal and Ageless Forever". *Classical Journal* **77**(2): 112–17.

Clements, A. 2006. "Aristophanes and the Philosophy of Sensory Perception". PhD dissertation, Faculty of Classics, University of Cambridge.

Cocteau, J. 2001. *The White Book*, M. Crosland (trans.). San Francisco, CA: City Lights Publishers.

Collingwood, R. G. 1938. *The Principles of Art*. Oxford: Oxford University Press.

Conklin, H. 1955. "Hanunóo Color Categories". *Southwestern Journal of Anthropology* **11**(4): 339–44.

Connolly, J. 2007. "Virile Tongues: Rhetoric and Masculinity". In *A Companion to Roman Rhetoric*, W. Dominik & J. Hall (eds), 83–97. Oxford: Blackwell.

Connolly, W. E. 2010. "Materialities of Experience". In Coole & Frost (2010), 178–200.

Considine, J. 2009. "'Les voyelles ne font rien, et les consonnes fort peu de chose': On the History of Voltaire's Supposed Comment on Etymology". *Historiographia Linguistica* **36**(1): 181–9.

Conte, G. B. 1994. *Latin Literature: A History*, J. B. Solodow (trans.). Baltimore, MD: Johns Hopkins University Press.

Coole, D. & S. Frost (eds) 2010. *New Materialisms: Ontology, Agency, and Politics*. Durham, NC: Duke University Press.

Cooper, G. L. & K. W. Krüger 2002. *Greek Syntax: Early Greek Poetic and Herodotean Syntax*, 3 vols. Ann Arbor, MI: University of Michigan Press.

Coote, J. 1992. "'Marvels of Everyday Vision': The Anthropology of Aesthetics and the Cattle-Keeping Nilotes". In *Anthropology, Art and Aesthetics*, J. Coote & A. Shelton (eds), 245–73. Oxford: Clarendon Press.

Corbin, A. 1986. *The Foul and the Fragrant: Odor and the French Social Imagination*. Cambridge: Cambridge University Press.

Cowgill, W. 1960. "Greek *ou* and Armenian *očʻ*". *Language* **36**(3.1): 347–50. Reprinted in *The Collected Writings of Warren Cowgill*, J. S. Klein (ed.), 99–101 (Ann Arbor, MI: Beech Stave, 2006).

Crawford, J. W. 1994. *Cicero. The Fragmentary Speeches*. Atlanta, GA: Scholars Press.

Csordas, T. J. 1993. "Somatic Modes of Attention". *Cultural Anthropology* **8**(2): 135–56.

Culler, J. [1981] 2001. *The Pursuit of Signs: Semiotics, Literature, Deconstruction*. London: Routledge.

Culler, J. 1986. *Ferdinand de Saussure*, revised edn. Ithaca, NY: Cornell University Press.

Cusset, C. 2002. "Poétique et onomastique dans les *Phénomènes* d'Aratos". In *Palladio Magistro: Mélanges Jean Soubiran*, Pallas 59, 187–96. Toulouse: Presses Universitaires du Mirail.

Cytowic, R. E. 2002. *Synesthesia: A Union of the Senses*, 2nd edn. Cambridge, MA: MIT Press.

Cytowic, R. E. 2003. *The Man who Tasted Shapes*, new edn. Cambridge, MA: MIT Press.

Cytowic, R. E. & D. M. Eagleman 2009. *Wednesday is Indigo Blue: Discovering the Brain of Synesthesia*. Cambridge, MA: MIT Press.

Dalí, S. 1933. "Interprétation paranoïaque-critique de l'image obsédante 'L'Angelus' de Millet". *Minotaure* **1**: 65–7.

Dalí, S. 1998. *The Collected Writings of Salvador Dalí*. H. N. Finkelstein (trans.). Cambridge: Cambridge University Press.
Dancy, R. M. 2004. *Plato's Introduction of Forms*. Cambridge: Cambridge University Press.
Dann, K. 1998. *Bright Colors Falsely Seen: Synaesthesia and the Search for Transcendental Knowledge*. New Haven, CT: Yale University Press.
Davies, J. L. & D. J. Vaughan (eds) 1879. *The Republic of Plato: Translated into English with an Analysis and Notes*. Oxford: Clarendon Press.
de Man, P. 1981. "Hypogram and Inscription: Michael Riffaterre's Poetics of Reading". *Diacritics* **11**(4): 17–35. Reprinted in *The Resistance to Theory*, 27–53 (Minneapolis, MN: University of Minnesota Press, 1986).
de Man, P. 1983. *Blindness and Insight*, 2nd edn. Minneapolis, MN: University of Minnesota Press.
Descartes, R. 2008. *A Discourse on the Method*, I. Maclean (trans.). Oxford: Oxford University Press.
Detienne, M. 1994. *The Gardens of Adonis: Spices in Greek Mythology*, J. Lloyd (trans.). Princeton, NJ: Princeton University Press.
Di Marco, M. (ed.) 1989. *Timone di Fliunte: Silli*. Rome: Edizioni dell'Ateneo.
Donno, E. (ed.) 1963. *Elizabethan Minor Epics*. New York: Columbia University Press.
Dörrie, H. 1965. "Emanation: Ein unphilosophisches Wort im spätantiken Denken". In *Parusia: Studien zur Philosophie Platons und zur Problemgeschichte des Platonismus. Festgabe für Johannes Hirschberger*, K. Flasch (ed.), 119–41. Frankfurt: Minerva.
Dover, K. J. (ed.) 1980. *Plato: Symposium*. Cambridge: Cambridge University Press.
Dover, K. J. (ed.) 1993. *Aristophanes: Frogs*. Oxford: Clarendon Press.
Drobnick, J. 2006. "Introduction". In *The Smell Culture Reader*, J. Drobnick (ed.), 1–6. Oxford: Berg.
Dubrow, H. 2006. "The Interplay of Narrative and Lyric: Competition, Cooperation, and the Case of the Anticipatory Amalgam". *Narrative* **14**(3): 254–71.
Duffy, P. L. 2001. *Blue Cats and Chartreuse Kittens: How Synesthetes Color their Worlds*. New York: Times Books.
Dunbar, N. (ed.) 1998. *Aristophanes: Birds* (abridged edition). Oxford: Clarendon Press.
Dupuis, M. 1977. "À propos des anagrammes saussuriennes". *Cahiers d'analyse textuelle* **19**: 7–24.
Durozoi, G. 2002. *History of the Surrealist Movement*, A. Anderson (trans.). Chicago, IL: University of Chicago Press.
Dwyer G. & R. Cole (eds) 2007. *The Hare Krishna Movement: Forty Years of Chant and Change*. London: I. B. Tauris.
Eco, U. 1985. "How Culture Conditions the Colours We See". In *On Signs*, M. Blonsky (ed.), 157–75. Oxford: Blackwell.
Edmunds, L. 2001. *Intertextuality and the Reading of Roman Poetry*. Baltimore, MD: Johns Hopkins University Press.
Edwards, C. 2007. *Death in Ancient Rome*. New Haven, CT: Yale University Press.
Effe, B. 1977. *Dichtung und Lehre: Untersuchungen zur Typologie des antiken Lehrgedichts* (Zetemata 69). Munich: Beck.
Eliot, T. S. 1975. "The Metaphysical Poets". In *Selected Prose of T. S. Eliot*, F. Kermode (ed.), 59–67. New York: Harcourt.
Elsaesser, T. 2009. "Freud as Media Theorist: Mystic Writing-Pads and the Matter of Memory". *Screen* **50**(1): 100–113.
Emerson, R. W. 2003. "Experience". In *Nature and Selected Essays*, L. Ziff (ed.), 285–312. New York: Penguin.
Erren, M. 1967. *Die Phainomena des Aratos von Soloi: Untersuchungen zum Sach- und Sinnverständnis*. Wiesbaden: Steiner.
Evans, E. 1941. "The Study of Physiognomy in the Second Century AD". *Transactions and Proceedings of the American Philological Association* **72**: 287–98.
Fakas, C. 2001. *Der hellenistische Hesiod: Arats Phainomena und die Tradition der antiken Lehrepik*. Wiesbaden: Reichert.
Farrell, J. 1999. "The Ovidian Corpus: Poetic Body and Poetic Text". In *Ovidian Transformations: Essays on Ovid's Metamorphoses and its Reception*, P. R. Hardie, A. Barchiesi & S. E. Hinds (eds), 126–41. Cambridge: Cambridge University Press.
Farrell, J. 2007. "Horace's Body, Horace's Books". In *Classical Constructions: Papers in Memory of Don Fowler, Classicist and Epicurean*, S. J. Heyworth, P. G. Fowler & S. J. Harrison (eds), 174–93. Oxford: Oxford University Press.

Fedeli, P. 2006. *Manualetto di campagna elettorale*, 2nd edn. Rome: Salerno.
Feeney, D. 2009. "Becoming an Authority: Horace on his own Reception". In *Perceptions of Horace: A Roman Poet and His Readers*, L. B. T. Houghton & M. Wyke (eds), 16–38. Cambridge: Cambridge University Press.
Fehr, J. 1996. "Saussure: cours, publications, manuscrits, lettres et documents. Les contours de l'œuvre posthume et ses rapports avec l'œuvre publiée". *Histoire Epistémologie Langage* **18**(2): 179–99.
Fehr, J. 2000. *Saussure entre linguistique et sémiologie*, P. Caussat (trans.). Paris: Presses Universitaires de France.
Feld, S. 2005. "Senses Placed, Places Sensed". In *Empire of the Senses: The Sensual Culture Reader*, D. Howes (ed.), 179–91. Oxford: Berg.
Feuillerat, A. 1925. "Scholarship and Literary Criticism". *The Yale Review* **14**(2): 309–24.
Florman, L. C. 2000. *Myth and Metamorphosis: Picasso's Classical Prints of the 1930s*. Cambridge, MA: MIT Press.
Foley, H. P. 1994. *The Homeric Hymn to Demeter*. Princeton, NJ: Princeton University Press.
Foley, H. P. 2000. "The Comic Body in Greek Art and Drama". In *Not the Classical Ideal*, B. Cohen (ed.), 275–311. Leiden: Brill.
Foley, H. P. 2008. "Generic Boundaries in Late Fifth-Century Athens". In *Performance, Iconography, Reception: Studies in Honor of O. Taplin*, M. Revermann & P. Wilson (eds), 15–36. Oxford: Oxford University Press.
Ford, A. L. 2002. *The Origins of Criticism: Literary Culture and Poetic Theory in Classical Greece*. Princeton, NJ: Princeton University Press.
Fortenbaugh, W. 1995. *Theophrastus of Eresus: Sources for his Life, Writings, Thought and Influence. Commentary*, vol. 8. Leiden: Brill.
Foster, S. L. 2011. *Choreographing Empathy: Kinesthesia in Performance*. London: Routledge.
Fowler, P. 1997. "Lucretian Conclusions". In *Classical Closure: Reading the End in Greek and Latin Literature*, D. H. Roberts, F. M. Dunn & D. Fowler (eds), 112–38. Princeton, NJ: Princeton University Press. Reprinted in *Oxford Readings in Classical Studies: Lucretius*, M. R. Gale (ed.), 234–54 (Oxford: Oxford University Press, 2007).
Franko, G. F. 1999. "Imagery and Names in Plautus' *Casina*". *Classical Journal* **95**(1): 1–17.
Frede, D. 1992. "Disintegration and Restoration: Pleasure and Pain in Plato's *Philebus*". In *The Cambridge Companion to Plato*, R. Kraut (ed.), 425–63. Cambridge: Cambridge University Press.
Frede, D. 1997a. *Platon: Philebos (Platon Werke* III.2). Göttingen: Vandenhoeck & Ruprecht.
Frede, D. (trans.) 1997b. "*Philebus*". In *Plato: Complete Works*, J. Cooper (ed.), 398–456. Indianapolis, IN: Hackett.
Freud, S. 1955. "Beyond the Pleasure Principle". In *The Standard Edition of the Complete Psychological Works*, vol. 18, J. Strachey (ed.), 7–64. London: Hogarth.
Freud, S. 1957a. "Leonardo Da Vinci and a Memory of His Childhood". In *The Standard Edition of the Complete Psychological Works*, vol. 11, J. Strachey (ed.), 57–137. London: Hogarth.
Freud, S. 1957b. "On Narcissism: An Introduction". In *The Standard Edition of the Complete Psychological Works*, vol. 14, J. Strachey (ed.), 67–102. London: Hogarth.
Freud, S. 1958. "Psycho–Analytical Notes on the Autobiographical Account of a Case of Paranoia (Dementia Paranoides)". In *The Standard Edition of the Complete Psychological Works*, vol. 12, J. Strachey (ed.), 1–82. London: Hogarth.
Freud, S. 1961. "A Note Upon the 'Mystic Writing-Pad'". In *The Standard Edition of the Complete Psychological Works*, vol. 19, J. Strachey (ed.), 225–32. London: Hogarth.
Freud, S. 2003. *The Uncanny*, D. McLintock (trans.). New York: Penguin.
Friedländer, P. 1969. "Pattern of Sound and Atomic Theory in Lucretius". In his *Studien zur antiken Literatur und Kunst*, 337–53. Berlin: De Gruyter.
Fritz, K. von 1938. *Philosophie und sprachlicher Ausdruck bei Demokrit, Plato und Aristoteles*. New York: Stechert.
Furley, D. 2007. "Nothing to us?". In *The Norms of Nature. Studies in Hellenistic Ethics*, M. Schofield & G. Striker (eds), 75–91. Cambridge: Cambridge University Press.
Gage, J. 1998. "Synaesthesia". In M. Kelly (ed.), *Encyclopaedia of Aesthetics*, vol. 4, 348–51. New York: Oxford University Press.
Galeyev, B. M. & I. M. Vanechkina 2001. "Was Scriabin a Synesthete?". *Leonardo* **34**(4): 357–61.
Gallop, J. 1982. "Lacan's 'Mirror Stage': Where to Begin". *SubStance* **11**(4)/**12**(1): 118–28.
Gandon, F. 2002. *De dangereux édifices: Saussure lecteur de Lucrèce. Les Cahiers d'anagrammes consacrés au De rerum natura*. Louvain: Peeters.

Gandon, F. 2006. *Le Nom de l'absent: épistémologie de la science saussurienne des signes*. Limoges: Lambert-Lucas.
Gardiner, M. 1999. "Bakhtin and the Metaphorics of Perception". In *Interpreting Visual Culture: Explorations in the Hermeneutics of the Visual*, I. Heywood & B. Sandywell (eds), 59–76. London: Routledge.
Gee, E. 2000. *Ovid, Aratus and Augustus: Astronomy in Ovid's Fasti*. Cambridge: Cambridge University Press.
Gell, A. 1995. "On Coote's 'Marvels of Everyday Vision'". *Social Analysis* 38: 18–30.
Gladstone, W. E. 1858. *Studies on Homer and the Heroic Age*, vol. 3. Oxford: Oxford University Press.
Glauthier, P. 2011. "*Census* and *Commercium*: Two Economic Metaphors in Manilius". In *Forgotten Stars: Rediscovering Manilius' Astronomica*, S. J. Green & K. Volk (eds), 188-201. Oxford: Oxford University Press.
Gleason, M. W. 1995. *Making Men: Sophists and Self-Presentation in Ancient Rome*. Princeton, NJ: Princeton University Press.
Godel, R. 1960. "Inventaire des manuscrits de F. de Saussure remis à la Bibliothèque publique et universitaire de Genève". *Cahiers Ferdinand de Saussure* 17: 5–11.
Goldhill, S. 2000. "Placing Theatre in the History of Vision". In *Word and Image in Ancient Greece*, K. N. Rutter & B. A. Sparkes (eds), 161–79. Edinburgh: Edinburgh University Press.
Goodman, N. 1968. *Languages of Art: An Approach to the Theory of Symbols*. Indianapolis, IN: Bobbs-Merrill.
Goold, G. P. (trans.) 1992. *Manilius: Astronomica*. 2nd edn. Cambridge, MA: Harvard University Press.
Gordon, W. T. & H. G. Schogt 1999. "Ferdinand de Saussure: The Anagrams and the *Cours*". In *The Emergence of the Modern Language Sciences: Studies on the Transition from Historical-comparative to Structural Linguistics in Honour of E. F. K. Koerner. Volume 1: Historiographical Perspectives*, S. Embleton, J. E. Joseph & H.-J. Niederehe (eds), 139–50. Philadelphia, PA: Benjamins.
Gosling, J. C. B. (ed.) 1975. *Plato: Philebus*. Oxford: Clarendon Press.
Gottlieb, C. 1966. "Picasso's 'Girl Before a Mirror'". *The Journal of Aesthetics and Art Criticism* 24(4): 509–18.
Gottschalk, H. 1964. "The *De Coloribus* and its Author". *Hermes* 92(1): 59–85.
Gow, A. S. F. 1951. "Notes on Noses". *Journal of Hellenic Studies* 71: 81–4.
Gowers, E. 1993. *The Loaded Table: Representations of Food in Roman Literature*. Oxford: Oxford University Press.
Green, S. J. 2011. "*Ardua ad astra*: The Poetics and Politics of Horoscopic Failure in Manilius' *Astronomica*". In *Forgotten Stars: Rediscovering Manilius' Astronomica*, S. J. Green & K. Volk (eds), 120–38. Oxford: Oxford University Press.
Gregoric, P. 2007. *Aristotle on the Common Sense*. Oxford: Oxford University Press.
Griffith, T. (trans.) & G. R. F. Ferrari (ed.) 2000. *Plato. The Republic*. Cambridge: Cambridge University Press.
Gronas, M. 2009. "Just what Word did Mandel'shtam Forget? A Mnemopoetic Solution to the Problem of Saussure's Anagrams". *Poetics Today* 30(2): 155–205.
Gronas, M. 2011. *Cognitive Poetics and Cultural Memory: Russian Literary Mnemonics*. New York: Routledge.
Gulick, C. B. (trans., ed.) 1941. *Athenaeus, The Deipnosophists: Books 14.653b–15*. Cambridge, MA: Harvard University Press.
Gunderson, E. 2000. *Staging Masculinity: The Rhetoric of Performance in the Roman World*. Ann Arbor, MI: University of Michigan Press.
Gundert, B. 2000. "*Soma* and *Psyche* in Hippocratic Medicine". In *Psyche and Soma: Physicians and Metaphysicians on the Mind–Body Problem from Antiquity to Enlightenment*, J. P. Wright & R. Potter (eds), 17–35. Oxford: Oxford University Press.
Habinek, T. N. 2005. *The World of Roman Song: From Ritualized Speech to Social Order*. Baltimore, MD: Johns Hopkins University Press.
Habinek, T. N. 2007. "Probing the Entrails of the Universe: Astrology as Bodily Knowledge in Manilius' *Astronomica*". In *Ordering Knowledge in the Roman Empire*, J. König & T. Whitmarsh (eds), 229–40. Cambridge: Cambridge University Press.
Habinek, T. N. 2011. "Manilius' Conflicted Stoicism". In *Forgotten Stars: Rediscovering Manilius' Astronomica*, S. J. Green & K. Volk (eds), 32–44. Oxford: Oxford University Press.
Hallenbeck, J. L. 2003. *Palliative Care Perspectives*. Oxford: Oxford University Press.
Halliwell, S. (trans., ed.) 1993. *Plato: Republic 5*. Warminster: Aris & Phillips.
Hamilton, J. T. 2003. *Soliciting Darkness: Pindar, Obscurity, and the Classical Tradition*. Cambridge, MA: Harvard University Press.
Hamlyn, D. W. 1959. "Aristotle's Account of Aesthesis in the *De Anima*". *Classical Quarterly* 9(1): 6–16.

Hampton, C. 1990. *Pleasure, Knowledge and Being: An Analysis of Plato's Philebus*. Albany, NY: SUNY Press.
Hardie, P. 1993. *The Epic Successors of Virgil: A Study in the Dynamics of a Tradition*. Cambridge: Cambridge University Press.
Harris, J. H. 2007. "The Smell of *Macbeth*". *Shakespeare Quarterly* **58**(4): 465–86.
Hartman, G. 2007. "Understanding Criticism". In his *Criticism in the Wilderness: The Study of Literature Today*, 2nd edn, 19–41. New Haven, CT: Yale University Press.
Hartog, F. [1980] 1988. *The Mirror of Herodotus: The Representation of the Other in the Writing of History*, J. Lloyd (trans.). Berkeley, CA: University of California Press.
Heath, J. 2005. *The Talking Greeks*. Cambridge: Cambridge University Press.
Henderson, J. (trans., ed.) 1998a. *Aristophanes: Acharnians, Knights*. Cambridge, MA: Harvard University Press.
Henderson, J. (trans., ed.) 1998b. *Aristophanes: Clouds, Wasps, Peace*. Cambridge, MA: Harvard University Press.
Herder, J. G. 2002. *Sculpture: Some Observations on Shape and Form from Pygmalion's Creative Dream*, J. Gaiger (trans.). Chicago, IL: University of Chicago Press.
Hersey, G. L. 2009. *Falling in Love with Statues: Artificial Humans from Pygmalion to the Present*. Chicago, IL: University of Chicago Press.
Hesseling, D. C. & H. Pernot (eds) 1913. Ἐρωτοπαίγνια *(Chansons d'amour) pub. d'après un manuscrit du XVe siècle : avec une traduction, une étude critique sur les Ekhatologa (Chanson des cent mots) des observations grammaticales et un index*. Paris: Welter.
Hetherington, K. 2003. "Spatial Textures: Space, Touch, and Praesentia". *Environment and Planning A* **35**(11): 1933–44.
Heubeck, A., S. West, J. B. Hainsworth, J. Russo & M. Fernández-Galiano (eds) 1988–92. *A Commentary on Homer's Odyssey*, 3 vols. Oxford: Oxford University Press.
Hexter, R. 1990. "What was the Trojan Horse Made of? Interpreting Vergil's *Aeneid*". *Yale Journal of Criticism* **3**: 109–31.
Heyd, M. 1984. "Dali's 'Metamorphosis of Narcissus' Reconsidered". *Artibus et Historiae* **5**(10): 121–31.
Hinard, F. 1985. *Les proscriptions de la Rome republicaine*. Rome: École française de Rome.
Hinds, S. 1998. *Allusion and Intertext. Dynamics of Appropriation in Roman Poetry*. Cambridge: Cambridge University Press.
Hollander, J. 1996. "The Poetry of Architecture". *Bulletin of the American Academy of Arts and Sciences* **49**(5): 17–35.
Hömke, N. 2010. "Bit by Bit Towards Death—Lucan's Scaeva and the Aesthetisization of Dying". In *Lucan's Bellum Civile: Between Epic Tradition and Aesthetic Innovation*, N. Hömke & C. Reitz (eds), 91–104. Berlin: De Gruyter.
Hope, V. M. 2000. "Contempt and Respect: The Treatment of the Corpse in Ancient Rome". In *Death and Disease in the Ancient City*, V. M. Hope & E. Marshall (eds), 104–27. London: Routledge.
Hope, V. M . 2009. *Roman Death: The Dying and the Dead in Ancient Rome*. New York: Continuum.
Hopkins, B. 1989. "Keats and the Uncanny: 'This Living Hand'". *Kenyon Review* **11**(4): 28–40.
Hort, A. (trans.) 1916. *Theophrastus: Enquiry into Plants*, 2 vols. Cambridge, MA: Harvard University Press.
Housman, A. E. 1903–30. *M. Manilii Astronomicon Libri*, 5 vols. London: Richards.
Housman, A. E. 1927. *M. Annaei Lucani Belli Civilis Libri Decem*. Oxford: Oxford University Press.
Howes, D. 1991. *The Varieties of Sensory Experience*. Toronto: University of Toronto Press.
Howes, D. 2003. *Sensual Relations: Engaging the Senses in Culture and Social Theory*. Ann Arbor, MI: Michigan University Press.
Howes, D. 2005. *Empire of the Senses: The Sensual Culture Reader*. Oxford: Berg.
Hubbard, M. E. (trans.). 1972. "Aristotle: *Poetics*". In *Ancient Literary Criticism*, D. A. Russell & M. Winterbottom (eds), 51–90. Oxford: Clarendon Press.
Hübner, W. 1984. "Manilius als Astrologe und Dichter". In *Aufstieg und Niedergang der römischen Welt* **2**(32): 126–320.
Hunter, R. 2008. "Written in the Stars: Poetry and Philosophy in the *Phainomena* of Aratus". In his *On Coming After: Studies in Post-Classical Greek Literature and its Reception*, vol. 1, 153–88. Berlin: de Gruyter.
Immerwahr, H. R. 1960. "*Ergon*: History as a Monument in Herodotus and Thucydides". *American Journal of Philology* **81**(3): 261–90.

Ingold, T. 2000. *The Perception of the Environment: Essays in Livelihood, Dwelling and Skill*. London: Routledge.
Ingold, T. 2011. *Being Alive: Essays on Movement, Knowledge and Description*. London: Routledge.
Irwin, E. 1974. *Colour Terms in Greek Poetry*. Toronto: Hakkert.
Jacques, J.-M. 1960. "Sur un acrostiche d'Aratos (*Phén.* 783–787)". *Revue des Études Anciennes* **62**: 48–61.
Jakobson, R. 1980. "Subliminal Verbal Patterning in Poetry". *Poetics Today* **2**(1a): 127–36. Reprinted in *Selected Writings III: Poetry of Grammar and Grammar of Poetry*, S. Rudy (ed.), 136–47 (The Hague: Mouton, 1981).
Jal, P. 1963. *La Guerre Civile a Rome. Étude littéraire et morale*. Paris: Presses universitaires de France.
James, E. 1995. *Light and Colour in Byzantine Art*. New York: Clarendon Press.
James, H. 2009. "Ovid in Renaissance English Literature". In *A Companion to Ovid*, P. Knox (ed.), 423–41. Oxford: Wiley-Blackwell.
Jarrell, R. [1951] 1999. "The Obscurity of the Modern Poet". In *No Other Book: Selected Essays*, B. Leithauser (ed.), 3–18. New York: HarperCollins.
Jeffords, S. 1993. *Hard Bodies: Hollywood Masculinity in the Reagan Era*. New Brunswick, NJ: Rutgers University Press.
Johansen, T. K. 1996. "Aristotle on the Sense of Smell". *Phronesis* **41**(1): 1–19.
Johansen, T. K. 1997. *Aristotle on the Sense-Organs*. Cambridge: Cambridge University Press.
Johnson, G. A. 2002. "Touch, Tactility, and the Reception of Sculpture in Early Modern Italy". In *A Companion to Art Theory*, P. Smith & C. Wilde (eds), 61–74. London: Blackwell.
Jones, C. A. & B. Arning 2006. *Sensorium: Embodied Experience, Technology, and Contemporary Art*. Cambridge, MA: MIT Press.
Joseph, J. E. 2007. "He was an Englishman". *Times Literary Supplement* **5459** (16 November): 14–15.
Joseph, J. E. 2008. "Undangerous Fair-mindedness: The Culmination of Two Men's Search for Saussure". *Historiographia Linguistica* **35**(1/2): 163–76.
Joseph, J. E. 2009. "Why Lithuanian Accentuation Mattered to Saussure". *Language and History* **52**(2): 182–98.
Jouanna, J. 1996. "Le vin et la médecine dans la Grèce ancienne". *Revue des études grecques* **109**: 410–34.
Jütte, R. 2005. *A History of the Senses*. Cambridge: Polity Press.
Kahn, C. H. 1966. "Sensation and Consciousness in Aristotle's Psychology". *Archiv für Begriffsgeschichte* **48**(1): 43–81.
Kaibel, G. 1894. "Aratea". *Hermes* **29**(1): 82–123.
Katz, J. T. 2009. "Wordplay". In *Proceedings of the 20th Annual UCLA Indo-European Conference, Los Angeles, October 31–November 1, 2008*, S. W. Jamison, H. C. Melchert & B. Vine (eds), 79–114. Bremen: Hempen.
Katz, J. T. 2010a. "Etymology". In *The Classical Tradition*, A. Grafton, G. W. Most & S. Settis (eds), 342–5. Cambridge, MA: Harvard University Press.
Katz, J. T. 2010b. "Inherited Poetics". In *A Companion to the Ancient Greek Language*, E. J. Bakker (ed.), 357–69. Malden, MA: Wiley-Blackwell.
Katz, J. T. 2010c. "*Nonne lexica etymologica multiplicanda sunt?*". In *Classical Dictionaries: Past, Present and Future*, C. Stray (ed.), 25–48. London: Duckworth.
Kennedy, D. F. 2011. "Sums in Verse or a Mathematical Aesthetic?". In *Forgotten Stars: Rediscovering Manilius' Astronomica*, S. J. Green & K. Volk (eds), 165–87. Oxford: Oxford University Press.
Kennedy, G. A. 1993. "Peripatetic Rhetoric as it Appears (and Disappears) in Quintilian". In *Peripatetic Rhetoric After Aristotle*, W. W. Fortenbaugh & D. C. Mirhady (eds), 174–82. New Brunswick, NJ: Transaction Publishers.
Kennedy, J. F. 1960. "The Soft American". *Sports Illustrated* **13**(26): 14–17.
Kenney, E. J. 1977. *Lucretius*. Oxford: Oxford University Press.
Kerr Borthwick, E. 1970. "P. Oxy. 2738: Athena and the Pyrrhic Dance". *Hermes* **98**(3): 318–31.
Kerr Borthwick, E. 2001. "Socrates, Socratics, and the word ΒΛΕΠΕΔΑΙΜΩΝ". *Classical Quarterly* **51**(1): 297–301.
Kidd, D. A. 1981. "Notes on Aratus, *Phaenomena*". *Classical Quarterly* **31**(2): 355–62.
Kidd, D. A. 1997. *Aratus: Phaenomena*. Cambridge: Cambridge University Press.
Kinser, S. 1979. "Saussure's Anagrams: Ideological Work". *MLN* **94**(5): 1105–38.
Kirby, J. T. 1997. "Aristotle on Metaphor". *American Journal of Philology* **118**(4): 517–54.
Kitto, H. D. F. 1956. "The Greek Chorus". *Educational Theatre Journal* **8**(1): 1–8.
Koerner, E. F. K. 1999. *Linguistic Historiography: Projects & Prospects*. Amsterdam: Benjamins.

Kövecses, Z. 2000. *Metaphor and Emotion: Language, Culture and Body in Human Feeling.* Cambridge: Cambridge University Press.
Kretzschmar, W. A., Jr. 2009. *The Linguistics of Speech.* Cambridge: Cambridge University Press.
Kristeva, J. 1967. "Pour une sémiologie des paragrammes". *Tel quel* **29**: 53–75. Reprinted in Σημειωτικὴ: *recherches pour une sémanalyse*, 174–207 (Paris: Éditions du Seuil, 1969). Published in English as "Towards a Semiology of Paragrams", in *The Tel Quel Reader*, R.-F. Lack (trans.), P. ffrench & R.-F. Lack (eds), 25–49 (London: Routledge, 1998).
Kühn, C. G. 1821–33. *Galeni Opera Omnia.* Leipzig: C. Cnobloch.
Kuipers, J. 1984. "Matters of Taste in Weyéwa". *Anthropological Linguistics* **26**(1): 84–101.
Kurke, L. 1992. "The Politics of ἁβροσύνη in Archaic Greece". *Classical Antiquity* **11**(1): 91–120.
Kyle, D. G. 1998. *Spectacles of Death in Ancient Rome.* London: Routledge.
Lacan, J. 1933. "Le problème du style et la conception psychiatrique des formes paranoïaques de l'expérience". *Minotaure* **1**: 68–9.
Lacan, J. 1949. "Le stade du miroir comme formateur de la fonction du Je, telle qu'elle nous est révélée dans l'expérience psychanalytique". *Revue Française de Psychanalyse* **13**(4): 449–55.
Lacan, J. 1977. *Écrits*, A. Sheridan (trans.). New York: W. W. Norton.
Lacan, J. 1998a. *On Feminine Sexuality: The Limits of Love and Knowledge*, B. Fink (trans.). The Seminar of Jacques Lacan 20. New York: W. W. Norton.
Lacan, J. 1998b. *The Four Fundamental Concepts of Psychoanalysis*, A. Sheridan (trans.). The Seminar of Jacques Lacan 11. New York: W. W. Norton.
Lacan, J. 2001. *Autres écrits.* Paris: Seuil.
Lacan, J. 2006. *Écrits*, B. Fink (trans.). New York: W. W. Norton.
Lacey, S., R. Stilla & K. Sathian 2012. "Metaphorically Feeling: Comprehending Textural Metaphors Activates Somatosensory Cortex," *Brain and Language* **120**: 416–21.
Lada Richards, I. 1993. "Empathic Understanding: Emotion and Cognition in Classical Dramatic Audience-Response". *Proceedings of the Cambridge Philological Association* **39**: 94–140.
Lada Richards, I. 1999. *Initiating Dionysus: Ritual and Theatre in Aristophanes' Frogs.* Oxford: Clarendon Press.
Lagrou, E. M. 2000. "Homesickness and the Cashinahua Self: A Reflection of the Embodied Condition of Relatedness". In *The Anthropology of Love and Anger: The Aesthetics of Conviviality in Native Amazonia*, J. Overing & A. Passes (eds), 152–69. London: Routledge.
Lakoff, G. 1987. *Women, Fire, and Dangerous Things: What Categories Reveal About the Mind.* Chicago, IL: University of Chicago Press.
Lakoff, G. & M. Johnson 1980. *Metaphors We Live By.* Chicago, IL: University of Chicago Press.
Lakoff, G. & M. Johnson 1999. *Philosophy in the Flesh: The Embodied Mind and its Challenge to Western Thought.* New York: Basic Books.
Lakoff, G. & M. Turner 1989. *More Than Cool Reason: A Field Guide to Poetic Metaphor.* Chicago, IL: University of Chicago Press.
Laks, A. 1999. "Soul, Sensation, and Thought". In *The Cambridge Companion to Early Greek Philosophy*, A. A. Long (ed.), 250–70. Cambridge: Cambridge University Press.
Landels, J. 1999. *Music in Ancient Greece and Rome.* London: Routledge.
Landolfi, L. 1999. "Οὐρανοβατεῖν: Manilio, il volo e la poesia. Alcune precisazioni". *Prometheus* **25**(2): 151–65.
Landolfi, L. 2003. *Integra prata: Manilio, i proemi.* Bologna: Pàtron.
Lapidge, M. 1979. "Lucan's Imagery of Cosmic Dissolution". *Hermes* **107**(3): 344–70. Reprinted in *Oxford Readings in Classical Studies: Lucan*, C. Tesoriero (ed.), 289–323 (Oxford: Oxford University Press, 2010).
Lapidge, M. 1989. "Stoic Cosmology and Roman Literature, First to Third Centuries AD". *Aufstieg und Niedergang der römischen Welt* **2**(36): 1379–1429.
Largey, G. & R. Watson 2006. "The Sociology of Odors". In *The Smell Culture Reader*, J. Drobnick (ed.), 29–40. Oxford: Berg.
Lasserre, F. (ed.) 1954. *Plutarque, De la musique. Texte, traduction, commentaire, précédés d'une étude sur l'éducation musicale dans la Grèce antique.* Olten: Urs Graf.
Latacz, J. 1966. *Zum Wortfeld "Freude" in der Sprache Homers.* Heidelberg: Winter.
Lateiner, D. 1998. "Blushes and Pallor in Ancient Fictions". *Helios* **25**(2): 163–89.
Lattimore, R. (trans.). 1965. *The Odyssey of Homer.* New York: Harper & Row.

Lausberg, H. 1998. *Handbook of Literary Rhetoric: A Foundation for Literary Study*, M. T. Bliss, A. Jansen, & D. E. Orton (trans.), D. E. Orton & R. D. Anderson (eds). Leiden: Brill.
Leder, D. 1990. *The Absent Body*. Chicago, IL: University of Chicago Press.
Le Feuvre, C. 2009. "Les Aèdes ioniens avaient-ils perdu l'oreille?". *Actes des sessions de linguistique et de littérature (LALIES)* **29**: 253-74.
Lehmann, A. G. 1950. *The Symbolist Aesthetic in France 1885-1895*. Oxford: Blackwell.
Lehrer, A. 1978. "Structures of the Lexicon and the Transfer of Meaning". *Lingua* **45**(2): 95-123.
Leonard, M. 2006. "Lacan, Irigaray, and Beyond: Antigones and the Politics of Psychoanalysis". In *Laughing with Medusa: Classical Myth and Feminist Thought*, V. Zajko & M. Leonard (eds), 121-39. Oxford: Oxford University Press.
Leonard, W. E. & S. B. Smith (eds) 1942. *T. Lucreti Cari De Rerum Natura Libri Sex, Edited with Introduction and Commentary*. Madison, WI: University of Wisconsin Press.
Levarie, S. 1977. "Noise". *Critical Inquiry* **4**(1): 21-31.
Levitan, W. 1979. "Plexed Artistry: Aratean Acrostics". *Glyph* **5**: 55-68.
Lewis, A.-M. 1992. "The Popularity of the *Phaenomena* of Aratus: A Reevaluation". *Studies in Latin Literature and Roman History* **6**: 94-118.
Lienhardt, G. 1960. *Divinity and Experience: the Religion of the Dinka*. Oxford: Clarendon Press.
Lilja, S. 1972. *The Treatment of Odours in the Poetry of Antiquity*. Helsinki: Societas Scientiarum Fennica.
Lissarague, F. 1987. *Un flot d'images: Une esthétique du banquet grec*. Paris: A. Biro.
Lloyd, G. E. R. 1987. *The Revolutions of Wisdom: Studies in the Claims and Practice of Ancient Greek Science*. Berkeley, CA: University of California Press.
Lloyd, G. E. R. 2003. "The Problem of Metaphor: Chinese Reflections". In *Metaphor, Allegory and the Classical Tradition. Ancient Thought and Modern Revisions*, G. R. Boys-Stones (ed.), 101-14. Oxford: Oxford University Press.
Lock, G. 2000. "Uror Amore Mei: Individual and Social Identity in Psychoanalytic Theory". In *Echoes of Narcissus*, L. Spaas & T. Selous (eds), 37-53. New York: Berghahn Books.
Lombardo, S. 1983. *Sky Signs: Aratus' Phaenomena*. Berkeley, CA: North Atlantic Books.
Long, A. & D. Sedley 1987. *The Hellenistic Philosophers*, 2 vols. Cambridge: Cambridge University Press.
Longo, O. (ed.) 1998. *La porpora: Realtà e immaginario di un colore simbolico (Atti del convegno di studio, Venezia 24 e 25 ottobre 1996)*. Venice: Istituto Veneto di Scienze, Lettere ed Arti.
Lotringer, S. 1973. "The Game of the Name". *Diacritics* **3**(2): 2-9.
Lovecraft, H. P. 2005a. *At the Mountains of Madness*. New York: Modern Library.
Lovecraft, H. P. 2005b. *Tales*. New York: Penguin Putnam.
Lühr, F.-F. 1969. "Ratio und Fatum: Dichtung und Lehre bei Manilius". PhD thesis, Johann Wolfgang Goethe-Universität, Frankfurt.
Luick, K. 1940. *Historische Grammatik der englischen Sprache*, vol. 1, pt. 2, F. Wild & H. Koziol (eds). Leipzig: Tauchnitz.
MacDowell, D. M. (ed.) 1971. *Aristophanes: Wasps*. Oxford: Oxford University Press.
MacPherson, F. (ed.) 2011. *The Senses: Classic and Contemporary Philosophical Perspectives*. Oxford: Oxford University Press.
Marincola, J. M. 1997. *Authority and Tradition in Ancient Historiography*. Cambridge: Cambridge University Press.
Marks, L. E. 1982. "Bright Sneezes and Dark Coughs, Loud Sunlight and Soft Moonlight". *Journal of Experimental Psychology: Human Perception and Performance* **8**(2): 177-93.
Marks, L. E., R. J. Hammeal & M. H. Bornstein 1987. *Perceiving Similarity and Comprehending Metaphor*. Monographs of the Society for Research in Child Development 52(1). Chicago, IL: University of Illinois Press.
Masters, J. 1992. *Poetry and Civil War in Lucan's "Bellum Civile"*. Cambridge: Cambridge University Press.
Mastromarco, G. 1988. "L'odore del mostro". *Lexis* **2**: 209-15.
Mastromarco, G. 1989. "L'eroe e il mostro". *Rivista di Filologia e Istruzione Classica* **117**: 410-23.
Maxwell-Stuart, P. G. 1981. *Studies in Greek Colour Terminology*, vol. 1: *Glaukos*; vol. 2: *Charopos*. Leiden: Brill.
May-Tolzmann, U. 1991. "Zu den Anfängen des Narzißmus: Ellis, Näcke, Sadger, Freud". *Luzifer-Amor: Zeitschrift zur Geschichte der Psychoanalyse* **4**(8): 50-88.

McCaffrey, P. 1994. "Freud's Uncanny Woman". In *Reading Freud's Reading*, S. L. Gilman, J. Birmele, J. Geller & V. D. Greenberg (eds), 91–108. New York: New York University Press.
McGlone, M. S. 1996. "Conceptual Metaphors and Figurative Language Interpretation: Food for Thought?" *Journal of Memory and Language* **35**(4): 544–65.
McGlone, M. S. 2001. "Concepts as Metaphors". In *Understanding Figurative Language: From Metaphors to Idioms*, S. Glucksberg (ed.), 90–108. Oxford: Oxford University Press.
Mehtonen, P. 2003. *Obscure Language, Unclear Literature: Theory and Practice from Quintilian to the Enlightenment*, R. MacGilleon (trans.). Helsinki: Finnish Society of Science and Letters.
Mejía Quijano, C. 2008. *Le Cours d'une vie: portrait diachronique de Ferdinand de Saussure*, vol. 1. Nantes: Defaut.
Melville, A. D. (trans.) 1986. *Ovid, Metamorphoses*. Oxford. Oxford University Press.
Mendelsohn, D. 1991-92. "Συγκερανόω: Dithyrambic Language and Dionysiac Cult". *Classical Journal* **87**(2): 105–24.
Merleau-Ponty, M. 1945. *Phénoménologie de la perception*. Paris: Gallimard.
Merleau-Ponty, M. 1962. *Phenomenology of Perception*, C. Smith (trans.). New York: Routledge.
Merleau-Ponty, M. 1964. *Sense and Non-Sense*, A. Dreyfus & P. A. Dreyfus (trans.). Evanston, IL: Northwestern University Press.
Merleau-Ponty, M. 1968. *The Visible and the Invisible*, A. Lingis (trans.), C. Lefort (ed.). Evanston, IL: Northwestern University Press.
Merleau-Ponty, M. 1969. "Cézanne's Doubt". In *The Essential Writings of Merleau-Ponty*, A. L. Fisher (ed.), 233–51. New York: Harcourt, Brace & World.
Merry, W. W. (ed.) 1895. *Aristophanes: The Knights*. Oxford: Clarendon Press.
Miller, W. I. 1998. *The Anatomy of Disgust*. Cambridge, MA: Harvard University Press.
Milner, J.-C. 1978. *L'Amour de la langue*. Paris: Éditions du Seuil. Published in English as *For the Love of Language*, A. Banfield (trans.) (Basingstoke: Macmillan, 1990).
Modrak, D. K. 1981. "*Koinē Aisthēsis* and the Discrimination of Sensible Differences in de Anima III.2". *Canadian Journal of Philosophy* **11**(3): 405–23.
Montaigne, M. de 1991. "An Apology for Raymond Sebond". In *The Complete Essays*, M. A. Screech (trans.), 489–683. New York: Penguin.
Montiglio, S. 2005. *Wandering in Ancient Greek Culture*. Chicago, IL: University of Chicago Press.
Montiglio, S. Forthcoming. "Hands Know the Truth Better than Eyes or Ears: Touch and Recognition".
Morales, H. 2004. *Vision and Narrative in Achilles Tatius' Leucippe and Clitophon*. Cambridge: Cambridge University Press.
Moretti, G. 2010. "Quintiliano e il *visibile parlare*: Strumenti visuali per l'oratoria latina". In *Quintilien: Ancien et moderne*, P. Galland, F. Hallyn, C. Lévy & W. Verball (eds), 67–108. Turnhout: Brepols.
Morgan, M. J. 1977. *Molyneux's Question: Vision, Touch and the Philosophy of Perception*. Cambridge: Cambridge University Press.
Morrison, S. 1998. "Skryabin and the Impossible". *Journal of the American Musicological Society* **51**(2): 283–330.
Most, G. 1992. "*Disiecti membra poetae*: The Rhetoric of Dismemberment in Neronian Poetry". In *Innovations in Antiquity*, R. Hexter & D. Selden (eds), 391–419. London: Routledge.
Mounin, G. 1974. "Les Anagrammes de Saussure". In *Studi saussuriani per Robert Godel*, R. Amacker, T. De Mauro & L. J. Prieto (eds), 235–41. Bologna: Il Mulino.
Munson, R. V. 1993. "Herodotus' Use of Prospective Sentences and the Story of Rhampsinitus and the Thief in the *Histories*". *American Journal of Philology* **114**(1): 27–44.
Murnaghan, S. 1987. *Disguise and Recognition in the Odyssey*. Princeton, NJ: Princeton University Press.
Murray, A. T. & G. E. Dimock (trans., eds) 1995. *Homer: Odyssey vol. II. Books XII – XXIV*. Cambridge, MA: Harvard University Press.
Murray, P. 2004. "The Muses and their Arts". In *Music and the Muses: The Culture of 'Mousikē' in the Classical Athenian City*, P. Murray & P. Wilson (eds), 365–89. Oxford: Oxford University Press.
Nancy, J.-L. 1996. *The Muses*, P. Kamuf (trans.). Stanford, CA: Stanford University Press.
Nancy, J.-L. 2000. *Being Singular Plural*, R. D. Richardson & A. E. O'Byrne (trans.). Stanford, CA: Stanford University Press.
Neil, R. A. (ed.) 1901. *The Knights of Aristophanes*. Cambridge: Cambridge University Press.

Nelson, R. S. 2000. "To Say and to See: Ekphrasis and Vision in Byzantium". In *Visuality Before and Beyond the Renaissance: Seeing as Others Saw*, R. S. Nelson (ed.), 143–68. Cambridge: Cambridge University Press.

Neuburg, M. 1993. "Hitch Your Wagon to a Star: Manilius and his Two Addressees". In Schiesaro *et al.* (1993), 243–82.

Obbink, D. (ed.) 1995. *Philodemus and Poetry*. Oxford: Oxford University Press.

Obrador-Pons, P. 2007. "A Haptic Geography of the Beach: Naked Bodies, Vision, and Touch". *Social and Cultural Geography* 8(1): 123–41.

O'Brien, D. 1984. *Theories of Weight in the Ancient World. Four Essays on Democritus, Plato and Aristotle: A Study in the Development of Ideas*. Paris: Les Belles Lettres.

Oliensis, E. 2009. *Freud's Rome: Psychoanalysis and Latin Poetry*. Cambridge: Cambridge University Press.

Olson, S. D. (ed.) 1998. *Aristophanes: Peace*. Oxford: Oxford University Press.

Olson, S. D. 1999. "Kleon's Eyebrows (Cratin. fr. 228 K-A) and Late Fifth-Century Comic Portrait Masks". *Classical Quarterly* 49(1): 320–1.

Olson, S. D. (ed.) 2002. *Aristophanes: Acharnians*. Oxford: Oxford University Press.

Olson, S. D. 2007. *Broken Laughter: Select Fragments of Greek Comedy*. Oxford: Oxford University Press.

Olson, S. D. & A. Sens (eds) 2000. *Archestratus of Gela: Greek Culture and Cuisine in the Fourth Century* BCE. Oxford: Oxford University Press.

Osborne, R. & A. Pappas 2007. "Writing on Archaic Greek Pottery". In *Art and Inscriptions in the Ancient World*, Z. Newby & R. E. Leader-Newby (eds), 131–55. Cambridge: Cambridge University Press.

Osgood, C. E. 1963. "Language Universals and Psycholinguists". In *Universals of Language*, J. Greenberg (ed.), 236–54. Cambridge, MA: MIT Press.

Padel, R. 1992. *In and Out of the Mind: Greek Images of the Tragic Self*. Princeton, NJ: Princeton University Press.

Page, D. L. 1955. *Sappho and Alcaeus: An Introduction to the Study of Ancient Lesbian Poetry*. Oxford: Clarendon Press.

Park, D. 1997. *The Fire within the Eye: A Historical Essay on the Nature and Meaning of Light*. Princeton, NJ: Princeton University Press.

Parker, H. 2009. "Books and Reading Latin Poetry". In *Ancient Literacies: The Culture of Reading in Greece and Rome*, W. A. Johnson & H. N. Parker (eds), 186–232. New York: Oxford University Press.

Paterson, M. 2004. "Caresses, Excesses, Intimacies and Estrangements". *Angelaki* 9(1): 165–77.

Paterson, M. 2007. *The Senses of Touch: Haptics, Affects and Technologies*. Oxford: Berg.

Paul, A. M. 2012. "Your Brain on Fiction". *The New York Times* (18 March): 6.

Payne, M. 2010. *The Animal Part*. Chicago, IL: University of Chicago Press.

Pearson, A. C. 1909. "Phrixus and Demodice: A Note on Pindar, *Pythian* 4.162 f.". *Classical Review* 23(8): 255–7.

Peirano, I. 2009. "*Mutati Artus*: Scylla, Philomela and the End of Silenus' Song in Virgil *Eclogue* 6". *The Classical Quarterly* 59(1): 187–95.

Pentcheva, B. V. 2007. "Epigrams on Icons". In *Art and Text in Byzantine Culture*, L. James (ed.), 120–38. Cambridge: Cambridge University Press.

Peponi, A.-E. 2009. "Choreia and Aesthetics in the *Homeric Hymn to Apollo*: The Performance of the Delian Maidens (Lines 156–64)". *Classical Antiquity* 28(2): 39–70.

Perloff, M. & C. Dworkin (eds) 2009. *The Sound of Poetry/The Poetry of Sound*. Chicago, IL: University of Chicago Press.

Petersen, E. 1917. "Rhythmus". *Abhandlungen der Königlichen Gesellschaft der Wissenschaften zu Göttingen, Philologisch-Historische Klasse* N.F. 16(5): 1–104.

Phillips, M. L. H. & M. Heining 2002. "Neural Correlates of Emotion Perception: From Faces to Taste". In *Olfaction, Taste and Cognition*, C. Rouby, B. Schaai, D. Dubois, R. Gervais & A. Holley (eds), 197–208. Cambridge: Cambridge University Press.

Platnauer, M. (ed.) 1964. *Aristophanes: Peace*. Oxford: Oxford University Press.

Pluth, E. 2010. "An Adventure in the Order of Things: Jean-Claude Milner on *lalangue* and Lacan's Incomplete Materialism". S: *Journal of the Jan van Eyck Circle for Lacanian Ideology Critique* 3: 178–90.

Politis, L. 1973. *A History of Modern Greek Literature*. Oxford: Clarendon Press.

Porter, J. I. 1995. "Content and Form in Philodemus: The History of an Evasion". In *Philodemus and Poetry*, D. Obbink (ed.), 97–147. Oxford: Oxford University Press.

Porter, J. I. 2009. "Is Art Modern? Kristeller's 'Modern System of the Arts' Reconsidered". *British Journal of Aesthetics* **49**(1): 1–24.
Porter, J. I. 2010. *The Origins of Aesthetic Thought in Ancient Greece: Matter, Sensation and Experience*. Cambridge: Cambridge University Press.
Potter, D. S. 2002. "Odor and Power in the Roman Empire". In *Constructions of the Classical Body*, J. I. Porter (ed.), 169–89. Ann Arbor, MI: University of Michigan Press.
Poulet, G. 1969. "The Phenomenology of Reading". *New Literary History* **1**(1): 53–68.
Poulet, G. 1970. "Criticism and Interiority". In *The Languages of Criticism and the Sciences of Man: The Structuralist Controversy*, R. Macksey & E. Donato (eds), 56–88. Baltimore, MD: Johns Hopkins University Press.
Powell, J. G. F. 1992. "Persius' First Satire: A Re-examination". In *Author and Audience in Latin Literature*, T. Woodman & J. G. F. Powell (eds) 150–72. Cambridge: Cambridge University Press.
Pretagostini, R. 1982. "Archiloco 'Salsa di Taso' negli *Archilochi* di Cratino". *Quaderni Urbinati di Cultura Classica* **11**: 43–52.
Prévot, A. 1935. "Verbes grecs relatifs à la vision et noms de l'oeil". *Revue de Philologie, de Littérature et d'Histoire Anciennes* **61**: 133–60, 233–79.
Prins, Y. 1999. *Victorian Sappho*. Princeton, NJ: Princeton University Press.
Purves, A. Forthcoming. "In the Bedroom: Interior Space in Herodotus' *Histories*". In *Space, Place, and Landscape in Ancient Greek Literature and Culture*, K. Gilhuly & N. Worman (eds). Cambridge: Cambridge University Press.
Pütz, B. 2003. *The Symposium and Komos in Aristophanes*. Stuttgart: J. B. Metzler.
Quint, D. 1993. *Epic and Empire: Politics and Generic Form from Virgil to Milton*. Princeton, NJ: Princeton University Press.
Rabaté, J.-M. 2003. "Lacan's Turn to Freud". In *The Cambridge Companion to Lacan*, J.-M. Rabaté (ed.), 1–24. Cambridge: Cambridge University Press.
Race, W. H. (trans., ed.) 1997. *Pindar*. Cambridge, MA: Harvard University Press.
Radici Colace, P. 1995. "Le voci delle stelle". In *Lo spettacolo delle voci*, F. de Martino & A. H. Sommerstein (eds), 231–42. Bari: Levante.
Ragland-Sullivan, E. 1986. *Jacques Lacan and the Philosophy of Psychoanalysis*. Urbana, IL: University of Illinois Press.
Rakoczy, T. 1996. *Böser Blick, Macht des Auges und Neid der Götter: Eine Untersuchung zur Kraft des Blickes in der griechischen Literatur*. Tübingen: Narr.
Rakova, M. 2003. *The Extent of the Literal: Metaphor, Polysemy and Theories of Concepts*. New York: Palgrave Macmillan.
Rastier, François 2009. "Saussure et les textes — De la philologie des textes saussuriens à la théorie saussurienne des textes". *Texto!* **14**(3): 1–26. www.revue-texto.net/index.php?id=2420.
Rastier, François 2010. "Saussure et la science des textes". In *Le Projet de Ferdinand de Saussure*, J.-P. Bronckart, E. Bulea & C. Bota (eds), 315–35. Geneva: Droz.
Rastier, Françoise 1970. "À propos du Saturnien: notes sur '*Le Texte dans le texte, extraits inédits des cahiers d'anagrammes de Ferdinand de Saussure*, par Jean Starobinski'". *Latomus* **29**(1): 3–24.
Reckford, K. 1962. "Studies in Persius". *Hermes* **90**: 476–504.
Redard, G. 1978. "Deux Saussure?". *Cahiers Ferdinand de Saussure* **32**: 27–41.
Redfield, J. M. 1985. "Herodotus the Tourist". *Classical Philology* **80**(2): 97–118.
Rée, J. 1999. *I See a Voice: A Philosophical History of Language, Deafness and the Senses*. New York: Harper Collins.
Regan, B., C. Julliot, B. Simmen, F. Viénot, P. Charles-Dominique & J. D. Mollon 2001. "Fruits, Foliage and the Evolution of Primate Colour Vision". *Philosophical Transactions: Biological Sciences* **356**(1407): 229–83.
Reichel-Dolmatoff, G. 1978. "Desana Animal Categories, Food Restrictions, and the Concept of Color Energies". *Journal of Latin American Lore* **4**: 243–91.
Reinhold, M. 1976. *The History of Purple as a Status Symbol in Antiquity*. Brussels: Latomus.
Richards, I. A., C. K. Ogden & J. Wood 1925. *The Foundations of Aesthetics*. New York: Lear Publishers.
Richlin, A. 1997. "Gender and Rhetoric: Producing Manhood in the Schools". In *Roman Eloquence*, W. Dominik (ed.), 90–110. London: Routledge.

Rindisbacher, H. J. 1992. *The Smell of Books: A Cultural-Historical Study of Olfactory Perception in Literature*. Ann Arbor, MI: University of Michigan Press.
Rix, H. 2001. *LIV: Lexikon der indogermanischen Verben. Die Wurzeln und ihre Primärstammbildungen*, 2nd edn. Wiesbaden: Reichert.
Rodaway, P. 1994. *Sensuous Geographies: Body, Sense, and Place*. London: Routledge.
Rodríguez Ferrándiz, R. 1998. *Semiótica del anagrama: la hipótesis anagramática de Ferdinand de Saussure*. Alicante: Universidad de Alicante.
Rodríguez Ferrándiz, R. 2000. "La semiología del nombre propio en Saussure: los *Nibelungen* y los *Anagrammes*". *Revista de investigación lingüística* 3(1): 181–205.
Rogers, B. B. (trans., ed.) 1913. *The Peace of Aristophanes*. London: G. Bell & Sons.
Rogers, B. B. (trans., ed.) 1915. *The Wasps of Aristophanes*. London: G. Bell & Sons.
Rogers, B. B. (trans., ed.) 1930. *The Knights of Aristophanes*. London: G. Bell & Sons.
Rojas, C. 1993. *Salvador Dalí, or The Art of Spitting on Your Mother's Portrait*, A. Amell (trans.). University Park, PA: Penn State Press.
Romano, E. 1979. *Struttura degli Astronomica di Manilio*. Palermo: Accademia di Scienze, Lettere e Arti di Palermo.
Rosen, R. M. 1988. *Old Comedy and the Iambographic Tradition*. Atlanta, GA: Scholars Press.
Rosen, R. M. 1990. "Hipponax and the Homeric Odysseus". *Eikasmos* 1: 11–25.
Rosen, R. M. 2000. "Cratinus' *Pytine* and The Construction of the Comic Self". In *The Rivals of Aristophanes: Studies in Athenian Old Comedy*, D. Harvey & J. Wilkins (eds), 23–39. London: Duckworth.
Rosen, R. M. 2007a. *Making Mockery*. Oxford: Oxford University Press.
Rosen, R. M. 2007b. "The Hellenistic Epigrams on Archilochus and Hipponax". In *Brill's Companion to Hellenistic Epigram*, P. Bing & J. S. Bruss (eds), 459–76. Leiden: Brill.
Rosen, R. M. 2008. "Badness and Intentionality in Aristophanes' *Frogs*". In *KAKOS: Badness and Anti-Value in Classical Antiquity*, I. Sluiter & R. M. Rosen (eds), 143–68. Leiden: Brill.
Rosen, R. M. 2013. "Iambos, Comedy and the Question of Generic Affiliation". In *Greek Comedy and the Discourse of Genres*, E. Bakola, L. Prauscello & M. Telò (eds), 81–97. Cambridge: Cambridge University Press.
Rosen, S. H. 1961. "Thought and Touch: A Note on Aristotle's *De Anima*". *Phronesis* 6(2): 127–37.
Rosenmeyer, P. A. 1992. *The Poetics of Imitation: Anacreon and the Anacreontic Tradition*. Cambridge: Cambridge University Press.
Rossi, A. 1968. "Gli anagrammi di Saussure: Poliziano, Bach e Pascoli". *Paragone* 19(218/38): 113–27.
Roudinesco, E. 1990. *Jacques Lacan & Co.: A History of Psychoanalysis in France, 1925–1985*. Chicago, IL: University of Chicago Press.
Roudinesco, E. 1997. *Jacques Lacan*. New York: Columbia University Press.
Roudinesco, E. 2003. "The Mirror Stage: An Obliterated Archive". In *The Cambridge Companion to Lacan*, J.-M. Rabaté (ed.), 25–34. Cambridge: Cambridge University Press.
Rouveret, A., S. Dubel & V. Naas (eds) 2006. *Couleurs et matières dans l'antiquité: textes, techniques et pratiques*. Paris: Éditions Rue d'Ulm/Presses de l'École Normale Supérieure.
Rowe, C. J. (trans., ed.) 1998. *Plato: Symposium*. Warminster: Aris & Phillips.
Ruffell, I. 2002. "A Total Write-Off. Aristophanes, Cratinus and the Rhetoric of Comic Competition". *Classical Quarterly* 52(1): 138–63.
Ruffell, I. 2008. "Audience and Emotion in the Reception of Greek Drama". In *Performance, Iconography, Reception: Studies in Honor of O. Taplin*, M. Revermann & P. Wilson (eds), 37–58. Oxford: Oxford University Press.
Russell, D. A. (trans., ed.) 2001. *Quintilian: The Orator's Education*, 5 vols. Cambridge, MA: Harvard University Press.
Russo, J., M. Fernández-Galiano & A. Heubeck 1992. *A Commentary on Homer's Odyssey*, vol. 3 (Books xvii–xxiv). Oxford: Oxford University Press.
Rutherford-Dyer, R. 1983. "Homer's Wine-Dark Sea". *Greece and Rome* 30(2): 125–8.
Sadovszky, O. J. 1973. "The Reconstruction of IE *pisko and the Extension of its Semantic Sphere". *Journal of Indo-European Studies* 1(1): 81–100.
Sadovszky, O. J. von 1995. *Fish, Symbol and Myth: A Historical Semantic Reconstruction*. Budapest: Akadémiai Kiadó.

Sahlins, M. 1995. *How "Natives" Think. About Captain Cook, For Example*. Chicago, IL: University of Chicago Press.
Salemme, C. 2000. *Introduzione agli Astronomica di Manilio*, 2nd edn. Naples: Loffredo.
Sanders, C. (ed.) 2004. *The Cambridge Companion to Saussure*. Cambridge: Cambridge University Press.
Sansone, D. 1975. *Aeschylean Metaphors for Intellectual Activity*. Hermes, Zeitschrift für klassische Philologie: Einzelschriften Heft 35. Wiesbaden: Steiner.
Sassi, M. 1993. "Fisiognomica". In *Lo Spazio Letterario della Grecia Antica*, G. Cambiano, L. Canfora & D. Lanza (eds), 431–78. Rome: Salerno.
Saussure, F. de 1879. *Mémoire sur le système primitif des voyelles dans les langues indo-européennes*. Leipzig: Teubner.
Saussure, F. de 1892. "Varia". *Mémoires de la Société de Linguistique de Paris* **7**: 73–93.
Saussure, F. de 1922. *Recueil des publications scientifiques de Ferdinand de Saussure*. Heidelberg: Winter.
Saussure, F. de 1997. *Linguistik und Semiologie: Notizen aus dem Nachlaß. Texte, Briefe und Dokumente*, J. Fehr (trans., ed.). Frankfurt am Main: Suhrkamp.
Scarry, E. 1999. *On Beauty and Being Just*. Princeton, NJ: Princeton University Press.
Schadewaldt, W. 1999. "Richard Wagner and the Greeks". *Dialogos* **6**: 108–41.
Schiefsky, M. J. (ed.) 2005. *Hippocrates' On Ancient Medicine*. Leiden: Brill.
Schiesaro, A., P. Mitsis & J. Strauss Clay (eds) 1993. *Mega nepios: Il destinatario nell'epos didascalico* (Materiali e discussioni per l'analisi dei testi classici 31). Pisa: Giardini.
Schindler, C. 2000. *Untersuchungen zu den Gleichnissen im römischen Lehrgedicht: Lucrez, Vergil, Manilius*. Göttingen: Vandenhoeck & Ruprecht.
Schlikker, F. W. 1940. *Hellenistische Vorstellung von der Schönheit des Bauwerks nach Vitruv*. Berlin: Archäologisches Institut d. Deutschen Reiches.
Scholtz, A. 2004. "Friends, Lovers, Flatterers: Demophilic Courtship in Aristophanes' *Knights*". *Transactions of the American Philological Association* **134**(2): 263–93.
Schöne, R. 1897. *Damianos, Schrift über Optik: Mit Auszügen aus Geminos*. Berlin: Weidmann.
Schrijvers, P. H. 1983. "Le chant du monde: remarques sur *Astronomica* I 1–24 de Manilius". *Mnemosyne* **36**(1/2): 143–50.
Schubart, W. 1941. "Über den Dithyrambus". *Archiv für Papyrusforschung* **14**: 24–30.
Schultz, W. 1904. *Das Farbenempfindungssystem der Hellenen*. Leipzig: J. A. Barth.
Schwarz, W. 1972. "*Praecordia mundi*: Zur Grundlegung der Bedeutung des Zodiak bei Manilius". *Hermes* **100**(4): 601–14.
Schweitzer, B. 1932. *Xenokrates von Athen: Beiträge zur Geschichte der antiken Kunstforschung und Kunstanschauung*, Schriften der Königsberger Gelehrten Gesellschaft. Geisteswissenschaftliche Klasse **9**(1). Halle (Saale): M. Niemeyer.
Scranton, R. L. 1964. *Aesthetic Aspects of Ancient Art*. Chicago, IL: University of Chicago Press.
Seaford, R. (ed.) 1984. *Euripides: Cyclops*. Oxford: Oxford University Press.
Segal, A. F. 2009. "The Afterlife in Modern America". In *Speaking of Death. America's New Sense of Mortality*, M. K. Bartalos (ed.), 78–101. Westport, CT: Praeger.
Segal, C. 1977. "Synaesthesia in Sophocles". *Illinois Classical Studies* **2**: 88–109.
Segal, C. 1990. *Lucretius on Death and Anxiety*. Princeton, NJ: Princeton University Press.
Segal, C. 2001. *Singers, Heroes and the Gods in the Odyssey*. Ithaca, NY: Cornell University Press.
Seidensticker, B. 1978. "Archilochus and Odysseus". *Greek, Roman and Byzantine Studies* **19**(1): 5–22.
Seremetakis, C. N. 1994. *The Senses Still: Perception and Memory as Material Culture in Modernity*. Chicago, IL: University of Chicago Press.
Serres, M. 2008. *The Five Senses: A Philosophy of Mingled Bodies*, M. Sankey & P. Cowley (trans.). London: Continuum.
Serres, M. 2009. "Epilogue: What Hearing Knows". In *The Re-Enchantment of the World*, J. Landy & M. Saler (eds), 259–76. Stanford, CA: Stanford University Press.
Shakespeare, W. 2006. *A Midsummer Night's Dream*, H. F. Brooks (ed.). London: Arden Shakespeare.
Sharples, R. W. 1985. "Theophrastus on Tastes and Smells". In *Theophrastus of Eresus: On his Life and Work*, Rutgers University Studies in Classical Humanities 2, W. W. Fortenbaugh, P. M. Huby & A. A. Long (eds), 183–204. New Brunswick, NJ: Transaction.

Shepheard, D. 1982. "Saussure's Vedic Anagrams". *Modern Language Review* **77**(3): 513–23.
Shepheard, D. 1983. "How many Saussures? The Question of the Anagrams". *Paragraph* **2**: 42–52.
Shepheard, D. 1986. "Saussures Anagramme und die deutsche Dichtung". *Sprachwissenschaft* **11**(1/2): 52–79.
Shepheard, D. 1990. "Saussure et la loi poétique". In *Présence de Saussure: actes du Colloque international de Genève (21–23 mars 1988)*, R. Amacker & R. Engler (eds), 235–46. Geneva: Droz.
Shklovsky, V. [1917] 1965. "Art as Technique". In *Russian Formalist Criticism: Four Essays*, L. T. Lemon & M. J. Reis (eds), 3–24. Lincoln, NE: University of Nebraska Press.
Shklovsky, V. [1921] 1965. "Sterne's *Tristram Shandy*: Stylistic Commentary". In *Russian Formalist Criticism: Four Essays*, L. T. Lemon & M. J. Reis (eds), 25–57. Lincoln, NE: University of Nebraska Press.
Shoptaw, J. 2000. "Lyric Cryptography". *Poetics Today* **21**(1): 221–62.
Shulman, D. 2006. "The Scent of Memory in Hindu South India". In *The Smell Culture Reader*, J. Drobnick (ed.), 411–26. Oxford: Berg.
Siegel, R. 1970. *Galen on Sense Perception*. New York: Karger.
Silk, M. S. 2000. *Aristophanes and the Definition of Comedy*. Oxford: Oxford University Press.
Silk, M. S. 2003. "Metaphor and Metonymy: Aristotle, Jakobson, Ricoeur, and Others". In *Metaphor, Allegory and the Classical Tradition: Ancient Thought and Modern Revisions*, G. R. Boys-Stones (ed.), 115–47. Oxford: Oxford University Press.
Simon, G. 1988. *Le regard, l'être et l'apparence dans l'optique de l'antiquité*. Paris: Éditions du Seuil.
Skutsch, O. 1985. *The Annals of Quintus Ennius*. Oxford: Oxford University Press.
Slater, W. J. 1969. *Lexicon to Pindar*. Berlin: de Gruyter.
Smith, J. A. (trans.) 2006. *Aristotle: On the Soul*. Stilwell, KS: Digireads.
Smith, M. M. 2007. *Sensing the Past: Seeing, Hearing, Smelling, Tasting and Touching in History*. Berkeley, CA: California University Press.
Smith, M. M. 2008. "The Touch of an Uncommon Man". *The Chronicle Review – The Chronicle of Higher Education*, 22 February, http://chronicle.com/article/The-Touch-of-an-Uncommon-Man/22272.
Smyth, H. W. 1920. *Greek Grammar*. Cambridge, MA: Harvard University Press.
Sommerstein, A. H. (trans., ed.) 1980. *Acharnians*. The Comedies of Aristophanes 1. Warminster: Aris & Phillips.
Sommerstein, A. H. (trans., ed.) 1981. *Knights*. The Comedies of Aristophanes 2. Warminster: Aris & Phillips.
Sommerstein, A. H. (trans., ed.) 1983. *Wasps*. The Comedies of Aristophanes 4. Warminster: Aris & Phillips.
Sommerstein, A. H. (trans., ed.) 1996. *Frogs*. The Comedies of Aristophanes, 9. Warmister: Aris & Phillips.
Sommerstein, A. H. (trans., ed.) 1998. *Ecclesiazusae*. The Comedies of Aristophanes 10. Warminster: Aris & Phillips.
Sommerstein, A. H. (trans., ed.) 2001. *Wealth*. The Comedies of Aristophanes 11. Warminster: Aris & Phillips.
Sommerstein, A. H. 2002. "Monsters, Ogres, and Demons in Old Comedy". In *Monsters and Monstrosity in Greek and Roman Culture*, C. Atherton (ed.), 19–40. Bari: Levante.
Sommerstein, A. H. (trans., ed.) 2009a. *Aeschylus Volume I: Persians, Seven Against Thebes, Suppliants, Prometheus Bound*. Cambridge, MA: Loeb.
Sommerstein, A. H. 2009b. *Talking About Laughter and Other Studies in Greek Comedy*. Oxford: Oxford University Press.
Sontag, S. 2001. "Against Interpretation". In her *Against Interpretation and Other Essays*, 3–14. New York: Farrar, Straus & Giroux.
Sorabji, R. 1971. "Aristotle on Demarcating the Five Senses". *Philosophical Review* **80**(1): 55–79. Reprinted in MacPherson (2011), 64–82.
Sorabji, R. 1993. *Animal Minds and Human Morals*. Ithaca, NY: Cornell University Press.
Spingarn, J. E. 1917. *Creative Criticism: Essays on the Unity of Genius and Taste*. New York: Henry Holt & Company.
Stanford, W. B. 1936. *Greek Metaphor*. Oxford: Blackwell.
Stanford, W. B. 1942. *Aeschylus in his Style: A Study in Language and Personality*. Dublin: Dublin University Press.
Starobinski, J. 1964. "Les Anagrammes de Ferdinand de Saussure: textes inédits". *Mercure de France* (February): 243–62.
Starobinski, J. 1971. *Les Mots sous les mots: les anagrammes de Ferdinand de Saussure*. Paris: Gallimard.

Starobinski, J. 1979. *Words upon Words: The Anagrams of Ferdinand de Saussure*, O. Emmet (trans.). New Haven, CT: Yale University Press.
Starr, R. J. 2001. "The Flexibility of Literary Meaning and the Role of the Reader in Roman Antiquity". *Latomus* **60**(2):433–45.
Stevens, B. 2008. "The Scent of Language and Social Synaesthesia at Rome". *Classical World* **101**(2): 159–171.
Stevens, W. 1990. "Notes toward a Supreme Fiction". In his *The Collected Poems of Wallace Stevens*, 380–410. New York: Vintage.
Stewart, S. 1999. "Prologue: From the Museum of Touch". In *Material Memories*, M. Kwint, C. Breward & J. Aynsley (eds), 17–36. Oxford: Berg.
Stewart, S. 2002. *Poetry and the Fate of the Senses*. Chicago, IL: University of Chicago Press.
Stoller, P. 1997. *Sensuous Scholarship*. Philadelphia, PA: University of Pennsylvania Press.
Stover, T. 2008. "Cato and the Intended Scope of Lucan's *Bellum Civile*". *The Classical Quarterly* **58**(2): 571–80.
Struck, P. T. 2004. *Birth of the Symbol: Ancient Readers at the Limits of their Texts*. Princeton, NJ: Princeton University Press.
Suetonius 1860. *C. Svetoni Tranqvilli praeter Caesarvm libros reliqviae*, A. Reifferscheid (ed.). Leipzig: Teubner.
Summers, D. 1990. *The Judgment of Sense: Renaissance Naturalism and the Rise of Aesthetics*. Cambridge: Cambridge University Press.
Sutton, D. E. 2001. *Remembrance of Repasts: An Anthropology of Food and Memory*. Oxford: Berg.
Sweetser, E. E. 1990. *From Etymology to Pragmatics: Metaphorical and Cultural Aspects of Semantic Structure*. Cambridge: Cambridge University Press.
Taillardat, J. 1965. *Les images d'Aristophane: études de langue et de style*. Paris: Les Belles Lettres.
Tallis, R. 1995. *Not Saussure: A Critique of Post-Saussurean Literary Theory*, 2nd edn. Basingstoke: Macmillan.
Tellegen-Couperus, O. 2003. "A Clarifying *Sententia* Clarified: On *Institutio Oratoria* 8.5.19". In *Quintilian and the Law*, O. Tellegen-Couperus (ed.), 213–21. Leuven: Leuven University Press.
Telò, M. 2013. "Epic, *Nostos* and Generic Genealogy in Aristophanes' *Peace*". In *Greek Comedy and the Discourse of Genres*, E. Bakola, L. Prauscello, & M. Telò (eds), 129–52. Cambridge: Cambridge University Press.
Telò, M. Forthcoming a. "Aristophanes vs. Typhon: Co(s)mic Rivalry and Temporality in *Knights*".
Telò, M. Forthcoming b. "On the Sauce: Cratinus, Cyclopic Poetics and the Roiling Sea of Epic".
Testenoire, P.-Y. 2010. "Des Anagrammes chez Homère? De Saussure aux commentateurs anciens". *Actes des sessions de linguistique et de littérature (LALIES)* **30**: 215–31.
Thiercy, P. 1993. "Les odeurs de la polis ou le nez d'Aristophanes". In *Tragedy, Comedy and the Polis*, A. H. Sommerstein, S. Halliwell, J. Henderson & B. Zimmermann (eds), 505–26. Bari: Levante.
Thomas, E. 2007. *Monumentality and the Roman Empire: Architecture in the Antonine Age*. Oxford: Oxford University Press.
Thomas, R. 2000. *Herodotus in Context: Ethnography, Science and the Art of Persuasion*. Cambridge: Cambridge University Press.
Thomas, R. F. 2011. *Horace, Odes, Book IV and Carmen saeculare*. Cambridge: Cambridge University Press.
Thordarson, F. 1971. "ὁρῶ, βλέπω, θεωρῶ: Some Semantic Remarks". *Symbolae Osloenses* **46**(1): 108–30.
Thurston, L. 1998. "Ineluctable Nodalities: On the Borromean Knot". In *Key Concepts of Lacanian Psychoanalysis*, D. Nobus (ed.), 139–63. London: Rebus Press.
Toohey, P. 1996. *Epic Lessons: An Introduction to Ancient Didactic Poetry*. London: Taylor & Francis.
Tordoff, R. L. 2011. "Excrement, Sacrifice, Commensality: the Osphresiology of Aristophanes' *Peace*". *Arethusa* **44**(2): 167–98.
Tsantsanoglou, K. 2009. "The λεπτότης of Aratus". *Trends in Classics* **1**(1): 55–89.
Ullman, S. 1957. *Principles of Semantics*. Oxford: Blackwell.
Usher, S. (trans.) 1974. *Dionysius of Halicarnassus: Critical Essays I*. Cambridge, MA: Harvard University Press.
Usher, S. (trans.) 1985. *Dionysius of Halicarnassus: Critical Essays II*. Cambridge, MA: Harvard University Press.
Vaan, M. de 2008. *Etymological Dictionary of Latin and other Italic Languages*. Leiden: Brill.
van Hook, L. 1905. *The Metaphorical Terminology of Greek Rhetoric and Literary Criticism*. Chicago, IL: University of Chicago Press.
van Noorden, H. 2009. "Aratus' Maiden and the Source of Belief". In *Nature and Science in Hellenistic Poetry*, M. A. Harder, R. F. Regtuit & G. C. Wakker (eds), 255–75. Louvain: Peeters.
Verity, A. (trans.) & R. Hunter (intro.) 2002. *Theocritus: Idylls*. Oxford: Oxford University Press.

Viberg, A. 1983. "The Verbs of Perception: A Typological Study". *Linguistics* 21(1): 123–62.
Vilela, I. 1998. "Saussure pró: a unidade saussuriana presente no *Curso*, nos *anagramas* e na psicanálise de Lacan". *Cahiers Ferdinand de Saussure* 51: 251–72.
Vilela, I. 1999. "Saussure *versus* Lacan: linguagem, discursos patológicos e formações do inconsciente". *Signótica* 11: 75–106.
Vilela, I. 2008. "Le Fonds Ferdinand de Saussure". www.item.ens.fr/fichiers/Theorie_linguistique/FondsSaussure.pdf.
Villard, L. (ed.) 2002. *Couleurs et vision dans l'antiquité classique*. Rouen: Publications de l'Université de Rouen.
Vinge, L. 1975. *The Five Senses: Studies in a Literary Tradition*. Lund: C. W. K. Gleerup (Liber Läromedel).
Voigt, E-V. 1971. *Sappho et Alcaeus. Fragmenta*. Amsterdam: Athenaeum – Polak & Van Gennep.
Volk, K. 2001. "Pious and Impious Approaches to Cosmology in Manilius". *Materiali e discussioni per l'analisi dei testi classici* 47: 85–117.
Volk, K. 2002. *The Poetics of Latin Didactic: Lucretius, Vergil, Ovid, Manilius*. Oxford: Oxford University Press.
Volk, K. 2009. *Manilius and his Intellectual Background*. Oxford: Oxford University Press.
Volk, K. 2010a. "Aratus". In *A Companion to Hellenistic Literature*, J. J. Clauss & M. Cuypers (eds), 197–210. Malden, MA: Wiley-Blackwell.
Volk, K. 2010b. "Literary Theft and Roman Water Rights in Manilius' Second Proem". *Materiali e discussioni per l'analisi dei testi classici* 65: 187–97.
Volk, K. 2012. "Letters in the Sky: Reading the Signs in Aratus' *Phaenomena*". *American Journal of Philology* 133: 209–40.
Wagner, R. 1995. *Opera and Drama*. Lincoln, NE: University of Nebraska Press.
Wallon, H. (ed.) 1938. *La vie mentale* (*Encyclopédie française* 8). Paris: Société des gestion de l'Encyclopédie française.
Walters, B. 2011. "Metaphor, Violence, and the Death of the Roman Republic". PhD dissertation, Department of Classics, University of California, Los Angeles.
Ward, J. 2008. *The Frog who Croaked Blue: Synesthesia and the Mixing of the Senses*. London: Routledge.
Warren, J. 2002. "Democritus, the Epicureans, Death, and Dying". *The Classical Quarterly* 52(1): 193–206.
Warren, J. 2004. *Facing Death. Epicurus and His Critics*. Oxford: Oxford University Press.
Watkins, C. 1995. *How to Kill a Dragon: Aspects of Indo-European Poetics*. New York: Oxford University Press.
Watkins, C. 2011. *The American Heritage Dictionary of Indo-European Roots*, 3rd edn. Boston, MA: Houghton Mifflin.
Weiss, M. 1994. "Life Everlasting: Latin *iūgis* 'Everflowing', Greek ὑγιής 'Healthy', Gothic *ajukdūþs* 'Eternity' and Avestan *yauuaēǰī-* 'Living Forever'". *Münchener Studien zur Sprachwissenschaft* 55: 131–56.
West, M. L. (ed.) 1966. *Hesiod, Theogony*. Oxford: Oxford University Press.
West, M. L. (trans., ed.) 2003. *Homeric Hymns. Homeric Apocrypha. Lives of Homer*. Cambridge, MA: Harvard University Press.
West, S. 2007. "Rhampsinitos and the Clever Thief (Herodotus 2.121)". In *A Companion to Greek and Roman Historiography*, vol. 2, J. Marincola (ed.), 322–7. Malden, MA: Blackwell.
Whitby, M. 2007. "The *Cynegetica* attributed to Oppian". In *Severan Culture*, S. Swain, S. Harrison & J. Elsner (eds), 125–34. Cambridge: Cambridge University Press.
Whitman, C. H. 1964. *Aristophanes and the Comic Hero*. Cambridge, MA: Harvard University Press.
Willi, A. 2003. *The Language of Aristophanes: Aspects of Linguistic Variation in Classical Attic Greek*. Oxford: Oxford University Press.
Williams, J. M. 1976. "Synaesthetic Adjectives: A Possible Law of Semantic Change". *Language* 52(2): 461–78.
Wilson, A. M. 1985. "The Prologue to Manilius 1". *Papers of the Liverpool Latin Seminar* 5: 283–98.
Wilson, N. 2007. *Aristophanea: Studies on the Text of Aristophanes*. Oxford: Oxford University Press.
Wimsatt, W. K. 1954. "The Affective Fallacy". In his *The Verbal Icon: Studies in the Meaning of Poetry*, 21–39. Louisville, KY: University of Kentucky Press.
Winkler, J. J. 1990. *The Constraints of Desire: The Anthropology of Sex and Gender in Ancient Greece*. New York: Routledge.
Wiseman, T. P. 1994. *Historiography and Imagination. Eight Essays on Roman Culture*. Exeter: University of Exeter Press.

Wohl, V. 2002. *Love Among the Ruins. The Erotics of Democracy in Classical Athens*. Princeton, NJ: Princeton University Press.
Wöhrle, G. 1985. *Theophrasts Methode in seinen botanischen Schriften*. Amsterdam: John Benjamins.
Wood, M. 2009. "A World Without Literature?". *Daedalus* **138**(1): 58–67.
Woolf, V. 1986. "How Should One Read a Book?". In *The Common Reader, Second Series*, A. McNellie (ed.), 258–70. London: Hogarth Press.
Woolf, V. 1987. "Creative Criticism". In *The Essays of Virginia Woolf*, A. McNeillie (ed.), 122–5. New York: Harcourt Brace Jovanovich.
Worman, N. 2008. *Abusive Mouths in Classical Athens*. Cambridge: Cambridge University Press.
Wunderli, P. 1972a. "Ferdinand de Saussure: '1er Cahier à lire préliminairement'. Ein Basistext seiner Anagrammstudien". *Zeitschrift für französische Sprache und Literatur* **82**(3): 193–216.
Wunderli, P. 1972b. *Ferdinand de Saussure und die Anagramme: Linguistik und Literatur*. Tübingen: Niemeyer.
Wunderli, P. 1972c. "Saussure et les anagrammes". *Travaux de linguistique et de littérature* **10**(1): 35–53.
Wunderli, P. 2004. "Saussure's Anagrams and the Analysis of Literary Texts". In Sanders (2004), 174–85, 264.
Zanker, G. 1981. "*Enargeia* in the Ancient Criticism of Poetry". *Rheinisches Museum für Philologie* **124**: 297–311.
Zanker, P. 1988. *The Power of Images in the Age of Augustus*, A. Shapiro (trans.). Ann Arbor, MI: University of Michigan Press.
Zinn, E. 1956. "Die Dichter des alten Rom und die Anfänge des Weltgedichts". *Antike und Abendland* **5**: 7–26.

INDEX

Ackerman, D. 35
Aeschylus 20–21, 68–9
    Agamemnon 21
    Seven Against Thebes 6, 20–22, 74, 86
    Prometheus Bound 21
    see also Life of Aeschylus
aesthetes 89–90, 91, 95, 97–8, 100, 155–6
aesthetics 1–2, 6, 9–26, 44, 51–2, 91, 93, 95, 97, 100, 102, 129, 135, 137–8, 156–7, 161
    and *aisthēsis* 1, 14–15, 156
        Aristotle on 1, 15
    and *aisthanomai* 1
    modern usage of 1, 25–6
    Plato on 89–93, 100
    and sensory pleasure 2, 5, 157–61, 163–4; *see also* aesthetes
Afranius 59(*n*27)
afterlife/underworld 9, 115(*n*2), 120, 195, 200
aisthanomai see aesthetics
aisthēsis see aesthetics
Alberti, L. B. 188
ambrosia *see* smell
Anacreontea 86
anagrams *see* writing, wordplay
animals 6, 43–52, 129, 130, 135–7
    see also Aristotle; nonsense; smell
Apuleius, *Metamorphoses* 135(*n*31)
Aratus, *Phaenomena* 6, 106–9, 113
Archestratus 77(*n*23)
Archilochus 54–6, 62, 64–6, 67–8
architecture *see* art/arts, plastic
Aristophanes 6
    Acharnians 58–9, 64(*n*39), 72(*n*6), 74–5

Birds 46–51, 74
Clouds 78(*n*26)
    and Cratinus, compared 53–70
Ecclesiazusae 75, 77(*n*23), 78(*n*26)
Frogs 13, 21, 68–9, 75, 78, 86, 87, 90
Knights 53–70, 71–5, 78(*n*26), 87–8
Peace 58(*n*20), 59(*n*23), 74, 75, 77(*n*23), 78(*n*26), 84, 87
Thesmaphoriazusae 13
Wasps 58, 75, 78(*n*26), 83
Wealth 78, 83
Aristotle 6, 14–16, 80, 140, 142, 143
    on animal sounds 47–8, 51–2
    on common sensibles 14–16
    Eudemian Ethics 15
    History of Animals 52
    Metaphysics 16
    Nichomachean Ethics 15
    On Dreams 74(*n*12)
    On Sleep 15
    On Sophistical Refutations 86(*n*54)
    On the Soul 2(*n*3), 14–16, 29, 52(*n*15), 65(*n*46), 79, 80(*n*35), 132
    Parts of Animals 29, 47
    Poetics 15, 18(*n*32), 143(*n*11)
    Politics 48
    Rhetoric 14, 141, 149
    Sense and Sensibilia 14, 29, 76(*n*20)
    on sense faculties, interaction of 2, 14–16, 29, 83, 140
    see also aesthetics; colour; metaphor; oratory; smell; speech; taste; touch

art/arts 1, 156–9, 161
　creation of 189, 194, 195–7, 199–200
　　as loss 194, 200
　　as narcissism 194, 196–7
　as expression of perceptual experience 164–5
　plastic 12–13, 18–19
　　architecture 12, 13, 18–19
　　sculpture 13, 18, 19, 187, 194, 195
　　painting 16, 145, 164, 187, 188, 198
　sensual pleasure in *see* aesthetes; aesthetics
　synaesthetic approach to 10–11, 25–6
　see also Surrealism; touch
Ashton, D. 189
askēsis 89–90, 95, 97, 101(*n*26), 102
astrology *see* Aratus; Manilius; stars/constellations
Athenaeus, *Learned Banqueters* 61(*n*33), 66, 67
Augustine, *Confessions* 163–4
Aulus Gellius, *Attic Nights* 131

Bakhtin, M. 53
Barthes, R. 156, 195
　"Death of the Author" 197
Baudelaire, C. 43
　"Correspondances" 3, 5, 43–4
Baumgarten, A. 1
beauty 15, 89–102, 157–60, 163, 165
　of the cosmos 103
　erotic 158–61
　immortal 63
　intellectual appreciation of 89–102
　in Plato 6, 89–102, 155
　　absolute beauty 90–91, 93–5, 97, 100, 102
　　ta kala 63, 89–93
　sensory appreciation of 5, 89–102, 157–61,
　　163–4; *see also* aesthetes
　and transcendence 90–91, 95, 97–8, 100–101
　see also aesthetics; music; vision
Bell, M. 115
Benveniste, E. 177, 181
Berlin, B. 130
Biles, Z. 61
blindness *see* vision
body/bodies 27–33, 35–8, 40
　as beautiful 93–4, 96
　commingling of 164
　cosmic 105, 113
　dead/dying 116–26
　as diseased/dysfunctional 37, 82–3, 125, 138
　dismemberment/mutilation of *see* mutilation
　and climate/environment 31–2, 134

　as fragrant/malodorous; *see* smell
　geography of 40
　and the grotesque/carnality 53, 56, 117–18, 123
　　bodily functions 53
　naked 40–41, 159
　physiology of 84, 86
　in relation to soul 121–2, 124
　taste of (a kiss) 160, 162
　text as 121, 124
　see also Descartes, R.; senses
brain *see* mind
Brenkman, J. 193
Breton, A. 189, 199

Callimachus 50(*n*14), 56
　Aetia 104
Caravaggio, M. M. da, *Narcissus* 188–9
Chapman, G., *Ovids Banquet of Sence* 7, 158–65
Cicero 106(*n*15), 117, 135, 144, 183
　Against Catiline 117(*n*12)
　On the Responses of the Soothsayers 135
　De natura deorum (On the Nature of the Gods)
　　111, 115(*n*2)
　For Plancius 143(*n*18)
　Handbook of Electioneering 116
　In toga candida 116
　On Divination 151(*n*73)
　On Oratory 143(*n*10), 151(*n*72)
　Orator 149
　Tusculan Disputations 115(*n*2), 120
Clarke, M. 130–31, 133
clarity *see* vision
Cocteau, J. 187, 189, 192, 195
　The Orphic Trilogy 187, 189, 192, 195
　The White Book 192
cold *see* temperature
colour 7, 96, 98–9, 100, 127–40, 145, 155, 197
　ancient terms denoting 7, 127–8, 131–5, 138
　　in Homer 127, 132
　　oinops 131, 132–3
　anthropological studies of 128–30
　Aristotle on 14, 132, 137
　blindness 127
　and grapheme-colour synaesthesia *see*
　　synaesthesia
　"colour organ" *see* Scriabin, A.
　and death 122–3
　dyes 127, 135–8
　experience of as object-centred 131
　philosophy of 132, 137

Plato on 99–100
  pure colour 97, 99–100
 purple/*porphura*/*purpura* 131, 135–8
 of skin 32, 132–4
 and senses
  hearing 1, 96, 100, 101(*n*26), 180
  smell 3, 127, 135, 137–8
  taste 3, 131
  touch 127, 135
 significance of 130, 133
 see also music; sound
Columella, *On Agriculture* 131
Comedy, Greek 6, 47–51, 53–70, 71–4, 88; *see also* Archilochus; Aristophanes; Cratinus; performance
common sensibles, theory of *see* Aristotle
consciousness 15, 18, 157, 182–3, 196, 197
 and reflexivity 187, 193, 199
 synaesthesia as higher state of 101(*n*26)
consonants/consonantism *see* sound, linguistic
constellations *see* stars/constellations
cosmology/cosmos 103; *see also* stars/constellations
Cratinus 55–69
  Archilochoi 65
  Didaskaliai 61–2
  Pytinē 56
  see also Archilochus; Aristophanes
Cytowic, R. E. 179

Dalí, S. 186–9, 191–2, 195, 200
  Archaeological Reminiscence of Millet's Angelus 188
  Metamorphosis of Narcissus 186, 188, 189–90, 191–2
 and Freud, S. 189–91, 192, 197, 200
 see also Lacan, J.
dance 12–14, 22; *see also* poetry, dithyrambic
darkness 7, 27–8, 34, 40, 118, 127, 141–54
Darwin, C. 127
De coloribus 135–6
death 2, 6, 38–40, 115–26, 138, 192, 195
 fear of 118–26
 see also afterlife; body/bodies; colour; Lucretius; metaphor; mutilation; poetry; reading; senses; smell; taste; temperature
Demetrius, *On Style* 18
Descartes, R. 155–6
 Cartesian dualism, theory of 130, 155–6, 165

desire 48, 92, 159–61, 163–4
Dionysiac ritual 55–7, 61–2, 65–6, 68, 131, 133; *see also* drunkenness
Dionysius of Halicarnassus
  On Literary Composition 19
  On the Style of Demosthenes 19
Diotima 90–6, 100, 102; *see also* Plato, *Symposium*
discus (from Cephallenia) 16–18, **17**
disease *see* body
dismemberment *see* mutilation
display/*ornatus* 149–51
Dolto, F. 190–91
Donne, J. 162–3
dress 135–8
drunkenness 55–7, 61, 62, 65–7; *see also* Dionysiac ritual
dreams 5, 61–2, 64, 65, 66, 164

Echo 159, 199–200; *see also* Narcissus
echolalia 199
Eco, U. 128–9, 130
ecphrasis *see* ekphrasis
ekphrasis 20–22, 51, 108, 139(*n*37), 194
Eliot, T. S. 162–3
Ellis, H. 190, 192
Elsaesser, T. 196, 198
Emerson, R. W. 155–6
emotion/feeling 45–8, 84–5, 97, 107
 and audience of Comedy 54
 and knowledge 157–8, 161–2
 as nonverbal utterance 45, 47–8, 50–51
 physicality of 74, 84–5, 106, 110–11
  anger 84–6; *see also* humours, bile
  blushing 134
  grief/lamentation 50, 133
  sympathy 51
 and sound 44–5
 see also taste; touch; senses; stars/constellations
enargeia 143–4
Ennius, *Annales* 117, 121
Epicureanism 6, 120, 122, 125; *see also* Lucretius
Eupolis 53(*nn*23, 25)
Euripides 68(*n*65), 69, 79
  Cyclops 78, 86
Eustathius, *Commentary on Homer's Odyssey* 78(*n*26), 179(*n*51)

feeling *see* emotion/feeling
Feuillerat, A. 156–7, 164

INDEX

Flournoy, T. 180
Freud, S. 38(*n*29), 189–90, 191, 192, 200
    "A Note Upon the 'Mystic Writing-Pad'" 196
    Beyond the Pleasure Principle 190, 197–8
    on homosexuality as narcissism 190, 192–3
    Leonardo da Vinci and a Memory of his Childhood 190
    as media theorist 196
    On Narcissism 190, 192
    and the self/Ego 190, 193, 196–8
    on the senses 197–8
    see also Dalí, S.; Lacan, J.
Fuller, T. 27

Galen 133–4
    On the Properties of Foodstuffs 72(*n*3)
    On Simple Drugs 83(*n*42)
Gallop, J. 186
garlic *see* taste
gesture 45, 47
Gladstone, W. 127
Godel, R. 177
Goethe, J. W. 127
Gorgias 14
Gratidianus *see* Lucan

Hamilton, J. 152
haptics *see* touch
hardness/softness *see* metaphor; touch
Hartman, G. 156
hearing *see* sound
heat *see* temperature
Hegel, G. W. F. 15(*n*23), 193
Herodas 86
Herodotus, *Histories* 6, 27–41
    story of Candaules and Gyges in 40–41
    story of Rhampsinitus and the Thief in 27–8, 36–40
    story of Smerdis in 27–8, 34–6
Hesiod
    Theogony 9, 78(*n*27)
    Works and Days 182
Hippocratic Corpus 66(*n*54), 81–2, 83, 84–5, 86(*n*55), 133–4
Hipponax 68
historiography 6, 28–34
Homer 6, 9–10, 16, 127, 132, 178–9, 181
    Iliad 9, 21, 51, 78, 84, 85(*n*47), 86(*n*53), 132, 182
    Odyssey 9, 10, 40, 54, 58, 62–4, 66–9, 74(*n*12), 85, 86, 132, 179

Homeric Hymn to Demeter 63, 64(*n*40)
Hopkins, G. M. 182
Horace
    Epistles 57(*n*15), 66(*n*53)
    Epodes 131
    Odes 183
Housman, A. E. 103
humours, theory of 84–7, 133–4
    bile 85–6, 133

imagines 195–6
intertextuality 121, 123, 191
intuition *see* senses, sixth sense
intellectus see mind
Isocrates, *Evagoras* 147

Jakobson, R. 181, 183
Jones, E. 185
Jonson, B. 162
Joseph, J. E. 179–81

Kay, P. 130
Keats. J., "This Living Hand" 38
Kidd, D. 107
kinaesthesia 28
Kitto, H. D. F. 14

Lacan, J. 170(*n*10), 177(*n*41), 185–200
    and Dalí, S./Surrealism 186–7, 190–91, 195, 199, 200
    and Freud, S. 190–91, 192–3, 196, 200
    and the "mirror stage" 185–8, 191–5, 197, 200
    on the Imaginary, Real, and Symbolic 194
    and Poe, E. A. 186
language
    clarity and obscurity in use of 141–54
    and communication between species 43–52
    materiality of 6, 198
    and sensation
        hearing/sound 199, 200
        synaesthetic 2, 3, 7, 179–81
        touch 30–31
        vision 199
    as social institution 180, 198–9
    as translation of experience 5
    see also linguistics; nonsense; orality; speech; sound, linguistic; wordplay; writing
Lapidge, M. 111
Leder, D. 37
Lessing, G. E. 15

Life of Aeschylus 20–21
light/luminosity 127, 141–54, 163; *see also* colour; darkness; metaphor
linguistics 167–84
  diachronicity and synchronicity 169, 171–4
  etymology 1, 168, 172–4, 190
  linearity of language 173, 175, 176
  linguistic fickleness 173, 183
  phonetics/phonemes 169, 170, 178–9, 182, 198
    laryngeals 170–71
    phonic patterning 170, 172
  semantics 45, 47, 78–9, 81–2, 84, 88, 130, 169, 173, 182
Lovecraft, H. P. 48, 52
Lucan, *Civil War* 6, 115–26
  story of Marius Gratidianus in 115–19, 121, 123–4
Lucian, *How to Write History* 60(*n*29)
Lucretius, *On the Nature of Things* 6, 115–26, 132, 183
  on death 118–20, 124–5
Lycophron 152

magic 46, 64(*n*41), 104–5
Manilius, *Astronomica* 6, 103–14
  on aspect 110
  compared with Aratus, *Phaenomena* 106–9
  as didactic 112–13
  panaesthetic worldview of 106
  proem in 104–6, 113
  and Stoicism 103, 111
  sensual cosmos in 104–14
    and music/song 104–5, 106
    and vision 110–14
  see also stars/constellations
Martial 137–8
material world 92–7, 99, 100–102, 130; *see also* language; sound
medicine *see* physicians
Mehtonen, P. 142
Meillet, A. 171, 175, 181
memory 5, 6, 195; *see also* smell
Menander 59(*n*27)
Merleau-Ponty, M. 16, 29, 30(*n*13), 33(*n*18), 37–8, 69, 200(*n*53)
metaphor 1, 77–9, 80–81
  Aristotle on 79–80, 87–8
  astrological 104–5, 110
  "bright" as 80(*nn*34, 36), 107; *see also* light/luminosity

  and death 115, 122–5
  "hard" and "soft" as 30–33, 169; *see also* touch
  "hot" as 80–81(*nn*32, 36–7), 82–3, 106
  intersensal/intersensual 1, 2, 73, 87–8
  as literal 79–81, 87–8
  poetry as 12–14, 18–19, 115–26, 160–61, 194
  Quintilian on 7, 141–54
  sensation/synaesthesia as 110, 128, 164
  of taste 77–81, 87–8
  visual 141–54
  see also darkness; death; mirrors; poetry
metamorphosis 64, 189; *see also* Ovid
metonymy 25, 63, 72(*n*7), 73, 148(*n*46)
Millet, J-F. 186, 188
mind 5, 15
  as brain 198
  mind's eye/mental images 15, 96, 112, 144, 146–7, 149
  and intellection of knowledge 155
  as *intellectus* 147, 151–2
  noetic/*noēsis* 1, 94–6, 97, 98
  see also Descartes, R.; senses, and reason
Minotaure see Picasso
mirrors 7, 159, 160, 161, 187, 192–6, 200
  and homosexuality 190, 192
  the "mirror stage" *see* Lacan, J.
  and reflection 187, 193, 199
  writing as 187, 194, 199–200
  see also Echo
Montaigne, M. de 155, 165
Most, G. 118
motion 12, 14–15, 18, 105
Muses, the 9–11, 14, 25, 61, 182, 200
music 11, 155, 159, 200
  and beauty/transcendence 100–102
  and colour 43, 128
  of the spheres 106, 162
  and Wagner's "ear/eye of hearing" 44, 45, 49
  see also poetry, dithyrambic; song; sound, rhythm
mustard *see* taste
mutilation 6, 36–40, 116–21, 123–5

Näcke, P. 190, 192
Nancy, J-L. 9–10
Narcissus 7, 159, 185–200
narcissism 190–93, 196–7; *see also* Freud, S.
noēsis see mind
nonsense 7, 43–52, 200
  as animal utterance 6, 46–52

as nonverbal exclamation 47–52
 visually expressed 6, 22–5
 see also vase, Chazen; echolalia
nose/nostrils 82–4, 86, 117; *see also* smell

Obrador-Pons, P. 29
obscurity *see* vision
olfaction *see* nose/nostrils; smell
Oliensis, E. 183
oracles 60–62, 64, 142
 Delphic 12, 29–30, 199
orality 18, 169, 179, 182
oratory 7, 128, 141–54
 Aristotle on 141–3
 and vision 141–53
ornatus see display/*ornatus*
Ovid 7, 106(n15), 121, 158–65, 189–90, 193–4, 196, 199–200
 Amores 134(n27)
 Art of Love 135, 158–61, 164
 Fasti 139
 Metamorphoses 37, 104(n6), 118, 189, 194, 199–200
 reception of 189–90
 see also Chapman, G.
onomatopoeia *see* sound
Oppian/pseudo-Oppian 6
 Cynegetica 46–51

pain 5, 20–21, 28, 47–9, 83, 97, 99, 119
painting *see* arts, plastic
Paphlagon *see* Aristophanes
paraesthesia 43–52
Pater, W. 156
Paterson, M. 33
perception *see* senses
performance 18–19
 and audience, sensory experience of 45–6, 54–5, 67–9, 72–3, 77, 81, 87, 143–53
 oratorical 152–3
 theatrical 18, 20–22, 53, 89–90
Petronius 145(n25)
phainomena 91, 98, 107, 108, 113
Pherecrates 59(n25)
Philonides, *On Perfumes and Wreaths* 66–7
physicians/medicine 32, 66, 72, 82–4, 133–4; *see also* Galen; Hippocratic Corpus
physiognomy 71, 133–4
physiology *see* body

Picasso 187–9
 cover for *Minotaure* 186–8, **188**
 Deucalon and Pyrrha Creating a New Human Race 189
 Girl Before a Mirror 187, 189
 Sacrifice of Polyxena 189
Pindar 18, 60(n28), 152
 Nemean 5 13
 Olympian 6 12
 Pythian 1 13
 Paean 8 12
Plato 6, 21, 81–3, 89–102, 137, 167, 172
 Philebus 97–9, 100
 Republic 78(n26), 87(n58), 89–91, 93, 97–8, 155
 Statesman 78(n26)
 Symposium 6, 90–95, 97–8, 100
 Theaetetus 78(n26), 80(n35), 167
 Timaeus 77(n23), 81–3
 see also aesthetics; beauty; colour; pleasure; taste
Plautus 59(nn26, 27), 66(n52)
pleasure
 Plato on 89–90, 92, 97–9
 "true" pleasure 97–100
 in poetry 151, 153
 sensory, pursuit of *see* aesthetes
 and sound 49
 see also aesthetics
Pliny
 Natural History 35(n22), 72(n3), 134, 135–8
 Panegyric 134
Platonius, *On the Differences in Character of the Comedians* 65
Plutarch 13
 Morals 21
Poe, E. A., "The Purloined Letter" 186
poetry 2, 3–5, 68–9, 141–54
 as architecture 12–14, 18–19
 as death 115–26
 didactic *see* Manilius
 elegy 150
 epigram 189
 exploration of synaesthesia in 5, 43
 images in 157; *see also* mind
 poetic metre 200
  dithyrambic 18(n32), 56, 61–2, 66
  hexameter 142
  iambic 56, 62, 64–6, 68
  Stabreim 44, 45, 49(n13)
 as mirror 160–61, 194
 obscurity of 141–54

INDEX

Saturnian 175, 178
truth of 7, 141–54, 155–65
visual depiction of 22–5
see also sound
Poulet, G. 160–61, 162
Propertius 152
proprioception 28
psychoanalysis 7, 186–8, 190–94, 196, 199–200
Pythagoras 106

Quintilian 7
The Orator's Education 21, 108, 141–54
clarity/obscurity in 7, 143–4, 145, 148, 150–53
see also metaphor

reading 7, 158, 160, 161, 162–3
as death 121–3, 124–5
as epistemological process 7
sensory experience of 6, 158, 160, 163
learning processes of 198
as performance 17–18
practices of 7, 19
reception, classical 7
as syn-aesthetics 2, 9–26
reflexivity, *see* consciousness
rhetoric 145, 149, 157
Rhetorica ad Herennium 143(n10)
rhuthmos 12; *see also* sound, rhythm
rhyme *see* sound
Richards, I. A. 157
Riegl, A. 16
Rimbaud, A., "Voyelles" 43

Sallust
Histories 116
War with Catiline 115(n2)
Sappho 3–5, 9
Sausage-Seller *see* Aristophanes
Saussure, F. de 2, 7, 167–84
Cours de Linguistique Générale 174
as synaesthete 179–80, 183
theory of signifier-signified 172–3, 175, 194
Scriabin, A. 1, 89, 100–102
Mysterium 101
Prometheus 100–101
sculpture *see* arts, plastic
Seneca
Controversies 145(n25)
Epistles 134
Hercules on Oeta 132(n12)

On Anger 116, 134
senses 14, 40
absence/death of 6, 115–26
Aristotle on 14–15, 140
anachronism of 77, 88, 127
collaboration/unity of 6, 16, 91
confusion of 22, 200
distal/proximal 7, 161, 162
distrust of 137, 155–6, 165
failure of 147, 159, 161
Epicurean theory of 120
five, assumption of 128, 140
hierarchy of 2–3, 53, 80
isolation/segregation of 41, 72(n7), 87–8
insensate 120, 156, 199
and knowledge 7, 91, 92, 95, 137, 140, 155–9, 160–61, 162–3, 164–5
and literary criticism 18–19, 90, 141–2, 156–7, 162, 165
as mediators 158
overload/overwhelm of 13–14, 55
philosophy of 155–6
pleasure in *see* aesthetes
and reason 113–14, 155–6
sixth sense/intuition 5, 200
subjectivity/objectivity of 156–8, 159–62
transcendence of 6, 90–91, 95, 96, 97, 98, 100–102, 155–6
transgression of sensory boundaries 64, 79–80, 91
see also smell; sound; taste; touch; vision
"sensuous geography" 29, 32–3
Serres, M. 52
sex and sexuality 190–93
Shakespeare, W.
Merchant of Venice 73
A Midsummer Night's Dream 164
Shklovsky, V. 13, 15
Shoptaw, J. 183
sight *see* vision
simile 148, 151
Simonides 13
skin *see* colour; touch
smell 6
Aristotle on 83
and aromatherapy 66–7
and construction of self/other 53–70
of death 122–3
as fragrance 54, 59–66
of ambrosia 54, 61, 62–4, 66, 68

anointing with 60, 63–4
  of bodies 63–4, 159
  of incense 3, 4, 122, 161
  of perfumes/unguents 63, 66, 135, 163
  and memory 6, 54, 68
  moral valuations of 54, 57–9, 60, 61, 64–6
  as malodour
    of animals 58–9, 60, 66
    of bodies 57, 58–9, 64, 78
    of garlic 61, 64–6, 84
    of purple 135, 137–8
  pungent *see* taste, *drimus*
  and vision 3, 64, 69, 137–8
  and taste 65(*n*48), 83, 87–8
Socrates 90–95, 99, 167, 199
song 12, 22, 104–5, 163
Sontag, S. 156–7
sophists 14, 142; *see also* Plato; Socrates
Sophocles, *Philoctetes* 47–8, 49, 50–51
soul 15, 101, 119–22, 124
  as insensate 120
  see also body; Descartes, R.
sound 3, 5, 43–52, 100, 162
  as colour 96, 101(*n*26), 180
  and ears 35–6
  echo *see* Echo; echolalia
  linguistic
    alliteration 182–3, 200
    assonance 44, 49(*n*13), 182, 200
    onomatopoeia 50
    consonants/consonantism 44–6, 50, 171, 173, 181–2
    "sound strings" 24, 47–9
    vowels 44–6, 50, 173, 179–80; *see also* Rimbaud, A. "Voyelles"
  made visible 12, 22–4, 100–101
  materiality of 12, 23–4
  non-verbal utterances 45–52, 173
  of pain 47–8
  of poetry 153, 200
  rhyme 182
  rhythm 12, 20, 22, 24, 25, 200
  and "soundness" 167–8
  and text 18
  and vision 7, 12–13
  Wagner's "ear/eye of hearing", and "understanding ear" 6, 44–52
  see also music; nonsense; orality; speech; wordplay
spectacle 138–9, 155; *see also* display/*ornatus*

speech 6
  Aristotle on 52
  in astrology 108–9
  Wagner's "word-tone-speech" 44
  see also linguistics; writing
Spingarn, J. E. 157
Stanford, W. B. 1, 78–9
stars/constellations 6, 103, 106–12
  and the cosmic spheres 105, 108
  as divine 105, 112–14
  and divine/human communication 108–9
  emotions of 110
  interactions of 103, 109–12
    impact on humans 104–5, 111–12
    as sensory 110–12
  and knowability of the universe 113–14
  and signification 108–10
  and touch 105
  as writing 108
  zodiac 103, 109, 110
Stewart, S. 29
Stevens, W. 155
Stoicism 6, 103, 106(*n*18), 111, 114, 118, 137; *see also sympatheia*/"sympathie"
structuralism 171–2, 174, 176
  deconstructionism 171
  post-structuralism 176, 177
sublime 94, 165
Suetonius
  Lives of Grammarians and Rhetoricians 151(*n*72)
  Pratum 147
Surrealism 7, 186–91, 194, 199
  Freud, S., and 189–90
  see also Dalí, S.
sympatheia/"sympathie" 6, 103, 111, 160, 163
synaesthesia
  associative/symbolic 101(*n*26)
  clinical 1–2, 11–12, 95–6, 101(*n*26), 128, 179–81
    grapheme-colour 43, 96, 180
  and the cosmos 101, 103–14
  definition of 1–2, 53(*n*1)
  as delusion 164
  and God 163–4
  as inter-subjectivity 160–62
  as default mode of sensation 80(*n*35)
  philosophical 91, 93–4, 95–7, 100
  poetic 89–102, 115–26
  and *sunaisthanomai* 1
  and *sunaisthēsis* 1, 15, 91, 157

INDEX

synaesthetes 2; *see also* Baudelaire, C.; Saussure, F. de; Scriabin, A.
  as syn-aesthetics 2, 9–26
  and transcendence 91, 93, 95–6, 100–102
  as truth 163–4
  see also art; consciousness; language; poetry; metaphor; senses

Tacitus
  Agricola 134
  Dialogue on Orators 145(*n*25)
taste 2, 3, 5, 163
  Aristotle on 76(*n*20), 83
  ancient classifications of 75–7
    drimus 76–88
    "hot" *see* temperature
    issues of translating 73, 77, 83–4
    "looking mustard" 71–5, 87–8
    "looking oregano" 75, 87
  bitter/sour 73, 76, 77, 80, 85
  cross-modal 83, 87
  and death 117–18, 122–3
  and eating 57, 71–2, 75, 88
  and emotions 84–7
  and facial expression 71–3, 75(*n*15)
  and gluttony 56, 138
  and disease 82–3, 85
  Plato on 82–3
  pungent flavours 73; *see also* above, *drimus*
    of garlic 65–6, 72(*n*7), 84
    of mustard 71, 77, 87–8
    of orach 72
  and smell 65, 83, 87–8
  and tongue 52, 117–18
  and touch 162
  and vision 72–4, 75, 87–8
  see also body; metaphor, "hot"; metaphor, of taste
temperature
  cold, and death 122–3
  heat 80–81(*nn*32, 36–7), 82–3, 106
Thomas, R. 32
Tibullus 132(*n*11)
time 14–15, 68, 163, 195
Timon of Phlius 61
Theocritus 78(*n*26), 85, 86
Theophrastus 135, 149
  Causes of Plants 76(*n*20)
  Enquiry into Plants 72(*n*2), 75–7
tongue *see* taste
touch 6, 27–41
  Aristotle on 15–16, 29, 31(*n*16)
  in art 16
  elusiveness of 29
  erotic 36, 160
  "haptic studies" 28–9
  and hardness/softness 30–31
  and hearing 35–6, 79(*n*28)
  internal 6, 28
  and skin 27, 28, 30–2, 35, 37, 40, 51
  and truth 27–8, 34, 36, 40
  and vision 16, 111; *see also* vision, ancient theories of
  see also kinaesthesia; proprioception; vestibular system
Tragedy, Greek 22, 49–51, 69

underworld *see* afterlife/underworld

Valerius Maximus 183
Valéry, P. 141
vase, Chazen 22–4, **23, 24, 25**
Vergil
  Aeneid 118(*n*19), 132(*n*11), 134, 135(*n*31), 148(*n*46), 152, 183(*n*64)
  Eclogues 104–5, 148(*n*45)
  Georgics 106(*n*15), 121(*n*26), 152, 183
vestibular system 28
Vinci, L. da 196–7, 200
  Mona Lisa 196
vision 2, 7, 16, 193, 196, 198
  ancient theories of (intro/extramission) 14, 16, 41(n.37), 111
  Aratus on 106–9
  and beauty 89, 90, 91, 96
  and *blepō* 74–5
  blindness 42, 199, 200
  clarity/obscurity of 7, 141–54
  as gaze 95, 159–60
  Verweilung 15
  oneiric *see* dreams
  and sound 7, 22, 143–4
  and stars/cosmos 105, 107–8, 111
  and touch 16, 21, 41, 53(*n*1), 111–12
  and truth 144
  transcendence of 112–14
  "visual paradigm" 2–3, 106, 107, 128, 141, 178, 186
  see also beauty; colour; dreams; mind; *phainomena*
Vitruvius 134, 135
voice *see* speech
vowels *see* sound, linguistic

229

INDEX

Wagner, R. 6, 43–7, 101
   Opera and Drama 44–6
   Ring Cycle 44
      Siegfried 45–6
   Tannhäuser 43
Wilde, O. 156
Williams, J. M. 79
Wimsatt, W. K. 157, 162
wine 36, 55–7, 61, 66, 68, 92, 93; see also colour, *oinops*; drunkenness
Wood, M. 157
Woolf, V. 157
writing 2, 17–19, 199
   as *engrammatos phōnē* (engraved sound) 18
   experience of 158
   as image 196, 199
   layout/styles of 17–18, 22–3
   and legibility 196
   and orality/speech 169, 178, 198–9
   wordplay 170–79, 181–4, 198
      acrostics 109
      anagrams 7, 170(n10), 176–9, 183
      anaphonie 169, 174, 178–9, 181–4
      see also nonsense; stars/constellations
"writing-pad" see Freud, S.
Wunderli, P. 178

Xenocrates 77(n23)
Xenophon, *Memorabilia* 82(n38)